D0219580

THE AMERICAN MILITARY FRONTIERS

HISTORIES OF THE AMERICAN FRONTIER

Editor:
Howard Lamar, Yale University

Coeditors:
William Cronon, University of Wisconsin
Martha A. Sandweiss, Amherst College
David J. Weber, Southern Methodist University

THE American Military Frontiers ★

THE UNITED STATES ARMY
IN THE WEST, 1783–1900

Robert Wooster

UNIVERSITY OF NEW MEXICO PRESS   ALBUQUERQUE

© 2009 by the University of New Mexico Press
All rights reserved. Published 2009
Printed in the United States of America
First paperbound printing, 2012
Paperbound ISBN: 978-0-8263-3844-0

LIBRARY OF CONGRESS CATALOGING-IN-PUBLICATION DATA

Wooster, Robert, 1956–
The American military frontiers : the United States Army in the
West, 1783–1900 / Robert Wooster.
   p. cm.
Includes bibliographical references and index.
ISBN 978-0-8263-3843-3 (cloth : alk. paper)
1. West (U.S.)—History, Military—19th century.
2. United States. Army—History—19th century.
3. United States. Army—Military life—History—19th century.
4. United States—Territorial expansion—History—19th century.
5. Frontier and pioneer life—West (U.S.)
I. Title.
F592.w865 2009
355.00978'09034—dc22

                       2009021263

★

DESIGN AND LAYOUT: MELISSA TANDYSH
Composed in 10.5/14 Scala OT
Display type is Stempel Schneidler Std

CONTENTS

LIST OF ILLUSTRATIONS

MAPS

PREFACE

"To give protection to the citizens of the frontier against the Indians and to guard the long line of our Mexican border against robberies by Mexican citizens and Indians living in Mexico," wrote Major General Philip Sheridan in his 1873 annual report for his Division of the Missouri. Recording the many activities of the soldiers of his command, he continued, "To explore unknown territory and furnish escorts to surveying parties for scientific purposes and for projected railroads; to assist and guard the railways already built and other commercial lines of travel; to aid in the enforcement of the civil law in remote places; and to do generally all that is constantly required of our Army in the way of helping and urging forward everything which tends to develop and increase civilization upon the border, and at the same time to protect the Indians in the rights and immunities guaranteed them under existing treaties, has been the work of the troops in this military division."[1]

Such was a professional soldier's account of the army's activities for a single year in the borderlands. Modern scholars rightly shy away from using pejorative phrases like "the advance of civilization" to describe the expansion of the United States from the Appalachian Mountains to the Pacific Ocean. Nor do we share Sheridan's assumptions that development equaled progress or that his country's actions were inherently better than those of other peoples. Nonetheless, he accurately described the army's multiple duties in advancing and defending what the United States defined as its national interests.[2]

The present work argues that military affairs, in their varied dimensions, were of fundamental importance to the American frontiers and that the United States Army, as the federal government's most visible agent of empire, was central to that experience. Designed to complement earlier works in the Histories of the American Frontier series, it seeks to create a narrative synthesis that appeals to scholars as well as a broader literate audience and that both reflects and shapes our understanding of the role of the U.S. Army in the expansion of the nation. Although focusing on the army, the narrative remains multifaceted, for there were many sides to these military frontiers. Indians—some of whom fought alongside the army, more of whom fought against the army, and all of whom naturally sought to manipulate martial conditions in a manner that would further their own interests—are central to this story. Moreover, men and women of many backgrounds, races, and ethnic groups were part of these military communities, and their actions affected a similarly diverse civilian population. Acknowledging the multiple worldviews of these groups is essential to understanding the frontier military experience.

As a country born in war, the United States would long debate the best means of fashioning military forces suitable to republican government. In drafting the Declaration of Independence, Thomas Jefferson complained that George III had quartered "large bodies of armed troops among us," had allowed the army to dominate local civil authority, and was "transporting large armies of foreign mercenaries to complete the works of death, desolation and tyranny already begun." Moreover, the British people had permitted the king "to send over not only soldiers of our common blood, but Scotch and foreign mercenaries to invade and destroy us." Sam Adams warned that standing armies must "be watched with a jealouse Eye;" republican theorists thus preferred militias, comprised of able-bodied adult, male property holders.[3]

Wariness about a standing army did not mean that these Americans were pacifists. Responding to the struggle to control the borderlands and reflecting the racism that defined some people as humans and others as something less, colonists had conducted their wars against Indians (much like their cousins in Europe fought political rebels, infidels, or ethnic minorities such as the Irish) with a ferocity and brutality that would have been considered unacceptable in dealing with other enemies. These encounters, along with the competition for the resources necessary to secure weapons and other needed trade goods from the Euro-Americans, also changed the ways that Indians fought their wars, with conflict tending to become both more lethal and more intense.[4]

Despite their misgivings, the Confederation Congress quickly created a small regular army. Serving as the "sword of the republic," this force would eventually establish Washington's authority across the North American continent as it engaged in a series of tasks that encouraged expansion and development among non-Indians. Military roads and river improvements, for instance, involved the borderlands in the "communications revolution" that historian Daniel Walker Howe has identified as having transformed American life in the first half of the nineteenth century. Similarly, the army was essential in constructing the railroads that did much to create a nation that spanned the enormity of a continent.[5]

Much of this expansion came directly through force of arms. Combat action, whether it pitted the nation against Britain, Mexico, the Confederacy, or Indians, had meaning. Such was particularly the case when it came to the frontiers. Throughout these contested grounds, where virtually all parties recognized organized violence as an acceptable alternative to peace, failures and successes in battle alternately delayed and hastened civilian movement. Such was particularly the case when it came to Indians and non-Indians, neither of whom ever fully comprehended the mysteries of the others' worlds. Indeed, historian John Grenier has argued that the first truly American "way of war," which featured the destruction of an enemy's will and ability to resist through attacks on civilian population centers and economic infrastructure, evolved out of the long colonial and early republic struggles for military supremacy on the frontiers.[6]

For the U.S. Army, western experiences illustrated its role not only in ensuring national security but also in fostering national development. In so doing, its soldiers performed feats of great heroism, self-sacrifice, and humanity as well as acts of rank cowardice, selfishness, and cruelty. As an instrument of national policy, the army disrupted the lives of Indians, forcing many to accept removal to lands distant from those of their birth and nearly obliterating entire cultures. But at the same time, its presence paved the way for a new cast of characters and entrepreneurs steeped in western experiences. Responses within the United States to the army's frontier activities reflected a similar duality. Debates regarding the military's role in projecting Indian policy, the division of power between state and federal authorities, and the size of a professional military establishment revealed the inconsistency in the nation's views of its army, for the public demanded that the armed forces remain small even as it expected them to provide the services necessary to advance western migration.

The regulars were no more monolithic than the borderlands peoples they encountered—some soldiers eagerly embraced frontier associations, while others chose to focus on more conventional military operations. A sizeable minority of the army (roughly 10–15 percent between 1865 and 1885, for example) always garrisoned Atlantic seaboard defenses or government arsenals and thus had little to do with western issues. Similarly, there was, as Thomas W. Cutrer has argued, a "frontier military tradition" distinct from that of the regulars. Even as they questioned the habits and traditions of the army, warriors like Charles Scott, William Henry Harrison, Andrew Jackson, Alexander Doniphan, "Rip" Ford, Jack Hays, and Ben McCulloch played key roles in shaping the frontier military experience. Militias also served as a breeding ground for the democratization of the electorate and the formation of divisive political parties; they also provided a means by which men could honor their masculinity through demonstrations of independence, civic virtue, and martial prowess.[7]

These values, closely tied to concepts of patriotism, community, and manhood, were central to nineteenth-century Americans. But civilian warriors had little patience for the routine drudgery that characterizes many aspects of military life. Friedrich Wilhelm von Steuben, the former Prussian drillmaster turned Revolutionary War icon, had predicted as much when he explained that the needs of the frontiers "will be . . . so much more trying to patience than to valour." Although state militias often wielded tremendous political influence, they were usually replaced by looser associations of volunteers, bounty men, draftees, and substitutes when it came to actual military service. Indeed, such groups dominated the frontiers of the Mexican-American War and the Civil War.[8]

Americans—and westerners in particular—found their national

government a useful ally in a myriad of daily activities. In turn, federal officials recognized that the regular army served as an excellent means of advancing internal improvements and demonstrating support for and interest in frontier affairs. And in the process, the army helped to cement loyalties of far-flung borderlands residents to Washington. "Lands, mines, Indian affairs, Army affairs," explained Montana's Martin Maginnis, "constitute our great and close interest in the federal government." Through this confluence of factors, then, the regular army, rather than the militia or the volunteers, became the driving force behind national military policy in the West.[9]

Several definitions are in order. First, this book conceives of a frontier as series of zones of contact between persons representing the United States (either officially or unofficially) and others. These physical and psychic zones of contact changed over time; the regions of 1783 were much different from those of 1819, or 1848, or 1865. This book uses the term "borderlands" to capture the same idea. It does not intend to imply that the "frontier experience" explains American democracy or uniqueness or that it pitted "civilization" against "savages." Second, William A. Dobak and Thomas D. Phillips have recently demonstrated that African American regulars after the Civil War did not use the term "buffalo soldier" to describe one another, and so the present work does not use that phrase. Finally, this narrative uses the term "Dakota" to refer to the eastern, or Santee, Sioux (including the Mdewakantons, Wahpetons, Wahpekutes, and Sissetons). The western, or Teton, Sioux, are referred to as Lakotas. Seven *oyates* made up the Lakotas: Brulés (Sicangus), Hunkpapas, Oglalas, Minneconjous, Sans Arcs (Itazipcos), Sihasapas ("blackfeet"), and Two Kettles (Oohenunpas).[10]

Many institutions and people have assisted in this effort. I have received generous support from the Joe B. Frantz Fund, two College of Liberal Arts research enhancement grants, and a University Research Enhancement Grant from Texas A&M University-Corpus Christi. I am also grateful to Samuel J. Watson, associate professor of history at the United States Military Academy, for sharing sections of his book *Frontier Diplomats: The Army Officer Corps in the Borderlands of the Early Republic, 1815–1846* (forthcoming from the University Press of Kansas). Robert N. Watt, from the University of Birmingham in the UK also shared his unpublished manuscript on Victorio and the Warm Springs Apaches. David Blanke, my colleague in the history area at Texas A&M University-Corpus Christi, generously provided numerous suggestions that improved the final manuscript. Robert F. Pace, of Pace Academic Services, did a brilliant job making the first three maps, and I recommend him highly.

My mother and father, Edna and Ralph Wooster, have throughout my life given me their unconditional love, support, and wise counsel. My father, who recently retired after fifty-two years of teaching history at Lamar University, also carefully read the manuscript and supplied many useful corrections and suggestions. And my wife, Catherine I. Cox, remains a joyous addition to my life, a beloved comrade and fellow scholar who helps me to realize that every day is precious.

Robert Wooster
Corpus Christi, Texas

ONE

Defeat and Victory
in the Ohio Valley

"The peacemakers and our Enemies have talked away our Lands at a Rum Drinking," complained one Cherokee leader upon learning of the Treaty of Paris, whose provisional terms representatives of Great Britain and the newly recognized United States had agreed on in November 1782. Another observer described the Indians as being "Thunder Struck at the appearance of an accommodation So far short of their Expectation." Indeed, those who had sided with Britain during the war for independence had good reason to be angry, for their presumed allies had concluded a separate peace that paid scant attention to their interests. Moreover, in identifying the Mississippi River as the new country's western boundary, His Majesty's representatives had been extraordinarily generous to their former colonists. On paper, the United States now had claim to an enormous empire that contained American Indian, British, and Spanish contact zones.[1]

In the more populated regions along the Atlantic coast, the Revolution had generally followed the customary rules of limited warfare. Colonial, British, and French armies had for the most part avoided the wanton destruction of private property, the killing of noncombatants, or the torture or murder of enemy prisoners. Not so the war in the interior, where frequent acts of brutality had marked the conflict. In describing the war in the backcountry South, for example, Nathanael Greene

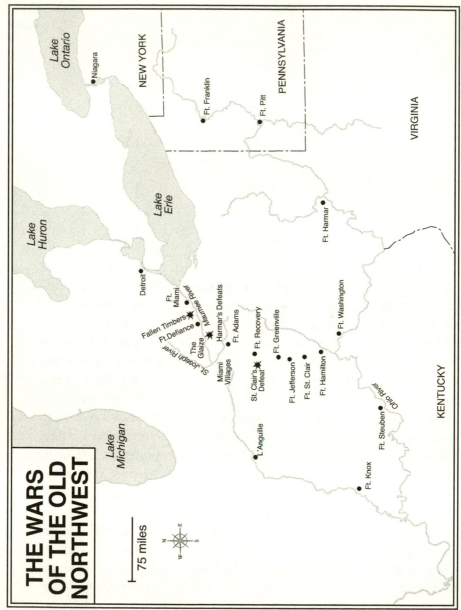

THE WARS
OF THE OLD
NORTHWEST

75 miles

Lake Michigan

Lake Huron

Lake Ontario

Lake Erie

Niagara

Detroit

NEW YORK

Ft. Franklin

Ft. Pitt

PENNSYLVANIA

VIRGINIA

Ft. Harmar

Ft.
Miami

Failen Timbers

Ft.Defiance

The
Glaize

Maumee River

St. Joseph River

Harmar's Defeats

Ft. Adams

Ft. Recovery

Ft. Greenville

Ft. Washington

Miami
Villages

St. Clair's
Defeat

Ft. Jefferson

Ft. St. Clair

Ft. Hamilton

L'Anguille

Ohio River

Ft. Steuben

Ft. Knox

KENTUCKY

Robert F. Pace

observed that "the whigs and tories pursue[d] one another with the most relentless fury[,] killing and destroying each other whenever they meet." In 1780, Shawnee, Wyandot, and Ottawa warriors had slaughtered two hundred men, women, and children at Ruddle's Station, Kentucky, reportedly burning alive mothers and their infants. A year later at Gnadenhütten in the Ohio country, Pennsylvania militia scalped and bludgeoned to death nearly a hundred Delaware Indians, many of whom had been seeking protection from the carnage at the mission there. No less a traditionalist than George Washington had warned of the fate that those Indians who fought the Patriots could expect: "The Cherokees and Southern tribes were foolish enough to listen to them [the British], and to take up the hatchet against us; upon which our warriours went into their country, burnt their homes, destroyed their corn, and obliged them to sue for peace."[2]

For the most part, at the close of the Revolution neither Indians nor white frontiersmen were ready for peace. Tactically, Indians of the eastern woodlands still enjoyed the advantage, as evidenced by victories at Oriskany Creek, Cherry Valley, and Blue Licks. Their superb physical conditioning, penchant for concealment and surprise, and willingness to withdraw from unfavorable battlefield situations made them formidable foes. Still, punishing attacks on their villages, farmlands, and trade routes had left the Ohio Valley tribes increasingly dependent on British arms, ammunition, and even food. For their part, many Patriots on the borderlands were determined to stamp out any challenges.[3]

To the south and southwest, conflicting international, national, state, and Indian goals resulted in what Reginald Horsman has called "a most confused and perilous state." Here, boundaries between the United States and Spain would remain unsettled for a quarter of a century, and former allies and enemies alike would joust with one another for the loyalties of borderlands residents. Hoping to check U.S. expansion, Spain signed treaties with most major tribes in 1784. Unconquered on the battlefield, Cherokees, Creeks, Chickasaws, and Choctaws claimed sovereignty of their own. Many saw the newly independent confederation as a potentially lucrative trading partner, one they might use to counterbalance European governments and preserve their own independence.[4]

The northwestern frontier, if perhaps less confused, posed an even greater potential threat to U.S. interests. The British were in no hurry to carry out their promises to withdraw their troops anytime soon, for the rapacious new confederation must be kept away from Canada, the profitable Great Lakes trade maintained, and Loyalist settlements given time to develop. Thus the Union flag of England and Scotland continued to fly over Lake Champlain, Oswego, Niagara, Detroit, and Mackinac. And even allowing for the disappointments of the Treaty of Paris, most tribes believed the king's men seemed a better bet than the shaky new republic. North as well as South, thousands of Indians—whether because of negotiations with Spain and Britain or a more self-conscious embrace of native cosmology—seemed sympathetic to notions of a pan-Indian opposition to the United States.[5]

The erratic performance of militias during the Revolution had convinced men like George Washington of the need for a professional army for the purposes of national defense. Washington and his allies understood, moreover, that an army could do more than simply fight. A regular force was necessary not only to "awe the Indians" and "prevent the encroachment of our Neighbours of Canada and the Floridas" but to "protect our Trade." Washington thus recommended that the Confederation create an army of 2,631 officers and men and that it maintain a well-organized militia to supplement the regulars.[6]

Congress, however, was in no mood to finance anything that might endanger the people's hard-won liberties. Only a dramatic appeal for patience by their commander in chief had quelled an incipient mutiny among Continental army officers stationed at Newburgh, New York in early 1783. The formation of Society of the Cincinnati, ostensibly organized to encourage fellowship among officers and comrades, reinforced suspicions that a tyrannical army might usurp civilian power. And that June, several hundred soldiers, fearing that they would be furloughed without their back pay, briefly barricaded Congress in the Pennsylvania State House. Although nothing came of the riot—other than that body opting to hold future sessions in the calmer clime of Princeton, New Jersey—it had hardly restored public trust in the army.[7]

Even so, affairs in the borderlands required military attention beyond the capacity of individual state militias to bestow. Thus a day after it dissolved the old Continental army in June 1784, Congress called on Pennsylvania, New Jersey, New York, and Connecticut to supply a total of seven hundred men for one year of national military service. Since

FIG. 1.
Massacre broadside.
Stories about attacks by
Indians against women
were long a staple of
the American media,
as exemplified in this
undated broadside.
LIBRARY OF CONGRESS,
USZ62-45716.

Pennsylvania would furnish most of these soldiers, it earned the right to name one of its own, Josiah Harmar, to command what would be known as the First American Regiment. An urbane Philadelphian and a Revolutionary War veteran, Harmar seems to have won the job because of his service as private secretary of Thomas Mifflin, then president of Congress. Most recruits, 55 percent of whom were immigrants, came from urban backgrounds and saw the military as a sound economic choice. Revolutionary veterans from middling families, often from southern New England and the middle states, dominated the officer corps.[8]

The army's first priority became the region drained by the Ohio River and its tributaries, where Indians challenged the Confederation's claims of empire. Thus the bulk of the army took garrison at Fort Pitt, their presence fostering a bustling market economy that would soon become Pittsburgh. From this early base, soldiers tried in vain to prevent their countrymen from entering contested lands north of the Ohio River. A new post, Fort Harmar (near present Marietta, Ohio), soon to become "a well constructed fort with five bastions and three cannon mounted," was erected 170 miles down the Ohio River. With military spending already consuming nearly 60 percent of the government's budget, in spring 1785 Congress named Henry Knox as secretary at war and extended terms of military enlistment to three years. The appointment of Knox, a bookseller-turned-artillerist weaned on the battles against Britain along the Atlantic seaboard, suggested that authorities had accepted the primacy of conventional, European-style forces.[9]

Insisting that only "the united voice of the confederacy" could authorize land cessions, few Indians recognized the treaties of McIntosh and Finney, in which the United States claimed much of the region from nondescript signatories. U.S. leaders initially sought to avoid open warfare, settling for additional stockades at Fort Franklin (present Franklin, Pennsylvania), Fort Steuben (near modern Louisville, Kentucky), and Fort Knox (present Vincennes, Indiana). In 1786, hoping to force the action, Revolutionary War hero George Rogers Clark led twelve hundred Kentucky militiamen on an unauthorized (and unsuccessful) expedition up the Wabash River. Another militia column attacked several Shawnee towns that October. Their brutality only solidified tribal opposition to the new republic. Further south, the treaties signed at Hopewell attempted, not always successfully, to make peace with Cherokees, Choctaws, and Chickasaws.[10]

The Confederation government's promotion of lands that Indians still claimed as their own added considerable kindling to the frontier fire and in the process reinforced the need for a standing army. The Ordinance of 1785 established a system for surveying and selling lands north of the Ohio River. Affirmed two years later, the Northwest Ordinance guaranteed residents certain rights and offered territories created from those lands a path to statehood. In so doing, it set an important principle of American development: western areas would be equal to the original thirteen states rather than merely colonial appendages. An act renewing the military establishment explicitly highlighted the army's roles in marketing these borderlands. "Stationed on the frontiers," the First American Regiment was instructed to protect settlers and "to facilitate the surveying and selling of the . . . [public] lands in Order to reduce the public debt and to prevent all unwarrantable intrusions."[11]

The new constitution of 1787 reinvigorated public debate over the army's place in U.S. society. It authorized Congress to "raise and support armies" but balanced that body's power by naming the president commander in chief. In an effort to foil the development of what twentieth-century observers would dub a military-industrial complex, military appropriations could be made for only two years. State militias would serve as a further check against the federal army. Still, anti-Federalists claimed such protections did not go far enough, deeming peacetime forces "dangerous to the liberties of a people."[12]

Not so, responded Federalist proponents of the new constitution. John Jay reasoned that foreign powers posed the greatest threat to American liberties and warned that the new nation must not "*invite hostility or insult*" by disarming its military. Alexander Hamilton mounted a more vigorous defense. To expect militias to garrison the frontier "against the ravages and depredations of the Indians" would be "impracticable" and "ruinous to private citizens." Claims that "the militia of the country is its natural bulwark" had nearly "lost us our independence," maintained Hamilton. A part-time militia, he argued, could never acquire the military skills necessary to defend the country.[13]

Shortly after ratification of the constitution, a standing army became a permanent feature of the American landscape. In April 1790 Congress approved a modest force of 1,216 rank and file to be organized into an infantry regiment and an artillery battalion. President Washington and Knox, now secretary of war in the first cabinet, agreed that the regulars must remain in the Northwest. The Ohio Valley, as Washington knew from his years as a surveyor, held enormous strategic and economic importance. Here the original states had ceded their western claims to the central government, which saw prospective land sales as a welcome boon to federal coffers. Soldiers would lend order to regional development; if left unregulated, squatters might usurp the property rights of others. Moreover, increasing the federal military presence would help

tie the region to the new constitutional government. Major General
Arthur St. Clair, a Society of the Cincinnati member who had recently
been named governor of the Northwest Territory, identified the situation accurately: "The People would derive Security, at the same time
that they saw and felt that the Government of the Union was not a mere
shadow . . . they would learn to reverence the Government." Still, costs
of an offensive in the Old Northwest would drain the Treasury, reasoned
Knox, who went on to warn that preemptive military action "would stain
the character of the nation." The government thus preferred to deal with
Indians with diplomacy rather than force.[14]

Even so, frontier tensions mounted. Long years of military struggle
in the woodlands made the Indians a formidable military foe, especially
when they received supplies of guns and powder from the British. They
had relatively small immediate logistical needs in combat, and their local
knowledge, tactical agility, stealth, physical endurance, and ambuscade
was well suited to the rough terrain, especially against the cumbersome
supply trains and rigid linear formations of more conventional foes. "I
must say that everything draws a picture of hostility in this quarter,"
wrote an officer from Fort Knox. In the face of escalating reports of Indian
attacks, in May 1790 Secretary Knox asked President Washington to authorize war against the "bad people" among the Shawnees and their allies,
estimated to be two hundred strong. The secretary envisioned launching
mounted regulars and militiamen to "strike a terror in the minds of the
Indians." Having won the president's approval, Knox the following month
instructed Harmar to "extirpate, utterly, if possible, the said Banditti."[15]

The situation quickly escalated beyond just the Shawnees, for the
Indians were developing what historian Gregory Evans has characterized as "a remarkable unity of purpose." From newly established Fort
Washington (present Cincinnati), Harmar determined that John F.
Hamtramck should push up the Wabash River from Fort Vincennes
and divert the attention of the Miami Indians, while his own command
marched to attack their village. But there were signs of trouble everywhere in the American camps. Even a seasoned Revolutionary War veteran like Hamtramck admitted, "I am apprehensive that I should not
come off so safe" in the face of what he believed to be a numerically
superior foe. Harmar refused to acknowledge the skills of his opponents, instead denigrating them as "merciless villains," "treacherous

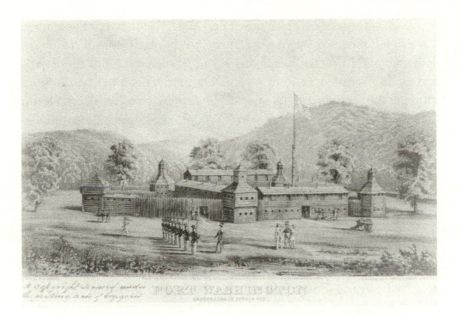

FIG. 2. Fort Washington. Constructed in 1789 with sturdy palisades,
Fort Washington was an important element in the early
growth of Cincinnati. LIBRARY OF CONGRESS, USZ62-1878.

. . . savages," and "scoundrels." Supplies were short and of dubious quality, and the fifteen hundred Kentucky and Pennsylvania militiamen
assembled for the campaign seemed criminally unprepared for battle.
Assuming that attempts to enforce discipline among these volunteers
would only spark mass desertions or a mutiny, regulars found it easier to
criticize their habits than to prepare them for the upcoming challenges
or to adapt looser, more flexible tactics suitable to the levees.[16]

Other developments further dimmed hopes for success. Under
orders to avoid an international incident, Governor St. Clair alerted
British officials to the upcoming campaign. The British undoubtedly
passed along this information to their Indian trading partners. Making
matters worse for Harmar was Knox's stern warning that his character
had been questioned in the highest circles of government. "You are too
apt to indulge yourself to excess in a convivial Glass," reported the secretary. Success in the upcoming campaign would "be [the] foundation
for your future professional prospects."[17]

With a heavy heart, Harmar left Fort Washington in late September, his 320 regulars bivouacking with 1,133 militiamen. Camp security was loose; as one historian has described it, "the character of the army's march . . . seemed more to resemble a herd of elephants tramping through the underbrush than the stealthy approach of a raiding column intent upon surprising their enemy." Finding the largest Miami villages empty, on October 18 Harmar's ill-disciplined men began to raze the surrounding fields. Leading a detachment of 180 militiamen and 30 regulars near the Eel River, Colonel John Hardin of Kentucky blundered into an ambush prepared by the Miami war leader, Little Turtle. Whereas the militia quickly panicked, the regulars stood their ground and were nearly annihilated. Two days later, Little Turtle snared Major John Palsgrave Wyllys's column. Only ten of the sixty regulars escaped as the frightened militia again bolted. Luckily for Harmar, many Indians took that evening's lunar eclipse to be a bad omen, allowing him to pull back the rest of his demoralized mob. United States losses numbered 75 regulars and 108 militiamen dead, with another 31 wounded.[18]

Shocked Kentuckians blamed the debacle on the regulars. Only mounted militiamen, "long accustomed to [Indian] methods of Warfare . . . and well Accustomed to the use of Riffles [sic] and Both aroused [sic] and put in motion by the most pressing of all obligations—the preservation of themselves their wives and children," could defeat the Indians. Regulars, by contrast, charged that the militia had behaved "like a rabble." Although a court of inquiry absolved Harmar of blame, President Washington pinned the defeat on the character of the expedition's commanding officer. "I expected *little* from the moment I heard he was a *drunkard*," noted the president. "I expected less as soon as I heard that on *this account* no confidence was reposed in him by the people of the West Country."[19]

Stung by the debacle and divided over what lessons should be learned, the new government readied to retaliate, fearing that inaction would encourage "sentiments of separate interests" among westerners. In January 1791, Secretary Knox called for funding to establish a fort at the Miami village and to raise another expedition. Seven hundred and fifty mounted militia should conduct a "desultory" strike designed to preempt Indian attacks against settlers. A second raid, consisting of as many as five hundred men, could follow if needed. St. Clair was to lead the main thrust, building a string of posts to ensure proper lines of supply and communication as he marched. "Disciplined valor will triumph over the undisciplined Indians," Knox assured his general. Alert to fragile regional loyalties, the secretary insisted that St. Clair remind westerners that the government was "making expensive arrangements for the protection of the frontiers, and partly in the modes, too, which appear to be highly favored by the Kentucky people."[20]

As St. Clair struggled to assemble the men and material necessary for the task, Brigadier General Charles Scott and eight hundred mounted Kentuckians crossed the Ohio River and sacked several Kickapoo villages. They brought back forty-one prisoners and claimed they had killed thirty-two Indians. Lieutenant Colonel James Wilkinson and five hundred militiamen left Fort Washington on August 1, "fainted boldly" toward the Miamis, then rode northwest and attacked L'Anguille, killing six men, two women, and a child, and capturing thirty-four prisoners. On their return, Wilkinson's men burned a Kickapoo village of about thirty lodges. The light losses in the twin raids—Scott admitted five wounded; Wilkinson, two killed and one wounded—were a result of the Indians having concentrated their defenses at the Miami villages, which the mounted raiders had studiously avoided.[21]

Deteriorating conditions at Fort Washington, however, suggested future disappointments. Private supply contractors and the army quartermaster alike seemed incapable of meeting the soldiers' needs. And the aristocratic St. Clair was anything but an inspirational leader. Overweight and wracked by gout, he neglected to collect solid intelligence about the strength, location, or intentions of his enemies. By fall, the respected Scott admitted to being "damn skittish" about serving under such an officer. To make matters worse, poor recruiting had forced the army to accept men "from the offscourings of large towns and cities; enervated by idleness, debaucheries and every species of vice." Knox and St. Clair thus pinned their nation's hopes on what they hoped would be a two-to-one numerical superiority.[22]

St. Clair lumbered forward in September, sending advance elements to construct a stockade at Fort Hamilton (present Hamilton, Ohio), twenty-three miles north of Fort Washington. Following the custom of the day, a swarm of camp followers, including many wives and children of the soldiers, accompanied the column. Lurching north, the soldiers paused again in mid-October to erect Fort Jefferson near modern Greenville, Ohio. Poor shoes, tattered clothing, leaky tents, and shortages of flour spawned rampant desertion, and officers found the militia and levees incapable of keeping any sort of discipline; though the command now lay deep within Indian country, even penalties of one hundred lashes could not prevent the disorderly throng from randomly firing their weapons into the wilderness. With many enlistments due to expire in early November, St. Clair needed to push ahead if he were to build a post at the Miami village that season.[23]

Leaving 120 men to garrison Fort Jefferson, St. Clair's column moved out on October 24. "The only prospect of effecting the purpose of the campaign is by immediately marching the army so far into the enemy's country that they [volunteers] may be afraid to return in detachments," admitted the expedition's exasperated adjutant, Winthrop Sargent. The march slowed to a crawl as "bilious colic" almost completely debilitated the gouty St. Clair. To protect long-overdue supply trains, the First U.S. Regiment was dispatched south. Though accompanied by some allied Chickasaws, St. Clair operated blindly; on November 1, he informed Knox that "the few Indians that have been seen were hunters only, who we fell upon by accident." A day later, a frustrated militiaman, Lieutenant Colonel William Darke, predicted to his wife: "I expect we shall march . . . towards the Indian towns, where we, I believe, shall not find an Indian."[24]

November 4 broke cold and clear along the Wabash River. St. Clair's men had neglected to fortify the previous night's camp. Over a thousand Wyandots, Shawnees, Miamis, Delawares, Ottawas, Chippewas, Potawatomis, and a smattering of Canadian militia, operating under Little Turtle's tactical guidance and enjoying an unusually strong degree of consensus, struck the intruders just after daybreak, routing the militia and the levees. Raw recruits in the Second United States Regiment hardly knew how to fire their weapons, and hidden Indian marksmen picked off officers as they tried to rally their men. Defending their families against the invaders, the Indians fought "like Furies"; an American described them as "hell hounds." By nine thirty that morning, St. Clair, who had to his credit rousted himself from his ailments to join the fighting, sounded a general retreat, which soon devolved into pandemonium. "The rout," he admitted, "continued quite to fort Jefferson, twenty-nine miles, which was reached a little after sun-setting."[25]

The worst defeat in the history of the U.S. Army's wars against the Indians—or, from another perspective, the greatest triumph of the Indians over the army—had just occurred at the Wabash River. "The fortunes of this day . . . will blacken a full page in the future annals of America," wrote Sargent, who calculated that 64 officers and 807 enlisted men of the 1,669 effectives in action had been killed or wounded. Casualties among the packers, artificers, and camp followers brought the human costs to over a thousand. The soldiers left behind 8 cannon, 1,193 muskets, 1,237 bayonets, 400 tents, 163 axes, 25 swords, and 24 pistols. Indians estimated their own losses at between sixty and eighty. Buoyed by strong kinship structures, having reached a near-unanimous agreement about the need for the battle and about how to conduct it, and boasting a qualitative superiority in their combat abilities, the confederated tribes merited their triumph just as much as St. Clair deserved the beating at the Battle of the Wabash.[26]

The debacle set off bitter acrimony among the Americans, who seemed unable to overcome the prejudices that left them certain of their innate superiority. Rather than admitting an Indian victory, many Americans found it more convenient to blame their own. True to form, westerners damned the regulars. In turn, St. Clair blamed his defeat on the contractors and on indiscipline among the militia and the levees. Exonerating St. Clair, a congressional investigation echoed similar themes. Secretary Knox blamed insufficient numbers of "good troops," poor discipline, and the lateness of the season. More prescient were the observations of General John Armstrong, twenty-year veteran of colonial borderlands conflict, who criticized St. Clair's determination to adhere "to regular or military rule." "In vain," wrote Armstrong, "may we expect success against our present adversaries without taking a few lessons from them. . . . We must, in a great degree, take a similar method in order to counteract them."[27]

Armstrong was correct, for the military had twice failed to either instill the stern discipline necessary to deploy in linear formations that could stand against an enemy skilled in the ways of woodlands warfare or to adopt more flexible tactics. Secretary Knox's initial response to the disaster on the Wabash nonetheless called for more of the same: a traditionally structured army of 5,196 enlisted men *disciplined according to the nature of the service* (Knox's emphasis). Until this force could be raised, equipped, and trained, mounted militia should conduct "desultory operations" against the Indians. In something of an afterthought, Knox suggested that allied Indians might accompany future expeditions.[28]

Skeptics variously denounced the proposed increase, proclaimed the virtues of the militia, called for additional diplomacy, and suggested that frontiersmen be restrained from moving further west. But the administration won a major victory in March 1792, when Congress passed An Act for Making Farther and More Effectual Provision for the Protection of the Frontiers of the United States. President Washington settled on Anthony Wayne, a Pennsylvania-born Revolutionary War hero who had captured British-held Stony Point in 1779 through a daring bayonet charge, to command the new force. A noted philanderer left penniless by recent efforts to establish a plantation in Georgia, Wayne needed the job. Though Washington acknowledged that Wayne was possibly "a little addicted to the bottle" and "more active and enterprising than judicious and cautious" as well as too "vain," the president respected his fighting abilities and reputation as a stern disciplinarian. Appointing a man as commander who had ties to both North and South also made good political sense.[29]

Wayne proved a superior choice. He would organize and lead a Legion of the United States, revolutionary in the application of a legion approach to an entire army. Based on dearly earned frontier experience, the writings of Colonel Henry Bouquet (a British officer who had served in the French and Indian War), and contemporary French notions of *petite guerre* (literally, "little war"), the legion was tailored to win control of the borderlands. Instead of adopting the single-arms formations of tradition, it was organized into four sub-legions, each of which was an integrated unit made up of a troop of dragoons, a company of artillery, two battalions of infantry, and a battalion of riflemen. As the primary maneuver unit, the sub-legion fostered a flexible, combined arms approach designed to meet the challenges of combat in the Ohio Valley.[30]

In order to help his men endure the shock of combat, Wayne enforced an iron discipline among his legion. If caught, deserters could expect one hundred lashes; one soldier who stole a horse from a widow was hung as an example to others. Instead of emphasizing mass volleys and

rigid linear tactics, as had traditionally been done, Wayne tailored training to the realities of the northwestern woodlands, paying careful attention to individual marksmanship. He worked to secure firearms that
would enable a mounted dragoon to "be constantly upon his Enemy,"
so that "he can *pursue* & load in full *trot*, without danger of loosing [*sic*]
any part of his powder." Wayne also put his troops through elaborate
war games: "We had a *sham* engagement—the rifle Corps (by reiter-
ated attacks and highly painted) acted well the part of Savages—which
required all the skill & fortitude of our little Legion to sustain."[31]

Aware that another disaster could fatally damage his new government's expansion into the Ohio country, Wayne convinced his superiors
to delay an offensive, thus allowing him time to expand his line of forts
toward the Miami villages, complete training of his legion, and stockpile
necessary resources. With the enemy's attention diverted by mounted
volunteer strikes at Sandusky and on the St. Joseph, the legion would
attack the Miami villages. Wayne promised to fortify his camp at the end
of every day, use scouts and Indian allies to prevent any ambushes or
surprises, and attack the enemy at night, when "I know from experience
that they are a contemptable [*sic*] enemy."[32]

Indecision among the Indians had allowed Wayne the luxury of
such a delay. Little Turtle's devastating November 1792 attack against a
supply column between Fort Hamilton and Fort St. Clair (near present
Eaton, Ohio) demonstrated the fragility of the army's logistical network
in the region, and the small garrisons (almost invariably less than two
hundred men) in unfriendly country seemed to invite attack. But assem-
bling large numbers of fighting men strained tribal economies, leaving
Indians even more dependent on British assistance. As thousands of
refugees from southern Ohio resettled at the Glaize, a watered plain
near present Defiance, Ohio, a grand council could not agree about what
to do. The Indians thus failed to follow up on their advantage against the
precarious U.S. outposts.[33]

The failure to follow up on their earlier successes meant the loss of an
extraordinarily good opportunity for the Indians of the Old Northwest,
because U.S. military power, and the regional economy necessary to sustain that power, was on the rise. By May 1793, the legion had advanced
to the environs of Fort Washington, where training stressed open-order
tactics and cooperation between dragoons, skirmishers, light infantry,

and infantry. Negotiations having again failed, on September 3 Secretary Knox unleashed Wayne, reminding his general to insure "that your force be fully adequate to the objects you propose to effect, and that a defeat in the present time and under present circumstances would be pernicious in the highest degree in the interests of our Country."[34]

By early October, Wayne had pushed ahead to Fort Jefferson. He had twenty-six hundred regulars and four hundred mounted volunteers for offensive operations, but outbreaks of smallpox and influenza and threats to his supply lines convinced him to delay any attack against the growing Indian concentration at the Glaize. Instead, his men built Fort Greeneville (about six miles north of Fort Jefferson) and subsequently the larger Fort Recovery (at the site of St. Clair's defeat). At least, he reasoned, the army's presence would deter attacks on U.S. settlements.[35]

As Wayne waited out the winter, the British, fearful that a U.S. presence so close to Lake Erie would endanger Canada, stepped up their support for the Indians. In April 1794, the British determined to reoccupy Fort Miamis, located on the trail from Lake Erie to the Glaize. Redcoats on a site clearly within the boundaries claimed by the United States were sure to provoke a response, even if neither country really wanted a direct confrontation. In mid-May, Secretary Knox thus ordered Wayne to deliver "some severe strokes" to the Indians. "I shall bring those haughty savages to a speedy explanation," wrote Wayne.[36]

Wayne found himself mired in a struggle with private contractors, and so the Indians took that opportunity to attack first. Buoyed by British assurances of support, fifteen hundred fighting men assembled to block the enemy occupation of the region surrounding the Maumee and Wabash rivers. Routing the escort of a supply convoy just outside of Fort Recovery, several hundred Indians then attempted to storm the fort itself. But their predilection for open-order skirmishing was no match for the defenders and their six cannon, secure behind the sturdy wooden walls of a stockade and detached blockhouse. Running low on food, the Indian army dissolved the following day. Their human losses—probably about three dozen—were not nearly as significant as the psychological impact of their having failed to carry even this exposed post.[37]

Buoyed by news from Fort Recovery, on July 28 Wayne set forth from Fort Greeneville with two thousand legionnaires, seven hundred mounted volunteers, one hundred allied Chickasaws and Choctaws, and

FIG. 3.
Anthony Wayne.
General Anthony Wayne
(1745–96), dubbed "Mad
Anthony" by one of
his soldiers. NATIONAL
ARCHIVES, 148-GW-468.

at least a dozen cannon. Another eight hundred volunteers guarded his
supply convoys. Like St. Clair before him, painful gout attacks weakened
Wayne's capacity to command, and a nasty whispering campaign instigated by Brigadier General James Wilkinson threatened his leadership.
Muttered Wayne: "We have had & shall have a many headed Monster to
contend with yet I have the most flattering hopes of triumphing over all
our Enemies both in front & *rear*." But in a break with the practices of
Harmar and St. Clair, camp security was tight, no women with children
accompanied the column, and the troops fortified their camp after every
day's march. On August 1, Wayne paused to build Fort Adams at the
Saint Mary's River; a week later, upon reaching the abandoned Glaize,
his men erected Fort Defiance and began destroying the lush fields that

had once fed thousands of refugee Indians. Having occupied the "Grand Emporium of the hostile Indians of the West," Wayne rewarded his men with an extra ration of whiskey. He pushed ahead on August 15, pausing again four days later to construct Camp Defiance, which would serve as a safe haven for his baggage train.[38]

Ahead of Wayne's advance, Indians had moved their women and children to safer locations. Thirteen hundred fighters, along with a detachment of Canadian militia dressed as Indians, prepared an ambush about five miles southwest of Fort Miamis. Situated along the north bank of the Maumee River, the site was marked by thick underbrush and hundreds of trees uprooted by a great storm. Blue Jacket, a Shawnee, seems to have been the principal war leader; Little Turtle, an abler tactician, had lost influence for having doubted (correctly, as it turned out) British promises of support. The warriors had expected Wayne to arrive earlier, and so they had eaten only evening meals for several days in the belief that empty bowels would reduce the impact of stomach wounds. By the morning of August 20, hundreds of hungry men had left their designated positions to find food.[39]

Wayne's army broke camp that morning about seven o'clock, marching in close order through the late summer heat and humidity. Four miles into their march, skirmishers fell back in confusion under heavy fire. Close on their heels came the pursuing Indians, only to meet the disciplined ranks of the legion. After several volleys, the regulars advanced with the bayonet; with dragoons and mounted volunteers enveloping their flanks, the Indians broke. "We could not stand against the sharp end of their guns [the Legion's bayonets]," recalled one Ottawa fighter. Had those men who had left the camp to gather food remained, the outcome might have been different, but the Indians at the Battle of Fallen Timbers were beaten in less than an hour. The 900 Americans engaged had suffered 133 casualties. Estimates of Indian losses vary widely; Wayne claimed to have inflicted over 250 casualties, but one British observer admitted only 40 killed.[40]

The tactical setback—which seemed especially shocking in light of previous successes against the United States—soon turned into a strategic disaster for the once-powerful alliance. As demoralized fighters streamed back toward Fort Miamis, the British commander, Major William Campbell, closed the stockade gates, not wanting to risk his exposed two-hundred-man garrison in a shooting war against Wayne's legion. Hungry, angry at their leaders who had insisted on war, and resentful that the British had once again forsaken them, most warriors returned to their families. Organized resistance dissolved. For three tense days, Wayne's army remained on the outskirts of Fort Miamis, destroying the surrounding cornfields and villages as he and Campbell exchanged a series of saber-rattling messages. Lacking supplies to conduct a siege or the heavy artillery required for an assault on this British outpost on United States soil, Wayne's army then withdrew by easy marches, laying waste to remaining fields as they went. The Indians, bragged Wayne, had been "taught to dread" his legion.[41]

TWO

Sword of the Nation

The Legion of the United States had demonstrated that the new government could, for the time at least, control a regular army and meet the military challenges posed to its expanding frontiers. But with the conclusion of the immediate threat, would the republic still want a standing army? If so, how large would that force be, and who would man its ranks? Would it be designed to fight potential European foes, or would it be tailored to deal with conditions in its western borderlands? And would it be relegated to its barracks, or would it take an active role in developing the nation and in promoting its territorial expansion?

In August 1794, from his field camp near British-held Fort Miamis, Anthony Wayne had little time to ponder such questions, for he had much to do. The lands surrounding the great Indian gathering at the Glaize—what twenty-four-year-old Lieutenant William Clark had earlier described as "one of the most beautiful landscapes ever painted"—now lay in smoldering ruins. As Wayne began the slow trek back to Fort Defiance, his troops destroyed any last vestiges of the shattered Indian economies. At Fort Defiance, three hundred men set about rendering the post capable of defying "all the artillery of Canada." Three weeks later, Wayne and a strong column pushed on to the now-abandoned Miami villages and began erecting another palisade, Fort Wayne.[1]

Northern Ohio nonetheless remained a dangerous place. Wayne had beaten the Indians at Fallen Timbers, but the coalition that had embarrassed Josiah Harmar and Arthur St. Clair still posed a formidable threat to an army far from home. The British presence loomed large, and the enlistments of many of Wayne's men were set to expire. Supplies presented "a continued source of difficulty & perplexity," complained Wayne, "ten fold more than contending with all the Savages in the Wilderness." His open rivalry with his subordinate James Wilkinson divided loyalties even among the legion. Indeed, Wayne came to believe that his rival had attempted to assassinate him, and some suspected that Wilkinson had conspired with the British to sabotage the campaign.[2]

That fall, however, the implications of the triumph at Fallen Timbers became increasingly apparent. Despite his complaints about supplies, Wayne enjoyed the benefits of a much more stable economic infrastructure than anything the Indian confederacy could muster. Dispirited and hungry, and with many of their most defiant leaders dead or discredited, Indians did not challenge the new U.S. bastions in their heart of their former Ohio Valley homelands. The Treaty of Greeneville recognized Washington's control over southern, central, and eastern Ohio. Annuities, to be distributed by select Indian leaders among their people, gave the federal government further influence over tribal affairs. And in Jay's Treaty, signed on November 19, 1794, Britain agreed to evacuate its northwestern posts.[3]

By forcing the Ohio Valley peoples to accept the U.S. presence, the army had done much to establish the constitutional government's legitimacy. As historian Andrew Cayton has emphasized, the decision to commit the army almost exclusively to the Northwest had profound consequences, for it represented the government's largest deployable resource. With military garrisons came better protection from Indian attacks, supply contracts, a market for local goods and services, and a better transportation network. The non-Indian population of the Northwest Territory, estimated to be about fifteen thousand in 1795–96, had more than tripled by 1800. Moreover, the army's presence had ensured that these migrants understood that their allegiances lay with the government in Washington.[4]

Relations with the federal government differed in Tennessee, the Carolina borderlands, and Georgia. Like the British, Spain had attempted

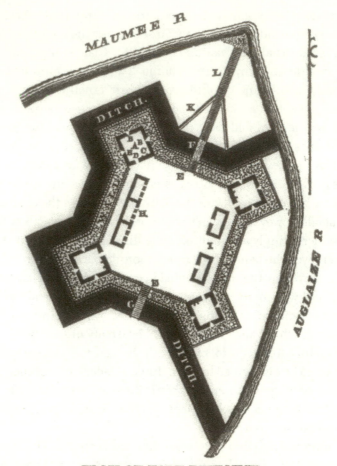

FIG. 4. Fort Defiance. Established by Anthony Wayne following the Battle of Fallen Timbers, Fort Defiance was supposed to be capable of defying "all the artillery of Canada." LIBRARY OF CONGRESS, USZ62-52576.

to counter U.S. expansionism with bribes to well-placed officials (most notably General Wilkinson) and numerous Indian alliances. The Spanish also occupied strategic positions at present-day Memphis and Vicksburg, Natchez, the confluence of the Tombigbee and Black Warrior rivers, and Fort St. Stephens (north of Mobile). Even after Pinckney's Treaty (1795), in which the Crown agreed to withdraw its posts north of the thirty-first parallel and granted Americans use of the Mississippi River, Spain remained a threat to the new republic's southern empire.[5]

In the face of such challenges, southerners cried out for more federal assistance. Only "a regular force," wrote one South Carolinian, could secure the "Dignity, wealth, & Power" of the national government against Spain and the Indians. Some backcountry folk had created the quasi-autonomous state of Franklin, and the wholesale pillaging of several Cherokee, Creek, and Chickamauga villages by Tennessee militiamen reinforced western faith in a more savage way of war ("your chastising them, by which I mean your killing of them will afford me great pleasure," went one set of orders). Such actions, however, threatened to inflame all of the borderlands into a war that the national government did not want. Secretary Knox resisted these calls for blood vengeance, reasoning that the nation could not afford a second conflict while Harmar, St. Clair, and Wayne were engaged in the Ohio River country. In a belated effort to restrain radicals on both sides of the frontier, regular troops occupied blockhouses southwest of Knoxville. The United States also invested in bribes sufficient to win the alliance of Creek leader Alexander McGillivray. Even so, whereas in mid-1794 nearly 3,000 regulars garrisoned the northwestern borderlands, only 264 patrolled the lands south of the Ohio River. Complained Andrew Jackson, soon to be elected Tennessee's first congressman, "this Country is Declining [fast] and unless Congress lends up more am[ple] protection this Country will have at length [to break] or seek a protection from some other Source than the present." It was no wonder, then, that residents of the Old Southwest had a distinctly different relationship with their federal government than did their northwestern cousins, who were profiting from the army's presence and the Northwest Ordinance.[6]

But the expectation that their government should provide military assistance nonetheless signaled a subtle shift in national attitudes. Just over a decade before, many Americans had questioned the need for any regular army; now, debate centered on the army's size and composition rather than on whether there should be one or not. In mid-1796, as the crisis in the Old Northwest eased, Congress reduced the army's authorized strength from over five thousand officers and men to about three thousand. Notably, however, Congress had *not* abolished the regulars entirely. Congress was also conferring to the War Department sweeping powers over Indian policy. In a series of measures known as the Trade and Intercourse Acts (frequently renewed and modified between 1790 and 1834), the federal government authorized agents, operating as civilian employees of the War Department, to regulate trade with Indians, stop private purchases of Indian lands, and stamp out the illicit liquor trade. Typically, these men set up operations near military bases and relied on the army to enforce their decisions. Similarly, the government established trading houses (known as "factories") to offer Indians access to goods free of the rough-and-tumble gouging of unscrupulous frontier entrepreneurs. Twenty-four of the twenty-eight factories were located at military posts, further reinforcing the army's influence.[7]

Even as Congress empowered the War Department to conduct Indian affairs, it did away with the combined-arms structure of the legion, which had been designed to meet military conditions along the frontiers. In its place, the army adopted the more traditional organization of a corps of artillerists and engineers, two companies of light dragoons, and four regiments of infantry. The shift may have simply been an easy way to slash expenses—military spending fell from over $2.4 million in 1795 to just over $1 million in 1797. But the cuts also suggest that Americans felt more comfortable with a European-style army than an institution designed to fight a less conventional foe. The legion would continue to have a broad impact: among its ranks were future president William Henry Harrison; future state governors John Adair, Charles Scott, and John Posey; explorers and administrators William Clark and Zebulon Pike; and William Eaton, destined to lead the Marines to victory over the Barbary pirates at Tripoli. And a few would pass on the lessons they had learned through word of mouth. Even so, the legion's demise signaled that the wars against Indians would have little impact upon army doctrine or organization.[8]

Deteriorating relations with France reinforced this trend. Europe, rather than the borderlands, now seemed the chief threat to national security. In 1798, when the United States was on the verge of war with France, Congress increased appropriations for coastal defenses, approved twelve new infantry regiments and six troops of dragoons, authorized the creation of a provisional army, and hastened naval construction. Solid Federalists all, the expanded army's senior generals— George Washington, Alexander Hamilton, and Charles Cotesworth

Pinckney—shared the former president's fears that "opposers of Government will stick at nothing to injure it." Hamilton admitted frankly that, as they assessed the backgrounds and reputations of 1,003 candidates for 370 line positions, "we were very attentive to the importance of appointing friends of the Govern[men]t to military stations." President John Adams, however, shared Republican suspicions that Hamilton might use the expanded army to further his own lofty ambitions. Returning to his earlier Whiggish roots, Adams satisfied himself with a greater emphasis on the navy and a return to diplomacy as radicals in France lost power. The new regiments were soon discharged.[9]

Despite the refocusing of attention elsewhere, the regular army remained central to the nation's borderlands. In December 1794, as he departed the War Department, Henry Knox pled for a fair and just Indian policy. Only by preventing "frontier white people" from seizing Indian lands "by force or fraud" could the nation enjoy peace in the West. To achieve this, he recommended that regulars occupy posts "out of the ordinary jurisdiction of any State." The old soldier was confident that disciplined regulars, commanded by officers of honor and virtue, could act as neutral brokers in defending the interests of Indians and United States citizens alike.[10]

Though evincing less concern for the rights and needs of Indians, Knox's successor, Timothy Pickering, based his policies on similar assumptions. With an eye to ensuring that Spain would continue to negotiate with the United States, the new secretary wanted to station a third of the entire regular force on the Georgia, Tennessee, and Mississippi frontiers. Further stimulated by the threat of war with France, American troops also built three forts: Pickering (Chickasaw Bluffs), Adams (on the Mississippi River south of Natchez), and Stoddert (just above the Spanish boundary line near Mobile). In the process, the War Department expected regulars "to preserve our influence with the Indians."[11]

The Adams administration also called attention to two themes that would profoundly influence future policy making: the desirability of concentrating scattered borderlands garrisons and of creating an educated officer corps. In 1799, James Wilkinson, now a brigadier general, recommended abandoning interior posts like Fort Wayne, Fort Washington, and Fort Knox, "for by such fritterings, we destroy the usefulness of both officer and soldier, and expose ourselves always to be beaten in detail." Following up on Wilkinson's report, Hamilton pointed out that stationing reserve forces at points easily accessible to transportation networks would promote economy and military efficiency as well as serve as a more impressive demonstration of national power. To improve officer training, Secretary James McHenry, successor to Pickering in the War Department, proposed a national military academy. Acknowledging "the occasional brilliant and justly celebrated acts of some of our militia" during the Revolution, McHenry noted that it was "universally felt, that regular and disciplined troops were indispensable, and that it was utterly unsafe for us to trust to militia alone the issue of the war."[12]

Although realities on the ground made it difficult to concentrate scattered garrisons, Thomas Jefferson's 1800 presidential victory rekindled interest in a military academy and reopened considerations of the army's role in national life. The new president had long realized that the army could be a potent source for nation building and for securing an expansive "empire for liberty." In 1783, for example, he had asked George Rogers Clark to organize a party "for exploring the country from the Missisipi [sic] to California." Nothing had come of the early idea, but as part of his broader efforts to challenge Federalist control of the government, Jefferson wanted to reform the army so as to assure its loyalty to his administration. To this end, he appointed party loyalist Henry Dearborn as secretary of war. Thanks to the long Federalist rule—and especially the efforts of Washington, Hamilton, and Pinckney to ensure that men of similar backgrounds and political philosophy would dominate the officer corps—the army did not reflect the nation's political diversity. President Jefferson thus needed a military academy to prepare a cadre of new Republican officers.[13]

These changes, however, needed to be made in the context of the new president's concurrent promise to slash federal expenditures. Jefferson thus embraced the Military Peace Establishment Act of 1802, which abolished the light dragoons and cut the army's strength to 3,287 officers and men, as a means by which the army could not only be reduced but also republicanized, as veteran Federalists became victims of the reductions in force. Military spending fell by about a third over the next three years. In a move destined to have even more lasting importance, Congress also authorized the president to establish a military academy at West Point, New York.[14]

The legislation correlated precisely with the administration's plans for western defense. The previous year, Secretary of War Dearborn had called for ten infantry companies (the equivalent of one regiment in the reorganized army) to be stationed in the northwestern borderlands and ten infantry companies (the second regiment) in the Southwest. Soldiers were also put to work carving out military roads from the Tennessee River to Natchez and between Lake Erie and Lake Ontario. At the request of the postmaster general, they would also construct a road from Fort Hawkins, Georgia, to Fort Stoddert, Alabama. The increased resources devoted to the nation's southwestern borderlands, which had overwhelmingly supported Jefferson and the Republican Party in the recent election, represented a sharp break from Federalist practice.[15]

Private investment followed the army into the southwestern borderlands, albeit somewhat more slowly than had been the case in the Ohio River valley. "I think the priviledge [sic] of suttling to the troops will be profitable," predicted the contractor responsible for supplying the troops who were building the Natchez Trace. In 1804 and 1806, John Smith (based in Ohio) and Oliver Ormsby (based in Pennsylvania) won army contracts to provide rations in Mississippi and Louisiana. Lexington, Kentucky, merchants like Elijah Galusha, John Seitz, and James Morrison came to dominate contracts in other regions. With each daily ration including one and a half pounds of fresh beef or three-quarters of a pound of salt pork, eighteen ounces of bread, one-half gill of alcohol, and soap, vinegar, salt, and candles, such contractors provided a welcomed market for the region's farmers, transporters, and craftsmen and regular infusions of money into cash-starved frontier economies.[16]

Anticipating the reductions stemming from the 1802 legislation, the president had tasked his private secretary, Captain Meriwether Lewis, with compiling a confidential assessment of every officer in the army. Politically reliable, Lewis's work as paymaster and special messenger to Anthony Wayne provided him a close familiarity with army personnel and needs. Captain Lewis classified 59 of the 256 officers as "first class, as esteemed from a superiority of genius & military proficiency," while deeming 43 as "unworthy of the commissions they bear." Lewis also divided commissioned personnel according to political suasion, describing forty-six as "opposed to the administration more decisively" or "opposed most violently to the administration and still active in its vilification." When the reduction in force came, the administration generally attempted to adhere to Secretary Dearborn's promise to "retain such as merit alone," but by the fall of 1802, a quarter of officers were Republican.[17]

Captain Lewis and the army would also be crucial in implementing Jefferson's Indian policy. The president saw an expanded Indian trade, overseen by the superintendents, agents, subagents, and interpreters who comprised the "Indian department" within the war office, as a means of improving relations with the Indians and encouraging tribal land sales. The army could also assist in the removal of Indians to lands west of the Mississippi River. To offset European threats to the Trans-Mississippi, Jefferson secured money for Lewis to outfit a corps of soldiers to promote commerce and "advance the geographical knowledge of our own continent." As Lewis made his preparations, astonishing news came from Paris: France, which had reclaimed Louisiana from Spain in 1800, had agreed to sell eight hundred thousand square miles to the United States for $15 million. The United States made the purchase; to consummate it, the army had to occupy Louisiana, and quickly.[18]

Jefferson initiated a two-pronged campaign to claim this valuable empire. Army personnel would conduct and support a series of explorations that would give them the opportunity to show the flag, meet with Indians, and begin to understand the region's geography. Most famous was that undertaken by Lewis and his associate, William Clark, a veteran of the Battle of Fallen Timbers and the younger brother of George Rogers Clark. Among their Corps of Discovery were twenty-five soldiers, two interpreters, Clark's slave, several voyageurs, and a Shoshone Indian named Sacagawea. In late May 1804, Lewis and Clark set out from St. Charles (present Missouri). Maintaining strict military discipline, they returned to St. Louis twenty-eight months and eight thousand miles later, having reached the Pacific Ocean and contacted many of the West's most prominent tribes along the way. Both men made it a point to comment on security issues upon their return in the hope that the government would act to minimize foreign influence. Clark recommended posts at "elegable Situations [sic]" along the upper Mississippi and Missouri rivers. Lewis focused on restricting British traders and in preventing unauthorized civilians from entering the Indian country. Military garrisons would be necessary, he observed, because "the first principle of governing the Indians is to govern the whites."[19]

FIG. 5. Meriwether Lewis. Most famous for his role in the Lewis and
Clark expedition, Lewis (1774–1809) also compiled a confidential
analysis of army officers for President Thomas Jefferson. This
engraving was made from a portrait by Charles Saint-Mémin.
LIBRARY OF CONGRESS, USZ62-105848.

Other southwestern expeditions were also afoot. Civilians William
Dunbar and George Hunter, escorted by "one Sober discreet active
Serjeant [sic] & ten faithful sober Soldiers," spent four months exam-
ining the Ouachita River in the region of present Arkansas. Another
civilian, Thomas Freeman, probed the commercial possibilities and diplomatic status of the upper Red River country. Accompanied by Captain
Richard Sparks and forty-five regulars, Freeman ventured northwest of

Natchitoches until encountering a much larger Spanish force, which ordered their withdrawal.[20]

Convincing the diverse Mississippi River valley residents to accept Washington's authority represented the second prong of Jefferson's efforts. Once again, he turned to the army. The administration appointed Captain Amos Stoddard as commandant of Upper Louisiana. Instructed to "conciliate the feelings" of St. Louis residents as he occupied the city, Stoddard would exercise civil as well as military powers until a territorial government could be organized. Using the army as a perk to help cement loyalties, Jefferson saw to it that six members of leading St. Louis families received appointments to the new military academy. To the south, 450 United States troops took formal possession of New Orleans on December 20, 1803. Overseeing the process, General Wilkinson screamed for reinforcements: "The formidable aspect of the armed Blacks & Malattoes [sic], officered & organized, is painful & perplexing," wrote Wilkinson, "and the People have no Idea but of Iron domination at this moment."[21]

By the end of 1804, 686 soldiers and 81 Marines—about 20 percent of the nation's ground forces—occupied nine sites in the newly acquired lands. From New Orleans, W. C. C. Claiborne inherited leadership of the newly created Territory of Orleans. The president named Wilkinson the first governor of the new Territory of Louisiana (formerly Upper Louisiana). Jefferson admitted considerable doubts about the wisdom of combining military and civil functions under one soldier—especially a scoundrel (characterized as a "vile assassin" by Anthony Wayne) who had been implicated in an attempted cabal against George Washington during the Revolutionary War and who was widely rumored to have taken Spanish bribes (though that was not proven until a century later). But he reasoned that military issues would for the moment dominate the position's responsibilities. Indeed, Spain and the United States had not agreed on the boundaries of the Louisiana Purchase, leading Secretary Dearborn to order Wilkinson to develop contingency plans for an offensive into Mexico. Referring to his ambitions in a letter to a fellow expansionist, Wilkinson explained frankly, "I shall ascertain every devious as well as direct route."[22]

Slippery but hardly stupid, the much-maligned Wilkinson was a shrewd judge of presidential character. Recognizing Jefferson's predilection for western exploration, the governor/general quickly launched several explorations—two led by Lieutenant Zebulon Pike, a third by Lieutenant George Peter, and a fourth by his son Lieutenant James B. Wilkinson—into the Trans-Mississippi West. Questions about Wilkinson's trustworthiness and motives, however, should not obscure the larger point: in naming a general to the post, Jefferson recognized that only the army possessed the resources necessary to confirm national sovereignty over an area he badly wanted. By fall 1805, Wilkinson's gubernatorial appointment had assumed new importance, for rumor had it that he and the discredited former vice president, Aaron Burr, were hatching a scheme to establish an independent western nation or to foment a war with Spain. In a sharply worded missive, Secretary Dearborn warned the general against becoming "too intimate" with Burr. "You ought to keep every suspicious person at arms length, and be as wise as a serpent and as harmless as a dove." But faced with a possible conflict with Spain over Louisiana's unsettled western boundaries, the administration, defeated in a ham-handed effort to promote one of its political favorites to a lieutenant colonelcy, had no option but to trust to Wilkinson's uncertain loyalties.[23]

Arriving at Natchitoches in September 1806, Wilkinson readied his troops for action. "Every man and every officer, should hold himself in readiness to march, to fight, and to die at a minute's warning," he warned. His correspondence reflected his characteristic desire to please different audiences while promoting his private interests. To a friend of Aaron Burr, he bragged that "the time . . . has now arrived for subverting the Spanish government in Mexico." With thirty thousand men, he could take everything. But when writing to Secretary Dearborn, Wilkinson advised that logistical problems and manpower shortages would preclude any extended campaign. Meanwhile, to a Senate ally, the general lambasted Dearborn as a man "utterly unqualified for his place."[24]

In late 1806, both the international crisis along the Louisiana-Texas border and question of the loyalty of the nation's ranking military officer were resolved. Despite Wilkinson's bellicose letters to confidantes back east, he and his Spanish counterpart, Colonel Simon de Herrera, agreed to respect a neutral ground between the Arroyo Hondo and the Sabine River until a more permanent settlement could be reached. Wilkinson also distanced himself (as did an overly impetuous Andrew Jackson) from Burr, whose intrigues had attracted Jefferson's closest

FIG. 6. James Wilkinson. Talented but loyal only to his own self-
        interests, Wilkinson (1757–1825) nonetheless played a key role
        in establishing U.S. authority over key parts of the Louisiana
        Purchase. DURRETT COLLECTION, SPECIAL COLLECTIONS
        RESEARCH CENTER, UNIVERSITY OF CHICAGO LIBRARY.

scrutiny. Impressed by the general's handling of the crisis, the president retained his faith in Wilkinson, who in the end had remained loyal
to Washington. Jefferson's deft actions reveal his appreciation for the
army's importance to national development as well as his keen grasp of
its internal politics.[25]

In June 1807, the HMS *Leopard*'s forcible seizure of suspected

deserters aboard the USS *Chesapeake* just off the Virginia coast reaffirmed congressional support for a larger standing army. President
Jefferson, frustrated in his attempts to goad Congress into improving the state militias, proposed raising twenty-four thousand volunteers and nearly tripling the regular army. Supporting the larger force,
Representative Josiah Quincy (Fed-Mass.) proclaimed "that there is no
rational ground to fear that it can become dangerous to our liberties
and independence." Army critics such as Representative John Randolph
(R-Va.) sought to counter such proposals by emphasizing Wilkinson's
dalliances in the borderlands. But the mood of Congress had clearly
evolved; one of the bill's opponents expressed "painful surprise . . . that
he should be in a minority unusually small." The House passed the
administration bill by a ninety-five-to-sixteen majority. Each of the nine
congressmen from the trans-Appalachian states (Kentucky, Ohio, and
Tennessee) supported the increase, a clear signal of western recognition
of the regular army's importance to regional development.[26]

Moreover, the composition of this force suggests it truly was a people's army. Thanks to the research of J. D. A. Stagg, we have a remarkably
comprehensive social portrait of the individuals who made up this army.
The average enlistee was about twenty-six years old. Between 1802–11,
artisans made up nearly 40 percent of all enlistees, whereas farmers constituted less than 29 percent. Another 22 percent were laborers. A handful of African Americans joined the army, even after an 1820 regulation
barred their service. Nineteen percent of recruits were immigrants, of
whom nearly two-thirds were Irish. Of the native born, Virginia and
Pennsylvania combined to contribute nearly 36 percent. Most soldiers
were poorer, had fewer prospects, and had weaker ties to the communities of their birth than the average American. An unemployed George
Ballentine, for instance, later admitted that he enlisted "as sort of a last
resource." The large number of skilled craftsmen, however, highlights
the wrenching changes that gripped the national economy. Foreign and
domestic embargos and blockades badly shook trade, and artisans—
especially shoemakers and carpenters—suffered as changing means of
production threatened their former economic independence. Enlistment
patterns indicate that many future soldiers had left home in the East and
moved to the frontier. Finding uncertain chances for advancement and
lured by an immediate bonus, they signed up for military service.[27]

The Jefferson administration's support for a larger army did more than reinforce the nation's acceptance of a regular military establishment, for in adding over three hundred new officers, it supplied a rich harvest of opportunities for party patronage. As Secretary Dearborn reasoned, "patriots" should receive preference. By the time Jefferson left office, over 60 percent of officers were safely Republican, a clear shift from the earlier Federalist dominance.[28]

All, however, was not well, for the blatant partisanship by both Federalists and Republicans over the preceding fifteen years had had a predictable effect on this institution that was so influential in the borderlands. Officers openly espoused their partisan beliefs, and the lack of job security and repeated political machinations hurt morale and discipline. Although several members of the officer class of 1808–9—most notably Winfield Scott, Henry Atkinson, and Zachary Taylor—would go on to make important contributions to the frontier army, the institution as a whole risked paralysis. "The old officers had, very generally, sunk into either sloth, ignorance, or habits of intemperate drinking," charged Scott, who characterized those in his appointed class as mostly "swaggerers, dependants, decayed gentlemen, and others . . . *utterly unfit for any military purpose whatever.*" Precious little attention was paid to training and military doctrine. A veteran of Wayne's campaign, noting that army regulations should incorporate maneuvers applicable "to real warfare," complained "that all officers do not agree in the mode of fighting Indians." The floundering military academy, described by another officer as being a place "of ignorance & illness," lent no inspiration. Complaining about the administration's economic and intellectual neglect, the first superintendent resigned in 1803, allowed himself to be talked into returning two years later, only to quit once again in 1812.[29]

President James Madison's new administration offered little promise of rejuvenating the armed forces. Although Jefferson had initially reduced the regular army, he understood its value to the government in the West, supported the military academy, and eventually oversaw a substantial army increase. Madison, by contrast, seemed indifferent to military affairs; Zachary Taylor later described him as being "a man perfectly callous[ed] & unacquainted with the noble feelings of a soldier." It was not surprising, then, that Madison's first secretary of war, William Eustis, was a genial former army surgeon from Massachusetts who owed his appointment to his party loyalty and longtime association with the Society of the Cincinnati rather than to any military expertise. Disgusted by the "leaden-headed ignorance" that permeated the military establishment, one quartermaster concluded: "Nothing but the most powerful political friends can bring an officer into notice. A knowledge of military science is no recommendation to him."[30]

Such disrepair seemed especially perverse in light of increasing signs of trouble at home and abroad, for London had redoubled its efforts to solidify its Indian alliances. "Keep your eyes fixed on me," urged one British diplomat to an Indian delegation. "My tomahawk is now up; be you ready, but do not strike until I give the signal." Sparked by the energetic Shawnee brothers Tecumseh and Tenskwatawa (the Prophet), many tribes now embraced a militant opposition to U.S. expansion. "War belts have been passing through all the Tribes from the Gulf of Florida to the lakes," warned William Henry Harrison, now governor of the Indiana Territory, in 1807. "A general combination of the Indians for a war against the United States is the object of all these messages and councils," he predicted. New factories at isolated Fort Madison (on the upper Mississippi at the mouth of the Des Moines River) and Fort Osage (near present Sibley, Missouri) represented only feeble attempts to assert federal sovereignty.[31]

The U.S. feud with many peoples of the Old Northwest intensified following the Treaty of Fort Wayne (1809), in which envoys from the Delaware, Potawatomi, Miami, and Eel River Indians (and, in separate treaties, the Weas and Kickapoos) ceded huge grants of land in return for miserly annuities worth about two cents per acre. Denouncing the agreements, Tecumseh redoubled his efforts to organize a pan-Indian coalition; to confront this growing strategic threat, Governor Harrison called for improved military preparedness. Dismissing militia musters as "generally devoted to riot and intemperance," he lambasted frontiersmen for refusing to admit the value of discipline, an educated officer corps, or the bayonet charge. Breaking with tradition, Harrison proposed to tailor the army according to regional specialization: westerners might form the "corps avance" of riflemen and light cavalry, the eastern and middle states the artillery and line infantry, and southerners the regular cavalry and light infantry. In case of an Indian war, the United States must launch a mounted strike into the hostile district. Such a

FIG. 7. Tecumseh. Although not a contemporary likeness, this image
captures some of the power and magnetism of the Shawnee leader
Tecumseh (1768–1813). LIBRARY OF CONGRESS, USZ62-8255.

move would discourage other tribes from joining the fray and relieve pressure on the state militias, which "would inevitably be beaten" unless they enjoyed surprise or overwhelming numerical superiority.[32]

By the late summer of 1811, Governor Harrison determined to deliver the first blow in a war that seemed inevitable. When Tecumseh went south to recruit additional support, Harrison organized about a thousand regulars and militiamen to strike against the Prophet's town. Ignoring Washington's suggestion that launching such an offense amounted to profligate spending, Harrison marched north from Vincennes on September 19. The troops constructed an advanced base near present Terre Haute, Indiana, and by late October, Harrison deemed his soldiers to be in readiness. "I do not hesitate to pronounce them so perfect as Genl. Wayne's army was on the day of his victory," boasted Harrison, who mimicked his predecessor's insistence on strict march discipline and careful reconnoitering.[33]

On November 6, as he reached the Prophet's principal village at Tippecanoe Creek, Harrison halted in order to allow final peace talks. Early the next morning, a sudden Indian attack routed the sentinels along Harrison's left flank. Initially stunned by onslaught, the Americans then rallied. "The Indians manifested a ferocity, uncommon even with them," explained Harrison breathlessly. "To their savage fury, our troops opposed that cool and deliberate valor which is characteristic of the Christian soldier." A bayonet charge and cavalry assault finally drove back the Indians, estimated to be about six hundred strong. His troops having torched the Prophet's village and laid waste to the surrounding farmlands, Harrison claimed "a complete and decisive victory" at Tippecanoe, but one that even he admitted had come at a terrible price: 188 casualties, or about 20 percent of his entire force. Three dozen Indian bodies were found on the field, and many others, it was believed, had already been removed.[34]

War had once again come to the borderlands. Although Tenskwatawa's influence would wane, his brother Tecumseh stood defiant, and Indians remained a potent military challenge to further U.S. expansion. The militia, in "defending and protecting the country," reasoned Representative Peter B. Porter (R-N.Y.) as Congress debated preparations in case the conflict expanded to include Britain, served as "the shield of the nation." Reflecting a new political consensus, however, Porter expanded his vision of national defense to include the regular army. In exploring and occupying a vast new western empire, asserting national boundaries, building roads, promoting regional economic development, and fighting Indians, the regulars had, in Porter's view, become "the sword." Events would soon sorely test both shield and sword.[35]

THREE

Sharpening the Nation's Sword

War with Britain in 1812 would severely try the nation's armed forces. Over-optimism, a woefully inadequate infrastructure, and dismal leadership characterized the army's performance in the conflict's first eighteen months. Neither regulars nor militia did well until new officers, better training, and an improved system of production and supply helped the Americans—backed by a few Indians, most notably their former enemies, the Iroquois—to secure a military stalemate against the British and their Indian allies. However embarrassing the army's early ineptitude, the War of 1812 had an enormous impact on the borderlands. Indian threats to the Ohio River valley region were extinguished and Creek military power in the south shattered. Following the war, scattered frontier garrisons asserted U.S. authority, and fears of a standing army were temporarily quieted in the heady nationalism of the postwar years. Many looked to the regulars as a convenient means of improving the nation's transportation system, a trend that held huge potential for the non-Indian development of the West. Ironically, however, the army refused to fully embrace these frontier duties, taking instead its inspiration from the traditions of Europe.

In early 1812, as relations between the United States and Britain deteriorated and "War Hawks" gained political ascendancy, Congress increased

FIG. 8. "A Scene on the Frontiers as Practiced by the Humane British and
their Worthy Allies." This American cartoon portrays a British officer
accepting a scalp from an Indian ally. The scene may have been inspired
by the August 1812 slaughter outside Chicago. LIBRARY OF CONGRESS,
USZ62-5800.

the army's authorized strength to thirty-five thousand and permitted
President James Madison to mobilize a hundred thousand militiamen
for federal service. Having concluded that Britain's economic blockades,
assistance to Indians, and impressments of American soldiers imper-
iled the republic's existence, Congress declared war that June. Such a
move flew in the face of military reality, for Secretary of War William
Eustis and the eleven overworked clerks in his office were unprepared
for a conflict. Early appointments to high command, made with more
consideration for politics than military ability, were consistently bad.
"We shall never be successful while our troops are commanded by such
men," advised future secretary of war William H. Crawford. "For God's
sake . . . endeavor to rid the army of old women and blockheads."[1]

Optimists in Washington had envisioned a three-pronged invasion
of Canada. But the absence of proper planning, the presence of intra-
party Republican factionalism, the reluctance of many New Englanders

to support the war, and gross incompetence allowed Britain to seize the initiative. Since late 1811, Major General Isaac Brock, commander of British forces in Upper Canada, had envisioned a preemptive strike in case of war. Boasting twenty-six years of military experience, the forty-one-year-old Brock believed that seizure of Detroit and Mackinac would ensure the loyalty of Canadian militia and Indian allies as well as counterbalance Yankee frontiersmen, who he characterized as "an enterprizing hardy race, and uncommonly expert on horseback with the rifle." He could then mount "a protracted resistance," which his undisciplined enemies would "soon tire" of battling. A mixed command of regulars, militia, and Indians indeed forced the outnumbered garrison at Fort Mackinac to surrender shortly after the war began, securing for Britain control of northwestern Lake Michigan. "I never saw so determined [a] Set of people as the Chippewas & Ottawas were," noted one officer, who concluded that had the Americans not capitulated, "not a Soul of them would have been Saved."[2]

News of Fort Mackinac's fall completed the collapse of Brigadier General William B. Hull, who had been organizing an army at Detroit. Though boasting a distinguished Revolutionary War record, Hull seemed too old and never gained the confidence of his militia. He feared that the loss of Mackinac had "opened the Northern hive of Indians" and that they now would be "swarming in every direction." Badly outnumbered, Brock cleverly dressed some of his Canadian militia in cast-off redcoat uniforms and exploited the traditional dread of his Indian allies. "It is far from my intention to join in a war of extermination," Brock warned direly, "but you must be aware, that the numerous body of Indians . . . will be beyond controul the moment the contest commences." In mid-August, paralyzed by the prospect of a massacre, Hull surrendered his twenty-five hundred soldiers and twenty-five cannon to a force about half his size. "Even the women were indignant at so shameful a degradation of the American character," protested one subordinate.[3]

Another debacle at Fort Dearborn (Chicago) completed the disastrous month for the United States. Following the fort's surrender, several hundred Indians ambushed the hundred-odd Americans trying to make their way back to safety, killing thirty-eight soldiers and at least fourteen women and children. British officers, acknowledging the slaughter as having been "disgraceful to Humanity," nonetheless sung the praises of

Tecumseh, symbol of the pan-Indian movement. "A more sagacious or a more gallant Warrior does not exist," exuded Brock. Added another, "He [Tecumseh] has shewn [sic] himself to be a determined character and a great friend to our Government."[4]

Affairs further east were going just as badly for the Americans. Having assembled six thousand men, the aging Henry Dearborn gingerly crept into Canada but fell back after a single skirmish. Another ill-fated attempt to invade Canada at Queenston failed when New York state militia refused to cross the Niagara River, forcing a thousand regulars stranded on the other side to surrender. Brock's death in the fighting there offered the dispirited Americans little comfort. Brigadier General Alexander Smyth charged that the Pennsylvania militia "disgraced the nation," after his subsequent attempt to strike British-held Fort Erie came to naught because it refused to participate. Assessing the year's failures, the *National Intelligencer* acknowledged that the militia's "services have been found to be most inefficient when most necessary."[5]

Peripheral campaigns along the western and southern borders, save for Captain Zachary Taylor's spirited defense of Fort Harrison, Indiana Territory, offered no consolation. Major General Samuel Hopkins and two thousand mounted Kentucky volunteers rode into the Illinois River and Wabash River valleys but failed to engage the Indians in any major battles. Forays from Illinois volunteers did only marginally better. To the south, President Madison had hoped that filibusters might snatch East Florida from Spain, but Congress steadfastly refused to sanction such a move in light of the disasters to the north. Anxious to protect slavery and to continue American expansion, southerners would for two years nonetheless engage in a desultory "Patriot War" along the Georgia–East Florida border.[6]

To pick up the shattered pieces in the Old Northwest, in fall 1812 Madison reluctantly turned to the hero of Tippecanoe, William Henry Harrison. Harrison's extravagant spending antagonized his critics—chief among them being the newly appointed secretary of war, John Armstrong Jr.—but the infusion of federal dollars at least helped to maintain popular support for the war. Unable to undertake any major offensives that winter, Harrison sent out several columns designed to threaten Indian supply lines and sources. Leading one such thrust, Brigadier General James Winchester—a sixty-year-old Revolutionary

War veteran—took it on himself to march to the Raisin River to protect the isolated residents of Frenchtown (present Monroe, Michigan). The British and Indians caught Winchester's thousand-man column in an exposed position and forced their capitulation; three hundred Americans were killed following the surrender.[7]

With the federal government funneling resources elsewhere, Harrison assumed a defensive stance at newly constructed Fort Meigs (modern Perrysburg), located on the Maumee Rapids in Ohio. On May 1, 1813, 900 British regulars and Canadian militia, along with 1,200 Indians, initiated a siege of Harrison's 550-man garrison. They routed a twelve-hundred-man Kentucky relief force five days later (the "excessive ardour" shown by the Kentuckians, wrote Harrison, "was scarcely less fatal than cowardice"), but the fort's stout palisades convinced the Indians and Canadian militiamen that the effort was fruitless. "There will be no Hull business here," boasted one newspaper. On May 9, the enemy withdrew. Though U.S. losses (320 killed or wounded and 600 captured between the attack on Fort Meigs and the failed Kentucky relief effort) were nine times heavier than the enemy's, the defense of Fort Meigs boosted American morale. A similar British failure against Fort Stephenson (present Fremont, Ohio), defiantly maintained by Major George Croghan's 160-strong garrison, further dispirited the Indians.[8]

Despite the federal government's emphasis on affairs further east, the United States was slowly regaining the initiative in the borderlands. In September, Oliver Hazard Perry's naval triumph at Lake Erie ended the threat of further British inroads into the Ohio Valley and opened Upper Canada to an American counterthrust. The overmatched and outnumbered Colonel Henry Proctor, who took over command of British forces in the region following Brock's death, fell back into Canada. Mustering over three thousand men, Harrison reoccupied Detroit and captured Fort Malden. Proctor, characterized by Tecumseh as a "fat animal, that carries its tail upon its back, but when affrighted . . . drops it between his legs and runs off" finally turned to face the Americans along the Thames River near Moraviantown. On October 5, Harrison, battle tested by years of frontier warfare, launched Colonel Richard Johnson's regiment of mounted Kentucky volunteers against the enemy's overextended lines. Explaining his unorthodox maneuver,

Harrison wrote: "The American backwoodsmen ride better in the woods than any other people. . . . I was persuaded too that the enemy would be quite unprepared for the shock." This "irresistible force" shattered the British lines, and over six hundred surrendered. Tecumseh was killed (symbolically, he had fought in traditional Indian garb, and attackers had mutilated his body) in the mêlée. Harrison, trumpeted one proadministration newspaper, had delivered to the enemy a "lesson on backwoods tactics."[9]

The Niagara front appeared less hopeful for the United States. In May 1813, Winfield Scott had seized Fort George. But subsequent defeats at Stoney Creek and Beaver Dams, along with repeated British raids against American supply lines, led to the removal of the aging Dearborn from theater command and the fort's abandonment. Fort Niagara fell to a surprise assault in December, throwing open western New York to British and Indian attacks. Blaming "criminal negligence" and the "cowardly" behavior of the local militia, Brigadier General Lewis Cass described Buffalo as "a scene of distress and destruction such as I have never before witnessed."[10]

By early 1814, when Britain was freed from European obligations by Napoleon's collapse, thousands of sturdy British redcoats were arriving in North America. "Chastise the savages," urged the *Times* of London, "for such they are, in a much truer sense, than the followers of Tecumseh or the Prophet." In the United States, recruiting lagged behind projections, and abuses associated with supply and ordnance contracts were legion. The sack of Washington by British raiders in August 1814 assured the demise of Secretary Armstrong. Once again revealing his startling inability to manage the conflict, Madison appointed Secretary of State James Monroe—whose lack of understanding of military affairs rivaled his own—to oversee the war office.[11]

Embarrassing as these setbacks were, a glimmer of hope was belatedly emerging along the Niagara frontier. The able Major General Jacob Brown moved into Canada and captured Fort Erie in early July. Having benefited from a rigorous training program, Brown's thirty-five hundred troops drove the British from the field at the Battle of Chippewa. Amazed at the performance of his enemies, a grizzled British officer reportedly cried: "Those are regulars, by God." Brown then fought the British to a draw during a bloody slugfest at Lundy's Lane. Subsequent action saw the British recoup their territorial losses, but the campaign had demonstrated that well-trained, well-led American units could stand up to the world's best in conventional battles.[12]

Along the southern borderlands, civil war had broken out among the Creeks. Lower Creeks tended to favor accommodation with Washington, whereas most Upper Creeks—especially the militant Red Sticks—had joined Tecumseh. "Let the white race perish," Tecumseh had told one Creek gathering in 1811. "They seize your land; they corrupt your women; they trample on the bones of your dead!" In July 1813, Mississippi militiamen attacked a party of Red Sticks at Burnt Corn Creek, then fell back to Fort Mims, Alabama, where several hundred squatters, mixed-blood farmers, slaves, and allied Indians had collected for safety. About midday on August 30, Red Eagle and a thousand Red Sticks routed the unprepared garrison and butchered many of the residents.[13]

Outraged backwoodsmen vowed to revenge the atrocities at Fort Mims. "We hope, we trust in God," screamed one newspaper, that the "government will never be at peace with those hell hounds until they are made to feel the weight of its mighty power." Major General Andrew Jackson of the Tennessee militia was equally blunt: "We must hasten to the frontier, or we will find it drenched in the blood of our fellow-citizens." Volunteers from Georgia and Mississippi failed to penetrate the heart of Creek country, but the Tennesseans, fired by Jackson's exertions and unyielding discipline, were made of sterner stuff. In early November, a detachment led by General John Coffee struck the Red Sticks near their village at Tallushatchee. As Hannibal had done at Cannae two thousand years earlier, and as Indians had done on countless occasions on the American frontiers, Coffee lured his foes into the center of his position, then enveloped the exposed enemy on both flanks. "We shot them like dogs," boasted Davy Crockett. One hundred eighty-six Red Sticks were found dead; another eighty-four women and children were taken prisoner. Coffee counted five dead and forty-one wounded. Six days later, Jackson tried to employ the same tactics against a Creek force roughly half the size of his at Talladega. This time the Red Sticks broke out of the trap, at a cost of three hundred dead left on the field. Immobilized by "the negligence of The contractors," Jackson then broke off the campaign.[14]

Emboldened by 850 reinforcements, in January 1814 Jackson again took the field. Five days' march from his base camp at Fort Strother (near Ohatchee, Alabama), however, he narrowly averted defeat in two sharp skirmishes. Chastened, Jackson retreated; the following month, after his army had been augmented by new volunteers and stiffened by the arrival of the Thirty-ninth Infantry Regiment, he resumed his stalled offensive with two thousand infantry, seven hundred mounted troops, six hundred Cherokee and Creek allies, and two small cannon. Learning that one thousand Red Stick warriors and some three hundred women and children held a fortified position inside Horseshoe Bend, formed by a loop in the Tallapoosa River, he reportedly predicted that "they have penned themselves up for slaughter." The attack began on March 27, with Jackson's Cherokee allies swimming the river and cap-turing the Red Sticks' canoes, cutting off their intended mode of retreat. His light artillery was unable to pierce the sturdy Red Stick breastworks, and so instead his infantry launched a frontal assault. "The *carnage was dreadfull*," he later admitted. Quarter was neither asked nor offered during the frenzied struggle, which claimed the lives of nine hundred Creeks. Among Jackson's 276 casualties were 23 allied Indians killed and 47 wounded.[15]

Having grown up amid the violence of the frontiers and the Revolution, Jackson embraced a ruthless willingness to shunt aside Indians—even those who had fought alongside him in battle—and Europeans alike to open up new lands for his countrymen. Following the contest at Horseshoe Bend, he established Fort Jackson (present Wetumpka, Alabama) in the heart of a region held sacred by the Creeks. That August, he forced both friendly and hostile Creeks to cede twenty-three million acres in Alabama and Georgia. Jackson also vowed to eliminate British and Spanish influence, and that November he swept into Spanish-held Pensacola to destroy a British depot. Early the fol-lowing year, the general secured an even more famous victory over the British in the Battle of New Orleans. Defending a fortified position anchored by the Mississippi River and Louisiana swampland, his mixed force of regulars, marines, sailors, militiamen, pirates, and slave volun-teers threw back a poorly managed assault by British regulars, inflicting nearly two thousand casualties at a cost of less than a hundred of their own number. "I could have walked on the dead bodies of the British for one quarter of a mile without stepping on the ground," reported

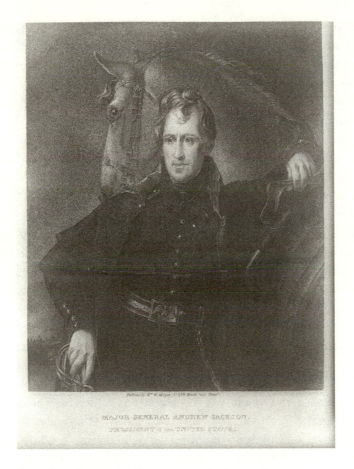

FIG. 9. Andrew Jackson. Jackson (1767–1845) was a lawyer, politician, and soldier whose frontier military successes against the Creeks and the British helped to propel him into two terms as president. LIBRARY OF CONGRESS, USZ62-435.

one Tennessee militiaman. Unknown to those on the blood-stained fields along the Mississippi, diplomats across the Atlantic at Ghent had already concluded a peace agreement that restored the status quo ante bellum. But since many Americans heard of Jackson's victory first, they wrongly assumed that the British had been driven to the peace table by force of arms.[16]

Although Washington and London had fought to a military draw, the War of 1812 forever altered the balance of power between the United States and Indians east of the Mississippi River. Battlefield setbacks, internal divisions, and economic stress had badly hurt the Creeks in the South, and convinced the Wyandots, Shawnees, Delawares, Miamis, Senecas, Ojibwas, Ottawas, Potawatomies, Sauks, and Winnebagos in the North to make peace with Washington. Blue-ribbon panels, featuring old western hands like Harrison and William Clark and $20,000 worth of presents, negotiated a new round of negotiations throughout the Old Northwest. Ended were considerations of pan-Indian confederations between northern and southern tribes, and alliances between the northern woodlands peoples and Britain also seemed a thing of the past. "The whole of the Western Indians are completely hemm'd in," concluded one British officer from Mackinac, "thoroughly in the power of the Americans, & their assistance in any future war, *hopeless, & not to be expected.*" Moreover, a greater sense of patriotic self-righteousness now permeated American attitudes toward war and diplomacy. Believing that republics were pacific because the people ruled, they assumed that their wars would, by extension, be only those of righteous self-defense.[17]

A strong military and economic presence accompanied the diplomatic offensive, for it was concluded that the army must interdict British trade routes from Canada. U.S. commissioners thus instructed Indians in Michigan, Wisconsin, and Minnesota "that it is intended to establish strong posts very high up the Mississippi, and from the Mississippi to Lake Michigan, and to open trading-houses at those posts, or other suitable places for their accommodation." Similarly, inhabitants of Ohio, Illinois, and Indiana learned that the army would occupy a line of forts from Chicago to St. Louis. Reinforcements hurried to Detroit, and Fort Mackinac was reclaimed from the British. Fort Howard and the reconstructed Fort Dearborn guarded the burgeoning communities of Green Bay and Chicago. Fort Edwards (present Warsaw, Illinois) and Fort Armstrong (present Rock Island) commanded the Mississippi River north of St. Louis, and further upriver Fort Crawford came to dominate the old French community at strategic Prairie du Chien.[18]

To the south, several Cherokee groups in 1817 and 1819 reluctantly exchanged their lands in North Carolina for territory in Arkansas and a promise of federal protection. Soldiers duly erected Fort Smith, in the heart of the Ozark Mountains, to shield the emigrants from the resident

Osages, but the garrison found it impossible to prevent white encroachments. Agent William L. Lovely complained that "whites of the worst character in this country" were stoking the fires of war. Authorities insisted that regulars take the lead over the more expensive, and less disciplined, militia in quelling potential conflicts. "Protection is the first object," went typical orders to Brevet Major General Edmund P. Gaines, stationed along the volatile Georgia-Florida border, "and the second is protection by the regular force."[19]

The army had profoundly influenced the nation's borderlands. But the frontier had little impact on army organization or doctrine in the nationalistic years following the War of 1812. Harrison, whose victories at Tippecanoe and the Thames had transformed the balance of regional power, resigned from the service, angrily denouncing those who had dubbed him an "artificial general." In the reorganized postwar force, Andrew Jackson and Jacob Brown were named the army's two major generals. The fiery, nationalistic Jackson certainly understood the frontier ways of war. But while Old Hickory would parlay his military feats all the way to the White House, he disdained those that smacked of professionalism. Brown, a former Quaker, had likewise emerged from the volunteer militia but was in most ways very much a conventional warrior, as evidenced by his failure to make effective use of his Indian allies at Chippewa.[20]

Frontier experiences also had little impact on army tactics. A board of officers headed by Brigadier General Winfield Scott adopted a new manual, the *1815 Regulations*. Essentially a translated version of an older French work, the *Regulations* (later revised in 1824 and again in 1835) reflected the army's penchant for conventional operations and tight linear formations. As Indians were presumed to be less than equal, it was assumed that warfare against them did not merit systematic analysis. Lessons learned in the forest warfare of the republic's early years—the value of combined arms, tactical flexibility, reconnaissance, and Indian allies—thus failed to make the pages of these manuals. Neither did West Point redress the problem. As historian John Waghelstein has concluded, the academy "largely ignored" the Indian wars. "If the hard won lessons of the past were not in the curriculum," adds Waghelstein, "they would be re-learned the hard way, in the Everglades or on the Little Big Horn."[21]

Sobered by the war's many disappointments, in early 1815 James

Monroe, interim secretary of war, had asked for a twenty-thousand-strong peacetime army. Understandably, Monroe stressed the threats posed by Spain and Great Britain rather than Indians. Given the weakened condition of the tribes along the nation's western borders, such a tack accurately reflected near-term strategic conditions but disregarded the army's historic constabulary duties. Representative James Fisk (R-Vt.) gamely evoked frontier experiences in an effort to rally support for the administration's proposal. "Who could recollect the disasters of Harmar, the defeat of St. Clair, and not fear similar results of similar circumstances?" wondered Fisk. But the Battle of New Orleans, during which Jackson's volunteers had faced down the vaunted British redcoats, had reconfirmed the popular belief in the militia's efficacy. Others invoked the long-standing fear of a professional army. "If there was only one principle which might be called fundamental to our civil institutions," insisted Richard Stockton (Fed.-NJ), "it was this—that a standing army was not to be tolerated in time of peace." In the end Congress authorized an army of 12,383 officers and men, which translated to an army that was 25 percent larger than that of 1808 but significantly smaller than what Monroe had requested.[22]

Elected president in 1816, Monroe, perhaps having learned from his own mistakes as war secretary, made improved national defense a cornerstone of his first inaugural address, insisting that the regular army be sufficient "to garrison and preserve our fortifications and to meet the first invasions of a foreign foe." He convinced John Calhoun, an outspoken champion of military interests during his tenure in the House of Representatives, to become his secretary of war. An energetic South Carolinian, Calhoun compensated for his lack of combat experience with imagination and intelligence. "Mr. C. will I have no doubt bring great decision into the Dept. & grt. weight & ability into the cabinet," observed a former officer. "He is considered one of the most promising men in the country." Eager to showcase his administrative abilities, Calhoun oversaw the development of a more effective staff system and the consolidation and centralization of the Corps of Engineers and helped his department clear millions of dollars of unsettled accounts. The secretary also backed the forceful new superintendent of West Point, Captain Sylvanius Thayer, who transformed the military academy into a powerful agent for army professionalism.[23]

FIG. 10. "The Nation's Bulwark." By the 1820s, most objective
observers had concluded that the militia had become more
useful as a political tool than a first line of national defense.
This satire, by Edward Williams Clay, lampoons the
Philadelphia militia. LIBRARY OF CONGRESS, USZ62-7752.

Calhoun's support for government-sponsored improvements promised tangible benefits to westerners. Following the War of 1812, analysts
pointed out that a better transportation system would improve national
security, and many looked to the army for assistance. Andrew Jackson
thus won President Madison's approval to construct a road from Nashville
to Madisonville, Louisiana (on Lake Pontchartrain, just north of New
Orleans). Madison also agreed to a military road from Detroit to Fort
Meigs; proud of his work on the latter thoroughfare, Brigadier General
Alexander Macomb declared it "highly beneficial" to the national government as well as the local population. "Besides greatly adding to the
defence and strength of this frontier," explained Macomb, "the road has
been the means of developing the nighness of the publick lands in this
territory and greatly augmenting their value."[24]

Despite their approval of these specific thoroughfares, the Virginia
presidents both opposed broader federal programs on constitutional

grounds. Carefully withholding his opinion on constitutional questions, in early 1819 Calhoun linked a national system of roads and canals with public prosperity, national defense, and the consolidation of the union. "The road or canal can scarcely be designated which is highly useful for military operations," he reasoned, "which is not equally required for the industry or political prosperity of the community." General Brown added that engagement in such projects would enable the army to "achieve a victory over some of the prejudices of the country by their useful labors in peace if they could not by their deeds of arms in War." Pointedly, however, Calhoun insisted that these measures protect against attack from a European foe. Wrote the secretary, "All our great military efforts, growing out of a war with a European power, must for the present be directed towards our Eastern, Northern, or Southern frontiers."[25]

The army's involvement in western economic development did not come without cost, for enlisted personnel provided much of the labor. Lieutenant Colonel Zachary Taylor complained that the nation's "passion" for using his soldiers to make internal improvements left little time for them to practice the art of war. Eighteen months' road work had left enlisted personal "without discipline, subordination or harmony." Following his 1820 inspection of Fort Mackinac, Colonel John Wool complained that it had been over a year since the garrison had undertaken any military drills. "The army has become a complete fatigue party and the duties of soldiers do not enter into their calculations," grumbled another veteran.[26]

In addition to building roads, regulars constructed most of the barracks, officers' quarters, hospitals, storehouses, and stables that marked the frontier forts, using locally available wood and stone. Others tilled post gardens. Soldiers, complained one inspector, represented "the pack horses of the republic, upon whose backs everything of an offensive nature is to be piled." Some officials claimed that moderate amounts of such labor would improve discipline, but the real reason for substituting soldier labor for hired civilians was to save money. Work on the second Fort Crawford, for example, forced inspector George Croghan to call off his review of the garrison in 1830. Upon his return three years later, Croghan again canceled the inspection. "The barracks erected here are certainly the best in the country," he acknowledged ruefully, "but they have as certainly built at the cost, I may say, of one of the best regiments that we have ever had."[27]

Enlisted men established for themselves communities largely separate from those of commissioned personnel. During off-duty hours, they hunted, fished, played games, and organized races in a manner that earned them little notice from their officers, who commented much more frequently on their drinking and gambling. A few made use of nascent post libraries, schools, and religious services, amenities that would receive more institutional support following the Civil War. Others joined glee clubs and produced lively, if not entirely polished, theatrical performances. "Music dancing and exhibition in the quarters of the men, once or twice during each week," sniffed one post surgeon. Using monies from post funds (collected from taxes paid by officially recognized sutlers) and revenue generated from the sale of excess rations, they organized hops and special holiday dinners in their company barracks and dining halls, by tradition inviting some of their officers to help inaugurate such proceedings.[28]

The typical regular engaged in remarkably little military training. "In fact U.S. soldiers on the frontiers a little in advance of its settlements are rather hewers of wood and diggers of ground than soldiers," explained Captain James J. Archer, "and it is very seldom that they are able to indulge in military exercises enough to enable them to preserve any of the appearance of a regular army." Periodically, the army attempted to funnel recruits through training depots (typically at Fortress Monroe, Virginia; Fort Columbus, New York; Carlisle Barracks, Pennsylvania; or Newport Barracks, Kentucky) before sending them to their units, but the process was at best haphazard. New recruits, complained one officer, "appear never to have had a firearm in their hands" before joining their unit. Once they got to their respective companies, soldiers found that drills emphasized close-order tactics designed to secure the most benefits from current military weaponry. Carrying flintlock smoothbore muskets (typically a .69-caliber weapon, using patterns adopted in 1816 and 1835), even the most skilled contemporary marksmen found it difficult to hit a target. Faced with chronic budget shortages, army officials thus saw no need to implement costly marksmanship practice, which they believed would have limited combat value anyway. Rigid discipline, tight linear formations, mass volleys, and bayonet charges instead seemed the order of the day. Introduction of more reliable percussion cap ignition systems in the 1830s and 1840s, along with production of the Model 1841 rifle (often called the Mississippi rifle), led to no discernable shift in attitude.[29]

The nationalistic Secretary Calhoun championed western expansion, as did the administration he served. Soldiers complemented the efforts of U.S. fur traders to broaden their foothold in the upper Missouri River country. In 1817 and 1818, peace treaties were signed with delegations from the Otos, Pawnees, and Poncas. To the east, policy focused on either removing Indians from lands desired by whites or on "civilizing" the Indians so as to avert their extinction. Many military and political leaders hoped to achieve these ends without resorting to force, but their claim that Indian hunters made less efficient use of land than U.S. farmers led them to insist that territorial expansion continue. As President Monroe reasoned in his first annual message, "No tribe or people have a right to withhold from the wants of others more than is necessary for their own support and comfort." The government must pursue a "liberal and humane policy," but Americans demanded that they be allowed to secure what they perceived to be their empire for liberty.[30]

Calhoun and many officers saw the British—especially the powerful Hudson's Bay Company (which merged with its rival, the North West Company, in 1821)—as major rivals to expansion into the northern plains and Oregon country. Although the two nations had agreed to jointly occupy Oregon in the Treaty of 1818, memories of past conflicts ran deep. One military inspector, Arthur P. Hayne, averred that fifteen thousand Indian warriors in the upper Missouri region were "completely under the control of the British Companies," who in turn were "incessantly Cabaling" them to oppose U.S. interests. Hudson's Bay Company posts dotted the region, and American fur traders and lobbyists peppered Washington with demands for assistance. To counter the continuing influence of British traders and new settlements along the Red River of the North, Calhoun called for new posts at the falls of St. Mary's (between Lake Superior and Lake Huron) and along the upper Missouri River to the mouth of the Yellowstone River. The United States should adopt a carrot-and-stick approach: in addition to "kind treatment and a proper distribution of presents," three regiments of regulars should accompany this diplomatic offensive. Such moves, he pronounced exuberantly, would allow the nation unfettered access to "the most valuable fur trade in the world."[31]

FIG. 11. John C. Calhoun. A capable, energetic administrator and
        nationalist, Calhoun (1782–1850) ranked among the best of the
        nineteenth-century secretaries of war. After leaving the War
        Department, he became much more interested in defending
        states' rights and slavery. LIBRARY OF CONGRESS, USZ62-102297.

Nationalists joined in the celebratory chorus. In a widely reprinted
editorial, the *St. Louis Enquirer* declared that a military post on the
Yellowstone River

will be an era in the history of the West. . . . The North West and
Hudson's Bay companies will be shut out from the commerce

of the Missouri and Mississippi Indians; the American traders will penetrate in safety the recesses of the rocky mountains in search of its rich furs; a commerce yielding a million
per annum will descend the Missouri; and the Indians, finding their wants supplied by American traders, their domestic
wars restrained by American policy, will learn to respect the
American name.

Seizing on the issue, President Monroe recognized that westerners saw
such a military effort as being more important "than any other which
has been taken by the government."[32]

Between 1818 and 1822, then, the army established three forts:
Snelling (at the junction of the Minnesota and Mississippi rivers),
Atkinson (Council Bluffs), and Brady (Sault Ste. Marie). Calhoun also
dispatched Major Stephen H. Long to explore the Missouri River and
its tributaries. Reflecting the era's giddy optimism, orders to Long
instructed the major to "acquire as thorough and accurate knowledge as
may be practicable . . . [and] permit nothing worthy of notice to escape
your attention." A graduate of Dartmouth College and member of the
army's Topographical Bureau, Long enjoyed considerable frontier experience; for his party he had recruited a botanist, a zoologist, a geologist, a
naturalist, and a painter. He could count on the regulars to provide him
with "every aid & protection which may be practicable."[33]

The architecture of many of these newer forts further reflected the
increased national confidence. Earlier posts had usually been crudely
constructed square enclosures, with roughly hewn timber palisades and
rude blockhouses guarding the corners. "I cannot conceive it to be useful
or expedient to construct expensive works for our interior Military posts,
especially such as are intended merely to hold the Indians in check,"
Secretary Dearborn had written in 1804. Newly commissioned Fort
Snelling, on the other hand, would have massive stone towers and palisades. Fort Atkinson boasted "good-looking, white washed buildings,"
according to one foreign observer, who was especially impressed by the
burgeoning military community's beehive of associated garden, sawmill, gristmill, smithy, and distillery. "The American military establishment must be looked upon as a great industrial center," he explained.
The republic, it seemed, was sharpening the nation's sword.[34]

FOUR

Asserting National Sovereignty

With the War Department now headed by the innovative, energetic, and ambitious John Calhoun, the army seemed poised to assume an ever-larger role in asserting national sovereignty across the borderlands. Seizing on a series of public relations disasters, the economic panic that swept the country in 1819, and the reduced military threat resulting from new agreements with Spain and Great Britain, however, Calhoun's political rivals joined forces with conservative congressmen to reduce the army and to block the secretary's efforts at organizational reform. The public expected the army to help secure the nation's imperial designs, but its role in implementing the government's controversial Indian policy, its composition, and the embarrassing behavior by some officers and enlisted men buttressed the case of its critics. Indeed, the inconsistencies between public expectations of and attitudes toward the army would continue to haunt the frontier regulars for decades to come.

In the late 1810s, explosive events in Florida highlighted the army's historic affiliation with the borderlands. About a thousand Red Sticks had migrated to Florida following the disaster of Horseshoe Bend. Believing that Indian alliances with Spain or Britain still posed a significant threat, Andrew Jackson, now commanding the Southern Division,

Brigadier General Edmund P. Gaines, heading the military department facing the Florida frontier, and Lieutenant Colonel Thomas S. Jesup, stationed in Louisiana with his Third Infantry Regiment, were ready to use any excuse to act. In late summer 1816, for example, Jesup breathlessly announced that he had "positive information" about an impending Spanish attack against New Orleans and insisted that "abundant evidence" indicated that the British would strike against Florida and Cuba. If these attacks were allowed to occur, the United States would "find the tomahawk constantly raised and actively employed against us." To forestall these threats, Jesup developed plans to invade Cuba.[1]

The predicted assaults never came, but skirmishing between Seminoles, escaped slaves, Red Sticks, Lower Creeks, state militiamen, and U.S. regulars along the Georgia borderlands continued even after the destruction of Negro Fort, once a center for dissident activities. In 1813, Georgia militia had established Fort Mitchell (Russell County, Alabama), and the government would add a trading factory four years later. In early 1818 Jackson and Gaines mustered three thousand volunteers and Creek allies to supplement their regulars. Disregarding orders, Jackson invaded Florida that March. At St. Marks, he executed two Britons suspected of aiding the Seminoles, then pushed on to Pensacola, proclaiming "that sound national Policy will dictate holding Possession as long as we are a republick." His preemptive strike, Jackson added, "puts an end to all Indian wars."[2]

More than anywhere else in the three decades following the War of 1812, military action in Florida would determine the course of national expansion. Jackson's belligerence was a key factor in Spain's decision in 1820 to ratify the Transcontinental Treaty, in which it agreed to cede Florida to the United States. But it also had unintended consequences in Washington. The general's high-handed actions infuriated Calhoun, and some in Congress compared Jackson's activities to the usurpation of civil power by Caesar, Cromwell, and Napoleon. Others pointed to the diminished international threats to security resulting from the new pact with Madrid as well as to recent agreements with Great Britain that demilitarized the Great Lakes (the Rush-Bagot Treaty) and resolved long-standing Canadian border disputes east of the Rocky Mountains (the Convention of 1818). In light of these developments, antiregular sentiment indeed seemed to be on the rise. "A most noble competition exists

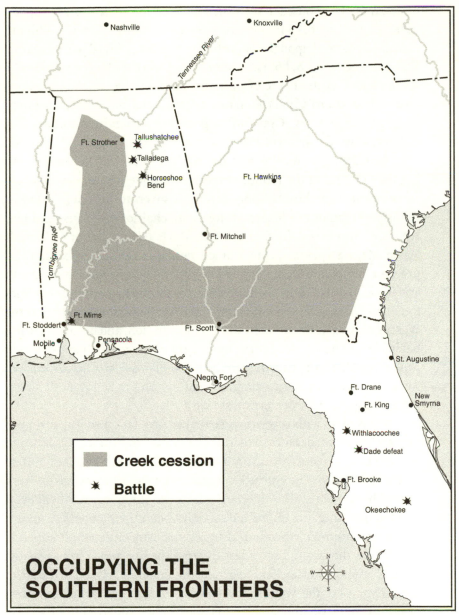

Nashville

Knoxville

Tennessee River

Ft. Strother   Tallushatchee
                Talladega
                Horseshoe
                Bend

Ft. Hawkins

Tombigbee River

Ft. Mitchell

Ft. Mims

Ft. Stoddert

Mobile

Pensacola

Ft. Scott

St. Augustine

Negro Fort

Ft. Drane
        Ft. King   New
                        Smyrna

Withlacoochee

Dade defeat

Ft. Brooke

Okeechokee

Creek cession

★ Battle

OCCUPYING THE
SOUTHERN FRONTIERS

Robert F. Pace

between the two houses to see which shall do the army the most spite," observed the caustic Winfield Scott. Secretary of the Treasury William Crawford pounced upon the opportunity to score political points against Calhoun and Jackson, both of whom he saw as rivals for the presidency. As the shock of the Panic of 1819 and the sectional acrimony associated with Missouri's application to enter the union as a slave state swept through the country, Crawford urged sharp spending cutbacks by Calhoun's war department.[3]

The shifting political winds also dashed Calhoun's hopes of planting the U.S. flag at the mouth of the Yellowstone River. Scandals concerning the sweetheart supply contracts given to Kentucky's James Johnson—brother of Richard M. Johnson, chair of the House Military Affairs Committee—further tainted efforts to implement Calhoun's vision. Major Stephen H. Long's much-vaunted scientific expedition also proved a disappointment. Plagued by illness, desertions, carelessness, and inadequate funding, the party failed to ascend to the source of either the Platte, Arkansas, or Red rivers. Moreover, Long's description of the West as an area "almost wholly unfit for cultivation, and of course, uninhabitable by a people depending upon agriculture for their subsistence" would long discourage interest in the Great Plains. Thus Fort Atkinson, Iowa, rather than a more extended position up the Yellowstone River, remained the army's westernmost post.[4]

In May 1820, with government expenditures far exceeding revenues and sectional tensions increasing, the House instructed Calhoun to devise a plan to reduce the army's authorized strength by about half, to six thousand men. The embattled war secretary summoned advice from each of his generals, who vigorously defended the army. Winfield Scott pointed out "that our troops have always been the pioneers & guardians of expanding civilization." But a consensus emerged: if cuts had to be made, they should come largely from the line and among enlisted men. Reductions elsewhere, warned the generals, risked a repeat of the early days of the War of 1812, when poor leadership and an enfeebled bureaucracy had nearly led to catastrophe. Adopting their advice, on December 12 Calhoun proposed what has come to be known as an "expansible army." Existing units, top-heavy with professional officers, could quickly absorb additional recruits in case of war. Calhoun's point of reference in constructing his plan, which emphasized the inability of

FIG. 12. Winfield Scott. A capable diplomat and rightly acclaimed for
his brilliant military service against conventional enemies like
Britain and Mexico, Scott (1786–1866) was extraordinarily
difficult to get along with and never grasped the nuances of
borderlands conflict. LIBRARY OF CONGRESS, USZ61-7.

untrained militiamen to stand against regular armies, was the perceived
threat from conventional European enemies.[5]

Whatever its merits, Secretary Calhoun's scheme was unrealistic
in light of contemporary political and diplomatic realities. Voicing old
fears, Senator Mahlon Dickerson (R-N.J.) claimed that "a large army

must at all times . . . be anti-republican." Even Dickerson, however, recognized that practical politics, rather than Republican dogma, now had the most impact on his fellow congressmen. A coalition of those desirous of slashing federal spending, denying Calhoun a chance to win a political victory, removing Jackson from the army, and securing a peace dividend from the recent agreements with Spain and Britain eliminated two infantry regiments, consolidated the artillery and ordnance departments, and purged three general officers. Little of Calhoun's proposal remained; infantry companies would have forty-nine enlisted men, rather than the thirty-seven he had suggested. "The vote on the army bill beats all I could have imagined," wrote one disappointed officer. "If reduction was to be made, the project of the Secretary is the only one in which system & science were incorporated and which had the singular advantage of lowering our numbers without weakening our means."[6]

Often forgotten in analyses of Calhoun's proposal was its failure to link the army's cause with potentially popular matters of western defense and nation building. In passing, the secretary acknowledged that some regulars would be needed to occupy "certain commanding posts in our inland frontier to keep in check our savage neighbors, and to protect our newly formed and feeble settlements in that quarter." But the overwhelming weight of Calhoun's argument centered on the needs of conventional warfare. It was foolhardy, he judged, to use militia as anything more than post garrisons or auxiliaries against "the regular troops of Europe." To save as many regulars as he could, Calhoun conceded that the rifle regiment—what General Brown dismissed as being "rarely valuable but in partisan warfare"—could be made a standard infantry unit as a cost-cutting gesture. Given this disinterest in military affairs pertaining to the borderlands and in light of the reduced international security threats, it was hardly surprising that 61 percent of frontier states representatives and senators joined those rejecting Calhoun's plan.[7]

Congress became a convenient scapegoat for the army's problems. One regular, for example, attributed Long's failure to the "detestable parsimony" of Congress. But such pleas ring hollow. The inflated costs associated with Calhoun's Yellowstone projects during a time of economic depression hardly inspired confidence in the Department of War, and the disappointing results of Long's expeditions did nothing to help. Moreover, the secretary's failure to associate his proposed restructuring with what might have been more popular plans for western empire seems a stunning oversight in an otherwise imaginative term in the War Department. Nowhere did he effectively link the army's role in promoting borderlands commerce and development with his protests against military cutbacks, nor did he attempt to capture western assistance for his expansible army concept by designing a force consistent with frontier realities. The failure to "sell" the army in the court of public opinion had devastating results for the military. It would be seventeen years before the army again reached ten thousand men and a decade before the War Department's percentage of federal spending regained levels of the late 1810s.[8]

The army's ambivalence toward Indian removal—a nineteenth-century version of ethnic cleansing—did nothing to improve the public's estimation of its image as an obedient agent of expansion. Most soldiers shared the ethnocentric prejudices of their countrymen; Lieutenant William Wall's views of Indians was typical: "I take them to be naturally indolent, very revengeful, and far inferior to the whites intellectually." After visiting one Indian camp, another diarist wrote, "I was most completely disgusted with their domestic life—and felt as though I never had more reason for thanking God that I was born civilized." Although there were exceptions, officers tended to rank Indians according to their degree of "civilization"—that is, according to the particular tribe's similarity with the practices of their own culture. But even as pressure to relocate Indians away from the onrush of American settlement swelled, many soldiers expressed reservations about the treatment of Indians, especially those that had adapted some elements of European-style civilization. Even avowed expansionists such as Brevet Major General Edmund P. Gaines, himself a product of a rough-and-tumble frontier environment and an outspoken supporter of western interests, complained of the unfair treatment accorded many Indians. As Gaines explained, he "would just as soon seek for fame by an attempt to remove the Shakers, or the Quakers, as to break up the Indians, take their lands and throw together twenty tribes speaking different languages." A racist, Gaines nonetheless insisted that his nation conduct its affairs honorably. "We must cultivate the friendship of these savages," he told the secretary of war, "be just to them, feed the hungry, clothe the naked, visit and heal the sick, and do unto them as we would that our strong civilized neighbors should do unto us. Otherwise we *must annihilate* them. This we cannot do without forgetting what is due to our own interests, and our own self-respect."[9]

Acting as borderlands policemen, regulars attempted to enforce loosely written and confusing federal laws, whereas most westerners expected them to adopt an avowedly proexpansionist stance. Soldiers who tried to prevent whites from trespassing or from engaging in the highly lucrative (but illegal) whiskey trade in Indian country did so at their own legal peril. Observed one traveler: "Every subaltern in the command knows, that if he interferes between an Indian and a white man, he will be sued instantly. . . . The Indian then despises the agent, because he is clothed with no military authority; and the pioneer despises the military, because their hands are tied by the local civil power." Knowing that friendly local judges and juries would usually support them, offenders scoffed at the regulars' policing efforts. "I was arrested," reported one trader, "went to the Fort, and laughed at the officers, and told them that I thought I was in a free country; and so believing, that I should go and come when and where I pleased, that they might all go to——."[10]

The army also continued to implement the nation's trade and intercourse laws, even after the 1822 abolition of the factory system. In 1824, Secretary Calhoun helped to create the Office of Indian Affairs, naming Thomas L. McKenney, long known as a champion of Indian education, to head the new office. War Department agents and military officers attempted to carry out policy through an intricate and often ritualized distribution of presents, annuities, and medals among influential Indian leaders. Military inspectors regularly labored to expose fraud, corruption, and mismanagement among contractors and agents; a typical report would conclude "that the Indians were deeply and unmercifully wronged." As could be expected, such meddling won the army few friends among private contractors, merchants, and fur traders anxious to take advantage of western economic opportunities, helping to explain the institution's uncertain status in the American psyche.[11]

Cognizant of the connection between public perceptions and congressional funding, in 1821 commanding general Jacob Brown urged officers to "cultivate intimate relations with society, and to attach the community to the interests of the army. . . . The affections of the nation constitute the only certain and permanent basis upon which the military

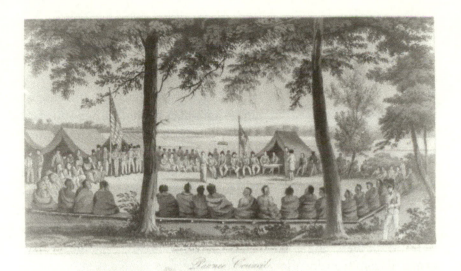

FIG. 13. Samuel Seymour, "Pawnee Council." Most early military
      expeditions included an illustrator. In the case of Stephen H.
      Long's 1819, 1820, and 1823 expeditions, it was Samuel Seymour,
      who depicted this meeting between Long and Pawnee leaders near
      what become Fort Atkinson. LIBRARY OF CONGRESS, USZ62-7778.

establishment can build its reputation." But national interests, at least
in the view of many soldiers, often differed from those of a particular
borderlands community, where the lure of the main chance sometimes
trumped legal or moral niceties. Likewise, the army met stiff opposition in its largely unsuccessful efforts to regulate lease programs among
lead miners. The regulars were thus placed in the unenviable position
of attempting to limit raw capitalism, making it difficult to defend the
army's interests in the court of public opinion.[12]

The open scorn some officers expressed about the rough-hewn
inhabitants of the borderlands added to civil-military rivalries. Better
educated, boasting more privileged backgrounds than most civilians
in and around the typical western garrison, and being members of an
institution that strongly valued hierarchy and order, commissioned personnel viewed with contempt the public displays of egalitarianism they
often witnessed. Frustrated in his efforts to check the whiskey trade,

Captain John Stuart dismissed the residents of the Arkansas Territory as either "adventurers" or as those who "have been all their Lives moving along in Advance of Civilization and good order. . . . And who have for the Governing Principles Self-Interest alone, Without regard to Law or honesty." Lieutenant Richard Ewell dubbed them "poor ignorant devils" and "brutes." "They want money—that's all," wrote another officer. "I have often d———d the Indians, and now I include the frontier loafers with all my heart."[13]

The flexible attitudes many soldiers had adopted regarding potential conflicts of interest further addled frontier competitors, who charged— sometimes with good reason—that regulars used their official status for their own personal gain. "I desired," declared one former officer matter-of-factly, "to make profit" out of the "special knowledge" of lands he had acquired from scouring them while in the service. Civilians asserted that even active-duty personnel spent more time looking out for their speculative ventures in mines and farmlands than they did in serving the national good. Residents near Fort Snelling, for example, criticized the "oppressive conduct of the military officers stationed on this frontier," who, "actuated by the most sordid and mercenary motives," had used an overly expansive military reservation to protect their private land claims.[14]

Unseemly feuding did nothing to improve the army's image. Although dueling had been forbidden since 1806, regulations carried only uncertain weight in an institution dogged by slow rates of promotion and filled with ambitious men for whom personal honor often had to substitute for tangible rewards. "The general talk was of duels," wrote Lieutenant Ethan Allen Hitchcock, "of what this one said and that one threatened." Disputes stemming from the War of 1812 led Major General Jacob Brown—himself entangled in a bitter spat with Brevet Major General Eleazer W. Ripley over the latter's conduct at the Battle of Lundy's Lane—to prohibit airing of the army's squabbles. Flouting the order, Ripley published a book defending himself. Though warning a subordinate against allowing himself "to become a mark for intriguing demagogues," Gaines became embroiled in a highly public feud with Scott, who responded by publishing a 150-page letter about the quarrel, labeling his foe as an "imbecile commander" and a "superannuated old martinet." The prickly Scott challenged both Gaines and Senator Henry Clay to duels despite having written the regulations that prohibited such conduct. Fed up with the bitter rancor between Scott and Gaines, President John Quincy Adams passed over both men following the death of commanding general Brown in 1828 in favor of their junior, Brevet Major General Alexander Macomb, for the army's top post.[15]

Soldier misbehavior extended beyond personal rivalries, further reinforcing tensions between westerners and the institution that was so crucial to their development. Many soldiers took Indian wives or lovers, leading one observer to label the army "a sink of iniquity, a school of vice." In 1798, headquarters had found it necessary to "request" that officers "forbear the bad example to the soldiery of drinking and rioting after dark." Stationed in the heart of the Creek Nation, the alcoholic Colonel Talbot Chambers, First Infantry, topped off his career when, during a drunken "fit" on the night of November 17, 1825, he assembled the entire garrison—including those men sick in the hospital—on the post parade ground and ordered them to begin firing their weapons. Awakened by the gunshots, most of the officers took cover behind their quarters. Unfortunately, J. J. Cosby, acting assistant surgeon, remained in his bed, nearly to be killed when one musket ball went through his bedroll and a second lodged in his coat. Finding Chalmers guilty of eight counts of drunkenness on duty, a court-martial cashiered him.[16]

Popular culture presented a similar image of enlisted men, who were now being recruited almost entirely from northern cities. By the 1850s, two-thirds had been born outside the United States. Although Irish-born John and William Wright, who each served a five-year stint in the regulars, claimed that their fellow enlisted men were "intelligent, and a considerable portion are the sons of gentlemen," most contemporary observers were more critical. A Pittsburgh newspaper described "the debaucheries and desertion" of the regulars there as exceeding "anything before known." One sergeant admitted that "the greater part of the army consists of men who either do not care to work, or who, because of being addicted to drink, cannot find employment." Voicing widely held prejudices, Charles Latrobe called the men "a rag-tag-and-bob-tail herd," consisting of "either the scum of the older States, or the worthless German, English, or Irish emigrants." The real problem for the army, of course, stemmed not from the ethnicity of its soldiers but from the high rates of illiteracy among them: between 25 and 40 percent of new recruits could not sign their names.[17]

Many officers shared these negative views, a result not only of the genuine misdeeds of some soldiers but of the widening social gulf between commissioned and enlisted personnel. In 1785, nearly a third of officers had once served as enlisted men; between 1817 and 1846, only twenty-three men from the ranks secured regular army commissions. Political affiliation and social status had become ever more important in the selection of officers in times of army increases, and West Point graduates now took almost every position made vacant by normal turnover. The officer corps had become a restricted club open only to selected members. "It appears to me that it is more difficult for one to advance themselves in a military life from a low position, in this republican government, than in any other," grumbled Sergeant Henry Hubbs, who besieged the War Department with letters of support from his commanding officer, several territorial officials, and his state's congressional delegation. A direct order from the secretary of war finally forced the army to organize a board of officers to investigate his suitability for a commission. Slamming the door on such challenges, the board declared Hubbs deficient in his knowledge of geography, U.S. history, mathematics, and astronomy.[18]

The abuse of alcohol caused many personnel problems. Before the mid-1830s, the government provided every enlisted man with about a quart of whiskey per week, a tradition that had been in place since the days of George Washington, who had once remarked that "the benefits arising from moderate use of strong Liquor have been experienced in all Armies, and are not to be disputed." Those seeking more alcohol could easily procure it from the legion of distributors who seemed willing to follow the army to the ends of the earth. "The men are so wicked constantly seeking occasion to drink & to get drunk," complained Brevet Lieutenant William H. Warfield.[19]

Alcoholism was in turn linked to desertion, the army's most consistent problem during the nineteenth century. Whereas 497 soldiers died between 1822–25, over three times that many deserted. Two-thirds did so during their first year of enlistment. Indeed, desertion rates averaged nearly 15 percent per year between 1820 and 1860. Although critics bemoaned the large number of immigrants serving in the army, the majority of deserters whose birthplaces were known had come from the United States. Occupation seemed to fit contemporary class stereotypes more closely, for more of those described as "laborers" deserted than any other single group. Reflecting the social gulf between enlisted men and officers, Adjutant General Roger Jones spoke for many when he blamed desertion on the poor quality of enlisted personnel. "The class from whence a majority of private soldiers are drawn scarcely regards the circumstance of desertion as an act of turpitude," proclaimed Jones.[20]

In reality, harsh and inconsistent systems of justice and punishment drove many from the service. As Sergeant George Ballentine explained, many soldiers believed "that they are not treated justly." Under the Articles of War of 1819, a regimental or garrison court of three or fewer officers could handle cases involving punishment of no more than one month's stoppage of pay, confinement, or hard labor. A general court-martial, comprised of between five and thirteen officers, investigated more serious offenses. Incident rates were high: in 1828, when the army numbered 5,702 officers and men, regimental courts heard 1,363 cases and general courts-martial another 113. Although regulations forbade "unusual" punishments, the sentences meted out by some courts—branding, shaving heads, iron collars, balls and chains, and bucking and gagging (placing a stick between a gagged soldier's arms and legs and tying him in that position)—tested the most extreme interpretations of the word. Until 1812, army courts could authorize that soldiers be given up to one hundred lashes. The practice was restored in 1833, when Congress authorized that deserters be given up to fifty lashes.[21]

Some officers concluded that such punishments merely "degrade the offenders and render them *incorrigible*," but others believed they enforced much-needed order, especially in isolated frontier garrisons where only a handful of commissioned personnel were present. Three soldiers attacked an officer at Fort Mackinac in 1829; four years later, an enlisted man at Fort Winnebago killed his company commander. Lieutenant Warfield left a revealing description of a near-mutiny at Fort Crawford in 1831. Less than two years out of West Point, Warfield sprang to the defense of a sergeant being attacked by three drunken soldiers. Slashing one assailant with his sword, Warfield, fearing that "the force I had to suppress the riot was too small," concluded that further action might lead to a full-scale riot. Taking the advice of one of his "best men," the young lieutenant let them sleep off their drunk and accepted their apology the next morning with a promise that they would "behave them-selves well."[22]

Although the army failed to link western realities to organization or doctrine, its main missions remained firmly tied to the borderlands. Between 40 and 50 percent of the army between 1821 and 1835 was sta-tioned in the West; another third patrolled the Southeast and Florida. The frontier army played its customary role—direct as well as indirect—in nation building. From 1818 to 1845, five departments (Adjutant General, Commissary General of Subsistence, Commissary General of Purchases, Ordnance, and Quartermaster General), each department dominated by a long-serving chief, formed what historian Cynthia Ann Miller has dubbed the army's "logistics complex." The army's recruiting, purchasing, manufacturing, and distributing agents developed reason-ably efficient systems that were well integrated into national markets and society. Former ordnance officers and workers transmitted the les-sons they had learned in crafting the army's weapons for other manufac-turers. Public and private arms factories thus did much to promote the much-vaunted "American system" in the nation's factories.[23]

The War Department, which controlled logistical networks for Indian affairs as well as the army, also played a fundamental role in dis-tributive politics. Authorizing the president to employ officers from the Corps of Engineers in projects deemed to be "of national importance," the General Survey Act of 1824 (which had won the unanimous sup-port of western congressmen) systematized the army's work on internal improvements. Freed from constitutional restrictions, army engineers surveyed roads, cleared rivers, and improved harbors across the country. Military posts were often established in advance of non-Indian settle-ment, then connected by roads following old Indian traces back east. The new transportation network then stimulated additional migration. As a former militia general and congressman representing western New York, Secretary of War Peter B. Porter (1828–29) was especially cogni-zant of the value this federal assistance to borderlands development. "There are probably no expenditures of the government which come so directly home to the interests and feelings of the great body of the people of the United States, or which are viewed with more lively and unquali-fied satisfaction," Porter observed in his annual report of 1828, "than those which relate to internal improvement."[24]

A military presence could prove a significant boon to regional prosperity. Dozens of steamboats carrying War Department goods plied
western rivers, and military roads allowed easier access between eastern and western markets and producers. Although a fort did not guarantee that a large, permanent civilian presence would result, Chicago,
Green Bay, and Des Moines benefited tremendously from their military
roots. As Francis Paul Prucha has noted, the army provided "a labor
force unequalled in compactness and unity of purpose by any group of
frontiersmen." Describing the effects of the Detroit–Fort Meigs road,
General Macomb proclaimed: "It will of itself form the best defence
ever afforded to this frontier and moreover be the means of introducing
a population which will forever hereafter secure it from the desolation
and distress to which it has been so recently exposed."[25]

Although most weapons and manufactured goods came from New
England and the middle Atlantic states, entrepreneurs closer to the
frontier garrisons supplemented these materials with foodstuffs and
other bulk goods. Army contracts for beef, pork, alcohol, flour, beans,
candles, vinegar, salt, and soap could mean the difference between the
success or failure of a fledgling borderlands merchant and his surrounding community. Sometimes, of course, government contracts could go
awry, as James and Robert Aull of Lexington, Missouri, found out in
1835. Assuming that locally available stocks of flour and salt would be
plentiful, they submitted the low bid for supplying Fort Leavenworth.
But a combination of bad harvests, the rejection of some goods by army
inspectors, and the government having exercised its option to reduce its
purchases (the garrison of Fort Leavenworth was diminished during the
year) cost the Aulls dearly.[26]

Luckier—or more adept—businessmen found the military a better
bet. "In its great variety of products and services," historian Michael
Tate has noted, "the army bidding system proved to be the Holy Grail
for many western civilians." Examples abound. Longtime Indian traders
John Dougherty and Robert Campbell formed a lucrative partnership by
dominating the military trade between Fort Kearny and Fort Laramie,
doing a brisk business with soldiers, emigrants, Indians, and the government. In 1841, J. M. D. Burrows, a general merchant in Davenport,
Iowa, noticed an advertisement for supplying Fort Crawford. Cash was
short in surrounding Scott County. "If I could accomplish it, and get a

contract and fill it from home production," Burrows remembered, "it would be a grand thing for both the town and the county." He won the bid, which would pay $8,280 (nearly $200,000 in 2006 dollars) for furnishing the garrison with its rations for the year. Burrows then sub-contracted locally, generating work and markets for the community's farmers, laborers, and coopers and turning a neat profit for himself. "I always considered this as the best and most successful operation I ever undertook," he reasoned, "and it benefited Scott County as much as it did me, as the money I obtained was scattered all over the county paying for produce."[27]

The Transcontinental Treaty of 1819 and the insatiable demands of land-hungry whites kept the army deeply engaged in southwestern affairs. Lieutenant Colonel Zachary Taylor moved into the old neutral ground between American Louisiana and Spanish Texas, establishing Fort Jesup about twenty-five miles southwest of Natchitoches, Louisiana. In the Arkansas Territory, tensions between resident tribes, emigrant Cherokees and Choctaws, and "lawless marauders" of white squatters threatened to ignite into open conflict on several occasions. Trying to keep the peace, soldiers reinforced Fort Smith, built Fort Gibson at the Arkansas River and Neosho (Grand) River junction, and Cantonment Towson near the mouth of the Kiamichi River in 1824.[28]

The threat of violence nonetheless remained very real, especially in the northwestern borderlands. The situation exploded in 1823 when Blackfoot and Arikara Indians, infuriated by repeated trespasses onto their lands, killed twelve fur traders, trappers, and boatmen. From Fort Atkinson, Colonel Henry Leavenworth organized regulars, civilian volunteers, and Yanktons and Lakotas anxious to see if the newcom-ers could help them expand their own interests into an expedition-ary force of about eight hundred men. In August, having taken nearly seven weeks to ascend the six hundred miles up the Missouri River, Leavenworth reached the Arikara villages. After some skirmishing with the seven hundred Arikara warriors, the Lakotas withdrew, disap-pointed by the lack of easy plunder and the soldiers' unwillingness to close with the enemy. Concerned about his exposed position and having lost two-thirds of his allies, Leavenworth refused to attack, instead offer-ing the Arikaras a hastily written treaty. That evening, the Arikaras fled their village. Insisting that his foes had been "very much terrified, and completely humbled," Leavenworth then retreated. Some of his civilian auxiliaries promptly burned the abandoned villages.[29]

Despite Leavenworth's proclamation of victory, northwestern peoples remained unbowed. Quietly, veteran frontiersman Colonel Henry Atkinson conceded that the upper Missouri was "shut against our traders" and that matters had been left "in a state of actual war." To make matters worse, the Lakotas were now evincing "some restlessness and much arrogance." One trader concluded that the Pawnees had only "contempt" for the armed effort and still believed "themselves to be more numerous warlike & brave than any other nation on earth"; in a biting attack against the "imbecility" of Leavenworth's retreat, the Missouri Fur Company's Joshua Pilcher charged that western Indians now had only "the greatest possible contempt for the American character."[30]

Few U.S. authorities understood the true nature of the military situation on the northern plains. For years, Lakotas, Yanktons, and Yanktonais had been expanding their reach, first into the middle Missouri River region, then further west and south. Less vulnerable to the ravages of diseases than their more sedentary rivals (most notably the Mandans, Omahas, Arikaras, and Hidatsas), the Lakotas needed to expand their buffalo hunting grounds to insure their food supplies and to replace the depleted beaver population east of the Missouri, which had fueled trade for firearms and other needed goods. Military domination of the village peoples, moreover, insured a source of supplementary food and trade. Thus it would be the Lakotas and Yanktonais who finally drove the Arikaras from the Missouri River.[31]

Blinded by their own ethnocentrism (Indians in the Columbia River region were, according to one congressman, "harmless, stupid, imbecile, good tempered, and unsuspecting"), Washington officials continued to attribute Indian troubles to British meddling. In 1823, Calhoun turned to Major Long to investigate the Minnesota River and Red River regions along the border with British Canada. Logging over fifty-four hundred miles, Long's expedition planted the flag at distant Pembina (present North Dakota). Always eager to promote the fur trade and western interests, in 1824 Senator Thomas Hart Benton prodded Calhoun to send a military force to the mouth of the Yellowstone River. Secretary Calhoun agreed, insisting that the removal of British and Russian traders along with either a permanent post or regular military expeditions were necessary to secure the fur trade for U.S. companies. An ambitious proposal to spend $44,000 to establish an outpost at the mouth of the Columbia went nowhere, but the Senate did allocate $10,000 to make treaties and a similar amount to dispatch a strong column into the furthest reaches of the Missouri River. In May 1825, Atkinson and nearly five hundred men thus began what would become a sixteen-hundred-mile journey, and commissioners signed peace treaties with many of the region's tribes.[32]

Upon his return, Atkinson concluded that supply difficulties made it "inexpedient" to establish a post above Council Bluffs. Instead, expeditions of three to four hundred men every few years into Blackfoot country would preserve good relations. But with British influence less pervasive than expected, the strong columns recommended by Atkinson were not forthcoming, and Fort Atkinson was abandoned in favor of Fort Leavenworth (present Kansas), which seemed better suited to encourage U.S. interests on the Santa Fe Trail. In an effort to promote intertribal peace (and to preempt the need for army intervention), the government hosted a council at Fort Crawford among the Sacs, Fox, Chippewas, Lakotas, Winnebagos, Menominees, Potawatomis, and Iowas. Thus instead of the regulars, it would be private enterprise—namely the American Fur Company and its short-lived rival, the Rocky Mountain Fur Company—that established the nation's earliest substantive presence in the upper Missouri regions. By the mid 1830s, the American Fur Company's network of trading posts and depots, anchored by substantial positions at the forts of Pierre, Union, McKenzie, and Laramie, housed upward of five hundred employees.[33]

Like officials before them, Secretary Calhoun and General Brown hoped to concentrate troops at centrally located posts. "Feeble positions" along the Indian borderlands, argued Brown, merely "invite attack." Dispersing units too broadly also made military instruction virtually impossible and inflated supply and transportation costs. Calhoun's successor as war secretary, Virginia planter James Barbour, agreed, and by late 1826 had concentrated nearly seven hundred men at Jefferson Barracks, located on the Mississippi River just below St. Louis. Large expeditionary forces could periodically sweep the borderlands to disperse "savages" and supply a demonstration of Washington's power.[34]

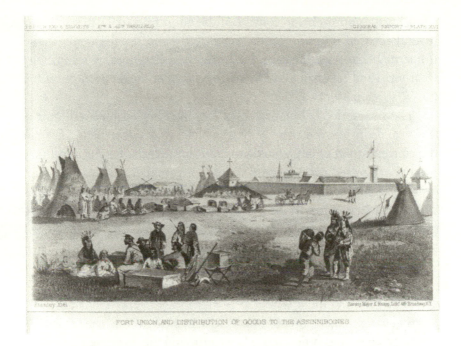

FIG. 14. "Fort Union and Distribution of Goods to the Assiniboines." Private
fur companies, most notably the American Fur Company and its
bitter rival, the Missouri Fur Company, took the lead in establishing
a U.S. presence in the upper Missouri country. Key to the former
company's activities was Fort Union (1828–67), where the Indian
trade was long a profit center. LIBRARY OF CONGRESS, USZ62-17615.

Among posts abandoned in conjunction with the concentration program were Fort Dearborn and Fort Crawford, the latter long plagued
by Mississippi River floodwaters. But troubles between the Winnebago
Indians and the miners, traders, and farmers who were pouring into
the area flared up in 1827. Responding to the "alarm and consternation" among the newcomers, territorial governor Lewis Cass called
for troops, and Secretary Barbour demanded that the Winnebagos "be
severely chastised for their insolence and violence." Atkinson led out
580 men from Jefferson Barracks that summer, joining up with several companies of militiamen and over two hundred Indian auxiliaries.
Resisting the popular clamor for violent action, Atkinson wisely adopted

a less hostile approach and convinced the outgunned tribe to hand over several accused murderers. But the threat—and the demands of the influential Cass—led the army to rebuild Fort Crawford, reoccupy Fort Dearborn, and construct Fort Winnebago at a strategic portage on the Fox-Wisconsin waterway.[35]

The misnamed Winnebago "war" of 1827 highlighted a dilemma that would long vex the army. Military efficiency and instruction favored the concentration of large garrisons, but local demands for a military presence required dividing commands into smaller packets across an ever-expanding frontier. Barbour bragged "that the prompt and efficient demonstration of force in the late Theatre of Indian hostilities will have given our frontier settlements security for the future." Better attuned to local politics, Governor Cass reached the opposite conclusion:

> The stockaded works erected in the Indian country, are important to overawe the Indians, and to restrain their perpetual disposition to war. Under any circumstances, in peace or war, they must be retained and supported. They command the great avenues of communication into the country; they cover the whole frontier; they protect our citizens in the various employment required by their duties, public and private, and they produce a moral effect upon the Indians, which is visible and permanent.[36]

Cass's view emerged ascendant, and momentum for concentration lost steam. Commanding general Brown died that February; his replacement, Alexander Macomb, was more interested in wresting direct control of the army from Secretary of War Barbour and his successors than in debating the particulars of frontier security. And Barbour, a confirmed advocate of closing small posts, left the cabinet several months later to become minister to Great Britain. The new war secretary, the old war hawk Peter B. Porter, denounced the concentration of troops at Jefferson Barracks as having invited hostilities. Determined to erect a line of mutually supporting posts just ahead of non-Indian settlement, Porter also condemned the idea of extending outposts like Fort Snelling and Fort Leavenworth too deep into Indian lands. The army's presence that far west, maintained Porter, served only to "invite wild and profitless adventurers into the Indian country." For their part, Plains tribes seem to have viewed these occasional encounters with the regulars with a mixture of contempt and hope—contempt for the bluecoats' failure to respect time-honored tradition of council and ways of war that relied on horses; hope that their abundant weapons and goods might make them useful allies against those who posed a more immediate military threat: rival Indians.[37]

FIVE

The Wars of Indian Removal

Andrew Jackson's presidential victory in 1828 accelerated the process of Indian removal. Hardened by the violence that had so often beset the nation's borderlands, the new president believed that the tribes represented a barrier to the spread of white civilization. Those Indians still living east of the Mississippi must be uprooted, Jackson contended, to save them from what would otherwise be their inevitable extinction, for if nothing were done they would be prey to the deadly predation by local whites. A lifetime of experiences along the nation's northwestern borderlands had also left Lewis Cass, Jackson's most influential secretary of war, a confirmed advocate of removal. "A tribe of wandering hunters, depending upon the chase for support, and deriving it from the forests, and rivers, and lakes, of an immense continent," Cass insisted, "have a very imperfect possession of the country over which they roam." To be fair, he hoped to implement the process humanely. To better manage the ongoing expulsion of the Choctaws, for example, he consolidated operations under the army's commissary general of subsistence, George Gibson. Cass also convinced Congress to create a commissioner of Indian Affairs, who, under the secretary of war's direction, would oversee more systematized bureaucracy.[1]

As the Jackson administration aggressively promoted removal, long-simmering disputes in northern Illinois (which had gained statehood in 1818) and the south central regions of the Michigan Territory (later Wisconsin, which was made a territory in 1836) boiled over into open conflict. In spring 1832, Black Hawk and eleven hundred allies (mostly Sauks and Foxes, but also a smattering of Kickapoos, Potawatomies, and Winnebagos) determined to resist demands that they exchange their lands for other territory west of the Mississippi River. Illinois governor John Reynolds called out sixteen hundred volunteers, among them a rawboned young captain, Abraham Lincoln. Regulars looked aghast at the antics of the amateurs, who, in the words of one officer, "were as active as a swarming hive; catching horses, electioneering, drawing rations, asking questions, shooting at marks, electing officers, mustering in, issuing orders, disobeying orders, galloping about, 'cussing and discussing' the war, and the rumors thereof."[2]

Negotiations between Black Hawk and Brigadier General Henry Atkinson, dispatched from Jefferson Barracks, collapsed in early May. Under orders to do "something decisive," Atkinson sent Major Isaiah Stillman with his mounted militia up the Rock River toward Black Hawk's followers. Support from the British and other Indians not having arrived as expected, Black Hawk had dispatched emissaries to secure a truce. Stillman's undisciplined rangers ignored the white flags and began pursuing the Indian negotiators, only to blunder into a hastily prepared ambush. The Illinois volunteers panicked; "Stillman's Run" ended downstream at Dixon's Ferry, at the cost of a dozen killed.[3]

Levees swelling his army to nearly four thousand, Atkinson began his much-delayed pursuit on June 28. Black Hawk fled north, but on August 1, soldiers aboard the steamboat *Warrior* turned back Sac and Fox attempts to cross the Mississippi River near the mouth of the Bad Axe. Some 150 Indians, including many women and children, were slaughtered in subsequent fighting the next day. "The loss of the squaws and children gives great regret," observed one officer, but, he rationalized, "fighting with an enemy who concealed themselves in the high grass and behind logs and the banks of the ravines and river, whose positions were designated by the flash and report of their guns . . . required that our fire should be directed to every point where an Indian appeared." The Black Hawk War had ended, and all tribes associated with this movement—including those who had not taken up arms against the government—eventually ceded still more land.[4]

Atkinson had sent mounted militia after Black Hawk because the regular army had been without cavalry since the War of 1812. Mounted troops, it had long been presumed, were not worth their extra expense. Now, however, the nation was encountering horse peoples of the prairies and plains justifiably proud of their military skills. Experiences along the Santa Fe Trail in 1829, when the War Department had assigned Captain Bennett Riley and four companies of infantrymen to exert their "moral influence" over the Indians, also pointed to the need for mounted troops. Leaving Jefferson Barracks in May, Riley's foot soldiers accompanied that year's caravan to the Mexican border, where they camped for two months until the traders returned. "It was a humiliating condition to be surrounded by these rascally Indians," recalled one soldier, "who, by means of their horses, could tantalize us with the hopes of battle, and elude our efforts; who could annoy us by preventing all individual excursions for hunting, &c., and who could insult us with impunity. Much did we regret that we were not mounted too."[5]

Cavalry advocates redoubled their efforts in March 1830, when Senator Thomas Hart Benton threw his support behind a bill that would have allowed President Jackson to mount ten companies of regulars. The expenses of such a move, explained Benton, would be minuscule when compared to the money spent for Atlantic coastal defenses. Although that measure failed, in 1832 Congress adopted a more politically attractive alternative. Employing rhetoric sure to be popular with his constituents back home, Arkansas Territory delegate Ambrose H. Sevier judged mounted volunteers to be superior to regulars, who "consisted generally of the refuse of society, collected in the cities and seaport towns; many of them broken down with years and infirmities." Frontier service, he explained, required men "who knew how to support themselves." Indiana senator John Tipton, a Jacksonian Democrat like Benton and Sevier, agreed: "The inhabitants of the frontier would have more confidence in being defended by their fathers, husbands, and brothers, many of whom are experienced in this kind of warfare, and who are emphatically of themselves, than by comparative strangers." With the Black Hawk War in full swing, Congress authorized six hundred Mounted Rangers, who would provide their own horses, arms, and equipment in return for pay of one dollar per day. President Jackson eagerly seized on the resulting patronage opportunities. He named fellow Democrat

Henry Dodge, an expansionist whose aggressive leadership in the Black Hawk War had won the acclaim of many borderlanders, to command the outfit, and stuffed the newly created officers' slots with westerners.[6]

Though politically attractive, the Mounted Rangers proved to be incorrigibly ill disciplined and twice as expensive to recruit and maintain as regulars. Encountering the Rangers during a western tour, Washington Irving described them as "a raw, undisciplined band, levied among the wild youngsters of the frontier. . . . None of them had any idea of the restraint and decorum of a camp, or ambition to acquire a name for exactness in a profession in which they had no intention of continuing." Evidence for once trumping popular mythology in the halls of Washington, Congress converted the Rangers into a regular regiment of more heavily armed dragoons. Dodge, aptly characterized as "a clever man, but not much of a soldier," remained as colonel, but the awkward mix of former Rangers and regular infantry officers pleased no one. Captain Ethan Allen Hitchcock, a West Point graduate who would spend four decades in the army, complained that Dodge had "taken sides with the Rangers against the army."[7]

Despite this infighting, Secretary Cass put the dragoons to work in earnest. In 1834, one company escorted that year's Santa Fe caravan, and the remainder were detached to "impress" the Plains peoples "with proper ideas of the power of the United States." Eager to take part in the adventure, artist George Catlin accompanied the expedition. Guided by thirty-two Indian scouts, Dodge and five hundred men trotted out of Fort Gibson on June 15. Sickness and heat decimated the ranks as the dragoons struggled to reach Wichita, Comanche, and Kiowa villages 250 miles to the west. "Perhaps there has never been in America a campaign that operated more severely in men and horses. The excessive heat exceeded anything I ever experienced," lamented the colonel. Less than two hundred soldiers reached their goal (Catlin pronounced the entire affair "most disastrous"). Dodge did manage to arrange a council at Fort Gibson among delegates representing the Kiowas, Comanches, Wichitas, Cherokees, Osages, Choctaws, Creeks, and Senecas. The following year, Dodge and 117 dragoons journeyed from Fort Leavenworth to the Rocky Mountains, visiting with representatives of the Otos, Pawnees, Omahas, Arikaras, Cheyennes, Arapahoes, Gros Ventres, and Blackfeet. Lieutenant Colonel Stephen W. Kearny

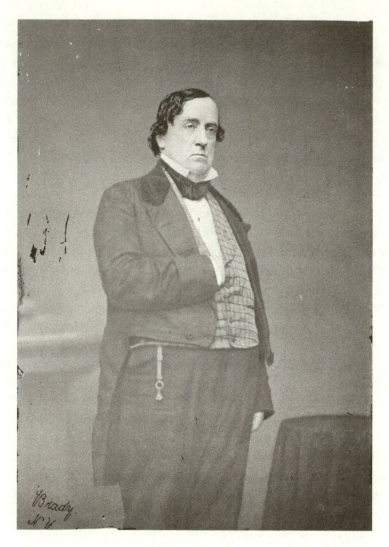

FIG. 15. Lewis Cass. A general in the War of 1812, Cass (1782–1866) was named the second governor of Michigan Territory in 1813. He resigned that post to become Andrew Jackson's secretary of war in 1831. Cass championed Indian removal and military roads and, later, popular sovereignty. The Democratic Party's nominee for president in 1848, he later served as secretary of state under James Buchanan. LIBRARY OF CONGRESS, DIG-CWPBH-02843.

and three companies of dragoons also reconnoitered the Des Moines River region. Finally, a few dragoons joined infantrymen in guarding peace talks at Cross Timbers.[8]

In early 1836, Secretary Cass unveiled a sweeping plan for border-lands defense. Indian removals, he claimed, would allow the nation to erect a barrier separating them from non-Indian settlements, which he presumed were approaching their natural limits. Cass proposed that the army construct an eight-hundred-mile military road from the Red River to present Minnesota. Eight or nine forts would guard the road, which would allow for easy communication along what he assumed would be a permanent frontier. Patrols of dragoons, "a species of force particularly dreaded by the Indians," could make the road "a barrier across which parties of hostile Indians would be very unwilling to pass." The package came with an estimated cost of $100,000 (roughly $2.2 million in 2006 dollars): $35,000 for the road, most of which might be built by soldiers, and $65,000 for the new forts.[9]

The military road was a logical culmination of Cass's experiences in the borderlands, where federal assistance had long been a prime stimu-lant for development. Between 1815 and 1831, the government had laced the frontiers with over twenty-five hundred miles of roads, three-quarters of which had been built by the army. As the House Committee on Military Affairs had concluded in 1826, westerners saw this network "not merely as a defensive measure, but as a measure of sound policy, calculated to build up, by proper encouragement, the settlement of that frontier with the sturdy yeomanry of the country." The War Department redoubled these efforts during Cass's tenure in Washington.[10]

A larger, more efficient army constituted the second leg of the Cass's vision for western security. Arguing that a better "moral culture" would bolster discipline, reduce crime, and check desertion, Cass, a founding member of the Congressional Temperance Society, abolished the tradi-tional whiskey ration (replacing it with sugar and coffee) and prohibited the sale of alcohol on military posts, save for soldiers on fatigue duty. The army also reduced terms of enlistment from five to three years and ended its practice of paying recruits a bounty; instead, privates saw their pay raised from five to six dollars a month. Reenlistees received a bonus equal to two months' pay. In 1838, Congress added another dollar to the salaries of all enlisted personnel.[11]

Early in his tenure as war secretary, Cass had taken the risky step of admitting that the militia "cannot be regarded as our most important means of safety in the event of war." Finding little support for a realignment along the lines of Calhoun's expansible model, Cass recommended that the army be increased from 7,194 to over 10,000. In addition, he sought to designate one infantry regiment as riflemen and another as light infantry, a move designed to meet the "imperative" needs of the borderlands. Welcoming the proposal, Senator Benton added that a larger military establishment "was a measure of western origin, and eminently called for by the present and prospective condition of the West."[12]

Events in Florida and Texas, however, soon diverted attention from the question of whether to build a western military road and the debate over how the army should be composed. In Florida, few Seminoles had recognized the treaties of Payne's Landing (1832) and Fort Gibson (1833), in which small delegations had agreed to move to present Oklahoma. Disputes between white slave owners, Seminoles, free blacks, and African Americans who lived in semibondage with the Seminoles further complicated matters. By late 1835, Brevet Brigadier General Duncan L. Clinch and fourteen companies of regulars were attempting to cajole the Seminoles into leaving. On December 28, Osceola and his Seminole supporters killed their agent and another officer outside of Fort King (near present Ocala); that same day, Seminoles and their African American allies ambushed Major Francis L. Dade's column near the Great Wahoo Swamp, slaying all but two of the eight officers and one hundred enlisted men present. Three days later at the Withlacoochee River, Osceola fought six hundred regulars and Florida volunteers to a standstill.[13]

"Great God! Such a wanton sacrifice of valuable lives to the mean, niggardly policy of our Government! It cries aloud for vengeance and vengeance it shall command," thundered the Fourth Infantry's Lieutenant Robert C. Buchanan. Experienced in the ways of frontier warfare, President Jackson dispatched General Scott to Florida, advising him to discover the location of the Seminole women and children and "proceed at any hazard & expense" to that point, where he might end the war with "one blow." The imperious Scott, who brought to Florida three wagonloads of camp furniture, wine, and his dress uniform, seems not to have listened, and his columns from Fort Drane (near present Silver Springs),

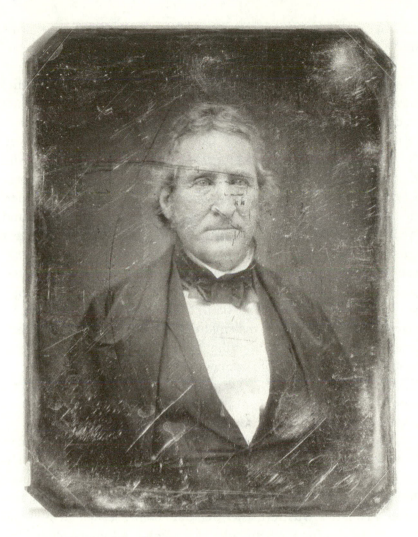

FIG. 16. Thomas Hart Benton. LIBRARY OF CONGRESS, USZ62-110024.

St. Augustine, and Fort Brooke (Tampa Bay) came back empty handed. The man who had literally written the book on early nineteenth-century American soldiering found the Florida terrain unsuitable for conventional operations. His nemesis, General Gaines, mocked his rival's "visionary plans" as being "excellent for operations against troops of civilized nations—but fruitless for wilderness swamp, against savages."[14]

Affairs in Texas further complicated debates regarding a larger army and a frontier road. Open warfare had broken out between Texans—many of whom had recently migrated from the United States—and Antonio López de Santa Anna's Mexican government. Early fighting had gone well for the Texans, but the loss of the Alamo (San Antonio) and a string of defeats in South Texas (culminating in the massacre of nearly four hundred captives at Goliad) had left them in full retreat. By spring 1836, the Texans' deteriorating situation, along with fears that Mexico might form an alliance with the Caddo Indians, prompted Gaines, charged with observing the volatile Texas-Louisiana border, to call up militiamen from Louisiana, Mississippi, Tennessee, and Alabama. Perhaps a hundred former U.S. regulars—mostly deserters from the Third and Sixth infantry regiments—also joined the Texas cause. In the House of Representatives, fur trader and western entrepreneur William H. Ashley (D-Miss.) feared that "a single spark might set . . . [the] whole frontier in a flame," leading to "the indiscriminate slaughter of men, women, and children." That April, the Texans' decisive victory over Santa Anna at the Battle of San Jacinto quieted fears that the United States might be drawn into an international conflict. In the end, Congress funded Cass's military road but rejected his call for a ten-thousand-man regular army, settling for a more modest addition of a second regiment of dragoons.[15]

Meanwhile, the quagmire in Florida continued. In May 1836, Scott happily accepted a transfer to Georgia, where in more predictable circumstances he completed the removal of the Creek and Cherokee Indians. Commanding over eight thousand regulars, volunteers, and Creek auxiliaries, Quartermaster General Thomas Jesup now assumed the job of defeating the Seminoles. Although the Indians eluded the bluecoats, the army's ceaseless harassment in the fall and winter of 1836–37 convinced hundreds of Seminoles to assemble near Fort Brooke as a prelude for what Jesup hoped would be a government-sponsored emigration. But on the evening of June 2–3, some of the younger chiefs, including Osceola and Coacoochee, led about seven hundred men, women, and children out of camp. Disgusted and discouraged, Jesup questioned his government's uncompromising removal demands. "To have made a durable peace would have been an easy matter. The Indians felt themselves beaten, and were tired of the war," declared the

FIG. 17. "A Bivouack in Safety or Florida Troops Preventing a Surprise."
Political cartoonists had a field day lampooning the army's
efforts during the Second Seminole War. In this one, attributed
to Henry Dacre, note especially the uniformed bloodhounds
to the right, under the standard that reads "Puppy Guard
Sentinel." LIBRARY OF CONGRESS, USZ62-49595.

beleaguered general. "To rid the country of them you must exterminate them. Is the government prepared for such a measure? Will public
opinion sustain it?"[16]

Insisting that removal be unconditional, Cass's successor in the War
Department, Joel R. Poinsett, funneled regular troops, militia, a riv-
erine naval squadron, and about a thousand Delaware, Shawnee, Sac
and Fox, Kickapoo, and Choctaw allies into Florida. In fall 1837, Jesup
thus renewed operations along the St. Augustine–St. John's River line,
and Colonel Zachary Taylor assumed command of operations in the
southwest from Fort Brooke. As morale sagged, complaints from white
Floridians mounted, and Seminole opposition remained unwavering,
Jesup's maneuvers assumed an increasingly desperate air. "The Indians

when they choose to run, escape our troops, so easily," sighed one officer. Plagued by "raw Irishmen" attempting to function as teamsters and
fearing that the rigors of campaigning in Florida would break the army,
Jesup arrested Osceola under a white flag and talked of using Cuban
bloodhounds to track down the Seminoles, which incited a storm of
humanitarian protest. In that season's largest contest, the Battle of Lake
Okeechobee, Taylor and 800 soldiers drove back a sizeable Seminole
force through knee-deep muck and five-foot high sawgrass on Christmas
Day, killing at least fourteen Indians at a cost of twenty-six dead and 112
wounded. Jesup was wounded in a sharp fight the following January
near the Jupiter River. Though Osceola had died of malaria while in
captivity, a disconsolate Jesup admitted that his efforts had "effected
absolutely nothing."[17]

By February 1838, Jesup again sought permission to allow the most
recalcitrant Seminoles to stay. "Wherever we come up with them, we
can fight and beat them," he told Taylor, "but from the nature of the
country our success is attended with no favourable results, because we
can destroy but few of them, even under the most favorable circumstances; and, from their abundant means of subsistence, we cannot
hope to starve them." He had whipped his enemies, Jesup claimed, just
as thoroughly as Jackson had in the first Florida war, and as Anthony
Wayne and William Henry Harrison had in the woodlands of the Old
Northwest. "It has been said that the national honor forbids any compromise with them," wrote Jesup on March 14. "Can there be a point of
honor between a great nation and a band of naked savages, now beaten,
broken, dispirited and dispersed?" But Poinsett steadfastly rejected any
compromises: truces must be temporary, designed only to protect white
settlers through the upcoming season.[18]

Taylor assumed command of Florida operations in mid-May. Like
his predecessor, Taylor was willing to try just about anything to cajole
the remaining Seminoles into surrendering. Initially, he hoped to starve
the Indians out of their Everglade haunts and backed the territorial government's acquisition of bloodhounds. But Taylor failed to consider the
region's plentiful stocks of native fish and fowl, and the dogs proved
of little practical assistance. Now commanding 3,300 regulars and 372
militiamen, in the winter of 1838–39 Taylor tried again, hoping that
five separate columns might drive the Seminoles south of a line from

Fort Brooke to New Smyrna. But the offensive uncovered few signs of Indians. "It is," he muttered, "a complete game of 'hide and seek.'"[19]

In spring 1839 Taylor unveiled a new scheme for occupying the region west of St. Augustine. Soldiers carved the area into military districts, each twenty miles long and twenty miles wide. An officer and twenty men (half of whom were supposed to be mounted) would establish a small post from which they could patrol their district every other day. Soldiers erected fifty-three such positions, along with 848 miles of wagon road and 3,643 feet of causeways and bridges. Advocates of such measures presumed that the improved security resulting from these operations would win civilian support and encourage immigration, foreshadowing twentieth- and twenty-first-century counterinsurgency doctrine.[20]

But the aggressive young republic lacked the patience necessary for such a long-term approach, especially after July 23, when Indians sacked a trading post on the Caloosahatchee River, killing eighteen soldiers and making off with considerable plunder. "Take my advice," warned Captain George H. Pegram, "& put off . . . thoughts of love or marriage until after this Florida war is ended. . . . The prospect of terminating this business seems as remote & gloomy as ever." After another season of fruitless campaigning, marked by near-epidemic rates of sickness among his command, Taylor was finally granted his long sought-after transfer. "The truth is that Florida is now bleeding at every vein and artery," complained one exasperated Floridian.[21]

Assuming command in Florida in summer 1841, Brevet Brigadier General William J. Worth adopted an even more belligerent stance. In an unofficial though widely recognized system, solders received $100 for every Seminole fighter killed or captured. Worth also kept troops in the field through the summer, squeezing the resistance out of many of the remaining Indians. Citing the "utter impracticality" of removing the last-ditch holdouts—an estimated 240 men, women, and children—in February 1842 Worth recommended that military operations be ended. This time, Washington officials relented, and three months later President John Tyler declared the long war to be over.[22]

The Second Seminole War had lasted through four presidential administrations, had cost about $20 million (over $500 million in 2006 dollars), and had claimed the lives of fifteen hundred soldiers. Three thousand Seminoles had been removed to the vicinity of Fort Gibson (present eastern Oklahoma). The army's inability to secure a quick tri-umph over a numerically inferior enemy had done nothing to impress skeptical Jacksonians already dubious about the merits of professional-ization, and probably added to the vigor of their attacks on West Point. For their part, regulars hated service in Florida, which one condemned as "a most hideous region to live in; a perfect paradise for Indians, alligators, serpents, frogs, and every other kind of loathsome reptile." Convinced that borderlands speculators had deliberately extended the war in order to line their own pockets with federal contracts and to use the army to explore what seemed to them a wilderness, many soldiers sympathized with the Seminoles. "The Indians were undoubtedly in the right, originally," added Major Ethan Allen Hitchcock, who later dubbed the conflict "a wicked waste of life & treasure."[23]

With much of the army tied down overseeing Indian removals from the Old Northwest and fighting the Seminoles in Florida, some feared that a pan-Indian alliance would overwhelm the thinly garrisoned west-ern frontiers. Even before leaving for Florida, Jesup had cautioned that twenty thousand Indian warriors lurked north of the Red River. "Even were the mass of them inclined to preserve peace with us," he continued, "danger is to be apprehended from the collisions among themselves, and their misunderstandings with frontier settlers." In 1838, Inspector General Croghan reported that the "entire frontier . . . can be laid waste whenever the restless tribes . . . may choose."[24]

Responding to these fears, Secretary of War Poinsett had deemed Cass's frontier road as being "entirely inefficient," complaining that hos-tile forces could easily cut any pathway running parallel to the frontier. Pressed by Congress for an alternative, the new secretary initiated a staff review. Taking a cue from his new civilian boss, Charles Gratiot, the chief of engineers, insisted that communication between connect-ing borderlands garrisons be perpendicular, rather than parallel, to the frontier. He envisioned a double line of military forts. Exterior posts (Snelling, Gibson, Towson, a new post on the upper Des Moines River, and a reoccupied position at Council Bluffs), would control "the great avenues leading into the Indian country." Eight inner fortresses would serve as "posts of refuge" for civilians. From a powerful St. Louis family, Gratiot had been one of Jefferson's appointments to the military acad-emy; not surprisingly, his plan would have greatly expanded the army's western presence and pumped hundreds of thousands of federal dollars into borderlands economies.[25]

In February 1838, General Gaines unveiled an even more grandiose vision for western defense. Fresh from an extensive western inspection tour, Gaines boasted that his system would solve the problem until the next century. He called for eleven frontier fortresses, constructed of stone or brick and covered with sheet iron. Each position would be garrisoned by 810 men behind sixteen-foot walls buttressed by two guard towers. Forty-two hundred miles of railroad would provide the means of communication. Total costs, Gaines estimated, would not exceed $70 million.[26]

Secretary Poinsett, a vocal supporter of Indian removal, summarily dismissed the Gaines proposal, favoring instead a scheme similar to that put forth by Gratiot and Trueman Cross, the acting quartermaster general, that called for a double line of military posts supported by a series of roads running perpendicular to the frontier and a strong reserve at Jefferson Barracks. The concentration of force at Jefferson Barracks, judged the secretary, would make it easier to deploy troops against a European invasion. He estimated that five thousand men could defend the borderlands. A board of officers, including Cross, Colonel Joseph G. Totten, Lieutenant Colonel Sylvanius Thayer, and Lieutenant Colonel George Talcott, later fleshed out more details, recommending $895,000 to build nine new posts and enlarge six others. The Van Buren administration's political influence had been badly hurt by the devastating Panic of 1837, however, and so the scheme went nowhere.[27]

Efforts to increase the army during the Second Seminole War had proved more successful. In late 1837, Poinsett backed a plan to enlarge the army to fifteen thousand. Such a force, stretched out along eight thousand miles of ground and maritime frontiers and officered by men "educated to reverence the laws and cherish the freedom of their country," he reasoned, posed no threat to civilian authority. Congress took up the issue the following year, the Senate considering an increase to 14,000 men and the House a more modest 12,500. "Country court lawyers," complained one Poinsett confidant, "think themselves qualified to decide on & change the arrangements proposed by the Secretary of War, after consultation with the General Officers." Missouri's Albert G. Harrison and Michigan's Isaac E. Crary, both Democrats, supported the increase but wanted to include a regiment of riflemen, who they believed

FIG. 18. Joel R. Poinsett. A Unionist, former minister to Mexico, and amateur botanist, Poinsett (1779–1851), a native South Carolinian, served as secretary of war in the Van Buren administration from 1837 to 1841. LIBRARY OF CONGRESS, USZ62-23834.

were the most effective Indian fighters. The House rejected the rifle regiment, but with the allure of a rich new mine of patronage commissions looming large, the conflict in Florida in full swing, and tensions between Britain and the United States running high along the Canadian border, Congress raised the number of regulars from just under 8,000 to 12,539.

The House had supported the crucial test vote by a 107–77 count, representatives from frontier states voting 14–1 in favor. New York, attuned to the Canadian border controversy, also emerged as a powerful force for augmenting the regular army, its delegation backing the measure by a twenty-five-to-eight margin. Congress authorized an eighth infantry regiment, but most of the increase came on the cheap by its expanding the number of privates per infantry regiment from 420 to 800.[28]

Jacksonians also succeeded in limiting a practice that had long offended their sensibilities. Since the General Survey Act of 1824, officers serving on detached duty had worked for state governments as well as private firms on internal improvement projects. Many then resigned their commissions to accept lucrative jobs in the private sector. Suspicious about the growing dominance of West Point–trained officers within the regular army, Democrats found it galling that such graduates stood to make a fortune from their government-financed educations even as officer shortages affected the army's prosecution of the Seminole War. Jackson's successor, Martin Van Buren, signed legislation that prohibited officers from leaving their regiments to serve on these detached assignments. Though these restrictions were entirely consistent with the party's determination not to privilege certain projects at the expense of others, their impact fell most heavily on the west, since borderlands states (and especially territories) depended on federal support for internal improvement projects.[29]

The flurry of proposals for western defense put forth by the military establishment during the 1830s had been unparalleled in the nation's history. Never before had officers spend so much time and energy trying to devise comprehensive systems specifically tailored for the borderlands—and they never would again. The army had retained its traditional role as agent of empire, engaging in a series of wars consistent with the public's demand for Indian removal. The relationship between the army and its frontier roots nonetheless remained contradictory and inconsistent. Responding to conditions on the prairies of the Midwest, Congress had added mounted units to the regulars' arsenal. But the army instituted few changes as a result of either the Black Hawk War or the seven-year conflict in Florida. Frustrated by this disjoint, some officers complained bitterly about the failure to adopt ordnance or methods to American conditions. Knee-deep in the Second Seminole

War, for instance, Jesup denounced the War Department's decision to model howitzers on French designs. "In nothing is our blind devotion to Europe more strikingly exemplified than in adopting into our service the mountain gun as used in France. It seems to have been adopted," he groused, "merely because it was French, without any inquiry as to the uses to which it was applied there, or the objects to be effected by it here." The irascible Gaines sounded a similar refrain: "We have loaded ourselves with French and English Books, uselessly ponderous Company & Regimental Books, and indulged in sedentary habits, until we find ourselves, or at least . . . most of our officers but illy qualified to cope with a savage foe."[30]

What passed for training ignored the converging columns, year-round campaigns, and strikes aimed at enemy food supplies that had been employed in Florida and that would become hallmarks of subsequent wars to the west. The Seminoles—and other Indians—seemed an uncivilized foe, unworthy of serious intellectual scrutiny. West Point was becoming a great engineering school, but the curriculum of math, French, drawing, science, philosophy, and drill would have little practical value for future officers serving in the borderlands. "A corps of women would be as serviceable against Indians as a corps of West Point graduates," scoffed Kentucky's Albert G. Hawes (D). The Dade disaster of late 1835 had inspired the legendary Professor Dennis Hart Mahan, whose "Engineering and the Science of War" served as West Point's senior capstone course, to develop one lecture on "Indian warfare." But a single lecture in a four-year curriculum, even when combined with the informal folkways that instructors with frontier experiences passed along to their students, hardly represented a systematic attempt to prepare officers for wars against the Indians. Henry Atkinson summed up the situation neatly: "Indian fighting is but an unprofitable business after all."[31]

Nor did the country demand any substantive change from the army. As historian Mary Ellen Rowe has demonstrated, the militia remained—in the public mind at least—"the bulwark of the republic." Zachary Taylor's mixed experiences following the Battle of Lake Okeechobee seem a classic illustration of the continuing symbolic power of the American volunteer. Taylor's victory earned him a brevet promotion, but his criticisms of Missouri volunteers ignited a political firestorm.

"They mostly broke," Taylor explained, "and instead of forming in rear of the regulars, as had been directed, they retired across the swamp to their baggage and horses, nor could they be again brought into action as a body."[32]

Angry champions of American manhood sprung to defend the volunteers against Taylor's charges. His claim that they had broken was "utterly unfounded," protested a petition signed by fourteen Missourians. The regulars, they complained, had subjected them "to the most continual and positive manifestations of their contempt and dislike towards us." Senator Benton accused Taylor "of exposing citizens to the fate of a forlorn hope" by stationing them as skirmishers ahead of his main body. Instead of Taylor's "censure," they deserved the thanks of a grateful nation. Missouri legislators charged that Taylor's report had been *intentionally* false." The aggrieved Taylor promptly demanded a court of inquiry to clear his good name. Wisely, Secretary Poinsett quashed the case, reasoning that no officers could be spared from Florida.[33]

SIX

Agent of Manifest Destiny

The late 1830s had seen an unparalleled articulation of comprehensive plans for frontier defenses. Although no consensus regarding the particulars of such proposals had been reached, they shared several common principles. A regular army was necessary but should be small, with reserves concentrated at strategic points. Participants in the debate also assumed that the nation had reached what they deemed its "permanent" boundaries and that Indians obstructed the civilized occupation of these regions. They often disagreed about the details associated with moving the tribes, but none of the principles doubted the righteousness of their nation's cause. As he left office, for example, Secretary of War Joel R. Poinsett pointed proudly to the removal of forty thousand Indians during his administration, asserting that the transplanted peoples were now "gradually advancing in the peaceful arts of life."[1]

Poinsett's views on Indians now seem repugnant. But in presenting an alternative to his predecessor's frontier road, the South Carolinian had stimulated a rare debate on borderlands defense. The conclusion of the Second Seminole War, President John Tyler's break with the Whig Party, and the antiestablishment passions of many within the old Jacksonian coalition, however, invited new assaults on the regulars and rendered large-scale defensive schemes moot. Having commanded militia during the Black Hawk War, Representative John Reynolds (D-Ill.)

avowed "that it was the border militia and volunteers that they [Indians] dreaded more than any United States troops." Ignoring the unanimous opposition of from the Arkansas, Louisiana, and Missouri delegations, in August 1842 Congress converted the Second Dragoons to a less expensive rifle regiment and slashed the number of privates in artillery and infantry companies to forty-two. The House voted one hundred to seventy in favor of the reductions. Borderlands representatives showed themselves to be only slightly more supportive of army interests than their eastern counterparts.[2]

Regulars lambasted Congress's actions. "Oh! Ye hypocrites—demagogues—who swallow a million squandered on a fraudulent contract, or on an Eastern palace," wrote Captain Philip St. George Cooke, "and strain at a cent for the protection and peace of the simple border States!" From its post–War of 1812 high of 12,449 men in 1837, the army's strength had fallen to 8,730 by 1844. Military spending consumed less than a quarter of that year's federal budget, the lowest since 1826. On a per capita basis, War Department expenditures had fallen to their lowest rates since Thomas Jefferson's first administration.[3]

Limited budgets dictated trying living conditions for the regulars in blue. Rations featured a monotonous fare of beef or salt pork, bread, and coffee, spiced occasionally with potatoes or cabbage. Food was ample in quantity, but notoriously poor in taste, texture, and appeal. Dragoon James Hildreth found "the pork rusty, the flour spoiled, and the beans of the meanest quality." Surgeon General Joseph Lovell complained "that even the laborers in our cities" enjoyed a greater variety of food. After much prodding, the War Department began substituting peas and beans for some of the meat and occasionally initiated mandatory programs obligating regulars to plant post gardens to add more fresh vegetables. Hunting and fishing parties sometimes complemented the soldiers' diets.[4]

Much the same could be said about uniforms. The cocked hats, bell-crowned leather caps, forage caps, and tall-cloth shakos of the early republic period were ill suited for borderlands service. "If the whole earth had been ransacked," observed one veteran in describing a particularly awkward model, "it is difficult to tell where a more ungainly piece of furniture could have been found." Leather boots and shoes could fit either foot, and white linen or cotton fatigue jackets appropriate for hot

summer climes only sporadically supplemented the official (and invariably ill-fitting) blue wool uniforms. Chronic shortages of uniforms and
equipment left frontier companies sporting an exotic mixture of various patterns. In the field, officers and enlisted men alike replaced their
regulation garb with a collection of more practical clothing. Lieutenant
Edmund Kirby Smith described the result to his mother: "Corduroy
pants; a hickory or blue flannel shirt, cut down in front, studded with
pockets and worn outside; a slouched hat and long beard, cavalry boots
worn over the pants . . . complete the costume as truly serviceable as it
is unmilitary."[5]

Lodgings varied widely, but officers and their families were always
strictly separated from enlisted personnel. Two-man bunks, often
stacked two and three high, remained the norm until the 1860s, and
miserly allotments for blankets, straw, and firewood left many soldiers
shivering through cold winter nights. Conditions seemed dreariest in
the borderlands; with budgets tight and the frontier in flux, officials
hesitated to build permanent housing on posts that might soon be abandoned. Quarters designed as temporary thus often had to suffice for
years. Winfield Scott, named commanding general in 1841, complained
that with few exceptions, "on the Indian frontiers . . . the troops are,
when they chance to be allowed short rests, either in tents (winter as well
as summer) or such miserable bush and mud huts as they have hastily
constructed for the moment."[6]

Military life was not without certain advantages. In his magisterial
study of army life, Edward M. Coffman has pointed out that, in rough
economic terms, antebellum enlisted men probably fared better than
contemporary farm hands or textile workers. Many soldiers received
extra duty pay (usually between ten and fifty cents per day) for their non-
combat labor, enjoyed considerable job security in an age of economic
uncertainty, and could not be imprisoned for debt.[7]

Regulations allowed each company to employ up to four laundresses, many of whom were married to soldiers. Authorized to receive
army rations and quarters, these women charged fees set by a board of
officers but depended on the whim of the commanding officer for the
quality of their housing. Some undoubtedly added prostitution to their
list of services; they "manage to make themselves as troublesome as all
the rest of the command put together," complained one officer. Another,

however, pointed out that they were "honest, married women, and their husbands apt to be our best soldiers."[8]

Other women worked as servants for officers, raising families and carving out lives for themselves as they accompanied their soldier-husbands across the west. In explaining his choice of an Irish immigrant bride to his father, Sergeant Charles Frances Clarke affirmed that she was "a good religious honest girl" who worked at Jefferson Barracks. Clarke admitted that he could "not say that she has the accomplishments of many of the ladies of England," but he stressed that "she has a good plain Education & is able & willing to work which is a great deal better out West here." In what was probably a typical case, Irish immigrant Jane Earl Thorpy bore four children while serving with her husband at nine different garrisons in six states and territories during his fourteen years in the service. At most posts they lived in a ubiquitous "Suds Row" off from the parade ground. "Situated on the outskirts of every military post," recalled one veteran, "may be seen a collection of huts, old tents, picket houses and 'dugouts,' an air of squalor and dirt pervading the locality, and troops of shock-haired children and slovenly looking females of various colors completing the picture."[9]

Life on the borderlands outposts was distinctly different for the wives of commissioned personnel, who, like their husbands, generally came from middle-to-upper-class backgrounds. Collectively, officers' wives formed the elite of garrison society. Their greater wealth allowed them to access considerably more daily comforts—better food, better quarters, and often an impressive collection of household goods befitting their status. Given that, as one officer's daughter recalled, "the garrison had to make its own entertainment," wives organized hops, sewing bees, reading circles, excursions by horseback and carriage to local sites of interest, and holiday celebrations. Correct military protocol insisted that visiting guests and dignitaries be fêted with the finest of a garrison's cuisine, furnishings, and entertainment, on the understanding that the treatment would be reciprocated when the circumstances were reversed.[10]

In the 1850 census, the twenty-three officers' wives residing in Minnesota and on eight Texas posts averaged twenty-six years of age. All were younger than their spouses. The majority hailed from the free states, with New York being the most common state of birth. Seven

FIG. 19. Alice Kirk Grierson. Wives of commanding officers
attempted to set a refined tone for frontier garrisons. Here is
Mrs. Grierson (1828–88), wife of Colonel Benjamin Grierson,
in the 1880s. She brought her piano to her West Texas stations.
FORT DAVIS NATIONAL HISTORIC SITE.

in ten of these couples had one or more children living with them.
Holding no official status, they nonetheless often enjoyed the services of
enlisted men working as "strikers" (personal servants) for their officer-
husbands. Others brought domestic help with them. Despite their privi-
leges, life on the military frontier was difficult; Martha Summerhayes,

wife of an Eighth Infantry officer, dubbed their existence one of "glittering misery." Probably the biggest single hurdle they confronted was loneliness, a result of the small nature of many garrisons as well as their own class biases. Teresa Vielé, wife of Lieutenant Egbert L. Vielé, reflected the sentiments of many when she described the situation at Ringgold Barracks, Texas: "I never saw a woman while there, except a Mexican peasant or a camp woman." Most nonetheless seem to have approached frontier life with the cautious determination of Mrs. Lydia Lane, who explained that she "had 'gone for a soldier,' and a soldier I determined to be."[11]

Roughly half of the officers in the 1850 census who were located in Texas and Minnesota were living with their wives. Those without spouses were, on average, nearly ten years younger than their married colleagues. Although the typical officer of the Jacksonian era hoped to find a wife who would become "a comforter" and did not want his prospective wife to work outside the home, in his individual relationships—especially with mothers and sisters—he revealed a surprising propensity to accept an expanded vision of female gender roles. The effects of these kinship relationships were particularly important in the intimate circle of antebellum army society, where as many as one-fifth of officers married a relative of a fellow soldier. Freed from the competition of the emerging market capitalism that marked the lives of civilians, officers were willing to allow their female kin greater individual autonomy than was the contemporary middle- and upper-class norm, and the need for a permanent companion seems to have led most to marry for love and happiness. Moreover, they were as likely to accept the trend toward more nurturing, child-centered parenting as their civilian counterparts.[12]

For their part, officers approached the borderlands with a mixture of a desire to help the nation attain its intended glory, an appreciation for the opportunities they found in the American West, and a longing for the refinements found back east. Most were frustrated by the tedium of daily garrison life and the painfully slow rate of promotion. "Military ambition however legitimate its bounds & laudable its object, is but the road to splendid poverty & neglect," wrote one officer. Seniority, rather than merit, dictated promotion through the rank of colonel, and there was no retirement system before the Civil War. In 1836, the adjutant general reported that in normal years it took new officers eight years to reach first lieutenant, another ten to secure a captaincy, and two more decades to gain elevation to major. Most adopted a philosophical attitude in light of their dim prospects for advancement. As Thomas Jesup put it, "I am a soldier. There is little speck of war in the political horizon; and, whatever my inclinations may prompt me to, my motto must still be, 'semper paratus' [always ready]."[13]

Fairly generous increases in emoluments (allowances for food, fuel, forage, quarters, and special duties that often tripled an officer's take-home pay) and the long-term stability of consumer prices were largely offset by the high costs of frontier living and officers' low base salaries, which for company-grade officers remained unchanged between 1798 and 1857: $300 per year for a second lieutenant (in 1856, this would have meant less than $7,500 in 2006 terms), $360 for a first lieutenant, and $480 for a captain. Bored with the monotony of garrison life and having little incentive to better themselves through private study, many turned to drink. In 1820, Surgeon William Beaumont complained about "very strong symptoms of dissipation among the officers"; three decades later, Lieutenant George Crook believed that almost all of his fellow officers at Benecia Barracks, California, got drunk every day.[14]

Sergeants comprised the backbone of the borderlands army, keeping order in the ranks, overseeing daily drills, handling paperwork, and passing along practical folkways. Officers selected personnel for these noncommissioned slots on the basis of their "special trust and confidence in the patriotism, valor, fidelity and abilities" of the individual. Each company had four sergeants and four corporals, with the first sergeant exercising "the management of all company affairs." Fresh out of West Point, John M. Schofield, a twenty-two-year-old brevet second lieutenant, described his initial encounter with First Sergeant Dominick Duffey, Company K, First Artillery:

> In the morning the first sergeant reported to me, with the quarterly and monthly returns prepared for my signature, and made out more beautifully than anything in writing I had ever before seen, and explained to me in detail all the business affairs of the battery . . . Next to General Scott and Colonel [Robert E.] Lee, with whom I had had the honor of some acquaintance, I was

quite sure there stood before me the finest-looking and most accomplished soldier in the United States Army. What a hard time young officers of the army would sometimes have but for the old sergeants![15]

Shut out from becoming officers, roughly one in every six soldiers during the antebellum period ended his military career as something other than a private. Several pay raises and new grades did much to keep them in the service. Legislation of 1833, 1838, and 1854 increased the monthly pay of sergeant majors from $9 to $21, sergeants from $8 to $17, and corporals from $7 to $13 (corporals in mounted units received an extra dollar). In 1832, Congress created the new position of ordnance sergeant, which the army interpreted as "a reward to those faithful and well tried Sergeants, who have long served their country." The five-dollar-per-month bonus served as an attractive inducement, and by the 1850s foreign-born noncommissioned officers probably outnumbered officers who were natives of the United States.[16]

Though incomplete, an emerging sense of professionalism among the officer corps also helped the army through these difficult times. Like physicians, lawyers, civil engineers, and scientists, commissioned personnel were developing a sense of group identity and consciousness, molded by common experiences at West Point (in 1830, 64 percent of commissioned personnel were West Pointers; by 1860 that figure stood at 76 percent), marriage and kinship ties, shared authoritarian social values, and a sense of isolation from the rest of society. The median career length for officers, only ten years in 1797, had doubled by 1830. And even as they remained involved in politics—voters elected Major General Zachary Taylor as president in 1848, and the Whig Party nominated commanding general Winfield Scott for that office four years later—by the middle of the century officers had at least accepted the primacy of civilian authority.[17]

The army now frowned on officers who entered local political squabbles, as evidenced in the reprimand given Captain Samuel P. Heintzelman for having involved himself in a dispute in Florida. "An officer of the army should not identify himself with the factions existing in either states or territories," insisted Quartermaster General Jesup. "He can be useful only so long as he acts with perfect impartiality to all." Moreover, the refusal of most officers to support either Canadian patriots or Texas revolutionaries belied charges that the regulars backed unbridled territorial expansion and filibustering. Even General Scott could, in some frontier matters at least, maintain a cool official dignity. Following his service in the Seminole and Creek conflicts, Scott helped to resolve several disputes with British Canada. In the Patriot Rebellion of upper Canada and the Aroostook War along the Maine–New Brunswick border, his imperious manner served the nation well. Intent on preserving order, his legalistic opposition to insurgents both north and south of the Canadian border set a fine example.[18]

But the move toward professionalization remained imperfect. Even as frontier issues consumed most of the army's resources, soldiers failed to engage in the rigorous, systematic analysis that might have produced training or tactics suitable to the borderlands environments. Nor could the haughty Scott absolve himself from the bickering more befitting a spoiled young child than the army's ranking officer. Taking advantage of a temporary absence of the secretary of war in April 1843, Scott took his long-running feud with Gaines directly to the president. Forwarding Gaines's correspondence, Scott pronounced that "this letter, like twenty other communications from Genl. Gaines . . . furnishes conclusive evidence that Genl. Gaines is, mentally, not fit for any responsible military duty or command" and recommended that Gaines be court-martialed or given a leave of absence so that "his *mental sanity*" could be checked. The president seems not to have acted on Scott's psychiatric analysis.[19]

Often critical of the society they were defending, officers nonetheless backed what they perceived to be the country's manifest destiny. Most concluded that unless Indians adopted more of the white man's ways, they were doomed to extinction. "It is only a question of time," asserted Captain William T. H. Brooks. "In the end, they are bound to be exterminated." Captain Thomas Williams also voiced the consensus view, which held that lasting peace could come only after the tribes had been whipped in battle. "I'm not sure that good policy would not decide they should receive a sound thrashing first, & peace afterwards," wrote Williams.[20]

Despite this paternalism, most soldiers took seriously their role in upholding what historian Samuel J. Watson has dubbed "the sovereign *pax Americana* asserted by treaty and national law." Thus when disputes

FIG. 20. Edmund P. Gaines. Veteran of the War of 1812 and the Second
Seminole War, Gaines (1777–1849) was a longtime rival of Winfield
Scott and would later be reprimanded for calling up volunteers
without authorization on the eve of the war with Mexico. He died
in New Orleans in 1849. LIBRARY OF CONGRESS, USZ62-57633.

between the Republic of Texas and Mexico spilled over to the Santa Fe
Trail in 1843, Captain Philip St. George Cooke and four companies of
dragoons rode out from Fort Leavenworth and Fort Scott to protect the
rich trading caravans. Encountering Jacob Snively and about 170 Texans
near the Arkansas River, the captain disarmed all but ten of the Texans.

Ignoring the Republic of Texas's protests, the army closed ranks in support of the actions of its own. "We must *destroy, arrest,* or *disarm* all such lawless combinations whenever found within or near our *unmarked boundary*," thundered Gaines.21

Similarly, most officers saw the reduction of intertribal conflict, especially in areas where white settlers had no immediate stake, as being entirely consistent with the national interest. Thus the army took great pains to root out corruption within the complex system of Indian annuities and to mediate disputes throughout the plains. Soldier-diplomats had much to do, for the "contested plains," as historian Elliott West has called the region, were changing. The increasing dependency on the fur trade and on an ecology straining against the pressures of growing numbers of humans was leading to increased militarization. Military leadership and skills proved even more valuable in this contest for limited resources. Indians responded in different ways to these realignments. Comanches, Kiowas, and Kiowa Apaches, for example, had become rich in horses but were now threatened from the north by Cheyennes, Pawnees, and Osages. Emigrant tribes, often better armed, exerted pressure from the east. Seeking easier and more lucrative targets, Comanches launched raids into Mexico, pushing even into San Luis Potosi. Many eventually concluded that intertribal agreements would free them to capitalize on new opportunities. Thus although wars against some foes—particularly with the emigrant tribes to the east, the Crows, the Osages, and the Pawnees—continued, west of the hundredth meridian former rivals like the Cheyennes, Arapahoes, Lakotas, Comanches, Kiowas, and Plains Apaches made a lasting peace in 1840. It would by no means be an active, cooperative alliance, but it did mean that they could focus their energies on other fronts.22

Such changes brought some unanticipated benefits to the army, as evidenced by the development of working associations with tribes like the Crows and the Pawnees. The experiences of the Crows, who had been badly hurt by the epidemics of the late eighteenth century, seem a classic illustration of the shifting dynamics of what Frederick Hoxie has aptly described as "life in a tightening circle." The Lakotas "are making war on us all the time," complained one Crow leader to one officer. Opportunistic and adaptable in their strategic needs, the Crows came to accept the Americans' professions of friendship, perceiving the newcomers as useful allies. In turn, the army regularly employed Crow auxiliaries in its wars against other tribes. Likewise, many Pawnees, badly weakened by disease and years of warfare, would join up with the army to fight their old enemies, the Lakotas and the Cheyennes. The United States, which had once dismissed the Pawnees as "beggars and thieves" who preyed on overland travelers, now welcomed a relationship with a suddenly valuable ally. This mutually profitable relationship by no means dictated that the Pawnees agreed to assimilate into American society; rather, in the words of one close student of Pawnee society, "they continued to count coups, take scalps, and practice their war-related ceremonies" and "remained distinctly Pawnee in their ways."[23]

Changing realities on the Great Plains put a special premium on mobility. As Winfield Scott surmised, "a warrior on horseback looks upon foot-soldiers, beyond musket-shot, without any danger." In 1844, Congress thus took up a proposal to remount the Second Dragoons. Representative James I. McKay (D-N.C.) objected, claiming that "no danger need be anticipated from them [the Indians], if they were but dealt with justly and kindly." Echoing traditional antimilitary sentiments, John Quincy Adams (Whig-Mass.) blasted the "magnificent appropriations" for military preparedness made by "the President and his two thunderbolts, the Secretary of War and the Secretary of the Navy." Despite such objections, the measure passed by a comfortable ninety-four to fifty-six count. Pointedly, supporters based their case on frontier needs.[24]

Thus the army slogged on. Thanks largely to Quartermaster General Jesup, who had proclaimed the project to be "of the highest national importance," Cass's military road was completed, if but with little fanfare. Along the Red River just west of Arkansas, which had been granted statehood in 1836, Fort Towson remained the southernmost anchor of the frontier garrisons. Fort Wayne and Fort Scott lay just west of the Arkansas and Missouri borders. Fort Leavenworth, erected in 1827, served as home to the First Dragoon Regiment. At the junction of the Des Moines and Raccoon rivers in the Iowa Territory, Fort Des Moines watched the Sac and Fox Indians. A new Fort Atkinson, established in 1840 at the present town bearing the same name, was designed to protect the immigrant Winnebago Indians from older residents. In the Wisconsin Territory, Fort Snelling remained a powerful presence, joined in 1844 by Fort Wilkins, built to support miners in the Copper Harbor region of Lake Superior. Key interior forts included Mackinac, Brady, Winnebago, Crawford, Jesup, and Gibson.[25]

Political considerations often influenced both the positioning of and allocations to western posts. Exceptional even under these circumstances was the saga of Fort Smith, Arkansas. Established at the confluence of the Arkansas and Poiteau rivers in 1817, the site was abandoned seven years later in favor of Fort Gibson. Despite opposition from most officers stationed in Arkansas, landowners smelling profits from the infusion of federal dollars into the local economy joined the garrison's former commander, Colonel Mathew Arbuckle, in lobbying for the army's return to Fort Smith. Bowing to pressure from the Arkansas congressional delegation, in 1838 the War Department began construction of a big new post there, featuring barracks for four companies, stables, two-story blockhouses, and twelve-foot-high stone walls. At the cost of $300,000 (roughly $7.5 million in 2006 dollars), the government had built what in essence served as an elaborate supply depot. The restored Fort Smith, admit its historians, was "an enduring tribute to resourceful border folk who labored mightily to keep this federal income-producing installation operational."[26]

Military affairs also played a major role in the neighboring Republic of Texas. Having won its independence by force of arms, Texans drew up plans for an impressive regular defense establishment, especially under President Mirabeau B. Lamar (1838–41). But spiraling costs, poor discipline, and frequent disputes between civilian and military leaders meant that the Lone Star Republic's regular army—officially numbering about one soldier for every fifty civilians—rarely met authorized standards and was disbanded as Lamar left office. Militiamen, volunteers, and rangers thus filled the brunt of the republic's security needs. These were quite large, for Mexico had recognized neither Texas's independence nor its claims that the Rio Grande represented its southern boundary, and most Texans—with the notable exception of Sam Houston, president from 1836 to 1838 and from 1841 to 1844—wanted to expel Indians from their midst.[27]

Incidental violence erupted into open warfare in 1839, when Texas demanded that emigrant tribes leave. On July 16, four hundred Texans defeated a Cherokee force less than half their size at the Battle of the

Neches. Further west, matters exploded the following year at San Antonio's Council House. The Penateka Comanches having failed to produce the expected white captives as a preliminary to peace talks, Texans shot down thirty-five of their number. The killings at the Council House convinced most Plains tribes that the Texans could not be trusted, and so they organized a raiding party, which swept through central Texas as far south as Victoria, sacking the community of Linnville, capturing thousands of cattle and horses, and killing two dozen settlers. Following a running fight at Plum Creek on August 6, the Comanche army split up. Lured by the promise of booty, a dozen ranger expeditions combed north and central Texas between 1839 and 1841, attacking any Indians unfortunate enough to be in their wake. In the bloodiest encounter, Colonel John Moore, ninety Texans, and seventeen allied Lipan Apaches surprised a Comanche village on the upper Colorado River, gunning down at least 140 inhabitants and capturing 35 others at the cost of 2 wounded.[28]

President Lamar had also determined to resolve his republic's disputes with Mexico. An ill-fated effort to secure sovereignty over New Mexico met a disastrous fate in October 1841, when an expeditionary force originally numbering 321 men surrendered at Santa Fe. Mexican retribution for this invasion came the following year, as columns led by Rafael Vásquez and Adrián Woll briefly occupied San Antonio. Newly elected president Sam Houston had vetoed a declaration of war in the wake of the Vásquez raid, but Woll's column represented a more serious threat, as evidenced by sharp fighting at Salado Creek. As Woll fell back south, Texas volunteers followed him to the Rio Grande; seeking revenge and plunder, about three hundred Texans under Colonel William S. Fisher crossed into Mexico. Running low on powder following a hard-fought battle at Mier, they surrendered on December 26. Seventeen men were later executed. Houston, cognizant of the troubled state of the Texas economy and counting on annexation by the United States, resisted public clamor for both a new war against Mexico and the extermination of the Indians, instead reopening negotiations on both fronts.[29]

Although Houston's efforts to secure immediate annexation failed, James K. Polk's victory over Henry Clay in the 1844 presidential race led to a dramatic turn in U.S. foreign policy. Having run on a Democratic Party platform that promised the "reoccupation" of Oregon, the "reannexation" of Texas, and the acquisition of a Pacific port in California,

FIG. 21. "A War President." Support for expansion was by no means universal. Here former secretary of war Cass, the Democratic presidential nominee in 1848, is caricatured in a Currier and Ives print. LIBRARY OF CONGRESS, USZ62-10789.

Polk's razor-thin triumph harkened a redoubled American expansionism overseen by a president determined to fulfill his campaign promises. For years, the Hudson's Bay Company had attempted to stem the tide of American immigration into Oregon by creating a "fur desert" in the Snake River basin, hunting down every fur-bearing animal they could find. Less than a month after Polk's triumph, the lame-duck secretary of war, William Wilkins, asked Congress for $100,000 to establish a line of military posts from the Missouri River to the Rocky Mountains. Whereas officials had previously justified such requests by reference to the need to improve defense against Indian attacks, Wilkins stressed the need to protect claims to Oregon, still jointly occupied with Great Britain.[30]

With the administration set on expansion, Secretary of War William L. Marcy dispatched summer patrols into the Great Plains. In

1845, Colonel Stephen Kearny led the largest expedition—five companies of dragoons—out from Fort Leavenworth. Three months later, after
meeting with Pawnee, Sioux, and Arapaho delegations as well as a two-
thousand-strong emigrant caravan bound for Oregon, Kearny's men
returned, having marched twenty-two hundred miles. Roving columns
such as his, asserted Kearny, would protect travelers going to Oregon
more effectively than fixed posts. To deter white interlopers from provoking needless conflict, he recommended placing the entire Indian
country under martial law.[31]

The thirty-six officers of the Army's Corps of Topographical
Engineers were poised to exploit the national mood. Headed by the
ambitious Colonel John James Abert, the Topographical Engineers had
in 1838 been accorded status equal to that of the Corps of Engineers.
Blending good education, a generous dose of Romantic optimism,
and what Pulitzer-Prize-winning historian William Goetzmann
has described as an "essentially cosmic approach to the West,"
the Topographical Engineers represented "a new type of explorer,
self-consciously carrying the burden of civilization to the wilderness
and the lessons of the wilderness back into civilization." Most successfully capturing the public imagination was Lieutenant John C.
Frémont, West Point graduate and son-in-law of Senator Thomas Hart
Benton, who led expeditions into the far west in 1841, 1842, 1843–44,
and 1845. His reports—essentially semiscientific observations of a man
who sought to shape his country's politics—helped to convince a generation of Americans that the Trans-Mississippi West was deserving of
occupation by a great nation.[32]

In May 1846, Congress's declaration of war against Mexico directed
attention to the Southwest. Within a few weeks, Congress increased
the regular army to over seventeen thousand by creating a Regiment
of Mounted Riflemen (initially designed to help protect the emigrant
trails to Oregon) and by allowing the number of privates per company to
expand from forty-two to one hundred. Polk nonetheless had little faith
in the regulars, arguing that "the old army officers have become so in
the habit of enjoying their ease . . . that most of them have no energy."
Moreover, the Democratic president believed them to be "all Whigs and
violent partisans." Confident that "citizen soldiers" would "be ready . . .
to rush [to arms] with alacrity, at the call of their country," he secured

authority to call out fifty thousand volunteers, and made sure that each of the thirteen volunteer generals was a loyal Democrat.[33]

Polk also wanted to occupy the Mexican territories of New Mexico and California. Relations between Mexico City and its far-flung northern provinces had been especially strained since the revolution against Spain, and frontier defenses against Indian attack had fallen into disrepair as Mexican leaders focused on problems closer to home. Poorly trained militias and volunteers had largely replaced the old presidial regulars; raiding and slave hunting now seemed more profitable than the traditional (and mutually profitable) mechanisms of trade, gifts, and diplomacy. Even longtime allies like the Utes had turned against Mexico. Confronted by Navajos, Comanches, and Apaches who were better armed than he was, one New Mexican complained in 1844 that "we are surrounded on all sides . . . by many heartless barbarians." To establish American sovereignty, Colonel (soon to be awarded his general's star) Kearny left Fort Leavenworth with his Army of the West, which included three hundred of his First Dragoons, thirteen hundred Missouri volunteers, and sixteen cannon. Driving his men hard, the austere Kearny completed the long march to Santa Fe by mid-August. For many New Mexicans, who had for years ignored instructions from Mexico City anyway, military opposition to Kearny seemed not only futile but against their self-interest. His dusty column thus entered the city without firing a shot, erecting Fort Marcy as a demonstration of U.S. power.[34]

Meanwhile, an unauthorized military agent was busy in California. The dashing Lieutenant Frémont had arrived in California the previous year with an eye toward exploring Oregon. In March 1846, he provoked an international incident by hoisting the Stars and Stripes near Monterey. A group of U.S. immigrants at Sonoma declared themselves independent three months later. Frémont resigned his commission, took command of the Bear Flag movement, formed the California Battalion, and proclaimed his intention to conquer all of California.[35]

The U.S. Navy also joined the race. Fearful that Britain might grab California, Secretary of the Navy George Bancroft had issued discretionary orders to the commander of the Pacific Squadron, Commodore John D. Sloat, twelve months before Polk declared war. After concentrating his fleet (one frigate, four sloops, a schooner, a storeship, and their Marine complements), in the event of a conflict Sloat was to "at once possess . . . the port of San Francisco, and blockade or occupy such other ports as your force may permit." Anticipating a quiet retirement, the sixty-five-year-old Sloat by no means relished the opportunity to make history—or risk blemishing his three decades of naval service—with any derring-do. But on learning of reports of the Bear Flag revolt (and wrongly assuming that Frémont had Washington's authority for such action) the commodore landed parties at Monterey and San Francisco. The arrival of the more aggressive Captain Robert F. Stockton and two additional ships later that month gave the cautious Sloat the excuse to sail for home. Stockton and Frémont sent detachments to occupy San Diego and Los Angeles, and the former pronounced himself territorial governor.[36]

Back in New Mexico, General Kearny appointed Charles Bent, a well-known merchant, as governor, and in late September began the arduous march from Santa Fe to Los Angeles. As Kearny and his one-hundred-man escort rode west, Californios wrested control of Los Angeles, San Diego, and Santa Barbara back from the Americans. On December 6, Kearny's little command, bolstered by three dozen sailors and marines dispatched by Stockton, walked into a trap laid by Andreas Pico thirty miles northeast of San Diego at San Pascual. Expert horsemen and lancers (Kearny later described them as "mounted on fine horses" and as "the best riders in the world"), Pico's Californios killed or wounded a third of their enemy (including Kearny, twice wounded by a lance). "Day dawned on the most tattered and ill-fed detachment of men that ever the United States mustered under her colors," remembered one member of Kearny's battered command as they scrambled to secure a defensible position. Only on December 10, with the arrival of another 180 reinforcements from Stockton, was the siege lifted.[37]

Kearny staggered into San Diego two days later. Pausing long enough to give the five hundred dragoons (long dismounted), marines, sailors, and volunteers assembled there some quick drills in forming a defensive square, he then led this makeshift force, along with an artillery battery, toward Los Angeles. Low on powder and morale, Governor José Maria Flores deployed 450 men and four archaic cannon twelve miles south of Los Angeles along the San Gabriel River to meet the *yanquis.* On the afternoon of January 8 Kearny's makeshift command waded across the river, their square formation fending off the probing attacks of Flores's light cavalry. U.S. forces occupied Los Angeles on the tenth. Clarification of the tangle over local authority between the combustible trio of Stockton, Kearny, and Frémont—warriors and martinets all—did not come until the arrival of the navy's Commodore Branford Shubrick, who outranked everyone, and the army's Colonel Richard B. Mason, who bore orders proclaiming him governor once Kearny deemed California "pacified." By June, Stockton, Kearny, and Frémont had gone, leaving Mason in command.[38]

Consolidating U.S. authority in New Mexico also proved difficult. After helping to draft a territorial constitution and a legal code, Colonel Alexander W. Doniphan, commanding the First Regiment of Missouri Mounted Volunteers, engaged in a seven-week campaign against the Navajos, occupying El Paso on Christmas Day. Colonel Sterling Price's twelve-hundred-strong Second Missouri Mounted Volunteers and two hundred dragoons now provided the armed might behind Governor Bent's administration. Bent, however, failed to recognize the tensions between local residents and the American occupiers, and on January 19, 1847, he and several others were assassinated. In response, Price smashed through several hundred rebels at Canada, and then again at the pass of Embudo. Pitched fighting on February 3–4 at the Taos Pueblo mission, which had become the focal point of the rebellion, left an estimated 150 rebels dead, at the cost of at least 50 American casualties.[39]

Price having regained control over New Mexico, Doniphan pondered his next action from El Paso. His original orders had been to support an offensive against Chihuahua, but the troops slated for that campaign had instead been diverted to reinforce Zachary Taylor at Saltillo. A popular Whig lawyer, Doniphan was left with a stark choice: march unaided against Chihuahua, retrace his steps to Santa Fe, or remain in El Paso. The six foot five Doniphan chose the first and most dangerous option. Thus on February 8, his decidedly unmilitary-looking column, consisting of 924 Missouri volunteers, six artillery pieces, a baggage train, and 315 heavy trade wagons with their associated merchants and teamsters began the three-hundred-mile trek to the Mexican state capital. The ungainly command rolled south across two deserts. Fifteen miles north of Chihuahua, three thousand Mexican troops and ten light cannon, led by Major General José A. Heredia, blocked the road. Enjoying superior firepower, on February 28 Doniphan's men turned the enemy's left flank

FIG. 22. Alexander Doniphan. One of the most able volunteer soldiers of the
nineteenth century, Doniphan (1808–87) had as brigadier general of
the Missouri state militia forced Joseph Smith, founder of the Latter-
day Saints, to leave Missouri but disobeyed orders to execute him
and prevented vigilantes from harming him. During the war against
Mexico, Doniphan wrote a code of civil laws for occupied New Mexico
and captured Chihuahua. LIBRARY OF CONGRESS, USZ62-109945.

and unleashed a murderous enfilading fire. "The field was literally covered with the dead and wounded from our artillery and the unerring fire of our riflemen," wrote Doniphan in his after-action report; indeed, the estimated six hundred Mexican casualties dwarfed the U.S. losses, which were less than a dozen. Doniphan entered Chihuahua the next day.[40]

In nine months, the Missourians had marched over two thousand miles, occupied Santa Fe and El Paso, fought Navajos, and captured a Mexican state capital. But, as Doniphan reported from Chihuahua on March 20, "my position here is exceedingly embarrassing." His men had never been paid and their twelve-month enlistments would expire on June 1. "They are literally without horses, clothes, or money—nothing but arms and a disposition to use them," he continued, and were "wholly unfit to garrison a town or city." With food, women, drink, and gambling in ample supply, Doniphan feared that his Missourians would "soon be ruined by improper indulgences." They were eventually shipped back to New Orleans; one newspaper described them as resembling "the pictures of Robinson Crusoe." Hailed as heroes, they collected their pay and discharges and went home, one of the most successful volunteer forces in the history of the American West.[41]

As the United States helped itself to enormous chunks of the Southwest, primary operations against Mexico shifted from Zachary Taylor's army of occupation, which had captured Monterrey, to Winfield Scott's army of invasion, which had landed at Vera Cruz and would eventually occupy Mexico City. But troubling events along the Santa Fe Trail presaged future conflicts with Indians who also claimed the lands contested by Washington and Mexico City. In response to these threats—one observer calculated that summer's losses at forty-seven persons killed, 330 wagons destroyed, and sixty-five hundred stock lost on the trail—in July 1847 the War Department called up five more companies of Missouri volunteers. Dubbed the "Indian Battalion," these men patrolled the road through most of the following year.[42]

Treaties with Great Britain and Mexico restored international peace to the American West. The Polk administration had resolved long-standing disputes with Great Britain in the Buchanan-Packenham Treaty, under which both nations extended the forty-ninth parallel as the boundary to the Pacific Ocean and acknowledged joint navigation rights through the Strait of Juan de Fuca. In the Treaty of Guadalupe-Hidalgo,

Mexico gave up its claims to Texas and ceded the Southwest in return for an indemnity of $15 million, assumption by the U.S. of Mexican debts totaling $3.25 million, the promise of full citizenship rights to residents of the affected lands, and vows from that the United States that it would put an end to cross-border Indian attacks.

By adding nearly 1.2 million square miles to the United States—a geographic area roughly equal to that of Europe—the treaties had doubled the size of the republic and shattered earlier assumptions about a permanent frontier. The war against Mexico had witnessed the popularization of Samuel Colt's .44-caliber six-shot revolver among mounted troops and confirmed the influence of West Point–educated officers within the regular army. But in a larger sense the victory over Mexico, punctuated by the remarkable exploits of Doniphan's mounted Missourians, confirmed for many their faith in the American volunteer. Ever suspicious of a professional military establishment, President Polk reflected this sentiment in his homage to volunteers during his final State of the Union address:

> The events of the late war with Mexico have . . . demonstrated that upon the breaking out of hostilities not anticipated, and for which no preparation has been made, a volunteer army of citizen soldiers equal to veteran troops, and in numbers equal to any emergency, can in a short period be brought into the field . . . They are armed, and have been accustomed from their youth up to handle and use firearms, and a larger proportion of them, especially in the Western and more newly settled States, are expert marksmen. They are men who have a reputation to maintain at home by their good conduct in the field. They are intelligent, and there is an individuality of character which is found in the ranks of no other army.[43]

SEVEN

Constabularies in Blue

Despite President Polk's pronouncements, volunteers did not replace the regulars following the war against Mexico. In general, states and territories had little desire to spend their own money on rangers or volunteers. They were happy to raise such units and bill Washington, of course, but only rarely would Congress or executive officials agree to such terms, for most recognized that such state units were much more expensive—and difficult to control—than the regulars.

The army, then, remained the federal government's most visible instrument in the borderlands, its task complicated by administrative changes that deepened divisions between soldiers and civilian Indian agents. In a bow to the increasingly complex functions of the federal government, in 1849 Congress created the Department of the Interior under which was to be subsumed by the General Land Office, the Patent Office, the Pension Office, and the Office of Indian Affairs. With considerable justification, Indian agents often believed the army too willing to resort to force; army officers, with equal merit, saw their civilian counterparts as raw political hacks who had little appreciation for frontier subtleties. For the next half century, soldiers would regularly—and always unsuccessfully—call for the transfer of the Indian Office back to the War Department.[1]

Because of their huge size and diverse populations, Texas, the

Mexican Cession, and Oregon posed significant military challenges. Over eighty-five thousand Hispanics already resided in these lands, and the two hundred thousand Indians living there had no reason to relinquish their use to any newcomers. In 1847, establishment of the Mormon state of Deseret in the Salt Lake Valley heralded a carefully planned, religiously inspired mission to establish a haven for the Church of Jesus Christ of Latter-day Saints. The following year, the discovery of gold near Sutter's Mill in northern California instigated a flood of immigrants seeking the promise of more earthly riches. Subsequent mineral strikes brought more emigrants to much of the Mountain West. These migrations, along with the increased traffic on the emigrant trails to Oregon, resulted in greater contact between the outsiders and the seventy-five thousand resident Indians of the Great Plains and the eighty-four thousand souls whom the federal government had already uprooted from the east. Alternately protecting, controlling, fighting, and assisting these diverse groups would be the job of the army, a task made more difficult by the public demand that the United States immediately assert its authority. Not surprisingly, borderlands combat between the army and Indians escalated dramatically.

Fiscal conditions directly influenced relations between residents of these newly acquired regions and the regulars. For the most part, garrisons located in remote areas enjoyed friendlier ties with civilians than did those stationed in lands holding more immediate economic promise. In addition to providing a measure of security, an army post meant jobs for guides, mechanics, and laborers, along with lucrative mercantile opportunities. The case of Fort Davis, Texas, serves as an illuminating example. Established some 475 miles west of San Antonio in 1854, government salaries and emoluments paid to soldiers and employees there averaged about $55,000 per year (roughly $1.3 million annually in 2006 dollars) during the antebellum period, making possible a small local service industry. Pennsylvania native Alexander Young, who came to the area with the army, worked the system to its fullest. The government had long authorized post and regimental officers to select sutlers, who paid a small monthly tax (about five cents per man) to the post fund in return for the chance to sell their wares on base. Young held that position at Fort Davis from 1855 to 1861; in 1860, he also picked up the sutlership at nearby Fort Quitman. And in addition to serving as de facto post

FIG. 23. Thomas Nast, "The New Indian War." Rivalries between the Interior Department and the War Department over control of Indian affairs would continue to plague the United States throughout the last half of the nineteenth century. Thomas Nast's "The New Indian War," which graced the front cover of *Harper's Weekly* in December 1878, depicts the long-standing rivalry between the Interior Department (represented by Secretary Carl Schurz) and the army (represented by Phil Sheridan, with William Sherman lurking in the doorway). LIBRARY OF CONGRESS, USZ62-55403.

banker to military personnel between the army paymaster's infrequent visits, Young often sold the garrison wood, hay, and corn, having won supply contracts to do so. The community's wealthiest man, by 1860 his estate was valued at $28,000.[2]

Federal money served as an especially important economic multiplier in the arid Southwest. Although more established eastern firms typically secured the largest contracts, garrisons bought beef, hay, flour, wood, and building materials from local suppliers like Young. Between 1849 and 1860, army salaries in Texas added $7.7 million to the state's economy. Quartermasters spent another $3.7 million on forage, transportation, building repair and construction, civilian salaries, rents and leases (this was largely unique to Texas, which retained control of its public lands), purchases of horses and mules, and other miscellaneous activities. In neighboring New Mexico, the army became the largest civilian employer. Not surprisingly, lobbyists and politicians supported military garrisons with more concern for their economic benefit than national security. "It is quite natural that the inhabitants of the towns should desire to have troops stationed among them," wrote one secretary of war with unusual candor. "Sometimes from motives entirely distinct from the good of the public service, and their representations on this subject cannot always be implicitly relied on."[3]

Whereas non-Indian inhabitants in depressed or isolated regions generally welcomed the army, boomtown communities often resented the military presence. As outside capital poured into the Astoria, Oregon, region in 1850, Lieutenant Theodore Talbot observed: "The people here detest us and are straining every nerve to have us removed. . . . It would be a hard matter for any class of people to be more unpopular than army officers are in this country." Talbot responded to this antimilitary sentiment in kind. The locals had "lost all their energy." Warming to his subject, the lieutenant added: "You can't imagine how disgusting it is to be compelled to have intercourse with such people. No aristocrat with the blood of all the Howards coursing through his veins, ever swelled or strutted with half the importance of some of the purse proud, illiterate mobocrats round about us."[4]

The military's perceptions of borderlands residents were also influenced by prejudices of class, ethnicity, and religion. "[T]here never was a viler set of men in the world," according to Major John Sedgwick, than the miners who rushed to Fort Wise, Colorado Territory, "where no man's life is safe, and certainly if he has fifty dollars to tempt one with." Most officers were equally contemptuous of Hispanics. Lieutenant Richard Johnson described the citizens of the Rio Grande community of Eagle Pass as "ignorant, destitute of any refinement, and . . . [lacking] respect for law and order." And like many back east, soldiers condemned the Mormon practice of plural marriage and feared the concentration of power in the hands of a small group of church elders.[5]

Amid the changing geography of the nation's borderlands, certain themes would persist. Officers still blamed much of the violence on civilians. "All our Indian wars, with very few exceptions, are brought on either by our frontier settlers," opined Captain Thomas W. Sweeny, "or the traders in the Indian Country, who as a class, are an unmitigated set of scoundrels." In describing conflicts against the Jicarilla Apaches in New Mexico, another wrote: "We have got ourselves, I regret to say, in a turmoil that . . . I don't see the end of. We are waging a war of extermination against a poor set of devils that have only done as a large population of the Territory has always been doing, that is, stealing a few head of cattle to keep them from starving."[6]

Continued military misconduct did nothing to ease borderlands tensions. An army court in 1855 admitted that four privates in the First Dragoons "engaged in a drunken riot" at Taos, New Mexico, and "mutinied against a Major of the regiment." The problem, judged the court, was that their company commander had also been drunk. Five years later, men of the garrison at Fort Davis broke into the stockade to lynch a civilian they believed had stabbed one of their comrades at a nearby saloon. "The whole company have done it," reported one of the overpowered sentinels. Captain Alexander W. Reynolds, among the ringleaders of a political-military cabal in Santa Fe, undoubtedly ranked among the guiltiest of the miscreants. Holding several quartermaster positions, Reynolds engaged in enough double billing, contract overpayments, and outright theft to leverage his salary and emoluments into a family estate—including full or partial interest in two sawmills, two gold mines, four ranches, two houses, three hotels, and an assortment of town lots—valued at over $70,000. Auditors later estimated his fraud and embezzlement to have cost the government $122,000.

Though dismissed from the service in 1855, Reynolds used his political connections to win reinstatement three years later.[7]

However uneasy its alliance with western civilians, the army was expected to secure national authority throughout the continent. With less than a thousand troops at their disposal, California military governors Colonel Richard B. Mason and Brevet Brigadier General Bennett Riley found it impossible to fully maintain order over an area inhabited by immigrant groups that were switching national loyalties and by resident Indians and Hispanics who were being overwhelmed by newcomers flocking to the gold fields. Longtime Californios resented the new U.S. authority; mission Indians, seeking to escape attacks by "the wild Indians" and Californians alike, fled in droves to the mountains, from whence the cycle of violence continued. Fearing a disruption of public order, in 1849 Riley oversaw elections for a constitutional convention in which soldiers figured prominently. Among elected delegates were Brevet Captain Henry W. Halleck and Lieutenant Cave J. Couts. Captain Robert S. Garnett chipped in by designing the Great Seal of California.[8]

Meanwhile, gold rush fever was decimating the army. Annual desertion rates for troops in the region reached 40 percent; had not officers allowed their men short furloughs to dig gold for themselves, the figure would have been higher. Officers themselves could not resist the urge to try to get rich. Colonel Mason, for instance, joined lieutenants William T. Sherman and William H. Warner in a partnership in a store through which they promptly tripled each of their $500 investments. A slight pay raise accorded troops serving in Oregon and California in 1850 (two dollars a day for officers and bonus money for enlisted personnel distributed at the time of their honorable discharge) did little to alleviate the crisis.[9]

The years were lean under Polk, but Zachary Taylor's election in 1848 meant that the regulars now had a friend in the White House. "Old Rough and Ready" sought authorization to increase the number of privates per companies stationed in frontier garrisons from forty-two (fifty in the dragoons, and sixty-four in the mounted riflemen) to seventy-four and to mount some infantry units. Temporarily halting their impassioned debates over slavery, both houses took up the bill in May 1850. Representative Joshua R. Giddings (Ohio-Free Soil) blasted the army and hailed the successes of "hardy backwoodsmen . . . who understand the Indian character, who are acquainted with their habits and their modes of warfare," in fighting Indians. Humphrey Marshall (Ky.-Whig) sprang to the regulars' defense, accusing Giddings of having "forgotten much of the material part of the history of the West." Citing the exploits of Anthony Wayne and Zachary Taylor, Marshall thundered: "I was born in the West—I belong to the West—I know the gallantry of the West; but I also know the pride of the West. Her people will never forget the credit that is due to those who bravely assisted the West in the hour of need." The House passed the bill with a nearly two-to-one majority. Eleven (nine Democrats and two Whigs) of fourteen borderlands representatives favored the increase. Senator Jefferson Davis (D-Miss.) shepherded the measure through the Senate.[10]

Taylor's sudden death that summer brought Millard Fillmore to the oval office. The new president's war secretary, Louisiana's Charles M. Conrad, had supported the recent army increase while in Congress and would sponsor repeated efforts—always unheeded by his former legislative colleagues—to increase the number of regular cavalrymen. Conrad also sought to find "some other means besides the terror of our arms" to resolve the Indian question. Lands must be set aside for Indian use, he insisted. Given that "the resistless tide of emigration" was sure to continue, humanity and practicality both suggested "that it would be far less expensive to feed than to fight them."[11]

Soldiers frequently attempted to help execute such policies, perhaps never more dramatically than in 1851 negotiations at Fort Laramie, where regulars watched anxiously as Indian agent Thomas Fitzpatrick negotiated treaties with Lakotas, Cheyennes, Arapahoes, Crows, Gros Ventres, Assiniboines, Arikaras, and Shoshonis. Peace was duly agreed to and individual tribal territories designated. But with the estimated ten thousand Indians dwarfing the 270 regulars who attended the conference, the scope of U.S. military power was clearly limited. "You have split my land and I don't like it," warned one Lakota. "These lands once belonged to the Kiowas and the Crows, but we whipped these nations out of them, and in this we did what the white men do when they want the lands of the Indians."[12]

Although Conrad's advice might have been sound, Americans were unwilling to halt the nation's course of empire. In Texas, Brevet Major

General George M. Brooke established four forts along the Rio Grande: Brown, Ringgold, McIntosh, and Duncan. Five others—Martin Scott, Croghan, Gates, Graham, and Worth—guarded Texas's northern frontier. Along the upper Frio River, Fort Inge interdicted an Indian trail into Mexico. Yet these outposts, each garrisoned by about one hundred men, did not elicit peace from mounted Indians, who had long used warfare for economic and social advancement. Texans were particularly critical of the regular infantry, who editors of the *Texas State Gazette* believed to be "as much out of place as a sawmill upon the ocean."[13]

With Brooke's death in March 1851, Secretary Conrad transferred Brevet Major General Persifer F. Smith from California to Texas. Under orders to "revise the whole system of defense," Smith established a series of new posts ahead of non-Indian settlements. Seven forts—Arbuckle, Belknap, Phantom Hill, Chadbourne, McKavett, Terrett, and Clark—formed a huge arc from the Washita River to the Rio Grande. Texas now had a double line of forts along its borderlands. In theory, infantrymen holding the outer line could warn the interior of Indian raids. Mounted troops would garrison the interior posts, where cheaper forage was available. But Smith lacked the manpower to launch the offensives Texans so badly wanted, and the state's efforts to raise volunteers (to be paid for, of course, by Washington) met stiff federal opposition. Such troops, asserted Conrad, "have a tendency to create hostilities and rather to endanger the peace of the frontier than to preserve it."[14]

The situation in New Mexico, where the departmental commander also served as governor until 1850, seemed equally disconcerting. In August 1846, Kearny had promised that "my government . . . will keep off the Indians." The fourteen hundred regulars stationed in the region had not come close to fulfilling that pledge. Ute, Navajo, and Apache raids, designed to secure plunder as well as to deter the expansion of the sixty thousand Mexican nationals and the newly arriving Americans, had continued unabated. To shake up the lethargic garrisons, in April 1851 Conrad ordered Lieutenant Colonel Edwin V. Sumner to take command. Energetic, strong minded, and looking every inch the soldier, "Bull" Sumner brooked no nonsense and had the orders to boot. He was to get the troops out of the towns and into the borderlands and conclude no peace with the Indians "until they have been made to feel the force of our arms," all the while reducing expenses.[15]

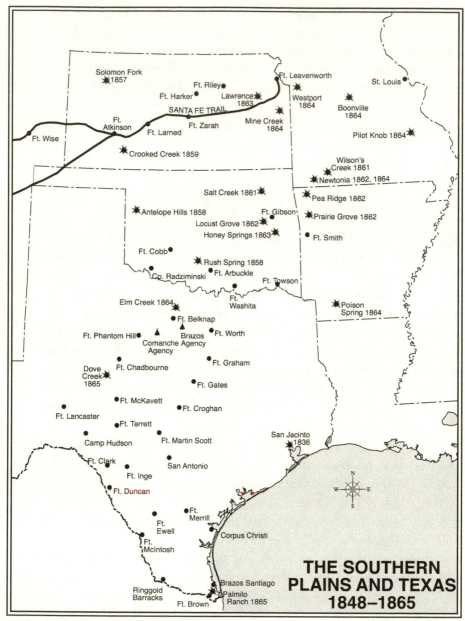

Solomon Fork 1857

Ft. Riley

Ft. Leavenworth

St. Louis

Ft. Harker

Lawrence 1863

Westport 1864

Boonville 1864

SANTA FE TRAIL

Ft. Atkinson

Ft. Larned

Ft. Zarah

Mine Creek 1864

Pilot Knob 1864

Ft. Wise

Crooked Creek 1859

Wilson's Creek 1861

Newtonia 1862, 1864

Salt Creek 1861

Pea Ridge 1862

Antelope Hills 1858

Ft. Gibson

Prairie Grove 1862

Locust Grove 1862

Honey Springs 1863

Ft. Smith

Ft. Cobb

Rush Spring 1858

Ft. Arbuckle

Cp. Radziminski

Ft. Towson

Elm Creek 1864

Ft. Washita

Poison Spring 1864

Ft. Belknap

Ft. Phantom Hill

Brazos Agency

Comanche Agency

Ft. Worth

Ft. Chadbourne

Ft. Graham

Dove Creek 1865

Ft. Gates

Ft. McKavett

Ft. Croghan

Ft. Lancaster

Ft. Terrett

San Jacinto 1836

Camp Hudson

Ft. Martin Scott

Ft. Clark

San Antonio

Ft. Inge

Ft. Duncan

Ft. Merrill

Ft. Ewell

Corpus Christi

Ft. McIntosh

THE SOUTHERN PLAINS AND TEXAS 1848–1865

Ringgold Barracks

Brazos Santiago

Palmito Ranch 1865

Ft. Brown

Robert F. Pace

Orders in hand, Sumner established Fort Defiance in the heart of the Navajo country. To the south, he built three new forts: Conrad, Fillmore, and Webster. Fort Union, northeast of present Las Vegas, guarded the Santa Fe Trail. Cantonment Burgwin protected the region north of Taos, and Fort Massachusetts observed the Utes. But Sumner seemed intent on alienating his Indian Office counterparts as well as the people of New Mexico, refusing to offer military escorts, flaunting ceremonial niceties that might have encouraged cooperation from agents and damning New Mexicans as "thoroughly debased and totally incapable of self-government." Bluntly, he advocated arming the residents and withdrawing the army. Secretary Conrad used his annual report of 1852 as a platform for exploring Sumner's recommendation. "Would it not be better," wondered the secretary, "to induce the inhabitants to abandon a country which seems hardly fit for the habitation of civilized man?" Even if it paid residents four times the value of their property, the federal government "would still . . . be largely the gainer by the transaction." Hoping that this radical proposal might shock Congress into action, Secretary Conrad hastened to add that a new regiment of mounted men would go far toward ameliorating the situation.[16]

Skyrocketing transportation expenses, which had risen from $120,000 in 1844 to $1.9 million in 1850, forced commanding general Scott to propose abandoning Fort Atkinson, Fort Kearny (established in 1848 on the Oregon Trail southeast of present Kearney, Nebraska), and Fort Laramie (occupied by U.S. troops in 1849) in the name of military efficiency. Scott contended that periodic columns of mounted men would "exert a greater pacific influence over the wild Indians, than would, perhaps, ten times the number of troops tied down . . . to a few fixed positions." Of course, such proposals flew in the face of strong congressional support for a permanent military presence along the Santa Fe and Oregon trails. Thus even as expenses grew, only Fort Atkinson, a collection of miserably constructed sod huts, was decommissioned. Indeed, rather than concentrating its scattered garrisons, the army was building new ones, providing business for local contractors and invaluable way stations for travelers. In 1853, work thus began on a new post, Fort Riley, at the junction of the Republican Fork and the Kansas River.[17]

To handle matters in the Pacific Division, Conrad turned to Ethan A. Hitchcock, now a brevet brigadier general. Hitchcock's fascination with philosophy seemed consistent with his beardless, balding profile and his lengthy diaries focused on alchemy and Spinoza rather than mundane matters of frontier defense. His ambitious orders paralleled those given Smith in Texas and Sumner in New Mexico: get the troops onto the frontier and "revise the whole system both of defence and administration" while cutting expenditures! In California, Hitchcock added the forts of Reading, Jones, and Humboldt to existing Yuma and Miller. In the Oregon country, a region terrorized by the recent murders of missionary Marcus Whitman and a dozen others, Fort Lane (near the Rogue River Indian Reservation) supplemented three older posts: Dalles, Steilacoom (south of present Tacoma), and Vancouver (also known as Columbia Barracks). The general blamed the violence on whites who first trespassed on Indian lands and then demanded military protection. But suggestions that civilians restrict their movements during the heady gold rush days in Oregon and California went unheeded. "Our people will go to the mines and they must have protection," reasoned Joseph Lane, Oregon's delegate to Congress.[18]

In this atmosphere, efforts to establish and honor Indian reservations failed miserably. Unable to prevent the region's fragmented Indians and the newcomers from killing one another, soldiers instead sought to overwhelm the divided hunter-gatherers with superior mass, discipline, logistics, and firepower. Captain Nathaniel Lyon thus described a particularly brutal campaign along the Russian River in matter-of-fact terms. His mixed force of infantry, dragoons, and a mountain howitzer twice stormed islands on which Indians had tried to make defensive stands, killing sixty of the enemy in the first encounter without a single casualty. The soldiers turned the second island into "a perfect slaughter pen," killing seventy-five Indians at the cost of two men wounded.[19]

The election of Franklin Pierce in 1852 brought to the war office Jefferson Davis, a West Point graduate, Mexican War hero, and former chair of the Senate Military Affairs Committee. As conscientious as he was insensitive, Secretary Davis made efforts to invigorate and reform the army that would rank alongside those of John C. Calhoun. Unfortunately, Davis clashed with commanding general Winfield Scott. Each possessing formidable measures of talent, military experience, and vanity, neither got along well with others even in the best of circumstances. And circumstances in this case could hardly be called

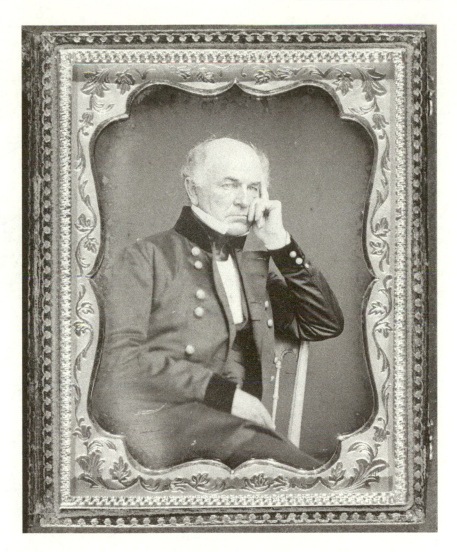

FIG. 24. Ethan Allen Hitchcock. Born in Vermont, Hitchcock (1798–1870) graduated from West Point in 1817 and served most of his four decades in military service on the frontiers. An avid musician and philosopher, he also published works on alchemy, Shakespeare, and Spenser. LIBRARY OF CONGRESS, USZ6-1970.

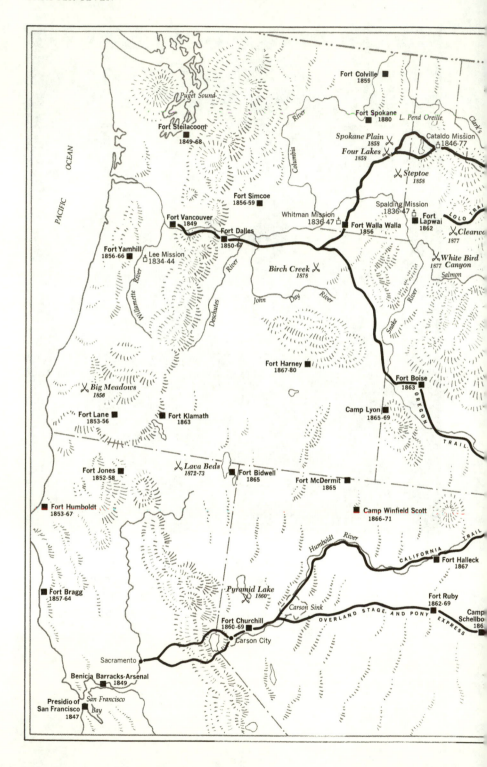

Fort Colville
1859

Fort Spokane
1880

L. Pend Oreille

Spokane Plain
1858

Cataldo Mission
1846-77

Four Lakes
1859

Fort Steilacoom
1849-68

Steptoe
1858

Fort Simcoe
1856-59

Spalding Mission
1836-47

Fort
Lapwai
1862

LOLO TRAIL

Whitman Mission
1836-47

Fort Walla Walla
1856

Clearwa
1877

Fort Vancouver
1849

Fort Dalles
1850-67

Fort Yamhill
1856-66

Lee Mission
1834-44

Birch Creek
1878

White Bird
1877 Canyon

Salmon

John   Day   River

PACIFIC OCEAN

Willamette River

Deschutes River

Fort Harney
1867-80

Big Meadows
1856

Fort Boise
1863

Camp Lyon
1865-69

Fort Lane
1853-56

Fort Klamath
1863

Fort Jones
1852-58

Lava Beds
1872-73

Fort Bidwell
1865

Fort McDermit
1865

Fort Humboldt
1853-67

Camp Winfield Scott
1866-71

Humboldt   River

CALIFORNIA TRAIL

Fort Halleck
1867

Fort Bragg
1857-64

Pyramid Lake
1860

Carson Sink

Fort Ruby
1862-69

Camp
Schellbo
186

Fort Churchill
1860-69

Carson City

OVERLAND STAGE AND PONY EXPRESS

Sacramento

Benicia Barracks-Arsenal
1849

Presidio of
San Francisco
1847

San Francisco
Bay

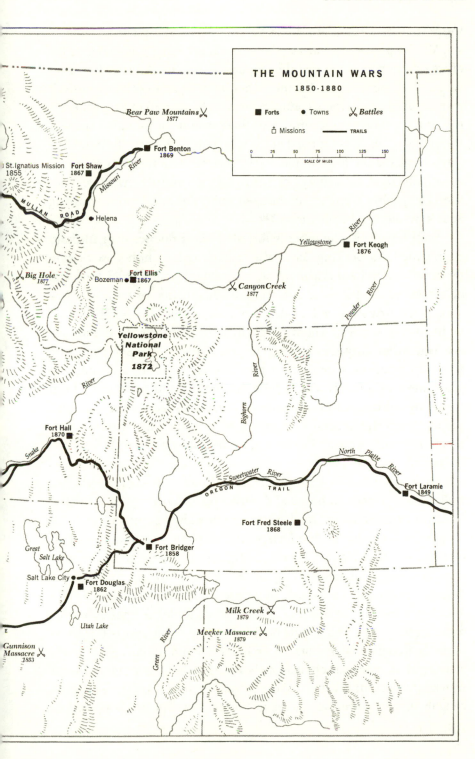

THE MOUNTAIN WARS
1850-1880

■ Forts   ● Towns   ⚔ Battles

⛪ Missions   ▬▬ TRAILS

0   25   50   75   100   125   150
SCALE OF MILES

Bear Paw Mountains ⚔
1877

■ Fort Benton
1869

St. Ignatius Mission   ■ Fort Shaw
1855   1867

Missouri River

MULLAN ROAD

● Helena

⚔ Big Hole
1877

■ Fort Ellis
Bozeman ● ■ 1867

Yellowstone River

■ Fort Keogh
1876

⚔ Canyon Creek
1877

Powder River

Yellowstone
National
Park
1872

River

Bighorn River

■ Fort Hall
1870

Snake River

North Platte River

Sweetwater River

OREGON   TRAIL

■ Fort Laramie
1849

Fort Fred Steele ■
1868

Great
Salt Lake

■ Fort Bridger
1858

Salt Lake City ● ■ Fort Douglas
1862

Utah Lake

Green River

Milk Creek ⚔
1879

Meeker Massacre ⚔
1879

Gunnison
Massacre ⚔
1853

the best. Scott's making a presidential bid as a Whig riled the partisan Mississippi Democrat, and the new war secretary's assertion of his office's authority infuriated the imperious soldier. At least the latter dispute had some merit, for the difficulty of squaring the executive's responsibility as supreme commander with the commanding general's role as the nation's senior military officer would confound Army–War Department relations for most of the nineteenth century. But Scott and Davis escalated the feud to new levels; their unflattering war of words, when published, totaled 254 printed pages of mutual invective, with Scott comparing Davis to "an enraged imbecile" and Davis censuring Scott's "malignity and depravity."[20]

Scott having in the process forfeited his influence over military affairs, the hard-working Davis was free to implement his own vision for remaking the American West. The army was his chief tool, and he supported the Pierce administration's acquisition of southern New Mexico and Arizona (the Gadsden Purchase) and its hands-off position on filibusters, many of whom sympathized with efforts to expand slavery. Thus when Brigadier General John E. Wool, a Free Soil Democrat trying to position himself as a presidential hopeful, attempted to prosecute a shady group of French émigrés forming around a local consul in California in 1854, Secretary Davis issued a stinging reprimand. When the Second Committee of Vigilance imposed a three-month reign of terror in San Francisco the following year, U.S. troops did not intervene.[21]

Davis also played a leading role in convincing Texas to create two Indian reservations. In hopes of dampening violence in the Lone Star State, the army had for several years been providing some Indians with food, reasoning that such efforts would alleviate the conditions that often led to war. Indeed, General Smith later attributed most depredations to hungry Indians stealing cattle "for food." In allowing Caddos, Wacos, Tawakonis, Tonkawas, Delawares, and even Comanches and Apaches to retain use of some of their lands under federal authority, formal reservations would build on this practice. In his efforts Davis was joined by Robert S. Neighbors, a former soldier and Indian agent turned state legislator who was often a lonely voice in trying to temper calls for unrestrained military action. In early 1854, the state legislature set aside roughly fifty-four thousand acres for the project. The resulting Brazos

FIG. 25. "A Bad Egg: Fuss and Feathers." The subject of many critical cartoon barbs, Winfield Scott, who was sometimes called "Fuss and Feathers," is portrayed here as a fighting cock in military uniform. The quotes refer to his Whig Party association with antislavery men such as William H. Seward. LIBRARY OF CONGRESS, USZ62-50949.

and Clear Fork (sometimes referred to as the Comanche) reservations temporarily reduced violence in the Lone Star State.[22]

The army also continued to work on internal improvements. With Congress's approval, soldiers carried on surveying, supervising, and building roads throughout the Trans-Mississippi. Similarly, the Corps of Topographical Engineers had undertaken extensive surveys of western rivers, the Great Lakes, international boundary lines, and emigrant routes. The corps' responsibilities further increased in 1853, when Congress allotted it $150,000 to identify the best course for a transcontinental railroad. Under this program, the corps surveyed four east-west routes as well as north-south trails up and down the Pacific coast. The unit's reports, written by current and former Topographical Engineers who were imbued with a can-do spirit and confident in their cause, invariably spoke positively about the particular pathway under scrutiny. Secretary Davis's recommendation of the route through Texas and New Mexico was predictable, as he was an outspoken advocate of southern interests. Northerners, of course, were in no mood to fund a project that would favor a rival section, so the railroad died in Congress, not to be resuscitated until the Civil War.[23]

Davis encouraged a variety of military innovations geared to meet frontier needs. Fueled by his belief that "a limit . . . has been reached, beyond which civilization has ceased to follow in the train of advancing posts," the secretary imported several dozen camels to the United States. Field experiments consistently demonstrated that the camels could carry heavier burdens and required less water and food en route than horses, mules, or oxen. But their unconventional habits and mannerisms won them few friends, and the army quietly forgot the program during the Civil War. More lasting were improvements in weaponry. Breech-loading rifled carbines for mounted troops began replacing the older musketoon, an unwieldy, ineffective muzzleloader condemned by one army inspector as "utterly unreliable for almost any range, and not fit to be put into the hands of troops." The infantry's Model 1855 .58-caliber Springfield rifles fired Minié balls, boasted modern percussion cap primers, and allowed the use of paper cartridges. Although the updated tactical manual, Captain William J. Hardee's *Rifle and Light Infantry Tactics*, focused exclusively on conventional warfare, the more accurate, longer-ranged weapons gave the regulars a distinct tactical advantage for over a decade.[24]

Secretary Davis also worked to expand the army's horizons. He prodded his old alma mater, the U.S. Military Academy, to add a fifth year of
study, with new courses in geography, history, military law, and Spanish
rounding out the older curriculum. In 1855, the War Department dispatched Major Richard Delafield, Major Alfred Mordecai, and Captain
George B. McClellan as military observers to Europe. In a striking departure from tradition, McClellan's subsequent report urged the nation to
tailor a force of light cavalry to fight Indians. In making his case, he
argued that American mounted service was "quite different from that
performed by any in Europe." As he reasoned, "we must be as light and
quick as they [Indians] are, and then, superiority of weapons and discipline must uniformly give us the advantage." From these bold state-
ments, however, McClellan then retreated; infatuated by the Cossacks,
he seems to have copied most of his tactical suggestions from those of
the Russians.[25]

Institutional reforms notwithstanding, the army needed more men
if it were to pave the way for borderlands development. "Our present
army is totally inadequate for the protection of our extended frontier,
not even enough to maintain a respectable game of bo-peep with the
Indians," wrote one disgusted officer. Davis noted that whereas the army
had increased by less than three thousand in forty-five years, the nation's
population had grown by eighteen million. Further, the country now
had to safeguard two seaboard coastlines, a three-thousand-mile Indian
frontier, and a twenty-five-hundred-mile border with Mexico. He might
have added that military spending had sunk to about 20 percent of the
total federal budget, its lowest point since 1824.[26]

The administration's calls for more troops fell on deaf ears, however,
until the reckless bravado of a green lieutenant provoked a war against
the Lakotas, now a dominant military power on the northern plains.
The region had been relatively free of Indian/non-Indian violence until
August 18, 1854, when a member of a Utah-bound wagon train reported
that a Sioux had killed one of his cows. The following day, Brevet Second
Lieutenant John L. Grattan marched out of Fort Laramie with twenty-
nine soldiers, two cannons, and a drunken interpreter to demand the
culprit's surrender. A year out of West Point where he had been a mediocre student and his poorest subject had been infantry tactics, Grattan
seems to have convinced himself that his tiny command could overawe

the thousand-odd lodges of the nearby Oglala, Brulé, and Miniconjou encampment who had gathered to receive their yearly government annuities. He was wrong, and he and every member of his party paid for this error with their lives.[27]

The First Sioux War had begun. Vowing to avenge what a typical newspaper dubbed a "treacherous slaughter," Davis recalled Brevet Brigadier General William S. Harney from leave in Paris to command the operation, which would be based at Fort Kearny. Though it would take over a year to collect the necessary forces, the brusque, profane Harney, standing six feet four, seemed to one observer "the beau ideal of a dragoon officer."[28]

Harney finally set forth on August 24, 1855, with five companies of infantry, two dragoon companies, a mounted infantry company, and a mounted artillery company. Efforts to recruit allies among Delawares, Potawatomies, and Shawnees failed, but most of the Lakotas had now renounced war against the United States. Thus about four hundred of Little Thunder's Brulé and Oglala supporters, whose attacks against emigrant parties that season had given away the location of their encampments along Blue Water Creek, stood alone. On September 3, the regulars struck. The infantry opened up first, their long-ranged rifle fire bewildering their surprised and outgunned foes. "Their arrows or the bullets from their poor flintlocks could not reach us," explained one enlisted man thankfully. The battle soon became a slaughter as women, children, old men, and warriors attempted to escape through the net laid by Harney's mounted contingent, which had swung behind the Indians to cut off their anticipated retreat. Harney reported eighty-six Indians killed—among which were many women and children, although accounts differ as to whether or not the firing had been indiscriminate—five wounded, and seventy women and children captured.[29]

Reaction among the Lakotas to Harney's uncompromising attack was mixed. Men from all but the Oglalas signed the treaty Harney demanded at Fort Pierre. After a year in prison at Fort Leavenworth, Spotted Tail, once a militant, determined that diplomacy would be the best means of defending his people's interests against U.S. expansion. On the other hand, five to ten thousand Lakotas attended a huge council meeting in 1857 at Bear Butte, at which they determined that they would

FIG. 26. William S. Harney. Quarrelsome, vain, profane, and an avowed Democrat, Harney (1800–89) was a fierce enemy of Seminoles, Mexicans, deserters, and Lakotas. LIBRARY OF CONGRESS, DIG-CWPB-04404.

defend the territory they now claimed for themselves. They would make no deals with Washington, and to secure access to more buffalos, they would move aggressively against the Crows. "If they went to war again they would not yield so easy as they did before," vowed one attendee. Lieutenant Gouverneur K. Warren predicted ominously that war with the Lakotas "at no distant day is probable."[30]

As Harney was making preparations for his offensive, a bill propos-
ing to add four regular regiments had been lurching through Congress.
Angry that the administration had not supported a railroad through
his beloved Missouri and attributing the most recent hostilities to
Grattan's bungling, Thomas Hart Benton, now a member of the House
of Representatives, had changed his tune regarding the army. "God
defend the West from these four new regular regiments," thundered
the old lion, who dubbed the bluecoats "school-house officers and pot-
house soldiers." Senator Sam Houston of Texas pointed out that "the
killing of a cow is not making war." But Secretary Davis had armed his
allies with reams of data demonstrating that regulars cost a third less
than a comparable number of volunteers, and the desire to retaliate
against the Sioux and to secure the borderlands proved insurmount-
able. Two-thirds of both Whigs and Democrats in the House supported
the increase, and the Senate voted thirty-two to seven in favor of the
new measure. Borderlands legislators, who increasingly were reliable
allies of army interests, backed the four-regiment bill by a twenty-two-
to-four count.[31]

The new regiments, so important to expanding the federal government's presence in the borderlands, offered the Pierce administration
significant patronage opportunities. It also opened up the prospect of
promotion to existing officers. Davis seems to have made selections
with both factors in mind, filling 116 vacancies with political appointees
(mostly Democrats), about 60 percent of whom claimed some form of
previous military service. But in an impressive bow to military professionalism, Davis reserved all of the field-grade appointments (major,
lieutenant colonel, and colonel) for regular officers.[32]

Even more troops, however, ultimately proved necessary, as the
uneasy peace in southern Florida had collapsed. The Swamp and
Overflowed Land Act of 1850 had returned to the state some twenty million acres, and developers were pressuring the government to remove
the remaining Seminoles. In December 1855, when a detachment of
soldiers led by Lieutenant George Hartsuff threatened a village loyal to
Chief Billy Bowlegs, the Indians retaliated, killing four and wounding
a similar number. Attacks across southwestern Florida followed; as had
been the case two decades earlier, efforts to track down the small raiding parties failed to meet the expectations of anxious Floridians. "What

has been done to remove or exterminate the Seminoles?" wondered the editor of the *Tampa Peninsular*. "We answer *nothing!*"[33]

Soldiers found the going to be miserable. Captain Abner Doubleday, later credited (incorrectly) with having invented baseball, described his patrols in the Fort Lauderdale region as "by far the most wearisome toil I had ever undertaken. . . . The men soon sank up to the middle in slimy mud and their progress became slow and laborious. . . . The men were often obliged to cross floating islands which could hardly bear their weight. In some cases they fell through and would have been drowned were it not for the prompt assistance of their comrades." Still, the army's clumsy pressure was unrelenting, and the introduction of shallow draft boats helped to improve the mobility of government forces. Thus, in March 1858, Billy Bowlegs finally agreed to move his people to a reservation in present Oklahoma. The reclusive Sam Jones and about 150 of his intractable Mikasukis remained, but the Third Seminole War was over.[34]

The Oregon frontier, where the Senate, Yakima Indians, and gold-hungry prospectors were united only in their common refusal to respect peace agreements reached in 1855, was also aflame. A massacre of twenty-three Rogue River Indian women, children, and old men by Oregon volunteers that October sparked a predictable retaliatory strike that left twenty-seven civilians dead. Indian threats to Puget Sound—many of which were trumped up by civilians seeking to insure the continuation of the lucrative federal military presence—reached a climax in January 1856, when volunteers and the sailors, marines, and sixteen guns of the USS *Decatur* threw back an assault on Seattle. "These inhuman butchers and bloody fiends must be met and conquered," fulminated the Portland *Oregonian*, "vanquished—yes, EXTERMINATED." Firing back, department commander Wool accused territorial officials of "running a race to see who can dip deepest into the treasury of the United States."[35]

As army-civilian relations collapsed, in March 1856 government troops moved into the Rogue River country. Regulars from the nearby forts of Humboldt, Orford, and Lane, along with a "Southern Army" of volunteers, scoured southwestern Oregon for two months. In late May, Indians trapped Captain Andrew J. Smith and eighty soldiers at Big Meadows, but the arrival of Captain Christopher C. Augur with reinforcements broke the back of the Rogue River resistance. That summer, the army transferred twelve hundred Indians to the Coast Reservation, establishing the new forts of Hoskins, Yamhill, and Umpqua to deter angry Oregon volunteers from seeking further retribution. But the conflicts—between Indians and non-Indians as well civil and military authorities—in the Pacific Northwest continued. Denouncing the regulars' inability to stamp out the Indian threat, Oregon's territorial governor, George Curry, requested Wool's dismissal, and Washington's Isaac Stevens lambasted the general's "utter and signal incapacity" and "criminal neglect." Wool countered by explaining that he did "not apprehend any further difficulties, and certainly not if the troops of Governors Curry and Stevens can be kept out of the field."[36]

Reinforcements were on the way, in the form of Colonel George Wright's new Ninth Infantry Regiment. A steady West Point graduate and veteran of the Seminole and Mexican wars, Wright, with the aid of volunteers, thirty-three blockhouses, and supporting fire provided by the guns of the USS *Massachusetts*, had by summer's end consolidated control over the Puget Sound. In July, Lieutenant Colonel B. F. Shaw and four hundred territorial volunteers destroyed a large Walla Walla, Cayuse, Umatilla, John Day, and Deschutes encampment, killing forty Indians. The army and Governor Stevens persisting in issuing recriminations against the other, peace talks that September yielded only an inconclusive armistice. The army occupied new positions at Fort Simcoe and at Walla Walla, and the federal government agreed to pay Oregon $2.5 million and Washington $1.5 million for their volunteers. Many of the region's Indians, however, remained defiant.[37]

Conflicts also continued in New Mexico. To replace the quarrelsome Sumner, Secretary Davis had selected Brevet Brigadier General John Garland, a veteran of wars against Britain, Black Hawk, the Seminoles, and Mexico. Simmering tensions exploded in March 1854, when Lieutenant John W. Davidson and a company of dragoons rode into an ambush laid by Chacón and his Jicarillas at Cieneguilla. Leaving twenty-two dead on the field, the soldiers limped into Taos bearing thirty-six wounded. Bent on revenge, mixed commands of regulars, largely Hispanic volunteers, and Pueblo and Mexican scouts crisscrossed northern New Mexico for several months. The Utes were drawn into the contest, and in the campaign's most significant combat engagement,

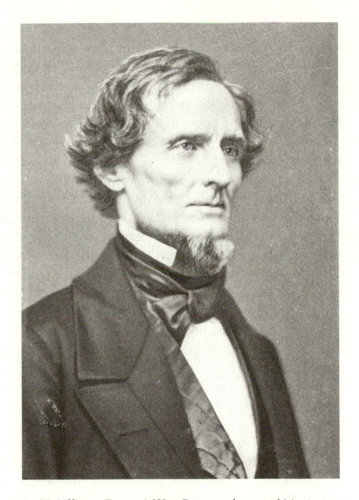

FIG. 27. Jefferson Davis. A West Point graduate and Mexican war
hero, Davis (1808–89) ranked among the nineteenth
century's most able and influential secretaries of war.
LIBRARY OF CONGRESS, DIG-CWPBH-00879.

Colonel Thomas T. Fauntleroy surprised one of their camps at Poncha
Pass. The soldiers' fire "swept the enemy like chaff before the wind";
forty Indians were killed and their property lost in the ensuing mêlée.
Ute resistance collapsed.[38]

In the arid Trans-Pecos to the east, Major John S. Simonson and
Major James Longstreet scoured the region for Mescalero Apaches

without success, but strikes led by Captain Richard S. Ewell and Lieutenant Samuel D. Sturgis diminished the war faction's influence. Learning a rarely recognized lesson, Ewell, commanding a mixed force of dragoons and foot soldiers, recognized that infantry, especially when carrying their new weapons, could be more durable than mounted troops if the march went on long enough. "The infantry were of invaluable service," he noted, "and towards the end of the campaign were able to outmarch the dragoons. The Indians were not aware of musket range until they paid for their experience." Tired of the grueling chases, about four hundred Mescaleros made peace that April. Secretary Davis also dispatched the newly created Second Cavalry Regiment to the Lone Star State. To better protect the lonely road west of San Antonio to El Paso, the government established Fort Davis (pleasantly situated in the Davis Mountains) and Fort Lancaster (located near the Pecos River).[39]

Amid the increasing violence, in his last annual report as secretary of war, Davis recommended sweeping changes in borderlands military operations. The limits of fertility, he argued, had been reached. Small, isolated garrisons had become prohibitively expensive and signaled the federal government's weakness rather than its strength. To change the dynamic, the secretary urged the army to concentrate its forces at larger posts, accessible by railroad or steamboat. Such a policy would improve morale, decrease expenses, and reduce desertion. Citing the French practice in Algeria, Davis suggested that strong forces patrol the Indian country during the grassy season, enabling the soldiers to undertake "the field practice of their profession, the temporary dangers and toils of which give zest to a soldier's life." In light of growing sectional tensions regarding slavery, however, it remained to be seen if the Davis program would be implemented.[40]

EIGHT

Frontier Regulars and the Collapse of the Union

In recommending the consolidation of small, isolated western posts into larger garrisons, Secretary of War Jefferson Davis had seized on a refrain; indeed, such an approach had been, and would remain, fundamental to assumptions about western defense. Yet the attempt to concentrate far-flung posts flew in the face of frontier realities, for such posts were too few and too distant to offer the economic benefits expected by so many communities and interests. Moreover, mounting Indian resistance to U.S. expansion reinforced civilian demands for a local military presence. In the midst of quarrels between older residents and newcomers, the army's multiple responsibilities of defending, governing, and developing the frontiers had reaffirmed its traditional importance in nation building. But not all had approved of the regulars' performance, and sectional rivalries would soon threaten the very existence of the nation the soldiers had sworn to defend.

New borderlands challenges—particularly in Kansas, where disputes between pro- and antislavery factions produced civil war, and in Utah, where many feared that the Latter-day Saints would wrest control from federal authorities—greatly complicated the military's work. In Kansas, populated by an ever-growing number of immigrants, the army could not use the same methods of establishing and enforcing peace as it did in areas dominated by Indians. As historian Tony R. Mullis has put it, lethal force, always an option against the tribes, was "neither person-ally nor politically palatable" to soldiers trying to check the movements of non-Indians. Widespread land speculation by army officers in the developing region, though perfectly legal so long as it did not affect their official duties or violate the public trust, further tested the uncertain alliance between the military and civilians.[1]

In November 1854 and March 1855, fraudulent elections in newly recognized Kansas Territory had produced a proslave territorial government, but escalating violence between free- and slave-state factions led Attorney General Caleb Cushing to broadly define the army's role in enforcing law and order. Galvanized into action by the violence in Kansas and Representative Preston Brooks's assault on Senator Charles Sumner (Colonel Sumner's cousin) in the capitol, President Franklin Pierce named a steady Pennsylvanian, James Geary, as new territorial governor. He also transferred another Pennsylvania Democrat, Brevet Major General Persifor F. Smith, to oversee military affairs there. Recognizing that the Democratic Party would not retain control of the White House if it did not quickly restore the peace, Geary convinced Smith to deploy the regulars in a preventative posture against extralegal forces from both sides. Smith also rescinded orders that would have shifted the First Cavalry Regiment to other duties, reasoning that keeping the peace in Kansas was more important than fighting Indians.[2]

In Washington, the administration scuttled a proposal to dispatch commanding general Winfield Scott, the Whig Party's last candidate for president, to Kansas. But a rebellious House refused to pass that year's army appropriations bill unless it expressly forbade the military from allying with the proslave territorial government. The Democratic Senate rejected such terms, forcing President Pierce to call a special session to fund the army. Notably, in justifying the money the president emphasized the demands of ongoing Indian conflicts on the "remote frontier," which he hoped would serve to unify legislators, rather than civil disorder in Kansas. On August 30 the House backed down and by a 101–98 vote accepted the bill shorn of its riders. The army finally had its budget, and the regulars brought the Democratic Party sufficient tranquility in Kansas to realize the election of James Buchanan.[3]

Almost to a man, soldiers resented having to referee the contest that pitted citizen against citizen, and they blamed radicals on both sides for making the army a scapegoat for their problems. Sagging morale probably explained high rates of resignations among officers, which by 1856 had grown to levels not seen since the Jackson administration. Reflecting on the widespread discontent from Texas, a depressed Lieutenant Colonel Robert E. Lee told his young nephew, Lieutenant Fitzhugh Lee, that "experience has taught me to recommend no young man to enter the service." Recognizing the problem, in February 1857 Secretary Davis secured for officers an across the board base pay raise—their first since 1798—of $20 a month.[4]

In naming John B. Floyd as his secretary of war, newly elected President Buchanan did the army, and the country, no favor. Floyd had neither military experience nor administrative competence, and his scandal-plagued tenure in Washington would end in his forced resignation. Scott, never a friend of those who sought to limit his unfettered control over the army, described Floyd as being "green as well as dilatory." Whatever his ethics and abilities, the secretary did not hesitate to deploy the regulars in a range of borderlands disputes. In Kansas, the Buchanan administration tried to use the army to legitimize popular sovereignty. By late 1857, over nineteen hundred regulars—fully one-seventh of the entire U.S. Army—were observing Kansas polling stations and patrolling the Missouri border to prevent armed bands from entering the territory. By no means were all of their actions impartial. In the Fort Scott region, for example, Captain George T. Anderson (a Georgian who would later become a Confederate brigade commander under James Longstreet) prosecuted antislavery "Jayhawkers" most vigorously. Despite the Buchanan administration's obvious sympathies with proslavery groups, Captain Nathaniel Lyon (a native of Connecticut and future commander of the Union Army of the West) gave the antislavery factions federal assistance. However unwittingly, the presence of the regulars, which gave Kansans the opportunity to determine their own fate, allowed Free-Soilers to demonstrate their majority at the polls, thus encouraging the very forces that President Buchanan had sought to suppress. Thus Kansas would be free.[5]

To the west, the federal government's relations with the Mormons had also deteriorated. Church president Brigham Young had been named Utah's first territorial governor, but his Gentile subordinates recoiled at the church's theocracy, resented the enormous power held by

Fig. 28. John B. Floyd. Former governor of Virginia but a poor administrator, Secretary of War Floyd (1806–63) was forced from his office under suspicion of financial malfeasance. He later became a Confederate general. LIBRARY OF CONGRESS, DIG-CWPBH-00887.

local probate courts, and ridiculed the practice of polygamy. On May 20, 1857, President Buchanan fired Governor Young and ordered the army to occupy the Salt Lake Valley. The president's motives remain unclear: perhaps he hoped this move would unite a divided country; perhaps he was trying to enrich some of his friends, such as the freighting firm of Russell, Majors and Waddell; perhaps he simply saw it as being necessary to the restoration of federal authority.[6]

As the Saints initiated a scorched earth policy and elements of their Nauvoo Legion stole army cattle, destroyed supply trains, and established roadblocks, advance columns made their way only to Fort Bridger, where they spent a miserable winter. The following spring, as the snows evaporated, Colonel Albert Sidney Johnston led nearly three thousand regulars into Utah. On June 26, 1858, they reached a deserted Salt Lake City. "It was like entering a Graveyard," wrote Private Charles A. Scott. "Silence reigned supreme." Peace was already at hand, for President Young had three weeks earlier promised Mormon loyalty to the federal government in exchange for presidential pardons. Many soldiers were dismayed that their labors had seemingly been for naught; as one disappointed lieutenant put it, the Mormons "went unwhipped by justice." That fall, the regulars began constructing Camp Floyd, forty miles south of Salt Lake City.[7]

Next spring, confirmation of a terrible atrocity nearly unraveled the uncomfortable peace. In September 1857, Mormon militiamen and Paiute Indians, angry at the abuses they had suffered and nervous about the impending invasion, had massacred at least 120 Arkansas emigrants and a band of "Missouri Wildcats" at Mountain Meadows. As part of a federal investigation into the incident, in May 1859 soldiers began uncovering the physical evidence. Talk of vengeance was rampant. From the scene, Captain James H. Carleton recommended that the Mormons be wiped from the face of the earth: "They are an ulcer upon the body politic. . . . It must have excision, complete and thorough extirpation, before we can every hope for safety or tranquillity."[8]

When dealing with Indians, the U.S. government routinely demanded that groups accept collective responsibility for the actions of individuals. On countless occasions, the refusal to turn over those suspected of criminal acts had triggered a swift military response. But the Mormons—believers in the Christian bible and perceived as

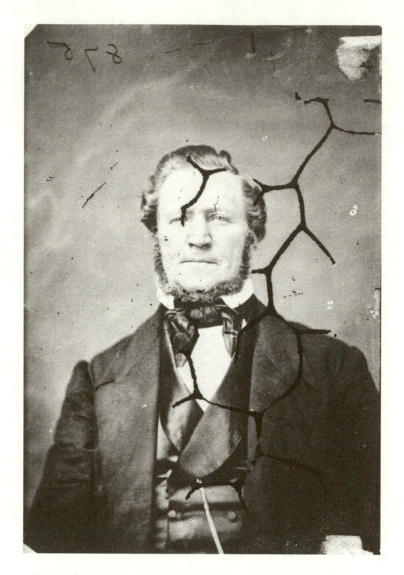

FIG. 29. Brigham Young. Longtime president of the Church of Jesus Christ of Latter-day Saints, Young (1801–77) oversaw a scorched earth retreat of his followers ahead of the U.S. Army during the Mormon War. LIBRARY OF CONGRESS, DIG-CWPBH-00825.

thrifty, orderly, and industrious—were different. And they were white. Moreover, as William MacKinnon, a perceptive student of the campaign, has pointed out, President Young "cultivated and used" military and political leaders in a manner that no Indian could possibly have conceived. Thus in the face of stony silence among the Saints about the affair at Mountain Meadows and Congress's refusal to commit new appropriations for this expensive exercise in federal sovereignty, President Buchanan backed down.[9]

Neither side had won the Utah War. Complete federal authority over Utah had not been established, nor had Buchanan unified the nation. The Mormons for their part had attempted to conceal a terrible secret that would stain the church they loved. Ironically, although the immediate impact of the mass flight was huge, the army's occupation brought with it a badly needed windfall of coin and treasure to Utah, for the soldiers employed hundreds of workers and spent thousands of dollars on food, grain, timber, and assorted nonmilitary products. The locals, observed one officer, were always "on the alert to profit at every point . . . from our presence." And when the regulars withdrew with the onset of the Civil War, the government would sell an estimated $4 million in property for about $100,000. But the temporary economic bonanza had come at a cost: a completely independent economy, long a vision of Young's, would be more difficult to achieve than before the army had come.[10]

During the Buchanan years, the military played a similarly active role along the nation's international borders. In the north, both Britain and the United States claimed sovereignty over the islands in the San Juan Archipelago, which lay between Washington and Vancouver Island. Commanding the newly created Department of Oregon and always ready for a fight, General William Harney ordered Captain George E. Pickett to occupy San Juan Island. The resulting "Pig War" of 1859—prompted by the refusal of an American to pay restitution for killing a Hudson's Bay Company pig that had eaten some of his potatoes—triggered a minor arms race off the coast of Washington Territory. Eventually, 450 U.S. soldiers, their hastily erected fortifications bristling with fourteen cannon, faced off against five British warships carrying 2,000 sailors, marines, and engineers. In no mood for war with Britain, Buchanan dispatched Scott, whose skills in international diplomacy matched the size of his enormous ego, to negotiate a peaceful end to the dispute. Scott did so, in the process taking every opportunity to humiliate Harney.[11]

Difficulties along the Rio Grande also tested the judgment of regular officers. In the early 1850s, the army had often winked at the movements of the San Antonio–born José M. Carbajal, who dreamed of carving out an independent nation from northern Mexico. Bands of Carbajal's fili-busters—typically a mixture of adventurers, army deserters, and occa-sionally a few furloughed Texas Rangers—used the United States as a base from which to engage the Mexican army. Responding to Mexican government protests, in late March 1853 Major Gabriel R. Paul and six companies of regulars captured Carbajal and disarmed three hundred of his men. Two years later, a company of Texas Rangers, chasing either Indians or runaway slaves, crossed the Rio Grande and burned sev-eral buildings in Piedras Negras. From Fort Duncan, Captain Sidney Burbank deployed several pieces of artillery in case the rangers needed cover as they recrossed the river. Although department commander Persifor Smith protested the "unlawful enterprises" of the Texans, the army had hardly maintained a strict neutrality.[12]

Ethnic tensions increased in 1857, when regulars intervened to restore peace after Anglos murdered several Tejano cartmen in an effort to seize control of trade between San Antonio and the Gulf of Mexico. But the real clash came two years later. Infuriated by the steady trans-fer of land and influence from Hispanics to Anglos in South Texas and perhaps emboldened by the army's recent withdrawal from Fort Brown, Ringgold Barracks, and Fort McIntosh, Juan N. Cortina and seventy-five men rode into Brownsville in the wee hours of September 28 and killed six men. Cortinistas then twice routed combinations of volunteers and Texas Rangers. The army selected Major Samuel P. Heintzelman, a thirty-three-year veteran, to reoccupy the Rio Grande Valley. Leading 165 regulars and 120 Texas Rangers, on December 14 Heintzelman skirmished ineffectually with about 350 Cortinistas, muttering that "we would undoubtedly have done better without the Rangers," whose lack of discipline and penchant for destroying property of friend and foe alike annoyed the professional soldier. A harder blow fell just after sunup two weeks later, when Heintzelman surprised Cortina at Rio Grande City. Here the rangers, now ably led by John "Rip" Ford, bore the brunt of the fighting. Heintzelman estimated enemy casualties at sixty killed; Ford put the count at more than three times that. Fourteen rangers had been wounded.[13]

Skirmishing on both sides of the Rio Grande continued into the spring of 1860. From Austin, Governor Sam Houston called for authorization to raise ten thousand Texas volunteers to "make reclamation upon Mexico for all her wrongs." To deter the Texans, the War Department dispatched the Third Infantry Regiment to South Texas and appointed the highly regarded Brevet Colonel Robert E. Lee to command the Department of Texas. Bearing authority to pursue the enemy "beyond the limits of the United States," Lee toured the lower Rio Grande that March, and Captain George Stoneman and Captain Rip Ford stormed into Mexico in an unsuccessful attempt to nab Cortina at Rancho la Mesa. With Mexican authorities having joined the hunt in earnest, on April 11 Lee pronounced the region free "of bands of armed men on either side."[14]

The actions of Texas Rangers highlighted an issue that would long divide federal and state authorities. Though generally complimenting the regular cavalry, Texans insisted that their mounted rangers were far superior to the army's infantry or artillery, and the establishment of a string of new posts, one camp (Hudson) and five forts (Stockton, Lancaster, Davis, Quitman, and Bliss) along the road from San Antonio to El Paso had done little to assuage them. Governor George T. Wood dubbed the foot soldiers "wholly unfit for the peculiar service required." Observing borderlands affairs during his extended tour of the slave states, Frederick Law Olmsted (who would soon design New York's Central Park) agreed with the Texans, likening the regulars' presence to "keeping a bulldog to chase mosquitos." On the other hand, the rangers, as described by Sam Houston, "are men who are acquainted with action; they are efficient; they are athletic; they are inured to toil, to enterprise, to danger; and they carry with them a spirit that is not to be found in the troops that are generally collected in the regular army." Regular soldiers and federal officials, however, charged that Texans merely wanted to secure more federal payments for security costs and blasted the state troops' lack of discipline. "I have an objection to placing rangers in immediate contact with the Indians on the frontier," complained Major General George M. Brooke, "as I am fearful, from their feeling . . . that they would be very apt to bring about what we wish to avoid—a general war."[15]

Disagreements over the relative merit of state troops, volunteers, and regulars symbolized the uneasy alliance between the army and non-Indian frontier residents. Demanding more immediate resolution, of course, were continuing conflicts in Indian affairs. The heavy demands of policing Kansas had forced the army to call off offensives against the Cheyennes in 1856, but by the next summer Bull Sumner, happy to be free of his controversial postings in New Mexico and Kansas and smug in his new rank as colonel, led a strike force that rendezvoused along the South Platte. Breaking camp on July 13, the colonel mustered three companies of the Sixth Infantry, six companies of the First Cavalry, four prairie howitzers, a handful of Delaware and Pawnee auxiliaries, and 180 mules. Sixteen days later, scouts spotted a few Cheyennes along the south fork of the Solomon River. Fearful that the enemy would flee, Sumner left the infantry and artillery behind and hurried his three hundred cavalrymen on ahead. These Cheyennes, roughly equal in number to the horse soldiers and having washed themselves in sacred waters reputed to protect them against the white man's bullets, were in no mood to run. Flanks protected by the Solomon River to the south and bluffs to the north, they waited atop their war horses.[16]

About one o'clock that afternoon, the cavalrymen rode into the valley. Sumner deployed his troopers into a line and began the advance at a trot. The Cheyennes, painted for war and sporting elaborate war bonnets, moved forward as well. "For perhaps the only time in the long history of Indian warfare," writes Robert M. Utley, "the contending forces acted their parts according to a script that a later generation of motion picture and television writers would enshrine in the folklore of the West." Both sides hastened their pace as they approached one another. Amid the din of thundering hooves and the excited war whoops of the Cheyennes, Sumner roared out: "Sling—carbine. Draw—saber." Then, "Gallup—march!" and "CHARGE!" Discipline triumphed over astonishment as the cavalrymen, flashing their rarely used sabers in the sun, pressed ahead. The sight of the steel weapons, against which they had no spiritual protection, took the fight out of the Cheyennes, who unleashed a ragged volley of arrows and musket balls before turning in flight. The pursuit continued for over seven miles, but Sumner could only report nine enemies killed and "a great number" wounded amid the isolated skirmishing. Two soldiers died; among the nine bluecoats requiring

FIG. 30. Edwin V. Sumner. Nicknamed "Bull" either for his booming voice or because a Mexican musket ball allegedly bounced off his thick head, Sumner (1797–1863) ranked among the most imposing officers in the antebellum army. During the Civil War, he commanded Union troops in the Peninsula, Antietam, and Fredericksburg campaigns. He died of a heart attack. LIBRARY OF CONGRESS, USZ62-115180.

medical attention was Lieutenant J. E. B. Stuart, who had taken a pistol shot in the chest at point-blank range.[17]

Sumner subsequently found a hastily abandoned encampment, and his soldiers destroyed enormous stores of cured buffalo meat and household possessions. The blow to morale and loss of winter stores represented a serious setback for the Cheyennes. "Colonel Sumner has worked a wondrous change in their dispositions toward the whites," reported Agent Robert Millar the following August. "They said they had learned a lesson last summer in their fight with Colonel Sumner; that it was useless to contend against the white man." Among militaristic Cheyennes such as the Dog Soldiers, however, the Solomon River engagement reinforced their determination to resist white encroachments.[18]

The truce between Indians and non-Indians in Washington Territory was also shattered. In May 1858, Brevet Lieutenant Colonel Edward J. Steptoe led five officers, 152 enlisted men, and two howitzers out of Fort Walla Walla, intent on reassuring residents of the federal government's presence and giving his new recruits a field exercise. After a "leisurely" march toward Colville, on the sixteenth the soldiers encountered about a thousand Spokane, Peolouse, Coeur d'Alene, and Yakima Indians, "all armed, painted, and defiant," near Tohotonimme Creek. Steptoe turned aside, and the next morning began to retreat back south. The Indians attacked about eight o'clock a.m.; badly outnumbered and his flanks crumbling, Steptoe barely managed to gather his shaken command on high ground. With ammunition running low, that night the soldiers buried the howitzers and their dead comrades and made a forced march to safety. Casualties numbered twenty-one.[19]

"This is a candid report of a disastrous affair," wrote Scott upon reviewing Steptoe's after-action report. But the Indian triumph was temporary. Demonstrating its enormous advantages in manpower and logistics, the army poured in supplies and reinforcements. In August, small commands led by Lieutenant Jesse Allen and Lieutenant George Crook found and summarily executed several men believed to be opposition leaders. Meanwhile, Colonel George E. Wright was organizing his main column—four companies of the First Dragoons, four companies of the Third Artillery (acting as infantry), two companies of his Ninth Infantry, a Third Artillery company handling two mountain howitzers, thirty Nez Perce scouts, and a four-hundred-mule packtrain. In high spirits following

FIG. 31. Cascades blockhouse. One of many blockhouses constructed
        in the federal government's efforts to establish military
        control over the Cascades River country during the late
        1850s. LIBRARY OF CONGRESS, USZC4-11412.

their victory over Steptoe, the Indians eagerly offered battle. But the bows,
spears, and muskets of the northwestern coalition were no match for the
longer-ranged rifles carried by many of their enemies. In early September,
Wright smashed the tribes at the battles of Four Lakes and Spokane Plain,
during which only a single regular was wounded. As a further demonstration of the army's power, Wright slaughtered nine hundred Indian ponies
and hung fifteen men judged to have been ringleaders. The next year,
the soldiers established Fort Colville to protect miners in northeastern
Washington. Superior resources, modern weapons, strong tactical leadership (among Wright's subordinates were seven future Civil War generals),
and the Indians' willingness to give battle on the enemy's terms had given
the regulars a convincing set of battlefield victories.[20]

In Texas, the Second Cavalry Regiment, commonly viewed as the army's best, boasted at least nineteen men who would eventually become generals.[21] With the two state reservations now in place, Indians found elsewhere were assumed to be enemies. But Lieutenant Colonel Lee's sixteen-hundred-mile campaign in summer 1856 had turned up few Indians of any sort. The following year, newly elected governor Hardin R. Runnels convinced the Texas legislature to raise additional companies of rangers. "What with the Utah War and Kansas," screamed the *Austin Intelligencer,* "the United States fails to afford Texas the protection necessary to save the scalps of our citizens. Let us, therefore, protect ourselves, and charge the bill to Uncle Sam." By May 1858, Rip Ford had assembled over two hundred rangers and Indian auxiliaries from the lower Brazos Reservation. They jumped Iron Jacket's Comanche village near Antelope Hills, reportedly killing seventy-six Comanches and admitting only two killed and three wounded of their own number. In describing his victory, Ford praised not only his rangers but the allied Indians, who, having "behaved most excellently on the field of battle[,] . . . deserve well of Texas."[22]

The commander of the Department of Texas, Brevet Major General David E. Twiggs, was embarrassed by the success of Ford's rangers and vowed to assemble an offensive strike of his own. In September, Brevet Major Earl Van Dorn led four companies of the Second Cavalry, a detachment of the First Infantry, and 135 allied Indians out from Fort Belknap across the Red River. Notorious for his womanizing, Van Dorn was also a determined officer carrying orders to "follow up the Comanches to the residence of their families." Establishing his infantrymen at Camp Radziminski, he received word of a Comanche presence near Rush Spring. Racing ninety miles east, Van Dorn's horsemen galloped into the Comanche encampment just after daylight on October 1. Surprise was complete, and for an hour and a half, deadly individual contests broke out throughout the valley's ravines as fighting men tried to cover the flight of their women and children. Van Dorn took an arrow in the stomach, but the soldiers and their allies killed fifty-eight Indians, captured three hundred horses, and burned 120 lodges. "Those who escaped did so with the scanty clothing they had on and their arms," reported Van Dorn, "and nothing was left to mark the site of their camp but the ashes and the dead."[23]

Reinforcements poured into Camp Radziminski as patrols scoured southwestern Oklahoma for the rest of the year. But Van Dorn had struck the wrong Comanches, for these were Buffalo Hump and his supporters, who weeks prior to the attack had disavowed any hostile intent in talks they initiated at Fort Arbuckle. Far from overawing the Indians, Rush Spring incited further depredations against the hated Texans. Twiggs and Van Dorn thus resumed the offensive, and on April 30, 1859, the latter led five hundred cavalrymen and several dozen Brazos River Agency Indians out from Camp Radziminski. The horse soldiers struck a Comanche camp two weeks later. Splitting the villagers from their horses in a brushy ravine near Crooked Creek, Van Dorn placed mounted troopers along the sides and moved in with dismounted skirmishers. The fighting left forty-nine Comanches (including eight women "unavoidably and unintentionally") killed, five wounded, and thirty-six taken captive. Van Dorn's command counted just two killed and fourteen wounded.[24]

Even in the wake of the success at Crooked Creek, the future for the Brazos Agency scouts was dim. Few Texans had accepted the reservations, and matters came to head in 1859, when John R. Baylor (a former Indian agent) and several hundred followers threatened to invade the Brazos Reservation even as a number of its men were fighting with Van Dorn. Although two companies of regulars and Indians at the agency frightened away Baylor's thugs, the days of the Texas reservations were numbered. In early August, accompanied by a strong army escort, the Texas Indians crossed the Red River to their new homes on the Washita.[25]

As the painful resettlement continued, soldiers abandoned Camp Radziminski for a new post, Fort Cobb, twelve miles west of the Wichita Agency. In spring 1860, eighteen companies from Fort Riley, Fort Cobb, and Fort Union combed the suspected enemy haunts. In July, Captain Samuel D. Sturgis's command from Fort Cobb struck several hundred Kiowas at Solomon's Fork, Kansas. Sturgis claimed that his men killed twenty-nine Kiowas, but the other warriors had managed to shepherd their women and children to safety. That summer's operations did establish two new posts along the exposed Santa Fe Trail: Fort Larned, where Pawnee Fork entered the Arkansas River, and Fort Wise, near present La Junta, Colorado. Still, the failure to inflict a decisive blow had been disappointing.[26]

In New Mexico, six treaties concluded by Governor David Meriwether did not end the hit-and-run raids that retarded regional growth. In 1857, thirteen companies took the field in southwestern New Mexico. The biggest fight came on May 27, when one column nearly annihilated the inhabitants of a Coyotero Apache camp on the Gila River, killing or capturing nearly ninety persons at the loss of ten wounded. "This is the first time that our troops have come into contact with these Indians," proclaimed the department commander, John Garland, "and the chastisement they have received will be long remembered by them."[27]

Further west, the bluecoats established Fort Buchanan about fifty miles southeast of Tucson in an effort to protect overland communications with California and to block Pinal and Chiricahua Apache raids into Mexico. In November and December 1859, Brevet Lieutenant Isaac V. D. Reeve swept through Pinal lands. Though one superior derided the effort as an "entire and utter failure," the Pinals made peace; to reinforce the government's authority, soldiers subsequently erected Fort Breckinridge on the San Pedro River.[28]

Regulars also joined volunteers in protecting and consolidating the newly opened Comstock Lode mines of western Nevada. Angry about the hordes of intruders flocking to Virginia City, Bannocks, Shoshonis, and Paiutes fought back, reportedly vowing to "clean out" the newcomers. On May 12, 1860, they ambushed about a hundred volunteers led by Major William Ormsby, killing half and scattering the remainder. Panicky locals convinced former Texas Ranger John C. Hays to take command of about five hundred volunteers and retaliate. Joined by two companies of regular infantry and two mountain howitzers under Captain Joseph Stewart, Hays pushed out from Virginia City on May 27. Six days later, his command drove the Indians from the field at Pinnacle Mount, claiming to have killed forty to fifty Indians at the cost of seven volunteers and four regulars killed or wounded. "Our Minié rifles kept them at too great a distance from us," reported Hays, "and it was quite apparent that they were astonished at the range of our guns." The outgunned Indians then scattered from their stronghold at Pyramid Lake. The volunteers being anxious to return to their diggings ("none of us wishes to remain in the service a day longer than the public interest requires"), Hays promptly broke up his command. To protect the region, the Federals soon established Fort Churchill.[29]

Open warfare also broke out that year against the Navajos, who one officer believed had "become quite insolent and require[d] a dressing." With perhaps twenty-five hundred fighting men and a long history of defending their lands against the encroachments of Spaniards, Mexicans, and rival Indians, the Navajos posed a formidable military challenge. In fall 1858 Lieutenant Colonel Dixon S. Miles initiated a series of operations into the tribe's Canyon de Chelly stronghold. Frequently assisted by Blas Lucero's Hispanic scouts, Miles's subordinates claimed to have killed or captured more than fifty Indians over the course of the offensive. "I have never known a more pacific disposition manifested by the Navajos," concluded Captain Oliver L. Shepherd from Fort Defiance.[30]

Shepherd was wrong. In the predawn hours of April 30, 1860, hundreds of Navajos crept down from the surrounding hills and assaulted Fort Defiance itself. Like most of the army's Trans-Mississippi posts, Defiance had no stockade, consisting instead of sod and adobe buildings organized around a parade ground. Brushing aside army sentinels, warriors occupied several outbuildings and stole some clothing from the sutler's store. But the Navajos, in no mood to slug it out in the face of the rallying three-company garrison, soon retreated. Slight casualties—one soldier killed and two wounded, and perhaps eight Navajos killed—belied the symbolic enormity of the challenge. A "lasting peace" must be "beaten into these Indians," reported a chastened Shepherd.[31]

As was the case in the Pacific Northwest, the federal government's logistical and numerical superiority would eventually overwhelm the Navajos. From Utah came two full infantry regiments as well as parts of a third and two companies of dragoons. Three columns from Fort Defiance and newly established Fort Fauntleroy, totaling six companies of cavalry, nine companies of infantry, and sixty "spies and guides," pushed into Diné bikéyah that fall with orders "to seize and destroy the crops of the Navajoes, and to surprise them while in their planting grounds." Skirmishing was indecisive, but the Navajos lost a thousand horses and seven thousand sheep to the invaders. Future losses would be even more devastating.[32]

As the regulars restored peace in Kansas, established federal authority in Utah, patrolled international borders, and chased Indians, their country was breaking apart. Officers' reactions reflected the deep divisions of the American people. From the Pacific Coast, Captain James J. Archer, a native of Maryland, angrily denounced his state's "dilatory course" in not immediately seceding. Assistant Surgeon DeWitt C. Peters, on the other hand, judged southerners to be "crazy as loonies." Lieutenant Theodore Talbot, a longtime frontier soldier now stationed at Fort Moultrie, South Carolina, placed his "strong abiding faith in the perpetuity of the Union, come what may." Posted in Texas, Lieutenant Colonel Lee, who had spent a lifetime in the service of his nation, reached a different conclusion. "I can anticipate no greater calamity for the country than a dissolution of the Union," wrote the stately Virginian, who nonetheless declared that "if the Union is dissolved, and the Government disrupted, I shall return to my native State and share the miseries of my people."[33]

In the end, 269 officers—roughly one quarter of the army's commissioned personnel—left the army and entered Confederate service. Twenty-six others refused to fight for either side. Enlisted men showed no such divided loyalties: less than three dozen of the fifteen thousand men in uniform are known to have joined the Confederate Army. As the war began, many of the regulars who had once garrisoned the West marched to Fort Leavenworth, either for assignment in Missouri or points further east. In Arkansas and the Indian Territory, the First Cavalry evacuated the forts of Washita, Arbuckle, Cobb, Smith, and Gibson. All ten companies from the Department of Utah soon joined them, as did most personnel from the Fifth, Seventh, and Tenth Infantry regiments previously stationed in New Mexico and Colorado. Four companies came from Fort Kearny and Fort Randall. Fort Breckinridge and Fort Buchanan were also abandoned.[34]

The most immediate crises came in Texas, California, and Missouri. In Texas, department commander Twiggs, though having one-sixth of the entire army at his disposal, surrendered shortly after that state's convention voted to secede from the Union. Under those terms, most soldiers in the Lone Star State got out before the Confederates fired on Fort Sumter, but about four hundred officers and men formerly stationed at Fort Bliss, Fort Quitman, Fort Davis, and Fort Stockton were taken prisoner just west of San Antonio as the war began. The officers were paroled within months, but it took nearly two years to work out an exchange for the enlisted men.[35]

To the west, nearly 40 percent of California's non-Indian residents had been born in slave states, and longtime Senator William H. Gwin avidly supported the expansion of slavery. Moreover, Brigadier General Albert Sidney Johnston, an adopted Texan, had recently taken command of the Department of the Pacific. Though Johnston remained loyal until the day he resigned to cast his lot with the Confederacy, the arrival of the more politically reliable Sumner as his replacement, along with news of the South's attack on Fort Sumter, solidified the northern cause on the West Coast. Fearful of secessionist strength, Sumner deftly transferred regulars from Indian duty to reputed secessionist strongholds at Los Angeles and San Bernardino. In stationing regulars near potential problem areas, he and his successor, George Wright, seem to have overawed Confederate sympathizers without having to revoke wholesale their civil liberties. The election of a staunch Republican, Leland Stanford, as governor later that year eliminated any possibility of the state's defection.[36]

In Missouri, General Harney commanded the military Department of the West from his headquarters in St. Louis. A Tennessean with many slave-owning friends, the veteran Harney seemed paralyzed as the Missouri state convention, which opposed leaving the Union, and the governor, who supported such a move, jockeyed for control. Unwilling to risk losing the most populous state west of the Mississippi River, the War Department sacked Harney in favor of Nathaniel Lyon (now a brigadier general), whose decisive action against secessionist forces threatening the St. Louis Arsenal negated any immediate possibility that the city would fall into enemy hands. Missouri, at least for the time being, remained under Union control.[37]

Now with an authorized strength of about eighteen thousand, during the late 1850s the army had undertaken major offensive operations against Indians in Texas, Oklahoma, Kansas, New Mexico, and Washington. Whereas the army had reported 42 combat engagements between regulars and Indians from 1840–49, that figure had nearly tripled (to 121) in the 1850s. Army casualties escalated accordingly, from 112 officers and men killed or wounded between 1840 and 1849 to 443 between 1850 and 1859. Attempting to implement policies of the Pierce and Buchanan administrations, the army had nearly come to blows with Britain in the Pacific Northwest, chased Cortinistas along the Rio Grande, invaded Utah, and quelled an incipient civil war in Kansas. Such actions were in harmony with its traditional functions, and the disposition of the army—in 1860, less than 7 percent of soldiers were stationed in the Department of the East, with the remainder in the departments of the West, Texas, New Mexico, Utah, Oregon, and California—clearly reflected its borderlands obligations. With the onset of the Civil War, many of the soldiers who had done so much to establish federal authority on the frontiers would be tested on battlefields far to the east. But during the years the white men fought one another, peace would not come to the West, and military affairs would remain central to the lives of many living in the borderlands.[38]

NINE

Civil Wars in the Borderlands

L ife on the nation's frontiers profoundly changed during the Civil War. Ignoring or fleeing the awful carnage in the East, farmers, miners, adventurers, and entrepreneurs flooded the West by the thousands. Spectacular prewar gold and silver strikes in California, Colorado (1858–59), and Nevada (1859) were followed by big new wartime discoveries in Idaho, Montana, and Arizona as well as by smaller finds in eastern Oregon and Washington. The expansion of stagecoach services, completion of a telegraph line to California, and better steamboat travel up the Missouri River further encouraged migration into areas already strained beyond their ecological limits. Political change accompanied these developments, Washington being eager to cement the West's ties to the Union. In the last days of the flagging Buchanan administration, Kansas belatedly received statehood, and Colorado, Nevada, and Dakota were granted territorial status. Congress recognized Arizona and Idaho as territories in 1863, with Montana joining them the following year. Seeking to create another safely Republican state and to reward mining interests, Congress also pushed through Nevada's statehood.

Military events—featuring a new set of characters—would be essential to these developments. The Lincoln administration kept the regular army intact, expanding it by eleven regiments (which amounted to just over twenty-two thousand more men). It also eliminated the archaic distinctions between cavalry, mounted riflemen, and dragoons by designating all mounted units as cavalry. The vast majority of the three million Americans who saw military service during the war, however, were volunteers. In the West, this mobilization also meant that the United States would field greater numbers of men: whereas about ten thousand regulars had been available for Indian campaigning in 1860, nearly twice that many were on hand four years later. Participation varied sharply by region. In Kansas, scene of bitter internecine guerrilla warfare as well as conflicts against Indians, nearly one in five persons saw military service, the highest percentage of any free state or territory in the country. Engaged in several ferocious campaigns against Indians, Nevada ranked second. By contrast, the six lowest rates of Civil War participation came from other borderlands regions: from lowest to highest, these included Utah (less than 1 percent), Oregon, California, New Mexico, Dakota, and Washington (under 9 percent).[1]

For the Confederacy, the West offered many strategic opportunities. Missouri, the most populous state west of the Mississippi River, was an especially important prize, ranking among the top ten states in its production of hemp, corn, and livestock. The largest lead-producing state in the Union, Missouri boasted a vibrant industrial base, and St. Louis controlled the strategic junction of the Missouri and Mississippi rivers. Many of the most favored overland routes from Washington to the Pacific were also vulnerable to a rebel strike, and there was no guarantee that the largely Hispanic population of New Mexico would remain loyal to the Union. Loss of this territory would in turn endanger southern California and Colorado, thus allowing the Confederacy to establish a Pacific outpost and to lay claim to rich mineral wealth. Although Richmond evinced little interest in a far-western strategy and could spare precious few resources for the war in the Trans-Mississippi, with a bit of luck and the cooperation of American Indians, even minor western thrusts offered the South a chance to trim the North's tremendous material advantages.[2]

American Indians, of course, had their own interests. For those tribes who had been removed to present Oklahoma, the division of the Union sharpened long-simmering internal rivalries. John Ross, the aristocratic, slaveowning principal chief of the Cherokees, initially tried to remain neutral. Others—like Stand Watie, who had supported the decision to move west, and John Jumper, a prominent Seminole minister—backed the Confederacy. Traditionalists such as the Cherokee leader Opothleyahola, on the other hand, preached loyalty to Washington. As the war opened, the Confederacy's Albert Pike, equal parts linguist, lawyer, and romantic, skillfully isolated the pro-Union factions, and seven Indian regiments—three Choctaw-Chickasaw, two Cherokee, one Creek, and one Seminole-Creek—eventually saw Confederate service. Opothleyahola and ten thousand loyalists fled north, suffering a major defeat at the hands of a mixed force of Texans, Arkansans, and pro-Confederate Indians at Salt Creek (Chustenahlah) before reaching the relative safety of Kansas.[3]

In nearby Missouri, Union troops overcame an early setback at the Battle of Wilson's Creek and gradually expanded the scope and reach of Washington's authority. In early 1862, Brigadier General Samuel R. Curtis and twelve thousand Federals met Major General Earl Van Dorn, the former Second cavalryman turned Confederate, with sixteen thousand men along the Missouri-Arkansas border. Van Dorn's command included three of Pike's poorly armed Indian regiments. On the bitterly cold morning of March 7, Van Dorn struck the outnumbered Yankees at Pea Ridge, Arkansas. Curtis's troops withstood the initial onslaught and drove the Confederates from the field the next day. In reporting the triumph, northern newspapers dramatized charges that Pike's Indians had scalped some Union soldiers. Plagiarizing from the *New York Tribune*, the *Dakota Republican* lambasted the "aboriginal Corps of Tomahawkers and Scalpers," denouncing Pike as "a ferocious fish" who "got himself up in good style, war paint, nose ring, and all."[4]

That spring also witnessed the passing of the Confederacy's high tide in the Southwest. Soon after the war began, John R. Baylor, now a lieutenant colonel of Texas state troops, occupied the deserted chain of Federal forts and moved up the Rio Grande with his secessionists. In late July 1861, leading 280 Texans, New Mexicans, and Knights of the Golden Circle, Baylor forced the humiliating surrender of 500 Union troops and set up headquarters at Mesilla. Baylor named himself governor of the new Confederate Territory of Arizona but knew that he needed aid from Richmond if he were to hold his gains. "The vast mineral resources of Arizona, in addition to its affording an outlet to the Pacific, make its acquisition a matter of some importance to our Government," he explained.[5]

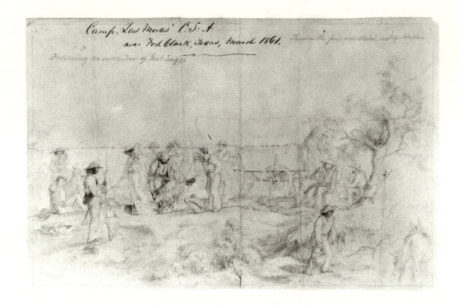

FIG. 32. Carl Iwonski, sketch of Texas state troops. After secession, Texas state troops quickly occupied former Union army posts in West Texas, putting abandoned supplies to good use. This drawing, by artist Carl G. Iwonski, was the first wartime sketch reproduced in *Harper's Weekly*. LIBRARY OF CONGRESS, USZ62-1062.

Brigadier General Henry Hopkins Sibley, a former dragoon who had convinced President Jefferson Davis to back his effort to raise the Stars and Bars across the Southwest, set out to do just that. Sibley's three thousand Texans filed into Confederate Arizona that winter and in February 1862 began moving up the Rio Grande toward Fort Craig, where his old friend Colonel Edward R. S. Canby (Sibley and Canby had been classmates at West Point, and Canby had served as best man in Sibley's wedding) had assembled about thirty-eight hundred regulars and New Mexico volunteers. On the afternoon of February 21, Sibley bested Canby at the Battle of Valverde, the Federals suffering four hundred casualties, twice those of the Confederates. Though a tactical victory, Valverde had little strategic importance: Union troops still held Fort Craig, the Texans were running low on supplies, and thirteen hundred regulars and Colorado volunteers were racing south from Fort Union. Sibley pushed

north and occupied Albuquerque and Santa Fe. Following an inconclusive clash with the Coloradans at Apache Canyon (March 26), the Texans
won a tactical victory on the field at Glorieta Pass (March 28), only to find
that their supply train had been destroyed by Major John P. Chivington's
Colorado cavalry during the main engagement. Far from home and short
of everything except the alcohol on which their commander had grown
dependent, the Texans' retreat soon became a rout, and Canby's Yankees
reoccupied New Mexico. Lead elements from among the exhausted
Texans finally reached San Antonio in August 1862.[6]

Confederate dreams of southwestern empire were collapsing. That
spring, Baylor and a hundred men had pursued Apache raiders deep into
Chihuahua. The U.S. consul in Mazatlán predicted that "the atrocities
of Baylor's men . . . will serve to revive the hatred of the Chihuahuans to
the Texans." Baylor accentuated the problem upon his return to Mesilla,
when, falsely claiming that the Confederate Congress had "passed a law
declaring extermination to all hostile Indians," he ordered a subordinate to "use all means to persuade the Apaches or any tribe to come in
for the purpose of making peace, and when you get them together kill
all the grown Indians and take the children prisoners and sell them to
defray the expense." Learning of the extermination order, Confederate
officials severed ties with Baylor and disavowed his subsequent plans to
regain Arizona.[7]

Elimination of the Confederate threat allowed the Federals to focus
on the Mescalero Apaches and the Navajos. In September 1862, Brigadier General James H. Carleton succeeded Canby as department commander. An autocratic disciplinarian, Carleton set about his task with
an unusual vigor. "The troops must be kept after the Indians, not in big
bodies, with military noises and smokes, and the gleam of arms by day,
and fires, and talk, and comfortable sleeps by night," he told one reluc-
tant junior officer, "but in small parties moving stealthily to their haunts
and lying patiently in wait for them; or by following their tracks day after
day with a fixedness of purpose that never gives up." Carleton also identified a subordinate capable of implementing the uncompromising new
regime: sixty-three-year-old Christopher "Kit" Carson, guide, Indian
agent, and frontiersman extraordinaire.[8]

First the duo faced the Mescaleros. If they tried to make peace,
instructed Carleton, "tell them fairly and frankly . . . that we believe if

we kill some of their men in fair open war they will be apt to remember that it will be better for them to remain at peace than to be at war." Nine companies of California and New Mexico volunteers and forty allied Pueblo scouts took the field from Fort Stanton, Mesilla, and El Paso. Unwilling to expose their families to such a determined onslaught, by March 1863 some four hundred Mescaleros had enrolled at Fort Sumner in the Bosque Redondo.[9]

Carleton next turned to the Navajos. Moving from recently established Fort Wingate and older Fort Canby (formerly named Fort Defiance), in summer 1863 Lieutenant Colonel J. Francisco Chavez and Carson launched a series of raids into Navajo country. Carson, Chavez, and their Ute scouts reported killing or wounding 118 Navajos, capturing another 196, razing hundreds of acres of cornfields, and seizing thousands of sheep, goats, and horses. In January 1864, Carson pushed through the snow into the securest holds of Diné bikéyah—the Canyon de Chelly. He returned sixteen days later, having killed twenty-three Indians. "But it is to the ulterior effects of the expedition that I look for the greatest results," explained Carson. "We have shown the Indians that in no place, however formidable or inaccessible in their opinion, are they safe from the pursuit of the troops of this command, and have convinced a larger portion of them that the struggle on their part is a hopeless one." By March 1864, six thousand dispirited Navajos had turned themselves in. Carleton packed them off to Bosque Redondo, throwing them together with their old enemies, the Apaches.[10]

In the Gila River district to the south, Carleton also made war on the Chiricahua and Mimbreño Apaches. Until early 1861, Chiricahuas of the Apache Pass region had cooperated with employees of the Overland Mail stagecoaches. That relationship was shattered when Lieutenant George N. Bascom, two short years out of West Point, attempted to arrest their headman, Cochise. The leader escaped, and the resulting tit-for-tat violence set off a bitter conflict that would last for a quarter century. To meet the threats, Carleton established several forts: Bowie, West (later replaced by Cummings), McRae, and Selden. In January 1863, Brigadier General Joseph R. West's Californians scoured the region, killing a few Mimbreños in battle and murdering even more (including the legendary Mangas Coloradas) whom they had lured in with false promises of negotiations and food. Even so, Apache resistance remained unbroken.[11]

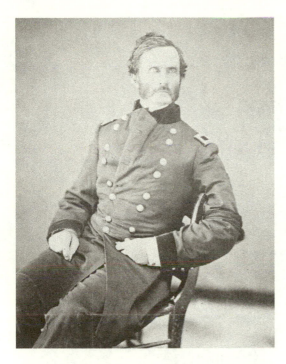

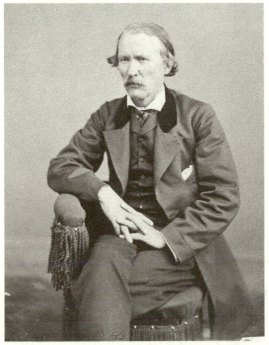

FIG. 33.
James H. Carleton

FIG. 34.
Kit Carson. Carleton
(1814–73) and Carson
(1809–68) made for a
ruthlessly effective team
fighting Indians in New
Mexico and Arizona
during the Civil War.
LIBRARY OF CONGRESS,
DIG-CWPB-07381 AND
DIG-CWPBH-00514.

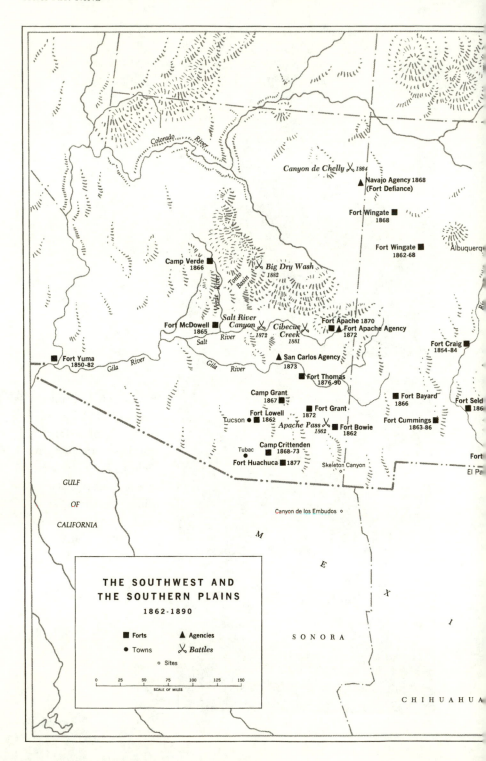

Colorado River

Canyon de Chelly ✕ 1864

Navajo Agency 1868
(Fort Defiance)

Fort Wingate ■
1868

Fort Wingate ■
1862-68

Albuquerqu

Camp Verde ■
1866

Big Dry Wash ✕
1882

Tonto Basin

Verde River

Salt River
Canyon ✕

Fort McDowell ■
1865

Cibecue ✕
Creek
1881

1872

Fort Apache 1870
▲ Fort Apache Agency
1872

Fort Craig ■
1854-84

Salt   River

Fort Yuma ■
1850-82

Gila   River

Gila   River

▲ San Carlos Agency
1873

Fort Thomas ■
1876-90

Fort Bayard ■
1866

Fort Seld
186

Camp Grant ■
1867

Fort Grant ■
1872

Fort Lowell
Tucson ● ■ 1862

Apache Pass ✕
1862

Fort Bowie ■
1862

Fort Cummings ■
1863-86

Fort

Tubac ●

Camp Crittenden ■
1868-73

Fort Huachuca ■ 1877

Skeleton Canyon ○

El Pa

GULF

OF

CALIFORNIA

Canyon de los Embudos ○

M

E

X

I

SONORA

**THE SOUTHWEST AND
THE SOUTHERN PLAINS**

1862-1890

■ Forts   ▲ Agencies

● Towns   ✕ Battles

○ Sites

0   25   50   75   100   125   150

SCALE OF MILES

CHIHUAHUA

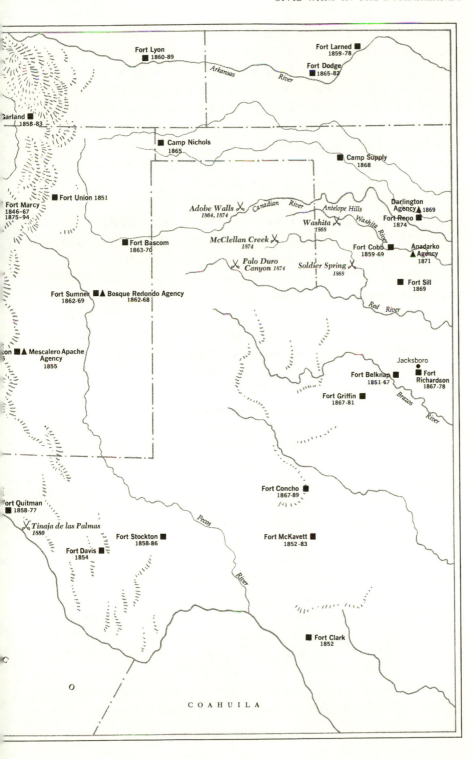

Fort Lyon
1860-89

Fort Larned
1859-78

Fort Dodge
1865-82

Arkansas River

Garland
1858-83

Camp Nichols
1865

Camp Supply
1868

Fort Marcy
1846-67
1875-94

Fort Union 1851

Adobe Walls
1864, 1874

Canadian River

Antelope Hills

Darlington
Agency 1869
Fort Reno
1874

Washita
1868

Washita River

Fort Bascom
1863-70

McClellan Creek
1874

Fort Cobb
1859-69

Anadarko
Agency
1871

Palo Duro
Canyon 1874

Soldier Spring
1868

Fort Sill
1869

Fort Sumner
1862-69

Bosque Redondo Agency
1862-68

Red River

Mescalero Apache
Agency
1855

Jacksboro

Fort Belknap
1851-67

Fort
Richardson
1867-78

Fort Griffin
1867-81

Brazos River

Fort Concho
1867-89

Fort Quitman
1858-77

Tinaja de las Palmas
1880

Pecos

Fort Stockton
1858-86

Fort McKavett
1852-83

Fort Davis
1854

River

Fort Clark
1852

COAHUILA

O

Embracing the cause of Manifest Destiny, Carleton enthusiastically employed military power to spur development. Seeking to demonstrate that "our country has mines of precious metals unsurpassed in richness, number, and extent by any in the world," the general established Fort Whipple near the soon-to-be Arizona territorial capital of Prescott. Demands from Arizonians to eradicate any threat from the local Yavapai Indians outstripped the capacity of the garrison, so self-appointed avenger King S. Woolsey instead proclaimed his intention to "fight on the broad platform of extermination" and organized a band of thirty territorial militiamen to hasten the task.[12]

Woolsey's murderers only inflamed the Yavapais and Apaches, so in May 1864 Carleton tried to organize a "general rising . . . to insure a lasting peace and a security of life to all those who go to that country to search for the precious metals." Five hundred soldiers would establish a new post, Fort Goodwin, in the upper Gila River country. Seeking the cooperation of the governors of Sonora and Chihuahua, Carleton authorized Mexican troops to pursue the Apaches into the United States. He also offered weapons to allied Pimas, Maricopas, and Papagos in return for their assistance. Arizona's governor, John N. Goodwin, should get "every citizen of the Territory who has a rifle to take the field. . . . Every man who has the development and prosperity of Arizona at heart must put his shoulder not only to the wheel, but to the rifle." Soldiers from the region's forts must travel light and use pack mules, rather than wagons, to carry their supplies. "To be encumbered with more is not to find Indians," insisted Carleton.[13]

Despite these entreaties, the campaign failed to break the Apaches. Man and beast sweated through the blistering summer heat in a series of largely futile explorations and chases. Most successful was a mixed column of just over a hundred soldiers escorting Lieutenant Colonel Nelson H. Davis out of Tucson. In the twenty-six-day operation, the expedition killed fifty-one, wounded seventeen, took sixteen women and children prisoners, and destroyed a ton of mescal, at a cost of one man wounded. But the majority of the soldiers' efforts came up empty: the Apaches were too skilled, the terrain too difficult, and the army's tactics too uninventive.[14]

Further west, veteran George Wright assumed command of the Department of the Pacific from Sumner (his brother-in-law) in October

1861. Wright's chief lieutenant was a combative Irishman, Colonel Edward Connor. The no-nonsense Connor had little use for secessionists ("Traitors shall not utter treasonable sentiments in this district with impunity, but must seek a more genial soil, or receive the punishment they so richly merit"), Mormons ("a community of traitors, murderers, fanatics, and whores"), or Indians ("hang them, and leave their bodies exposed as an example of what evil-doers may expect while I command this district"). In 1862, Connor built Fort Ruby and abandoned Fort Crittenden (formerly Camp Floyd) in favor of a more strategic position at Fort Douglas.[15]

Provoked by the harsh methods of the volunteers and the continuing flow of emigrants, Bear Hunter's Shoshonis took up the warpath. In January 1863, Connor set forth with three hundred men through heavy snows and bitter cold after Bear Hunter's people. Just after dawn on the twenty-ninth, they found a fortified encampment on the Bear River. Unleashing a deadly enfilading fire, the soldiers killed 224 Shoshonis (among them Bear Hunter), destroyed over seventy lodges, and captured 175 horses, leaving only "a small quantity of wheat" for the 160 women and children now abandoned in the numbing cold. "Of the good conduct and bravery of both officers and men California has reason to be proud," proclaimed Connor. Mormon officials who had accompanied the expedition saw it differently, reporting that the California volunteers had executed the wounded "by Knocking them in the head with an axe and then commenced to ravish the Squaws which was done to the very height of brutality." Sergeant William L. Beach, Second California Volunteers, added that "their [sic] was no quarters [sic] given that day."[16]

Promoted to brigadier general, Connor viewed the Bear River affair as just the first step in a larger campaign to assert Federal authority over Utah, whose residents he deemed "at heart disloyal." His sweeps through Shoshoni, Bannock, and Ute country through the first eight months of the year convinced the tribes to opt for the relative safety of government reservations. Seeking to counterbalance the Mormon influence, he encouraged his soldiers to search for mineral wealth and personally invested in several such ventures in Deseret. Fearing that such bellicosity would alienate the local citizenry, in July 1864 officials in the Department of the Pacific finally intervened, warning Connor that a war with the Mormons "would prove fatal to the Union cause."[17]

FIG. 35. Patrick E. Connor. A former enlisted man, Connor
(1820–91) rose to the rank of brevet major general of
volunteers. After the Civil War, he made his home in
Utah. LIBRARY OF CONGRESS, DIG-CWPB-06320.

Brigadier General Benjamin Alvord, a Vermont-born West Pointer,
commanded the District of Oregon. The steady stream of southern
emigrants and political influence of Copperheads alarmed Alvord, who
as late as 1864 requested permission to call up the militia to quell a
potential insurrection. Along the western boundary of present Idaho,

he established Fort Lapwai to separate miners from the Nez Perces, with whom he reached a peace agreement in 1863. Fort Boise guarded the emigrant trail and Fort Klamath deterred Modoc and Klamath Indians. But the non-Indian residents of the tristate corner of California-Oregon-Nevada were in no mood for halfway measures, leading the district commander in the Fort Humboldt region to complain that "no Indian can show his head anywhere without being shot down like a wild beast." Only the unrelenting campaigns by Lieutenant Colonel Stephen G. Whipple and locally raised California Mountaineers led to a peace, bought with the blood of almost all of the resident tribes and a few dollars spent in employing the small number left alive.[18]

Halfway across the continent, affairs in the Indian Territory were coming to no such definitive an end. In July 1862 Colonel William Weer, an alcoholic former Jayhawker, led Kansas troops and the First Indian Home Guard Regiment (mostly pro-Union Creeks) south into Indian lands. At Locust Grove, they trounced a regiment of Missouri Confederates. Capturing the hapless John Ross, who had most recently cast his lot with the South, they raised two more Indian regiments for the Federal government. Infuriated by Richmond's refusal to support his allies, Albert Pike submitted his resignation. But a mutiny of Union troops (a ringleader described Weer's actions as being "either insane, premeditated treachery to his troops," or possibly the result of "idiocy or monomania" induced by "his grossly intemperate habits long continued") prevented the North from consolidating its position, and the Kansans returned home.[19]

Loyalist Indians fell back along with the Kansans. With forty-three hundred Indians, Missourians, and Texans, Colonel Douglas H. Cooper, Pike's successor, surged ahead and won a sharp fight at Newtonia. Responding to the Confederate threat, Brigadier General James G. Blunt and Union reinforcements moved into southwestern Missouri and northwestern Arkansas, where they met Major General Thomas C. Hindman's Confederates at Prairie Grove. Each side had about ten thousand men engaged, and both suffered roughly 12 percent casualties, but Hindman, citing shortages of food and ammunition, fell back in what devolved into a demoralized rout. The Indian Brigade also drove Cooper back across the Arkansas River. On July 17, 1863, leading three thousand loyalist Indians, Coloradans, and black Kansans, Blunt (now a major general) attacked Cooper near Honey Springs. In the war's largest single battle in the Indian Territory, superior Union munitions and artillery broke the Confederate line. Fort Smith fell on September 1, and the Federals captured Little Rock nine days later.[20]

Yet all was not well for Union fortunes in western Missouri and eastern Kansas, where fierce guerrilla warfare had pitted neighbor against neighbor. State officials in Jefferson City and Topeka blamed one another for not doing enough to quell the internecine struggle. Revenge-minded borderlanders on both sides left no attack unpunished, and the return of proslavery ruffian Colonel William C. Quantrill exacerbated the terror. On August 21, Quantrill and four hundred men stormed into the abolitionist community of Lawrence, Kansas, and slaughtered 183 men and boys. "City in ashes," reported a furious Governor Thomas Carney. "I must hold Missouri responsible for this fearful, fiendish raid."[21]

Commanding the District of the Border, Brigadier General Thomas Ewing Jr. sought to impose an iron federal hand. Born to one of Missouri's most prominent families, he ordered residents of Missouri's Jackson, Cass, and Bates counties not in the immediate vicinity of a military station to leave within fifteen days, deeming them "all practically the servants and supporters of the guerrillas." The chief of the Department of Missouri (which then included both Missouri and Kansas), Major General John M. Schofield, tempered the predictable retributions that followed by revising Ewing's draconian evacuation order. Calls for Kansans to organize at Paola and "burn every living thing" in Missouri proved to be more bluster than reality. The ferocious regional conflict would continue nonetheless, as evidenced by the subsequent massacres of a hundred African American troops following the battle of Poison Spring, Arkansas, and of nearly 150 Union soldiers and militiamen at Centralia, Missouri, the latter horror courtesy of a pack of pathological killers led by "Bloody Bill" Anderson.[22]

More conventional Confederate raids still challenged Union authority in Missouri. In fall 1863, Colonel Jo Shelby led his six-hundred-strong Iron Brigade in a forty-one-day, fifteen-hundred-mile ride all the way to the Missouri River at Boonville, destroying nearly $2 million in railroad rolling stock and supplies and garnering hundreds of new Confederate recruits. Stand Watie, who earned a general's star for his daring capture of a Union supply ship in June 1864, followed up this success

September 19 by seizing a three-hundred-wagon supply train north of Fort Gibson. That same day saw the beginning of an even bigger incursion, made up of twelve thousand Confederates (a third of whom had no weapons) under Major General Sterling Price. But Price found the going tough. At fortified Pilot Knob (protected by a ten-foot-wide ditch, nine-foot earthen parapets, and sixteen cannons and mortars), General Ewing and just over a thousand Federals inflicted heavy casualties on attackers seven times their number. On October 23, in the war's largest engagement west of the Mississippi River, General Curtis drove back Price's outnumbered command at Westport, Missouri. Two days later, a Union cavalry assault at Mine Creek, Kansas, completed the defeat of Price's army.[23]

From Confederate Texas, state troops had occupied Fort Washita, Fort Arbuckle, and Fort Cobb and signed treaties with the Caddos, Chickasaws, Comanches, and Wichitas. An assortment of units—the Frontier Regiment, the Frontier Organization, and the Border Regiment—constituted their northern and western defenses. Commanded by Colonel James Bourland, a leader in the hanging of dozens of suspected Unionists at Gainesville, the Border Regiment took an especially harsh line against those unfortunate enough to be in their path. Despite (or perhaps because of) such measures, several tribes took advantage of the situation to settle old scores against the hated Texans. In December 1863, Comanches killed a dozen people and took a similar number captive in a sweep through north Texas. Kiowas and Comanches thundered into settlements near Elm Creek ten months later, killing twelve, seizing additional captives, and shepherding hundreds of livestock across the Red River. Shorn of their traditional federal defenses, borderlands residents had by this time taken to "forting up" in small stockades and blockhouses. Fearing another raid, on January 8, 1865, Captain Henry Fossett and Captain Silas Totten, commanding 360 militiamen and volunteers, blindly attacked an Indian encampment at Dove Creek (Fossett reportedly declared that he "recognized no friendly Indians in Texas"). It turned out to be several hundred Kickapoo men, women, and children en route to Mexico. The Kickapoos routed the poorly led Texans, killing twenty-three and wounding another nineteen.[24]

Affairs to the south were equally tumultuous. In August 1862, Texas Partisan Rangers cut down three dozen immigrant German Unionists along the Nueces River as they tried to flee the Hill Country for safer haunts in Mexico. On November 6, 1863, seeking to tighten the blockade of the Confederacy and neutralize the French-inspired effort to establish Ferdinand Maximilian as emperor of Mexico, the first Federal troops (which would ultimately number about six thousand) under Major General Nathaniel P. Banks splashed ashore at Brazos Santiago. Over the next two months they occupied Brownsville and moved as far north as Indianola and up the Rio Grande past Ringgold Barracks. Though the ambitious Banks proclaimed that his "most sanguine expectations are more than realized," the Confederates quickly rerouted the cotton trade upriver through Laredo, where Colonel Santos Benavides had repelled a Federal thrust. With the withdrawal of most Union troops to support Banks's unsuccessful Red River campaign in Louisiana the following spring, Rip Ford's Texans soon recaptured Brownsville.[25]

Ford's most immediate threat now came not from the Federals, who had retreated to Brazos Santiago, but from his old nemesis Juan Cortina, by this point self-proclaimed governor of the Mexican state of Tamaulipas. In September 1864, the approach of Mexican imperialist and French forces under General Tomás Mejía led Cortina to attempt an alliance with the Federals. On the eighth, Cortinistas cooperated with Union troops in skirmishing around Palmito Ranch, but the unpredictable Cortina then changed sides and donned the imperialist uniform. Even in the face of deteriorating Confederate fortunes elsewhere, a few of Ford's men fought to the bitter end. On May 13, 1865, over a month after Robert E. Lee had surrendered at Appomattox, they routed about eight hundred Union soldiers under Colonel Theodore Barrett at Palmito Ranch, the last battle of the Civil War.[26]

The war exacted a horrific toll on Missouri, Kansas, and the emigrant Indians of Oklahoma. Texas, like the rest of the former Confederacy, would suffer for generations. The loss of the normal infusion of federal monies into the southern-controlled areas compounded the region's economic problems, and local defenses in the Lone Star State were never as consistent as those formerly provided by the regular army. But nowhere in the borderlands did the war years bring such unmitigated terror as it did to the people of Minnesota and the Dakota Territory, non-Indian and Indian alike. Minnesota had been granted statehood in 1858, and three years later Congress organized the Dakota Territory (consisting

FIG. 36. 1863 Indian delegation to Washington. Indian delegations to
Washington were frequent throughout the nineteenth century.
Interpreter William Simpson Smith and agent Samuel G.
Colley are standing to the left of this group portrait, taken in
March 1863 in the White House Conservatory. Indians on the
front row are War Bonnet, Standing-in-the-Water, and Lean
Bear (Cheyennes) and Yellow Wolf (Kiowa). War Bonnet and
Standing-in-the-Water were massacred at Sand Creek, twenty
months later. LIBRARY OF CONGRESS, USZ62-11880.

of most of present North and South Dakota, Montana, and Wyoming).
In addition to the older posts at Abercrombie and Ripley that the army
had erected, it also had built Fort Ridgley. For the sixty-five hundred
Dakota Indians, maladministration by agents and government officials
following their 1858 removal to lands on the Minnesota River had led to a
disaster. Hundreds of thousands of dollars intended for the Indians had
instead lined the pockets of agents and traders like Alexander Ramsey
(Minnesota's first territorial governor) and Henry Hastings Sibley (no relation to the Confederate, Sibley was the state's first elected governor).[27]
   "We were in a starving condition and desperate state of mind,"

remembered one Dakota of the year 1862. Trader Andrew Myrick cru-elly suggested they should ameliorate their misery by eating "grass or their own dung." The slowly brewing cauldron finally boiled over on August 17, when a handful of young men murdered five whites north of the Redwood Agency. Rather than give up the offenders, Dakota soldier societies launched a preemptive strike ahead of the retaliatory blows they knew would follow. Among the most prominent of the fighters was Little Crow (Taoyateduta), the vain, courageous shaman who had once had preached accommodation. They swept through the Redwood Agency, stuffing the mouth of one of their first victims, Myrick, with grass. Others struck nearby towns and farms, slaughtering more than 350 whites the first day. As the pent-up orgy of revenge continued, over three hundred more Minnesotans were killed during the following week.[28]

The Minnesota frontier was aflame. Defenders barely turned back assaults against Fort Ridgely (August 20 and 22) and New Ulm (August 23). "Half the population of the State are fugitives," complained Governor Ramsey. From Yankton, Dakota Territory governor William Jayne (President Lincoln's former physician) reported that "a general alarm pervades all our settlements." But the Dakotas had lost the ini-tiative. Sibley gathered enough men to relieve the stricken Minnesota River Valley settlements. The War Department organized Wisconsin, Iowa, Minnesota, and the territories of Nebraska and Dakota into a new Department of the Northwest, headed by Major General John Pope. Recently beaten on the eastern front at Second Bull Run, Pope remained popular in the West owing to his earlier victories at New Madrid and Island No. 10. Most important, President Lincoln still had confidence in the veteran of two decades of military service.[29]

As Pope established his headquarters at St. Paul, Sibley took the field from Fort Ridgely. On September 23, his sixteen hundred men threw back an Indian attack in the two-hour Battle of Wood Lake. The twenty-five killed hardly suggested the magnitude of the defeat among the now-demoralized Dakota war factions, who fled west. That left the peace parties to turn over 269 white and mixed-blood captives and throw themselves to the uncertain mercies of the Minnesotans. A five-man commission handed out death sentences to 307 Indians and mixed bloods. Listening to the better angels of his nature, Lincoln slowed the hangman's noose, and Washington examiners culled the number to be executed to thirty-eight. On December 26, the nation's largest public hanging was conducted in Mankato.[30]

There remained the matter of the Dakotas who were still out. Amid reports that Little Crow was rallying support among the Lakotas for war, Pope, who declared it his "purpose to utterly exterminate the Sioux if I have the power to do so," organized a big new offensive for 1863. Hampered by shortages of water and a superabundance of three hundred wagons, Sibley's thirty-three hundred men crept into present-day North Dakota and established a supply depot south of Devil's Lake. In the battles of Big Mound (July 24), Dead Buffalo Lake (July 26), and Stony Lake (July 28), the Minnesotans claimed to have killed 150 Indians at the cost of a dozen of their own men. They also destroyed immense quantities of dried meat, buffalo hides, and household equipment. A second Federal column, twelve hundred Iowans and Nebraskans led by Brigadier General Alfred Sully, had gotten off to an even slower start, but on September 3 found several thousand Yanktonais, Lakotas, and Dakotas at Whitestone Hill. In a fiercely fought battle, Sully's troopers captured 156 prisoners (mostly women and children), claimed to have killed two hundred Indians and burned hundreds of lodges and half a million pounds of dried buffalo meat. On their return, his men established Fort Sully near present Pierre, South Dakota.[31]

Although victorious, neither Sibley nor Sully had won the definitive triumph that might have placated westerners. Thus 1864 saw the offensives resume. Soldiers established Fort Wadsworth (later renamed Fort Sisseton) southwest of present Lake City, South Dakota. In early July, Federals began erecting Fort Rice on the Missouri River. Sully and twenty-six hundred men then marched west and north, accompanied by—much to his discomfort ("I can't send them back. I can't leave them here, for I can't feed them. . . . Therefore I am forced to take them with me")— 123 civilian wagons bound for Montana. On the twenty-eighth, leaving an escort with the emigrants, Sully deployed his troops in a huge square, bristling with artillery, and methodically advanced on a Lakota village at Killdeer Mountain. Sully asserted that over five thousand warriors opposed him; Indian sources suggest a quarter of that. Whatever the actual numbers, the Hunkpapas, Sans Arcs, Sihasapas, and Minneconjous, as well as some Yanktonais and Dakotas, welcomed the fight. Effectively exploiting his infantry, cavalry, and artillery, Sully won the battlefield, destroying massive amounts of food stores and camp equipage. Marching back to Fort Rice, Sully then dispatched a column to rescue the beleaguered emigrant train, which had been besieged two hundred miles to the west.[32]

News of the Dakota uprising had inflamed prejudices throughout the West, but nowhere more so than in Colorado. Many Plains peoples refused to make the additional concessions called for in the Treaty of Fort Wise (1861), and new soldier forts had further strained the region's fragile environment. With bluecoats now occupying favorite watering holes and buffalo haunts, by spring 1864 Colorado officials had convinced themselves that an Indian war was eminent. Colonel Chivington, the ambitious former preacher whose earlier leadership against the Confederates in New Mexico had earned him command of the military district of Colorado, relished the chance for battle. "I think if great caution is not exercised on our part there will be a bloody war," an army inspector-general had warned that June, and field officers believed that they had had instructions to "kill Cheyennes whenever and wherever found."[33]

Alarmed by the violence along the southern plains trails, Chivington's superior in the Department of Kansas, Major General Curtis, rode west to Fort Lyon (formerly Fort Wise) with four hundred reinforcements to see for himself. Encountering no Indians, his men strengthened existing garrisons along the Santa Fe Trail and established the new posts of Harker (on the Smoky Hill River) and Zarah (near the Arkansas River). In September, General Blunt routed some Cheyennes and Arapahoes at Walnut Creek, but Price's Confederate raids into Missouri that fall once again turned Federal attention away from Indian affairs.[34]

Into the breech stepped the Coloradans, alarmed by tales of Indian depredations and the very real murder of five persons just ten miles outside of Denver. In late June, Governor John Evans instructed "the friendly Indians of the plains" to seek shelter near military posts, to prevent their "being killed through mistake." As raiding continued, an increasingly belligerent Evans raised a new regiment of hundred-day volunteers (the Third Colorado Cavalry). To the governor's surprise Black Kettle's band turned over four white prisoners and presented themselves at Fort Lyon, where Major Edward Wynkoop provided food and arranged a meeting with Evans and Chivington. Wynkoop and the Indians emerged from the talks believing that peace was at hand,

FIG. 37. Robert McGee scalped. Though the origins of scalping are disputed, by the eighteenth century both Indians and non-Indians had embraced the practice. Robert McGee was scalped by the Brulés outside Fort Larned in 1864. This photograph was taken about 1890 by E. E. Henry. LIBRARY OF CONGRESS, USZ62-105942.

but Evans, suspicious of an Indian-Confederate alliance, charged that "the great body of them are yet hostile." Any doubts that Chivington, described by one contemporary as "a crazy preacher who thinks he is Napoleon Bonaparte," might seek peace were dispelled by the words and deeds of his superior, Curtis, who recalled Wynkoop in favor of the more malleable Major Scott J. Anthony.[35]

Anxious to further his political fortunes and to use the new recruits before their enlistments expired, Colonel Chivington arrived at Fort Lyon on November 28 intent on attacking Black Kettle's camp of about 550 Southern Cheyennes and Arapahoes. During a rancorous conference, several officers objected to Chivington's upcoming assault, arguing that it would be "murder" and "a disgrace to the United States uniform." Chivington reportedly responded "that he believed it to be right or honorable to use any means under God's heaven to kill Indians that would kill women and children."[36]

That evening, Chivington rode out of Fort Lyon with 700 volunteers (including Major Anthony and 125 members of the garrison) and four mountain howitzers. As dawn broke on the twenty-ninth, they deployed into assault formations outside the Indian encampment at Sand Creek. An incredulous Black Kettle raised both a U.S. flag and a white flag above his tepee, but gunfire from the soldiers quickly disabused the Indians of the idea that further talks were possible. A few Indians made a brief stand in a creek bed above the village; elsewhere, with it "generally understood among the officers and men, that no prisoners would be taken," the volunteers indiscriminately slaughtered men, women, and children. The rabble of the Third Colorado then set about mutilating the corpses. "The bodies were horribly cut up," testified Sergeant Lucien Palmer, of the First Colorado Cavalry, "skulls broken in a good many. . . . I do not think I saw any but what was scalped; saw fingers cut off, saw several bodies with privates cut off, women as well as men." At a cost of nine men killed, thirty-eight others wounded, and a nation's honor lost, Colorado volunteers had butchered between 150 and 200 Cheyennes and Arapahoes, the majority of whom were women and children.[37]

From New Mexico, General Carleton was also endeavoring to secure the tenuous Santa Fe trails against Indian raids. To inflict "a severe drubbing" on the Kiowas and Comanches, he turned once more to his reliable friend Kit Carson. Carson left Fort Bascom on November 12 with 14 officers, 321 enlisted men, 75 Ute and Jicarilla allies, and two mountain howitzers, marching down the Canadian River into Texas. On the morning of the twenty-fifth, they surprised Little Mountain's village. The Kiowas fell back, turning to make a stand near Adobe Walls. Reinforced by several hundred well-armed Kiowas, Comanches, Apaches, and Arapahoes "mounted on first-class horses" and fighting with what Carson described as "more daring and bravery than I have ever before witnessed," the Indians nearly broke the Federal line, which seems to have been saved by the terrifying fire of the howitzers. The battle petering out about dusk, Carson destroyed the village and trudged back to Fort Bascom, stating that he would need a much larger force if he were to go after the same enemy again.[38]

"Feel assured," wrote one beleaguered subdistrict commander, "that this is no trifling Indian war." Indeed it was not, for the previous December perhaps fifteen hundred Cheyenne, Brulé, Oglala, and Arapaho fighters had smoked pipes and determined on war. In the first two months of 1865, they twice ransacked the stage station at Julesburg, Colorado, less than two miles from Fort Rankin. Not a single stagecoach or wagon train reached Denver for over a month, and the telegraph was cut in several places. Nearly fifty people were killed, over a thousand livestock stolen, and a hundred tons of government hay destroyed. A second council meeting, however, somewhat altered the original plan. The associated groups would flee the soldiers' columns and venture north, to join with the Lakotas and Cheyennes.[39]

To coordinate the fighting in the borderlands, general-in-chief Ulysses Grant turned to Pope to oversee a newly created Division of the Missouri, a massive expanse consisting of Missouri, Kansas, Wisconsin, Iowa, Minnesota, and the territories of Nebraska, Colorado, Dakota, and Utah (Arkansas was soon added). Pope began culling men from the fifty-two thousand soldiers in his military department for a major offensive against the Indians. Brigadier General James H. Ford would strike the villages of the Southern Cheyennes, Comanches, Kiowas, Apaches, and Araphaoes. Leading two thousand cavalrymen out of Fort Laramie, Connor, with orders to "bend all your energies to the common object and infuse life, discipline, and effectiveness into the forces under you," would drive north into the Bighorn Mountain country. Alfred Sully would enter the region from Fort Rice with twelve hundred soldiers.[40]

Although troops in Kansas would establish the new forts of Dodge, Wallace, and Hays, that year's campaign turned out to be a hugely expensive bust. Supplies were short, and with the Confederacy's collapse that summer, soldiers deserted in droves. Alarmed army inspectors questioned the skyrocketing costs of Pope's offensives, while revulsion over the Sand Creek massacre led many to question the justice of continued Indian wars. Ford's column thus went nowhere. To the north, ill-advised executions of Indian prisoners at Fort Rice and Fort Laramie, as well as the War Department's misguided attempt to transfer two thousand friendly Sioux from Fort Laramie to Fort Kearny—the latter squarely in the midst of the lands of their bitter enemies, the Pawnees—solidified war factions among the Lakotas, Cheyennes, and Arapahoes. On July 26, men from a huge allied village in the Powder River country swooped down and killed twenty-seven soldiers outside of the stockaded Platte Bridge Station (in present Wyoming). Honor satisfied and more hunting necessary before winter, the village broke up. Meanwhile, while Sully was tramping through the Devil's Lake region of northern Dakota, a rising leader named Sitting Bull convinced three hundred Hunkpapas, Yanktonais, and Sihasapas to make an unsuccessful assault on Fort Rice itself. Sully offered no pursuit as the Lakota and Yanktonai camps broke up for the winter.[41]

That left any tangible successes from the grand offensive in the hands of Connor, whose columns, slowed by three hundred wagons, were to rendezvous in the little understood Rosebud Creek area about September 1. No stranger to harsh methods, Connor had ordered his subordinates to "attack and kill every male Indian over twelve years of age." At the head of one column, Connor established a new post (eventually named Fort Reno) near the Bozeman Trail crossing of the upper Powder River. Probing the area, on August 29 he surprised an Arapaho village but barely held his own against a determined counterattack. As the other troops edged west across the badlands, they found themselves virtually dismounted by a devastating September norther. "Vulture like," Indians harassed the column as it edged its way up the Powder River. The Federal forces finally united on September 24 at Fort Connor, badly in need of fresh mounts, shoes, and uniforms.[42]

For the United States, the time for peace was at hand. Senator Benjamin Wade's Joint Committee on the Conduct of the War issued a scathing denunciation of the Sand Creek massacre, describing Chivington as having "deliberately planned and executed a foul and dastardly massacre which would have disgraced the veriest savage among those who were the victims of his cruelty." The huge costs of Pope's most recent offensive—estimated at $20 million exclusive of salaries— had added to the scandal, and on June 27, the massive Division of the Missouri was broken up. Further, Connor's appalling orders had suggested a nightmarish repeat of Sand Creek. "These instructions are atrocious," wrote Pope. "If any such orders as General Connor's are carried out it will be disgraceful to the Government, and will cost him his commission, if not worse. Have it rectified without delay." As governors busily mustered out their volunteers, more reliable regulars began returning to the frontiers. The civil wars in the borderlands were over.[43]

TEN

The Regulars Return

As Washington demobilized the armies that had preserved the Union and helped to end slavery, regulars replaced volunteers and resumed their vital role in western nation building. With them came a renewed infusion of federal dollars in military and ancillary projects, as well as the expansion in infrastructure, the emergence of long-term business opportunities, and the return of "normalcy" that so many Americans desired after their bloody civil war. Confident that his soldiers would restore order, Major General William T. Sherman assured his friend and superior Lieutenant General Ulysses S. Grant, that "as soon as the Indians see that we have Regular Cavalry among them they will realize that we are in condition to punish them for any murders or robberies."[1]

Cognizant of the army's varied services, in 1866 Congress increased the number of cavalry regiments from six to ten and infantry regiments from nineteen to forty-five. A fifth artillery regiment, created at the outbreak of the Civil War, was also retained. In the process, officers who wanted to remain in military service reluctantly exchanged their elevated Civil War volunteer status (many had accepted appointments in volunteer units) for lower regular army ranks. The War Department staff now included ten bureaus: Adjutant General, Inspector General, Medical, Ordnance, Pay, Quartermaster, and Subsistence departments; the Bureau of Military Justice; the Corps of Engineers; and the Chief

Signal Officer. Although the system made organizational sense, line officers charged that their cousins on the bureau staffs unfairly dominated plum jobs on the East Coast. As Zachary Taylor had lamented a quarter century earlier, "Most of them have been stationed there [in Washington, D.C.] so long that they have lost sight of, & know almost nothing of the wants of troops in the field or on the frontiers." In all, the new army could muster 54,302 officers and men, three times more than that of 1860.[2]

The majority of enlisted personnel continued to be immigrants or sons of immigrants (most had Irish or German roots), were recruited in northern cities, and came from marginal economic backgrounds. "The large majority are driven to enlistment by absolute want," explained one veteran officer. Although it appears there was little in the way of ethnic tensions within the ranks, class-conscious officers and public elites held the men in little esteem. Economically, enlisted personnel did less well than their antebellum predecessors, as a private's base pay ($192 per year before 1871 and $156 per year after that, the latter representing just over $2,600 in 2006 values) was only a fraction of that of a civilian laborer. The disparity was especially pronounced in the borderlands, where prices and wages tended to be higher. Small supplements allotted to soldiers working on extra duty assignments (typically fifty to seventy-five cents per diem) were useful but had the unintended consequence of reinforcing the chasm between civilian and military labor. The results were predictable: in 1874 and 1875, the army calculated that whereas 7,126 soldiers deserted, only 2,685 reenlisted.[3]

The racial composition of the regulars in blue, however, underwent significant change. In recognition of the contributions of 180,000 black soldiers during the Civil War, Congress reserved two cavalry and four (reduced to two in 1869) infantry regiments for African American enlisted personnel, almost all of whom were stationed in the West. Although historians William A. Dobak and Thomas D. Phillips have shown the army to be "one of the most impartial institutions of the day," the black men who joined in the Ninth and Tenth cavalries and Twenty-fourth and Twenty-fifth infantry regiments faced considerable segregation and personal discrimination. "We are not treated as . . . Soldiers but as a lot of dogs," protested one Twenty-fifth Infantry correspondent. Another regular stationed at Fort Shaw, Montana, complained

FIG. 38. Members of the Twenty-fifth Infantry near Fort Keogh, about 1890. African Americans—in this instance from the Twenty-fifth Infantry Regiment—comprised a significant part of the post–Civil War army. Their hodgepodge of different uniform patterns reflected the effect of chronic congressional underfunding of the army rather than an institutional effort to discriminate against them. Some are wearing buffalo robes. LIBRARY OF CONGRESS, USZC4-6161.

that officers "treat enlisted men worse than slaves because they are colored." And General Sherman's confession that the black infantry regiments had been sent to southern Texas and New Mexico "on the theory that that race can better stand that extreme southern climate than our white troops" helped to fuel suspicions that the army deliberately stationed them at unfavorable posts.[4]

African Americans nonetheless saw much to gain from their military service. With sharply restricted opportunities in the civilian sector, the army, with its equal pay and guaranteed food, housing, clothing, and medical care, seemed to many a reasonable option indeed. "To the colored man the service offers a career," explained Secretary of War Redfield Proctor. Most black recruits came from the rural South, and their ranks were leavened by perhaps three thousand Civil War veterans. Slightly younger at age of enlistment than their white counterparts, they deserted less frequently and reenlisted more often, providing a dependable source of manpower for an army desperately short of men. As a group, their greatest weakness was their low literacy rate (in 1870, for instance, the census enumerator at Fort Duncan calculated that 160 of the 222-man African American garrison could not read or write), often forcing officers to assume record-keeping tasks normally relegated to noncommissioned personnel. Many attempted to use the army's nascent system of post schools to correct this deficiency; as one observer put it, black troops were "too much interested in the Garrison School to find time for mischief."[5]

Military necessity and the shortage of quarters meant that black and white units often garrisoned the same post. One observer at Fort Duchesne, Utah, asserted that the different units "fraternize without any fine discrimination as to color." In 1881, the murders of two soldiers—one white and one African American—at San Angelo, Texas, united the mixed command at Fort Concho against a common threat. "We, the soldiers of the U.S. Army, do hereby warn Cow-Boys &c., of San Angela [sic] and vicinity, to recognize our right of way, as just and peaceable men" read a handbill surreptitiously printed on base. "If we do not receive justice and fair play, which we must have, some one will suffer," continued the warning, which was signed "U.S. Soldiers One and All." In other instances, however, the racism that permeated American society was reflected on post. At least one officer refused to allow black troops on the same parade ground as the white men of his unit, and another maintained strict racial segregation among troops assigned to guard duty under his command. And desertion among African American troops at Fort Davis, Texas, increased dramatically following the 1881 arrival of several companies of the all-white First Infantry, further suggesting racial tensions.[6]

Civilian reactions to black military personnel in the borderlands also varied. The relative absence of African Americans among the West's general population, along with the concentration of Indians, Chinese, Mexicans, and Mexican Americans in many communities, mitigated the racism directed at blacks. Adopting a pragmatic view, many residents saw the African American soldiers as being vital to their economic success and personal security. Nonetheless, race sometimes exacerbated the normal animosities between civilians and soldiers. Fearing "a serious conflict between the colored soldiers . . . and the white citizens" in San Antonio, Brigadier General Christopher C. Augur transferred a black company to more distant Fort Clark. In 1885, black troopers from Fort Meade clashed with some residents of nearby Sturgis, Dakota Territory, leading one community leader to label them "a set of reckless desperadoes."[7]

With one exception, the color line in the commissioned ranks in the frontier army barred African Americans from officership for nearly a quarter century following the Civil War. Henry Ossian Flipper, a former slave, overcame the social ostracism of his fellow cadets to become in 1877 the first African American graduate of West Point, ranking fiftieth in a class of seventy-six. Assigned to the Tenth Cavalry, Lieutenant Flipper served at Fort Sill, Fort Elliott, and finally Fort Davis. He seems to have been a good officer, but in handling commissary duties at Davis in 1881, Flipper came up short, and discrepancies in his accounts led to his arrest. Though cleared of embezzlement charges, he had repeatedly misrepresented the status of the accounts and had frantically attempted to conceal the discrepancies, and so a military tribunal found him guilty of five counts of conduct unbecoming an officer and dismissed from the service. The lieutenant subsequently claimed that he had been set up by the post commander, Colonel William R. Shafter, but recent scholarship suggests that "the evidence of his guilt was overwhelming," and that Flipper had "alone compromised his honor." Such was a tragedy, for Flipper's subsequent successes as a mining engineer, consultant, and translator seemed a clear demonstration of his considerable talents. The next African American to graduate from West Point would be John Hanks Alexander, who reported for duty as a second lieutenant in the Ninth Cavalry in 1887.[8]

Following the Civil War, the army continued to carve the nation into divisions, departments, and, as necessary, districts and subdistricts, basing the frequently changing system on an eclectic mix of geography, convenience, seniority, and the numbers of generals in service. That typically meant four divisions: Atlantic, South (or, in some years, the Gulf), Missouri and Pacific, and each was usually headed by a major general. The two latter divisions focused directly on the borderlands. The Missouri consisted of the departments of Dakota, Missouri, and Platte, and the Pacific broke down into the departments of Arizona, California, and Columbia. As part of congressional reconstruction, for a time the

War Department linked Texas (along with Louisiana) to the Fifth Military District, then shifted it to the Division of the Missouri. In normal years, a brigadier general headed each department, and officers engaged in indecorous behind-the-scenes skirmishing for preferred slots.[9]

Texas posed the most complex challenges. During the Civil War, Napoleon III had sent twenty thousand French troops into Mexico to help establish Archduke Ferdinand Maximilian's puppet government. With the collapse of the Confederacy, Grant dispatched Major General Philip Sheridan and fifty-two thousand veterans to the Rio Grande, suggesting that "he was not to be over-cautious about provoking" Maximilian's forces. Other schemes envisioned having Brigadier General John M. Schofield, a West Point graduate highly recommended by Grant, organize four divisions of volunteers (former Confederates as well as Federals) to cross the border in support of the ousted Benito Juárez regime. Eager to wrest control of foreign policy away from the army, Secretary of State William Seward arranged instead for Schofield's dispatch to Europe, with instructions "to get your legs under Napoleon's mahogany, and tell him he must get out of Mexico." Meanwhile, Sheridan shipped condemned or surplus military equipment to the Rio Grande for collection by Juárez's soldiers. The shaky empire indeed collapsed and Maximilian was executed in 1867; a satisfied Sheridan doubted "whether such results could have been achieved without the presence of an American army on the Rio Grande."[10]

Even with the restoration of Juárez, the Rio Grande remained an imperfect international barrier. The ebb and flow through the lands south of the Nueces River of emigrants and Indians, legitimate seekers of opportunity as well as those with more nefarious designs, challenged the social, political, and economic order. Cattle theft was endemic on both sides of the border. To patrol these regions, by 1868 soldiers had reoccupied forts that had been abandoned during the war, Duncan, McIntosh, Brown, and Ringgold Barracks.

The army also had to balance the expectations of congressional reconstruction against the desires of most white Texans. Operating through the Freedmen's Bureau, it offered African Americans and Unionists desperately needed assistance against the onslaughts of white racists and conservatives hoping to restore the antebellum order. But the bluecoats could not be everywhere; "Away from the influence of federal troops and federal bayonets," wrote William E. Strong, inspector general for the Freedmen's Bureau, "I assure you there is a fearful state of things. . . . [I]f the United States troops were removed from Texas no northern man, nor any person who had ever expressed any love for northern institutions or for the government of the United States, could remain with safety, and the condition of the freed people would be worse beyond comparison than it was before the war and when they were held in bondage." As a result, most troops in Texas were initially stationed with an eye toward reducing lawlessness rather than fighting Indians.[11]

Appointed to command the Fifth Military District in March 1867, Phil Sheridan, a combative Irishman who had been held back a year at West Point for punching out a fellow classmate, had been in the thick of the fighting at Perryville, Stones River, Chickamauga, Missionary Ridge, Winchester, and Cedar Creek. No friend of racial equality but determined to assert federal authority, the crusty Sheridan set about his task with his characteristic pugnacity. "It is strange that over a white man killed by Indians on an extensive frontier the greatest excitement will take place, but over the killing of many freedmen in the settlements nothing is done," he snorted. Similarly, Sheridan suspected that reported Indian depredations had been "manufactured wholesale . . . to affect the removal of troops from the interior to the frontier."[12]

As howls for protection from the Texas borderlands continued (the army attributed twenty-six civilian deaths to Indian attack during the first nine months of 1869), Sheridan and his successors shifted their emphasis toward the West. Increasing demand for livestock, diminishing buffalo herds, larger numbers of illegal whiskey and arms traders (*comancheros*), a wetter climate, and inconsistent government annuities had indeed sparked more Indian raids, especially from renegade bands of young men. After some initial reshuffling, bluecoats reoccupied Fort McKavett and built three new forts: Concho, Griffin, and Richardson. To patrol the long, lonely road from San Antonio to El Paso, regulars returned to other forts the Federals had vacated during the Civil War (Clark, Stockton, Davis, Quitman, and Bliss). These would by and large form the Lone Star State's basic defenses for the next two decades. Between 1867 and 1870, the army reported thirty-eight combat actions against Indians in Texas, at a cost of sixteen killed and twenty-six

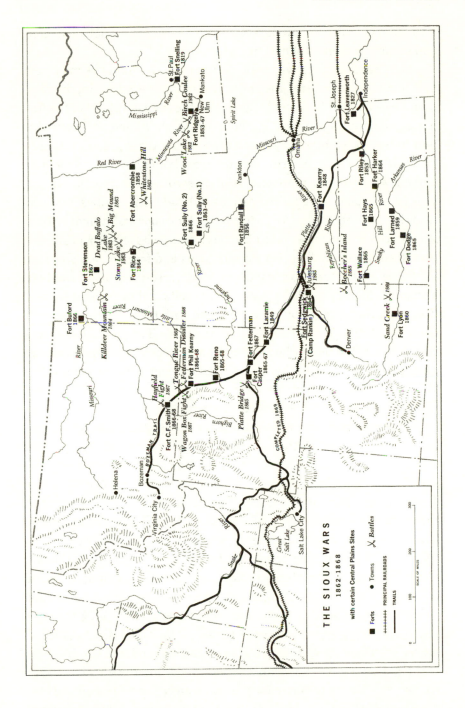

THE SIOUX WARS
1862–1868
with certain Central Plains Sites

■ Forts   ● Towns   ✕ Battles
+++++++ PRINCIPAL RAILROADS
———— TRAILS

SCALE OF MILES
0   100   200   300

wounded. Its claim to have killed 158 Indians was no doubt overstated, and security remained at best uncertain.[13]

Commanding the Division of the Missouri, William Sherman realized that railroads offered the key to controlling his sprawling jurisdiction. The Civil War had vividly illustrated the military utility of the iron horse and encouraged public funding for transportation. By promoting non-Indian development and affording his regulars greater mobility, railroads would help the army dominate the borderlands. And the partnership was mutually profitable: soldiers escorted construction teams, provided supplies, and policed distant railroad communities, and railroads in turn offered cheap transportation for troops and military stores, allowed the army greater latitude to concentrate its smaller posts, and furnished officers with lavish traveling cars and free passes. Sherman thus deployed the army to assist the railroads, asserting that it "would be a national calamity . . . if the work on the Pacific rail road should cease." Conveniently, railroad companies teamed with former Union officers. Grenville M. Dodge, chief engineer for the Union Pacific Railroad, was a close friend of Sheridan who had fought under both Grant and Sherman during the Civil War. In the Union Pacific Eastern Division, President William J. Palmer, Superintendent W. W. Wright, and Chief Engineer Eben Smeed had all served under Sherman.[14]

The partnership epitomized the army's promotion of frontier development, as revealed by the experiences of Cheyenne, Wyoming, and Omaha, Nebraska. In summer 1867, Dodge picked out the new town site of Cheyenne, shortly to become capital of a newly created Wyoming Territory, as a base for his Union Pacific laborers. Cooperating with the venture, soldiers established Fort D. A. Russell, and the associated Cheyenne Depot would become the region's military supply center. By year's end, four thousand people lived there. Similarly, in 1866 the War Department established headquarters for the Department of the Platte in Omaha, insuring the fledgling city a steady flow of federal dollars. Nebraska was granted statehood the following year, and in 1868 the army began erecting a big depot near the rail yards. The federal disbursements, predicted the *Omaha Weekly Herald*, "will go far to stimulate the now rapid settlement of our unoccupied lands, and the direct and indirect benefits we are to derive from it can scarcely be overestimated."[15]

The returning regulars were particularly valuable to borderlands

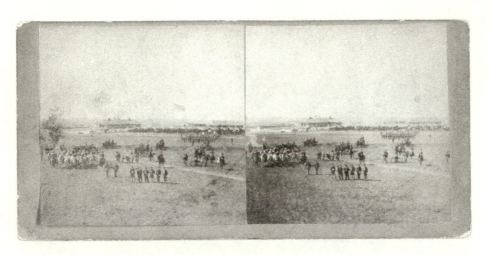

FIG. 39. Fort Harker. Following the Civil War, noted photographer
Alexander Gardner (1821–82), a former employee of Mathew Brady,
toured the west with the Union Pacific Railroad. Here he captures
the garrison of Fort Harker. Some of the post buildings are in the
background. LIBRARY OF CONGRESS, DIG-STEREO-1S00060.

economies strained by long years of civil war. As historian Darlis Miller
has observed, "the army was the single largest purchasing and employment agency in the Southwest." In 1867 alone, army spending in New
Mexico totaled about $2.5 million (roughly $35 million in 2006 terms)—
a figure equivalent to the total value of all livestock in the territory. The
army represented an even more significant part of the Arizona economy,
the roughly $1.5 million spent there in 1867 *alone* exceeding the assessed
property value of the entire territory. No wonder, then, that in calling
for a big new army depot for Denver, the editor of the *Rocky Mountain
News* proclaimed, "Our people have a right to some of the patronage of
the government."[16]

But the military did more than simply hire civilians and line the
pockets of contractors. In Alaska, purchased from Russia in 1867, the
two-hundred-man garrison, occasionally supplemented by a Treasury
Revenue vessel, handed out food to needy civilians and served as virtually the only law and order for hundreds of miles. In 1874–75, regulars assumed a leading role in responding to a locust infestation that

No. 17 Generals Grant, Sherman, Sheridan, Hooker, Harney, Dodge, Gibbon, and Potter at Fort Sanders.

FIG. 40. Army–Union Pacific meeting at Fort Sanders, Wyoming, 1868. The regular army was crucial to railroad construction in the Trans-Mississippi, as reflected in this army–Union Pacific meeting. Among the participants were Phil Sheridan (second to left), Ulysses S. Grant (seventh from left, with hands on fence), William T. Sherman (leaning on stile), William S. Harney (with white beard and cape), and Union Pacific official Thomas Durant (next to Harney, with hands clasped). LIBRARY OF CONGRESS, USZ62-110715.

devastated huge chunks of Kansas, Nebraska, Colorado, and the Dakotas. Brigadier General Edward O. C. Ord, commanding the Department of the Platte and vice chair of the Nebraska Relief and Aid Society, coordinated the distribution of sixteen thousand coats, twenty thousand pairs of shoes and boots, eight thousand blankets, and untold numbers of socks, hats, and pants from army inventories. Such missions could be dangerous: of an eighty-two-man patrol sent out from Fort Shaw in 1871 to arrest bootleggers along the Canadian border, seventy lost parts of either their feet or hands to frostbite.[17]

The post–Civil War career and services of John Schofield, the erst-
while diplomat in blue, exemplified the army's multiple interests. Upon
his return from his diplomatic mission to Europe, Schofield had overseen reconstruction efforts in Virginia before being named secretary of
war by the embattled President Andrew Johnson. From 1869 to 1870,
he commanded the Department of the Missouri, then served a six year
stint as head of the Division of the Pacific, a service broken by four
months (beginning in December 1872) spent inspecting the security
measures needed to defend a United States presence in the Hawaiian
Islands. Correctly identifying Pearl Harbor "as the key to the Central
Pacific Ocean," upon his return stateside, Schofield lobbied Congress
as to Hawaii's strategic importance.[18]

Immediately after the Civil War, many Americans had hoped
to avert further conflict in the borderlands. In late 1865, Cheyenne,
Arapaho, Kiowa, Comanche, and Plains Apache emissaries agreed to
withdraw south of the Arkansas River in exchange for annuities and
reservations in Kansas and present-day Oklahoma. An extended inspection tour of his sprawling command, however, convinced Sherman that
neither Indians nor non-Indians were ready for a permanent peace.
Skeptical of "parties of whites who would be benefited by an Indian
war," he suspected that "every little drunken quarrel or horse-thieving
is exaggerated into a big bug-bear." The misdeeds of his countrymen
notwithstanding, Indians must give way to what Sherman perceived to
be his nation's superior civilization.[19]

The general had good reason for his doubts about the peace talks, for
the influential Oglala leader Red Cloud was organizing dissident Lakotas,
Cheyennes, and Arapahoes into a formidable military coalition. On the
Bozeman Trail, Colonel Henry B. Carrington's Eighteenth Infantry
Regiment pushed northwest from Fort Reno (formerly Fort Connor) and
in 1866 established Fort Phil Kearny and Fort C. F. Smith. Reflecting
their exposed positions, each was stockaded—an unusual feature for
Trans-Mississippi forts. A corporate lawyer by training, Carrington had
spent most of the Civil War behind a staff desk; as Indian raids grew
more frequent, subordinates like Captain William J. Fetterman, a brazenly confident veteran twice brevetted for combat service, bristled at
their commander's inactivity.[20]

On December 6, having been prodded into adopting a more

FIG. 41. Major General William T. Sherman (1820–91). LIBRARY OF CONGRESS, DIG-CWPBH-00593.

aggressive posture, Carrington dispatched fifty-five men in response to an attack on a wood-gathering party at Fort Kearny. The regulars scampered back to safety after two were killed and five wounded. Fifteen days later the bluecoats would not be so lucky. Detailed to relieve another wood train that had come under attack, Fetterman and eighty men blundered into an ambush, orchestrated in part by a rising Oglala tactician, Crazy Horse. Every soldier and civilian died within an hour. Upon learning of the Indian victory, an angry and embarrassed Sherman wrote infamously: "We must act with vindictive earnestness against the Sioux, even to their extermination, men, women & children."[21]

Fortunately, such revenge would not transpire. In January 1867, Senator James R. Doolittle's joint congressional committee published a lengthy report documenting the government's missteps and recommending that the Indian Office be kept separate from the War Department. In the wake of the Doolittle Report and the sensational publication of Sherman's impolitic remarks, President Johnson dispatched a new peace commission and placed the army on the defensive in the north. The army consoled itself by building several new forts: Totten to the road from Minnesota to Montana, Buford and Stevenson to the Missouri River line, and Shaw and Ellis in Montana. Fort Fetterman reinforced the Bozeman Trail.[22]

No such directives prevented offensives to the south, so Sherman geared Major General Winfield Scott Hancock's Department of the Missouri for war. "Hancock the Superb" had turned back Pickett's charge at Gettysburg and hoped that a victory against the Indians would promote western development as well as his own lofty political ambitions. Concluding that the Cheyennes and Oglalas "intended to make war," he burned their abandoned lodges and dispatched Lieutenant Colonel George A. Custer with six troops of the Seventh Cavalry in futile chase. The expedition ground to an unceremonious halt, however, when troopers deserted in droves and Custer took an unauthorized absence in the midst of the campaign for a rendezvous with his wife. For a time, Hancock's belligerence only intensified attacks on the western travel lines, but peace factions among the southern plains tribes regained their ascendancy as economic realities dictated the shift of efforts from military affairs to winter preparations. In October, Kiowa, Comanche, Plains Apache, Arapaho, and Southern Cheyenne delegates affixed their marks to the Medicine Lodge Creek Treaty. As outlined in the complex document, they agreed to accept reservations in present Oklahoma and make peace in return for a mountain of alluring presents, renewed guarantees of government annuities, the promise of schools, teachers, and mechanics to assist in acculturation, and the right to hunt south of the Arkansas River "so long as the buffalo may range thereon in such numbers as to justify the chase."[23]

FIG. 42. Red Cloud. A charismatic warrior-statesman, Red Cloud (1822–1900) formed military coalitions that forced the government to withdraw its Bozeman Trail posts in 1868. Following these victories, he sought to protect his and his people's interests through diplomacy. LIBRARY OF CONGRESS, USZ62-91032.

The situation was significantly different in the north, where Indians attending that summer's sun dance agreed to target the forts in the Powder River country. The Cheyennes and Arapahoes directed their efforts against Fort C. F. Smith, and the Oglalas, Minneconjous, and Sans Arcs rode against Fort Phil Kearny. But resulting skirmishes in the Hay Fight (northeast of C. F. Smith) and the Wagon Box Fight (five miles from Phil Kearny) were in no way decisive, for the Indians' dividing their attacks, plus the newly modified breech-loading Springfield 1866 model rifles carried by the infantry, had minimized chances for any repetition of the previous year's spectacular triumphs. A defiant Red Cloud nevertheless set the abandonment of the Bozeman Trail posts as his price for peace. Ironically, accepting such terms, though humiliating to the regulars, was consistent with national objectives. Congress had determined to use the army to institute reconstruction throughout the former Confederacy (about 40 percent of the army was detailed to these duties in 1867), so few troops could be spared to fight Indians. Moreover, protecting Union Pacific railroad teams demanded higher priority than the Bozeman Trail. The army thus evacuated the forts of C. F. Smith, Reno, and Phil Kearny, prompting Red Cloud and other northern plains leaders to sign the Treaty of Fort Laramie (1868). Containing provisions similar to those of the Medicine Lodge agreements, the document promised "that the country north of the North Platte river and east of the summits of the Big Horn mountains shall be held and considered to be unceded Indian territory."[24]

Surprisingly, the truce reached at Fort Laramie would hold for nearly a decade. To the south, however, even Indian superintendent Thomas Murphy admitted that "war is surely upon us" after Cheyennes killed fifteen men and raped five women in a series of attacks on western Kansas ranches and farms between August 10 and 12, 1868. Sheridan, whose rigorous application of congressional reconstruction in Texas and Louisiana had led the more conservative President Johnson to insist on his transfer to the Department of the Missouri, had no doubts that the problem required a military solution: "I am of the belief that these Indians require to be soundly whipped, & the ringleaders in the present trouble hung, their ponies killed, & such destruction of their property as will make them very poor."[25]

Sheridan dispatched Major George A. Forsyth and fifty scouts to patrol the railroad line in western Kansas. Meanwhile, Lieutenant Colonel Sully marched south from Fort Dodge into Indian Territory with five hundred men supported by thirty supply wagons. Concluding that he could never chase down the Indians with his cumbersome wagon train, Sully withdrew after just a week in the field. But on September 17, seven hundred Cheyennes jumped Forsyth along the Arikaree Fork of the Republican River. Forsyth's men dug in on an island and held off the attackers for eight days, until they were relieved by African American soldiers of the Tenth Cavalry. Sheridan heated up his rhetoric. Not only should they be made poor ("Burn their lodges, kill their ponies"), but they should be exterminated: in dealing with these Indians of the southern plains, he told Lieutenant Colonel Luther P. Bradley, "I want you to kill all you can."[26]

By mid-October, broad plans for a winter campaign were complete. Near Fort Cobb, Colonel William B. Hazen would establish a refuge for those Indians seeking peace. Field operations would begin "as soon as the failure of the grass and the cold weather forces the scattered bands to come together to winter in the milder latitudes south of the Arkansas." As the campaign opened, Major Andrew W. Evans marched east from Fort Bascom with 563 men and four mountain howitzers. Major Eugene Carr led twelve troops of cavalrymen (about 650 men) east and south from Fort Lyon. These columns were designed to drive the Indians into the operation's main force, commanded by Sully and accompanied by Sheridan: eleven companies of the Seventh Cavalry, five infantry companies, a dozen Osage scouts, and, in a departure from the army's normal reluctance to use state troops, the Nineteenth Kansas Volunteer Cavalry.[27]

The winter operations, "deemed impracticable and reckless by old and experienced frontiersmen," produced notable results. The most significant combat action came against Black Kettle's Cheyennes. Having survived the disaster at Sand Creek four years earlier, Black Kettle had nestled the fifty-one lodges of his camp into a bend of the Washita River. Shortly after daybreak on November 21, Custer's Seventh Cavalry swept through the surprised village. The luckless Black Kettle, who had only a week earlier attempted to renew negotiations at Fort Cobb, fell early in the fray. Soldiers then began burning the lodges and slaughtering nearly nine hundred ponies so as to prevent their recapture. But in his determination to assault the community before its inhabitants escaped, Custer had not reconnoitered the area, and several Cheyenne, Arapaho, and Kiowa encampments lay just downstream. Hundreds of angry fighters now threatened Custer's scattered command, and no trace of Major Joel Elliott and a squad of seventeen men, who had ridden off in chase of some villagers, could be found. As the regimental band struck up "Ain't I Glad to Get Out of the Wilderness," Custer's troopers mounted up and rode to safety, taking fifty-three women and children as prisoners. Although Custer claimed to have killed 140 Indians, a figure of half that number seems more plausible, with the majority being women and children. Only later was it determined that Elliott's squad had been annihilated, bringing army casualties to thirty-three.[28]

Save for this dramatic early encounter, Sheridan's war soon became a contest of resources, one that the regulars were sure to win. Near the junction of the North Canadian River and Wolf Creek, regulars established Camp Supply, which would become central to future southern plains operations. As supplies ran out, the soldiers returned to field depots, refitted and recouped from their losses, and returned to the march, a luxury the Indians could not afford. On a snowy Christmas Day at Soldier Spring (present southwestern Oklahoma), Evans destroyed the property and winter stores of a Comanche village. Keeping up the pressure through the following summer, in July 1869 Major Carr whipped the Cheyenne Dog Soldiers at Summit Springs, Colorado. Comanches, Kiowas, Arapahoes, and finally Cheyennes turned themselves in at Camp Supply and Fort Bascom, Fort Cobb, and Fort Sill. Even so, from the army's perspective not all had gone well. Lurid tales of the affair at the Washita reinforced disenchantment among some quarters with the nation's armed forces. Leadership had been spotty; supply mix-ups and delays had been the norm rather than the exception; hundreds of animals had died of exposure; and the failure to attend to the Elliott party engendered enormous resentment among Custer's army rivals.[29]

Warfare had also broken out in the Department of the Columbia, where regulars, volunteers, and government officials initially seemed incapable of defeating the Northern Paiutes. "There was much dissipation amongst a good many officers, and there seemed to be a general apathy amongst them, and indifference to the proper discharge of duty," recalled Lieutenant Colonel George Crook, dispatched in 1866 to take charge of the troubled District of Boise. A mediocre student at West Point, Crook had served in the Rogue River campaigns before compiling a distinguished Civil War record. Keenly interested in Indian ways and manners, the energetic, bewhiskered Crook, whose endurance and skills as an outdoorsman were becoming legendary within the army, drove himself and his men hard. Between December 1866 and August 1868, he and his men reported forty combat engagements and claimed to have killed 329 Indians, wounded 22, and captured 225. Chastened by the horrific experience, eight hundred others surrendered. For his efforts, Crook was given command of the Department of the Columbia.[30]

In New Mexico and Arizona, scattered rancheros, mining ventures, and travelers on the road west of El Paso continued to pose lucrative opportunities for Apaches to seize plunder and exhibit their military skills. Fort Bayard, established in 1866 to guard the Pinos Altos mining region, deterred few raiders, and the return of the Chokonen war leader Cochise from Mexico three years later intensified the violence. Denouncing Washington's failure to exterminate any and all Indian threats, editors of Prescott's *Weekly Arizona Miner* charged that "the government skull is mighty thick, and its sympathies appear to be with the Indians." By 1870, the regulars had reported 170 combat engagements in Arizona and New Mexico since 1865, but with greater Apacheria now sliced into three separate commands—Texas, the Division of the Missouri (New Mexico), and the Division of the Pacific (Arizona)—coordinating military efforts was difficult.[31]

The army's dim views of the region and its inhabitants magnified the tensions. Residents of southern Arizona, muttered Brigadier General Edward O. C. Ord, were "a vicious renegade population of Texan Union haters" whose murders of innocent Indians provoked conflict. "Almost the only paying business the white inhabitants have in that Territory is supplying the troops," he added later. "Hostilities are therefore kept up with a view to protecting inhabitants most of whom are supported by the hostilities. Of course their support being derived from the presence of troops, they are continually asking for more." Echoing a refrain that Secretary of War Charles Conrad had sung nearly two decades earlier, Sherman recommended that the government abandon Arizona altogether.[32]

Frustrated by what they believed to be the public's ingratitude for

FIG. 43. George Crook. Crook (1828–90) was one of the
army's most successful borderlands campaigners.
NATIONAL ARCHIVES, 111-SC-87737.

their efforts, optimistic frontier regulars hoped that Ulysses S. Grant's
election as president in 1868 heralded better times. One of their own, the
unassuming Grant had promised to end the long-standing controversy
concerning the secretary of war's authority over the army and would
surely adopt the army's approach to Indian affairs. In some ways, Grant

performed as they had hoped, sponsoring efforts to return the Office of Indian Affairs to the War Department, appointing his longtime military secretary, Ely S. Parker, as commissioner of Indian Affairs, and naming former Major General Jacob D. Cox to head the Interior Department. Though Parker's office would be troubled by the financial scandals that permeated Grant's administration, both he and Cox were sympathetic to army interests.[33]

But Grant often disappointed his old comrades. The president rescinded instructions that would have given Sherman, his successor as commanding general, effective control over the army, a decision that embittered his old friend and left unresolved a problem that would haunt the army for the rest of the century. Soldiers also found Grant's much-heralded "Peace Policy" to be extremely unsettling. Attempting to transform the tribes and depoliticize the Indian Office, Grant handed over many agency appointments to religious groups, including the Quakers. Skeptical regulars dismissed the practice of relying on church-sponsored agents as dangerously naïve. "I am utterly powerless to help you by order or advice," fumed Sherman to one frustrated western subordinate. "Do the best you can."[34]

As the Grant administration attempted to implement the Peace Policy, Congress sought further military reductions even as it was depending on the army to reconstruct the former Confederate states. Ironically, the army received little political credit for this role; to many Democrats, reconstruction served to confirm fears that the army could be used as an instrument of federal tyranny. Recalling themes of old, New York's Fernando Wood declared it "contrary to the genius of the country to keep up a standing army in a time of profound peace." Officers were characterized as "idle vagabonds who are so well paid and do nothing." The Dakota Territory's delegate, former Indian agent Walter A. Burleigh, denounced the $30 million spent prosecuting the recent wars against the Sioux as having "had no good effect whatever." Quartermaster and commissary expenditures "might as well be thrown into the [Missouri] river." In a measure that enjoyed bipartisan support, Congress eliminated twenty infantry regiments in March 1869. Reflecting the deep national uncertainties about reconstruction, frontier representatives showed no more inclination to support a larger army than their more easterly counterparts.[35]

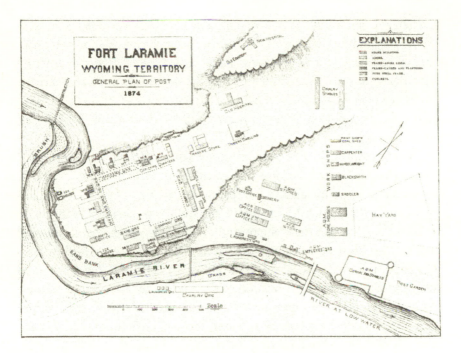

FIG. 44. Fort Laramie, 1874. Most army posts west of the Mississippi River had no stockades or interior defenses, but were loosely organized around a parade ground. NATIONAL ARCHIVES, 111-SC-101886.

Events in Montana further tarnished the army's reputation. Responding to depredations attributed to the Piegan Indians, Sheridan instructed Major Eugene M. Baker "to strike them hard." In early January 1870, Baker did just that, his men pouring a deadly fire into a Piegan village along the Marias River. Baker's command slaughtered 173 Piegans and rounded up 140 prisoners and lost only one man of its own. But Baker had attacked the wrong village, and this camp's chief, Heavy Runner, was gunned down while waving an agreement he had reached with the Indian Office. Equally embarrassing was the number of children and women killed: Baker admitted fifty-three; Vincent Colyer, secretary to the Board of Indian Commissioners, set the number nearly three times that.[36]

The public recoiled in the face of the massacre. Recalling controversy over the earlier affair at the Washita River, reform-minded Wendell Phillips identified "three savages upon the Plains . . . Baker, General

Custer, and at the head of all, General Sheridan." Editors of the *New York Times* branded the affair as "both a crime and a blunder"; Representative Daniel Voorhees (D-Ind.) charged Sheridan with being "stained with the blood of innocent women and children." A bitter administration critic, Voorhees vowed that he "shall not vote for one dollar of an appropriation that upholds such a system of warfare as the indiscriminate massacre of all ages and both sexes."[37]

Congressional critics of the regular army smelled blood. John A. Logan (R-Ill.), chair of the House Committee on Military Affairs, led the 1870 charge. A politician and lawyer by profession, "Black Jack" Logan possessed a flair for battle and during the Civil War had risen to the rank of major general. Yet many suspected that he was now seeking revenge against the West Pointers who had denied him further advancement. Claiming that the most recent reductions had left the army "the most numerously officered organization in the world," Logan sought to eliminate officers rendered supernumerary by the previous year's legislation. Current practice, he quipped, provided for "a brigadier general of bean soup." Congress agreed, cutting the number of major generals to three and brigadier generals to six, reducing the staff bureaus, and limiting enlisted personnel to thirty thousand. As had been the case a year earlier, borderlands senators, with the exception of Senator William M. Stewart (R-Nev.), who raised passionate objections, were no more inclined to support the army than legislators from other parts of the country.[38]

The new round of reductions stretched the army to the limit. Belatedly acknowledging that troubles in the "chronic sore of Arizona" were not going away, in April 1870 the War Department carved that territory into a separate military department within the Division of the Pacific. Commanding the new department, Brevet Major General George Stoneman offered food and protection to those Apaches who eschewed violence. But few white Arizonians appreciated these gestures, and twelve months later an ugly mob swept down on a Pinal and Aravaipa Apache *rancheria* at Camp Grant, slaughtering over a hundred Indians and carrying off twenty-nine children into slavery. At the insistence of Governor Anson P. K. Safford, the War Department transferred Lieutenant Colonel Crook from Oregon to replace Stoneman.[39]

Peace emissaries from Washington, in the form of the humanitarian Vincent Colyer and Brigadier General Oliver O. Howard, twice forced Crook to call off offensives as the government established reservations at Tularosa (New Mexico), Fort Bowie, San Carlos, Camp Verde, and Camp Date Creek. But depredations attributed to Apaches and Yavapais continued: in the year ending September 1872, fifty-four raids claimed forty-four lives, and over five hundred stock were stolen. On November 15, freed of Indian Office constraints, Crook finally took the field. Employing dozens of allied Indian scouts and using mules to carry supplies and enhance mobility, his columns swarmed over the Tonto Basin. "The trail must be stuck to and never lost," he insisted. The largest combat engagement came on December 28 at Skull Cave, where Captain William H. Brown trapped nearly a hundred of Nanni-Chaddi's Apache followers. "Never have I seen such as hellish spot as was the narrow little space in which the hostile Indians were now crowded," wrote Lieutenant John G. Bourke; after seventy-six Apaches were slain, twenty terrified women and children surrendered. The following March, the campaign culminated south of Camp Verde in the Turret Mountains, where soldiers and allied scouts killed another twenty-three Indians. Claiming to represent twenty-three hundred people, Chalipun now turned himself over to Crook. Bourke paraphrased the surrender speech:

> They had never been afraid of the Americans alone, but now that their own people were fighting against them they did not know what to do; they could not go to sleep at night, because they feared to be surrounded before daybreak; they could not hunt—the noise of the guns would attract the troops; they could not cook mescal or anything else, because the flame and smoke would draw down the soldiers; they could not live in the valleys—there were too many soldiers; they had retreated to the mountain tops, thinking to hide in the snow until the soldiers went home, but the scouts found them out and the soldiers followed them. They wanted to make peace, and to be at terms of good-will with the whites.[40]

Sections of the Pacific Northwest were also ablaze. In 1872, the Indian Office had insisted on removing several hundred Modocs from their homelands along the Oregon-California border to the Klamath Reservation. But the army bungled the job of disarming the Indians,

FIG. 45. Fighting the Modoc Indians. The army's failure to prepare for the
kind of tactical environments found in the borderlands often proved
embarrassing, as it did during the Modoc War. Here soldiers take
cover, observed by a reporter. NATIONAL ARCHIVES, 111-SC-82293.

who took refuge in the rugged lava beds south of Tule Lake. A January 17,
1873, attempt to storm what came to be known as the "Stronghold"
turned into an embarrassing defeat; thirty-seven regulars and volunteers were killed or wounded, while not a single Modoc was hit. On
April 11, Brigadier General Edward R. S. Canby, some peace commissioners, and two interpreters met with Modoc leaders. During the talks,
Kintpuash (Captain Jack) whipped out a pistol and shot Canby, a veteran
of three wars and the Utah expedition. Two other whites were also slain.
On the twenty-sixth, the Modocs mauled another reconnaissance force.

"We seem to be acting somewhat in the dark," admitted Major General Schofield, now head of the Pacific Division. "Let there be no more fruitless sacrifices of our troops. There can be no necessity for exposing detachments to such slaughter."[41]

Unrelenting pressure finally overwhelmed the Modocs, whose last holdouts surrendered in early June. Four, including Captain Jack, were hanged by order of a military court; President Grant commuted the sentences of two others to life imprisonment. The government shipped 155 others to present-day Oklahoma. But the entire affair reflected poorly on the army's tactical competence. For nearly six months, a few dozen fighters had held off as many as a thousand soldiers. Bad marksmanship and poor discipline hampered efforts of the enlisted men, and officers had failed to properly coordinate attacks against Modoc riflemen. "Those men don't know how to fight Indians," admitted one regular.[42]

The southern plains represented still another festering wound. Security gains attributable to Sheridan's war of 1868–69 quickly wore off, and Kiowas and Comanches used the Fort Sill Reservation as a sanctuary from which to strike Texas and Kansas. Representative Sidney Clarke (R-Kans.) characterized the army's response as "preposterously absurd and inefficient." In May 1871, Sherman set out from San Antonio with a small escort, determined to see the situation for himself. Near Salt Creek, a hundred Kiowas, including war leaders Satanta, Big Tree, and Satank, allowed the general's party to pass in favor of what seemed to be a much juicier target: ten wagons manned by just twelve teamsters. The Kiowas killed seven of the haulers, plundered the wagons, and herded forty-one captured mules back north. Enraged by news of the incident, Sherman hurried on to Fort Sill, and in a tense confrontation on the garrison commander's front porch, ordered the Kiowa leaders (who had brazenly returned to their reservation) arrested. A Jacksboro, Texas, jury convicted Satanta and Big Tree, but Governor Edmund J. Davis commuted their executions in favor of a term in the state prison. The affair gained national attention, with reformers and Indian agents blaming the trouble on the army's "demoralizing influence."[43]

Kickapoo, Mescalero, and Lipan Apache incursions from Mexico also disrupted security. The solution, army officials believed, lay in allowing regulars to enter Mexico in pursuit of fleeing raiders. To deal with the crisis, President Grant transferred Colonel Ranald B. Mackenzie,

FIG. 46. Ranald Mackenzie. Ulysses S. Grant called Mackenzie (1840–89), who graduated at the head of his West Point class in 1862, the army's "most promising young officer." Plagued by mental instability, Mackenzie would be forced into a premature retirement in 1884. LIBRARY OF CONGRESS, USz62-77935.

whom he would later dub the army's "most promising young officer," and seven companies of his Fourth Cavalry Regiment to Fort Clark. Acting on verbal assurances of support from Sheridan and Secretary Belknap, on the evening of May 17 Mackenzie led nearly four hundred troopers, a mule train laden with five days' rations, and a screen of allied

Seminole-Negro scouts across the Rio Grande. The next morning, they surprised some Indians at Remolino, forty miles west of Piedras Negras. Mackenzie knew that most of the warriors were away, but the attack went ahead nonetheless. The soldiers killed nineteen Indians, took another forty captive, and torched scores of lodges and camp supplies. "We just about exterminated what we did not bring back," wrote a civilian scout. "The village looked like a cyclone had struck it."[44]

Having ridden 160 miles in thirty-two hours, the regulars hustled back across the Rio Grande. Mackenzie remained bellicose; though he hoped to avoid a war with Mexico, he reasoned that "this plundering might as well be stopped now as later." Sheridan and the department commander, General Augur, backed Mackenzie's action, but other army men expressed considerable doubts regarding its propriety. In the end, Mexico's official reaction—which did not come until January 1874—was fairly muted, merely insisting that Texans had vastly exaggerated the size and scope of the Indian raids.[45]

Although the eight years immediately following the Civil War were less bloody than those between 1861 an 1865, they nevertheless reflected the longer-term increase in violent confrontations between Indians and non-Indians. Indeed, the frequency of combat actions (589 between 1866 and 1873, resulting in 367 soldiers killed and another 481 wounded) in Oregon, Texas, the far Southwest, the southern plains, and along the Bozeman Trail had badly strained army resources, and its leaders had not adopted any organizational or tactical changes that might have improved the army's effectiveness in borderlands combat. Buffeted by criticisms of its controversial (and largely unwanted) association with congressional reconstruction, this very conventional army was only barely able to handle its multiple responsibilities. As the borderlands became more populated, newcomers naturally demanded government services. The coming years would sorely test the army's ability to fulfill their expectations.[46]

ELEVEN

Testing the Peace Policy

"Get out, gentlemen, get out—the orders are to close our doors!" shouted a midlevel manager to a panicked crowd at Jay Cooke and Co.'s Washington branch office on September 18, 1873. That morning, the firm, having overreached itself in its efforts to finance the Northern Pacific Railroad, had been forced to suspend operations when it could not come up with a million dollars to meet the demands of several prominent creditors. Spooked by the failure of one of the nation's leading investment houses, shareholders immediately attempted to redeem their stocks, bonds, and bank deposits. "Everything went down," explained the *New York Times*. The nation's deepest economic depression to date had begun.[1]

The crisis directly impacted frontier military affairs. Faced with falling government revenues, Congress searched for ways to cut spending, and the House Appropriations Committee found the U.S. Army a convenient target. In early January 1874, committee chair William A. Wheeler (R-N.Y.) proposed slashing $4 million from army expenditures, largely by funding only twenty-five thousand enlisted men. In justifying a measure that would reduce the army's strength by five thousand soldiers, he wondered "how far the Government ought to go in protecting adventurous men, who push out beyond the bounds of civilization, often for the very purpose of inciting Indian outrages, in order that they may invoke the military arm of the Government, and then profit by the attendant pecuniary expenditures. It would startle the American people," he explained, "if they could mathematically compute the expense of protecting the very small minority of their population residing, for example, in the Territories of Washington, Montana, and Dakota." Commanding general Sherman's ill-timed quip that he would "knock two regiments of cavalry from our estimates" if Mexico would take back Arizona did the army's cause little good.[2]

Evincing a growing recognition of the military's importance to their region, western delegates howled in protest. "You cannot reduce the force of the Army along our western frontier," asserted Charles W. Kendall (D-Nev.), "without endangering the safety of those settlements and the lives of a people who found that vast country a wilderness, and have built up instead prosperous, powerful, and advancing commonwealths." Arizona's Richard C. McCormick (Unionist Party) pointed out the army's special importance to borderlands nation building. Added James Nesmith (D-Ore.), "I feel that my duty to my constituency requires me to enter my protest against any proposed reduction of the military forces now employed for the protection of the frontier." The army was "wholly inadequate" to meet the needs of his state, contended Nebraska's Lorenzo Crounse (R).[3]

Chairman Wheeler struck back angrily: "All gentlemen who speak on that side of the question [assume] that of necessity, we must have Indian troubles; that we are bound to have Indian wars, requiring additional troops to be sent to the frontier. Now, there is no ground whatever for assuming that such a necessity is to arise." Wheeler and the House leadership thus rammed through the cutbacks. In the Senate, army supporters—including eight of the ten frontier lawmakers who voted on the issue—also failed to delete language capping the number of enlisted men at twenty-five thousand. In June 1874 President Ulysses S. Grant signed the measure into law. In the preceding five years, the army had been reduced by half, and War Department spending as a proportion of the total federal budget (now roughly 15 percent) had fallen to levels not seen since Thomas Jefferson's administration. Regulars lamented that they were now scattered about in too many small posts to do anything very effectively. "Local interests everywhere on the frontier require protection," groused John Schofield. "Posts established for that purpose can not be abandoned without the most strenuous opposition from citizens in the vicinity . . . and their representatives in Congress."4

To make matters worse for the army, long-running disputes over the respective powers of the secretary of war and commanding general deprived it of its most prestigious defender, William Sherman. In 1869, Grant had selected William W. Belknap, formerly a brigade commander in Sherman's Army of the Tennessee, as his war secretary. Though Sherman had initially approved of the choice, the relationship quickly soured, Belknap infuriating his old chief by issuing orders, transfers, and leaves of absences without going through Sherman's office. In May 1874, Belknap happily granted Sherman permission to transfer his headquarters to St. Louis, effective in October. Though his comrades protested that the departure would only hurt the army, Sherman stuck to his guns. Kowtowing to a political hack was "beneath the dignity of my office and character," he grumbled. Packing up his family for St. Louis, the nation's highest-ranking officer thus divorced himself from routine matters of army administration and borderlands affairs.5

So it was that in the early days of summer in 1874, as Sherman prepared to leave Washington and Congress completed its latest army reduction, the fragile peace in Sheridan's Division of the Missouri was eroding. The previous October, Governor Edmund J. Davis had released Satanta and Big Tree from the Texas penitentiary in hopes of improving relations, but depredations attributed to Indians had increased, a surge fueled by the slaughter of thousands of buffalo by hunters cashing in on the latest fashion trends. One aide admitted that the Indians "have ample cause" for war. "The country along the Arkansas is filled with outlaws & desperados, who are killing the buffalos, selling liquor to the Indians, & killing white men when an opportunity offers," he explained. The blame nevertheless fell on the Indians, and in mid-July, the Interior Department authorized a military offensive. The campaign would incorporate troops from the departments of Texas, commanded by Brigadier General Christopher C. Augur, and the Missouri, still led by John Pope. Fearing that any delay might give the Indian Office the time to change its mind, Sheridan overrode Pope's suggestion that the attack be delayed until winter but generally allowed his subordinates broad operational latitude. "I will not sketch out any plan of operations for your cavalry," he notified Pope, "leaving you to exercise your good judgment in this respect."6

The department commanders adopted a similarly hands-off approach. In charge of Kansas, New Mexico, and parts of Colorado and Indian Territory, Pope organized two main columns. Major William R. Price and four troops of the Eighth Cavalry would march down the Canadian River from New Mexico. "If the circumstances . . . permit[ted]," Price was to link up with Colonel Nelson A. Miles, who was to lead four companies of his Eighth Infantry and eight troops of the Sixth Cavalry south from Kansas. "Guided by circumstances as they arise," they were to attack Indians wherever they found them. To spearhead operations from his Department of Texas, Augur brought Mackenzie and his Fourth Cavalry back from the Rio Grande to Fort Concho. Supporting Mackenzie were columns from Fort Griffin and Fort Sill, commanded by the lieutenant colonels George P. Buell and John W. Davidson, respectively.[7]

Operations got off to a confusing start. At Fort Sill, Davidson had been tasked with the ticklish job of separating Indians deemed friendly to the government from those believed to be hostile. In the wake of a skirmish between Davidson's African American troopers and Kiowas and Comanches near the Andarko Agency on August 22–23, nearly five thousand Indians, about a quarter of whom were fighting men, left their reservations. With soldiers now infesting the Texas Panhandle and present western Oklahoma, the struggle became a test of endurance against the summer's searing heat. "One man endeavored to open a vein to drink his blood and another tried to drink his urine," remembered a veteran of Miles's thirsty column. Torrential rains broke the drought on September 7, but the Indians were threatening Miles's supply lines. Captain Wyllys Lyman and the escort to a thirty-six-wagon supply train withstood a three-day siege, saved by Major Price's precipitous arrival from New Mexico. With supplies running low, Miles, Davidson, and Buell limped back to their base camps. As one journalist reported, "The whole country is alive with Indians."[8]

The aloof, meticulous Mackenzie was enjoying better success. At daybreak on September 28, his troopers surprised an encampment of several hundred lodges, mainly Mamanti's Kiowas, Ohamatai's Comanches, and Iron Shirt's Cheyennes, in the rugged beauty of Palo Duro Canyon. In their frantic dash for safety, the Indians abandoned their food, camp equipment, and animals. Burning the lodges and selecting about four hundred of the best Indian mounts as replacements for their own horses, the soldiers slaughtered the remaining one thousand ponies to prevent their recapture.[9]

By October, Buell, Miles, and Price had returned to the field. Buell burned two abandoned villages of nearly five hundred lodges. On November 8, escorting twenty-three empty supply wagons from Miles's column, Lieutenant Frank D. Baldwin discovered a camp of about a hundred lodges belonging to Grey Beard's Cheyennes. Baldwin positioned his tiny mounted contingent on the flanks, formed the wagons into two columns, loaded up his infantrymen, and rolled into the village, routing the inhabitants. Davidson rejoined the pursuit in November, and during one of that winter's devastating ice storms, he lost one hundred of his animals, and 26 of his 160 men reported frostbite. In a final defiant gesture, on January 2, Miles led three companies out west of Fort Sill in a five-week march.[10]

The representation of the Red River campaign in the formulaic western films produced a century later notwithstanding, in reality it had been a contest of logistics rather than open-order battles. The army's private contracting system, which often failed to deliver food and supplies on schedule, caused the soldiers considerable discomfort. But the inability of the more fragile Indian economies to replace losses suffered during their desperate flights took an even greater toll among the Kiowas, Comanches, and Southern Cheyennes. Peace factions returned to favor, and by February 1875 sizeable numbers were surrendering at the Darlington Agency and Fort Sill. Unable to fathom the bureaucratic infighting that delayed a final determination of their fate, about sixty Cheyennes subsequently fled north from Darlington. On April 23, Lieutenant Austin Henely and a troop of the Sixth Cavalry caught them in northwestern Kansas on Sappa Creek, where the soldiers cut down nineteen men and eight women and children. The last holdouts—407 Kwahadi Comanches—gave up on June 2.[11]

Indian military power in the southern plains had been destroyed, but violence continued to plague residents on both sides of the Mexican border. In March 1875, raiders from Mexico struck the little community of Nuecestown (just outside present Corpus Christi), leading the navy to dispatch two small vessels to patrol the lower Rio Grande. Amid mounting tensions with Mexico, Brigadier General Edward O. C. Ord,

Augur's replacement as commander of the Department of Texas, concluded that only strikes into Chihuahua would check Apache raids. Taking his cue from Ord, Captain James F. Randlett waded across the Rio Grande to assist a party of Texas Rangers as they returned from an incursion into Mexico. In May 1876, Ord approved Lieutenant Colonel William F. Shafter's request to cross the border in pursuit of Indians. "We have broken the ice," noted Ord triumphantly. But as demands for manpower on other frontiers mounted, Sherman, who had returned to Washington after a nineteen-month hiatus in St. Louis, reined in his overeager subordinate. "I cannot approve a deliberate purpose to invade Chihuahua," instructed Sherman, "on the theory that its Government is inefficient or in the hands of outlaws and rebels."[12]

Sherman had good reason for wanting to avoid a crisis in the Southwest; he feared a war in the northern regions was imminent, for the Northern Pacific's plan to construct a railroad through Dakota and Montana was causing considerable consternation among the Lakotas and Cheyennes. In 1871, seven infantry companies, accompanied by two Gatling guns, had escorted a surveying party into the Yellowstone River country. Even if Indian signatories to the Treaty of Fort Laramie understood its legal niceties (which obligated them to accept compensation for "the peaceful construction of any railroad"), most considered the destruction of the buffalo herds that would surely accompany the railroad's arrival to be unacceptable. As Red Cloud and Spotted Tail tried to balance requirements of life on reservations with traditional culture, the more defiant Sitting Bull was gathering support. "You are fools to make yourselves slaves to a piece of fat bacon, some hard-tack, and a little sugar and coffee," he admonished his kinsmen who accepted the agencies.[13]

But a nation bent on rapid expansion and development had little interest in discerning the nuances of the Lakota worldview. In the summer of 1872, another Northern Pacific survey team pushed west from Fort Rice, escorted by Colonel David S. Stanley, 586 men, a cannon, and three Gatling guns. A second group, accompanied by Major Eugene Baker and about five hundred soldiers, headed east from Fort Ellis. The two parties had planned to meet along the Powder River, but Baker, whose heavy drinking had dulled his taste for combat, broke off the proposed junction in the wake of a sharp skirmish at Pryor's

Creek (sometimes referred to as the "Battle of Poker Flat"). Anticipating further trouble, soldiers erected Fort Abraham Lincoln, just south of present Bismarck.[14]

The year 1873 saw an even larger foray. On June 20, thirteen hundred soldiers, nearly three hundred wagons, and 353 teamsters, herders, scientists, and newspaper correspondents pushed off from Fort Rice. The Cheyennes and Lakotas had begun to acquire modern firearms, and reports of Indian attacks on August 4 and 11 by the column's most celebrated figure, Lieutenant Colonel George A. Custer, heightened fears that stiff resistance would prevent the settlement that was crucial to the railroad's success. Already beset by unexpectedly high expenses, difficult engineering problems, and sagging bond sales, the Northern Pacific could endure no further trouble. Despite the military's support, the beleaguered company was forced into bankruptcy.[15]

For the Lakotas and Northern Cheyennes, however, the crisis had just begun. That year had seen them fight a pitched battle with their old rivals, the Crows and Nez Perces, and the continuing intertribal conflicts ensured that the army could hire hundreds of auxiliaries eager to reclaim access to their old hunting grounds. Diminishing buffalo herds—the result of greatly increased demographic and economic pressures rather than a consciously designed army plot—intensified the sense of foreboding as bluecoats erected Fort Robinson and Fort Yates to watch the Red Cloud and Standing Rock agencies. Sheridan also determined that the army must establish another fort somewhere in the vicinity of the Black Hills. Unspoken, at least officially, was the desire to follow up on rumors of mineral wealth, where, as the *Bismarck Tribune* promised, "the rills repose on beds of gold and the rocks are studded with precious metal." To lead the expedition, which would pierce the heart of the Great Sioux Reservation, Sheridan turned to George Custer.[16]

Thus on July 2, 1874, the Black Hills Expedition—twelve companies of regulars, over a hundred wagons, three Gatling guns, a cannon, sixteen musicians, sixty-one Indian scouts, four scientists, three journalists, a photographer, Lieutenant Colonel Fred Grant (son of the president), and two "practical miners"—rolled out from Fort Abraham Lincoln. More interested in hunting the ever-decreasing buffalo, Indians distanced themselves from the powerful column, which evolved into an expensive frolic as it wound its way through the spectacular Dakota terrain. The expedition returned to Fort Lincoln eight weeks later, wagons bulging with fossils, hunting trophies, and specimens of flora and fauna. The miners had also found traces of gold, which the press merrily inflated into a new El Dorado. "STRUCK IT AT LAST!" boasted the Yankton *Press and Dakotaian*, "The National Debt to be Paid When Custer Returns." Not to be outdone, the *Chicago Inter-Ocean* avowed "that there is gold here, in quantities as rich as were ever dreamed of." Boosters insisted that Indian title be extinguished as hundreds of prospectors braved the dangers of the Great Sioux Reservation in hopes of striking it rich. Citing "national good faith and honor," Brigadier General Alfred Terry, commanding the newly created Department of the Dakota, sought to check the onslaught of illegal immigration but enjoyed the support of neither Sheridan nor the American public.[17]

The transfer of the veteran George Crook, now a brigadier general, from Arizona to the Department of the Platte sent an unmistakable signal of the federal government's budding interest in the Yellowstone River country. In an effort to settle the debate over the mineral wealth of the Black Hills, the government authorized another scientific team to enter the region, this time from Fort Laramie. Escorting the 1875 party were Lieutenant Colonel Richard I. Dodge, seven troops of cavalry, and a company of infantry. Though deeming cheap-pan mining impracticable, the scientists' technical report predicted that systematic drilling, backed by moderate capital investments, would produce handsome returns; moreover, the area's "wonderfully healthy and invigorating" climate promised to yield "a world of wealth in the splendid grazing." The optimistic *Inter-Ocean* needed no disclaimers. "Golden Sands—That Is What the Black Hills Geological Exploring Expedition Have Found," blared its front-page headline.[18]

By late fall, the Grant administration determined that the Indians must go. On November 9, Indian inspector Erwin C. Watkins gave those seeking a military solution all they needed. Reporting that further diplomacy was useless, he went on to suggest that the army launch a thousand-man expedition that winter, "when the Indians are nearly always in camp and at which season of the year they are the most helpless." Watkins, a Republican Party hack who had served in Secretary of the Interior Zachariah Chandler's political machine in Michigan as well as under both Crook and Sheridan during the Civil War, probably

FIG. 47. Black Hills expedition, 1874. This photograph, by English-
born William H. Illingworth of Custer's camp at Hidden Wood
Creek, gives an idea of the massive size of some army columns.
To gain greater mobility, mules were often substituted for
wagons. NATIONAL ARCHIVES, 77-HQ-264-801.

did little more than sign the document that provided his bosses with
useful cover.[19]

The die was now cast. Correctly anticipating that the Interior Department would turn the matter over to the army, Terry, Crook, and Sheridan
outlined general plans. To converge on suspected Indian haunts, troops
from Terry's department would drive west from Fort Abraham Lincoln;
those from Crook's Department of the Platte would march north from
Fort Fetterman. Sheridan largely removed himself from operational

FIG. 48. Custer and his trophy. Soldiers on the Black Hills expedition of 1874 encountered few Indians, but it afforded them ample opportunities for big-game hunting. Lieutenant Colonel Custer (center) poses with one impressive specimen. LIBRARY OF CONGRESS, USZ62-47876.

oversight. "I am not well enough acquainted with the character of the winter and early springs in your latitude to give any directions," he told Terry, "and you will have to use your own judgment as to what you may be able to accomplish."[20]

But the scheme had failed to adequately account for the rigors of a northern plains winter. As his men shivered in their barracks, Terry, citing heavy snows, called off his effort. On March 1, Crook, Colonel

Joseph J. Reynolds, 883 officers and men, four hundred mules, and eighty wagons sloshed out from Fort Fetterman. They were slowed by the bitter cold, but Reynolds and a cavalry detachment did manage to destroy He Dog's Oglala encampment on the Powder River. In an embarrassing episode (Sheridan dubbed it "shamefully disgraceful"), however, Reynolds left the bodies of two soldiers behind as he hustled back to safety. "These winter campaigns in this latitude should be prohibited," complained Reynolds upon his return. "Cruelty is no name for them. The month of March has told on me more than any five years of my life."[21]

Discouraged army brass readied new summer offensives. This time, three columns—Colonel John Gibbon with 450 men from Fort Ellis; Terry with 925 men, 40 Arikara scouts, and three Gatling guns from Abraham Lincoln; and Crook with 1,047 regulars from Fetterman, later to be joined by 262 Crow and Shoshoni auxiliaries, would converge on the Lakotas and Cheyennes suspected to be in the Yellowstone River Valley. Sheridan nixed Sherman's suggestion that he establish unity of command by extending Crook's Department of the Platte to include all of the affected area, citing the protests that would accompany any shift of federal patronage away from the Department of Dakota. Encouraging his field commanders to rely on their own initiative and judgment, on May 16 he assured Terry of "the impossibility of any large numbers of Indians keeping together as a hostile body for even a week." Sheridan's belief that the Indian coalition would fall apart quickly accurately reflected the consensus view of seasoned frontiersmen.[22]

In that centennial summer, however, the consensus was wrong. That spring, the nonagency Lakotas and Cheyennes had determined to stick together and follow the leadership of Sitting Bull. Agency Indians coming out for their traditional summer hunts would be welcomed into the coalition. Remembered one Cheyenne:

> He [Sitting Bull] had come now into admiration by all Indians as a man whose medicine was good—that is, as a man having a kind heart and good judgment as to the best course of conduct. He was considered as being altogether brave, but peaceable. He was strong in religion—the Indian religion. . . . We supposed that the combined camps would frighten off the soldiers. We

hoped thus to be freed from their annoyance. Then we could separate again into the tribal bands and resume our quiet wandering and hunting.[23]

By early June, scouts brought word of the soldiers' approach, evidence confirmed by Sitting Bull's spiritual visions. The council selected Crazy Horse to organize the upcoming battle. On the afternoon of the seventeenth, outfitted in their finest war regalia, more than 750 Lakotas and Cheyennes fell on Crook along the Rosebud Creek. The government's Crow allies blunted the main assault, but the battle soon devolved into an elastic, mobile affair that gave the Lakotas and Cheyennes every advantage. Crook's subsequent retreat, and uncharacteristically cautious behavior over the next six weeks, suggests that the fight at the Rosebud had unnerved him. As he later admitted, "I am at a loss what to do."[24]

Sixty miles to the north, Terry and Gibbon, operating independently from Crook, had linked up on the Yellowstone River eight days before the fight at the Rosebud. Though unaware of Crook's fate, they knew of ominous political developments in Washington courtesy of Custer, whom Terry had insisted accompany the expedition. Earlier that spring, Custer had testified about War Department corruption in the scandal that had forced Secretary of War Belknap's resignation (which in turn made possible the return of General Sherman from his self-imposed exile). But House Democrats, enjoying their recently gained majority, were still on the warpath. In late March, the Military Affairs Committee, chaired by Representative Henry B. Banning (D-Ohio), had recommended eliminating five infantry and two cavalry regiments. Closely allied with the Democratic Party, Custer undoubtedly reported these prospective reductions to his fellow officers. Ignoring objections of Republicans and a few borderlands delegates, on June 1 House Democrats passed the Banning proposal by a 123–82 count; of the eight Democrats who broke with their party to oppose the army cutbacks, four represented Texas.[25]

Informed observers understood that the Senate, still safely Republican and more heavily tilted to the sparsely populated western states, would soften the House's reductions. Moreover, men like Senator Samuel Bell Maxey of Texas—a Democrat—could be counted on to support the army. "I cannot appreciate the sentiments of gentlemen who live in the interior, whose people are not exposed," proclaimed Maxey, "when they oppose a proper defense of the frontiersmen who make up the new States." In what was otherwise a straight party-line vote, Maxey joined twenty-four Republicans in passing a Senate measure more favorable to the army. Even so, some cutbacks seemed likely.[26]

As Congress awaited resolution of the political impasse, the military offensive continued. On the Yellowstone River aboard the steamer *Far West*, Terry, Gibbon, and Custer met for a final time on June 21. The enemy's exact whereabouts remained unknown, but a simple operational plan emerged nonetheless: Custer and the Seventh Cavalry would follow a suspected Indian trail along the Rosebud to the south. Gibbon and Terry would steam west along the Yellowstone River, then march south down the Bighorn. As Gibbon remembered, the object "was to prevent the escape of the Indians, which was the idea pervading the minds of all of us." Preferring not to slow his column—or to share any credit for the grand victory he expected—Custer rejected the offer of a battalion of the Second Cavalry and a battery of Gatling guns. Inexperienced in warfare against Indians, Terry intentionally left Custer with vague written instructions: "The Department Commander places too much confidence in your zeal, energy, and ability to wish to impose upon you precise orders which might hamper your action when nearly in contact with the enemy." Custer's African American cook, Mary Adams, offered a similar account of Terry's orders. "Use your own judgment and do what you think best if you strike the trail," she recalled Terry telling her boss. "And whatever you do, Custer, hold on to your wounded."[27]

The Seventh Cavalry—31 officers, 566 enlisted men, 35 Indian scouts, and a dozen civilian packers—and its lieutenant colonel broke camp at noon on June 22, each soldier armed with a Springfield single-shot carbine and a Colt revolver, carrying a hundred rounds for his carbine and twenty-four for his pistol. The pack train hauled fifteen days' rations and extra ammunition. Three-quarters of the men had at least a year of service, and over a quarter boasted more than five years' experience. Within the regiment, Custer's "family" consisted of brothers Thomas (now captain of Company C) and Boston (along as a guide); eighteen-year-old nephew Harry Armstrong Reed (on a summer adventure as a herder); and a retinue of loyalist captains—Myles W. Keogh, Myles Moylan, Thomas B. Weir, and George W. Yates—and lieutenants—"Jimmi" Calhoun, William W. Cooke, and Algernon E.

FIG. 49. Sitting Bull. Arguably the most famous of the army's Indian opponents, Sitting Bull (ca. 1831–90) proved a formidable political, military, and religious adversary. LIBRARY OF CONGRESS, USZ62-112177.

"Fresh" Smith. Outsiders included Major Marcus A. Reno and Captain Frederick W. Benteen, the latter of whom was especially antagonistic toward the Custer clique.

Having discovered signs of a large Indian presence, on the evening of the twenty-fourth Custer marched west toward the Little Bighorn River. A confusing nighttime ride of eight to ten miles left his troopers struggling into their bivouac at three thirty the next morning. The move reflected Custer's fear that the Lakotas and Cheyennes might escape and was consistent with the discretion granted him by Terry. He was unaware of the reality of the situation. Their numbers swollen to perhaps six thousand men, women, and children, these Indians, having whipped Crook at the Rosebud and agreed on Crazy Horse as undisputed war chief, were in no mood to run.

June 25 broke warm and cloudless. Still uncertain as to the size and location of the Indian encampment and worried that his command had been spotted, in late morning Custer and his men galloped ahead into a detached cluster of a dozen Sans Arc lodges, just missing the fleeing inhabitants. Suddenly came a shout from interpreter Fred Gerard: "Here are your Indians, General, running like devils." They were making their way toward the Little Bighorn. Sure that these Sans Arcs would lead him to the main camp and fearful that any delay would allow a mass escape, Custer judged that attacks from several directions would confuse and terrify his foes. Major Reno, with three companies, would cross to the south bank of the Little Bighorn and engage the enemy from the west. Continuing along the river's right bank, Custer would take five companies and pin the enemy against Reno. Completing the maneuver would be Captain Benteen's three-company battalion, supported by a final company escorting the pack train. As the magnitude of the enemy camp became apparent, Custer's adjutant, Lieutenant Cooke, scribbled a final message to the slow-moving Benteen: "Come on. Big Village. Be Quick. Bring Packs. W. W. Cooke. P. bring pacs."

Inexperienced in the ways of Indian warfare, Reno struck first, probably about three fifteen that afternoon. Having marched through much of the previous night and now another eighteen miles in the past three hours, Reno's exhausted command formed a dismounted skirmish line short of the village. Feverishly defending their loved ones, Indians threw the soldiers back across the Little Bighorn in

FIG. 50. George, Lizzie, and Tom Custer. The Custer "family" dominated the Seventh Cavalry Regiment. Here George Custer (1839–76), wearing a uniform befitting his Civil War rank of major general, is seated next to his wife, Elizabeth (1842–1933), and his brother, Thomas (1845–76). LIBRARY OF CONGRESS, USZ62-114798.

considerable disorder. They held on long enough atop Reno Hill, little thanks to their commander, to receive Benteen and reinforcements at about four twenty. "Where's Custer?" wondered Benteen, who had been in no hurry to march to the sound of the guns. "I don't know," replied a shaken Reno. Later that afternoon, their combined forces made a tentative foray toward sounds of battle but then quickly retraced their steps to the security of Reno Hill.

As gunshots echoed through the ravines and ridges of the Little Bighorn Valley, Custer seems again to have hoped that parallel attacks against their massive village might confuse his numerically superior foes. But the effort soon collapsed. The regulars fought hard, if not necessarily effectively, for the tangled terrain meant that individual martial prowess trumped whatever discipline and coordination the soldiers could have maintained as the hopelessness of their situation became obvious. Between 210 and 215 officers, enlisted men, scouts, and civilians died with Custer; 47 of Reno's men were killed and 53 were wounded. Half of the army's most famous regiment had fallen in a single afternoon. Indian casualties, often wildly overstated, were between thirty-five and fifty killed. How had the Lakotas and Cheyennes so badly whipped the army's most celebrated cavalryman? "The simplest answer, usually overlooked," writes historian Robert M. Utley with his usual acuity, "is that the army lost largely because the Indians won."28

Crook, Terry, and Gibbon were too shaken by the disaster to enthusiastically seek out combat again that summer. "The fact of the case is," admitted Sheridan, "the operations of Generals Terry and Crook will not bear criticism, and my only thought has been to let them sleep." But the Lakota–Northern Cheyenne victory was only fleeting, for even the tentative movements of the soldiers prevented the tribes from resuming their normal summer routines. And the world of the northern plains was changing: cattle were replacing buffalo; emigrants were claiming ever-increasing chunks of arable land; railroads were allowing the government to better exploit its enormous advantages of men and material. Six companies of the Twenty-second Infantry Regiment arrived from the Division of the Atlantic. Colonel Wesley Merritt's Fifth Cavalry trotted in from Kansas, skirmishing on July 17 with the Cheyennes on War Bonnet Creek, an encounter most noted for the "duel" between William F. ("Buffalo Bill") Cody and the subchief Yellow Hair. Colonel

Miles's veteran Fifth Infantry came by steamboat from the Department of the Missouri, and Mackenzie was transferred in with six companies of his Fourth Cavalry.[29]

Public furor over the Indian triumph at the Little Bighorn enabled the army to score some temporary political victories. "ONE OF THE BLOODIEST MASSACRES ON RECORD!" blared one headline. "We should like," the article went on to state, "to see the Indians turned over to the tender mercies of the war department and instructions issued to Gen. Sheridan to thrash the hostile Indians into submission." Editors of the *New York Times* opined that the disaster "has once more showed that the military arm cannot be weakened." The Interior Department granted the army control over the affected agencies, and Congress authorized funding for two big new military posts in the Yellowstone River region. In mid-August, with Democratic fury over the army's role in reconstruction temporarily abated amid the fresh news of Custer's defeat, Congress authorized the army to enlist twenty-five hundred additional cavalry privates.[30]

On September 9–10, a rejuvenated Crook engaged some Minneconjous, Hunkpapas, Oglalas, and Sans Arcs at Slim Buttes. The soldiers destroyed thirty-seven lodges and killed or wounded dozens of women and children. On the Yellowstone, regulars were hacking out a big new cantonment at the mouth of the Tongue River (later Fort Keogh). On October 21, Colonel Miles and 398 infantrymen, buttressed by a single cannon, turned back attacks by a group of Indians believed to have been twice the size of their contingent. Casualties were few—three soldiers were wounded and the bodies of five Indians recovered—but the ensuing pursuit suggested the increasing fragility of Sitting Bull's mighty coalition. "I believe we can wear them down," wrote Miles grimly.[31]

The winter months were indeed cruel. At daybreak on November 25, Mackenzie struck Dull Knife's Cheyenne camp a crushing blow. As was so often case in the army's wars against the horse peoples of the Great Plains, the furious charge into the surprised camp quickly scattered the confused defenders. Mackenzie's semiliterate orderly, Private William Earl Smith, put it this way: "When the Indins saw so meny soldiers coming over the hill they broke and run for the hills and this left us in a cross fire all day. When the Indins broke the squaws and young ons lit out for the timber." Soldiers and their Indian allies systematically

FIG. 51. Graveside marker of John J. Crittenden. Among the wooden headboards honoring the dead at the Little Bighorn was that for Lieutenant Crittenden (1854–76). From a prominent Kentucky family, Crittenden dropped out of West Point but successfully petitioned President Grant for a commission in the Twentieth Infantry. A serious eye injury forced him to take leave from his regiment, but his father, Colonel Thomas Crittenden, convinced Custer to take him along as second in command of L Company. He died on Calhoun Hill. LIBRARY OF CONGRESS, USZ62-51708.

looted, then torched, the two hundred lodges. Probably forty Cheyennes had been killed, and twice that number wounded. Those who survived had lost everything. "As our column moved out, it began to snow heavily. Two or three Cheyennes came into their ruined camp, almost as soon as our men had left, and sat down and wailed at the spectacle of their [devastated] home," wrote Lieutenant Bourke.[32]

The aggressive, ambitious Miles, his talented subordinate, Lieutenant Frank Baldwin, and the rugged foot soldiers of the Fifth Infantry were also hard at work from their Tongue River cantonment. A 120-mile march through the freezing Montana cold to the Fort Peck Agency in November and early December failed to yield tangible results, but as the year ended, Miles set out once again with 436 men and two cannon. Heavy snows and food shortages haunted their efforts. "I believe I can fight & whip them even if they run three or four to one," Miles assured Sherman, "but the danger of getting blocked up in two feet of snow without food is some thing that I have to be careful about." Yet the combination of his tenacity, the on-again, off-again possibility of a negotiated settlement, and the winter weather was eroding Indian morale. Amid a swirling blizzard on January 8, 1877, Crazy Horse and five to six hundred men attacked the soldiers in the Battle of Wolf Mountains. Throwing back the assault, Miles claimed fifteen enemy dead and thirty wounded, setting his own casualties at three killed and eight wounded.[33]

The cumulative effects of the savage campaigns were taking a terrible toll among the Indians of the northern plains. Inefficient though it was, the government's logistical network dwarfed the capacities of tribal economies disrupted by the incessant marches. That spring, about three hundred Indians surrendered to Miles, with perhaps ten times that number coming in throughout Crook's Department of the Platte. On May 1, heading four companies of cavalry, six companies of infantry, and some recently enlisted Cheyenne scouts, Miles set out in pursuit of Lame Deer's defiant Minneconjous. A week later, soldiers found the village along Muddy Creek. Brief peace parleys nearly resulted in Miles's murder; the resulting fighting cut down Lame Deer, Iron Star, and a dozen other Minneconjous. The soldiers also rounded up most of the camp's ponies, and final army sweeps that summer convinced the remaining Lakotas to either turn themselves in or take flight to Canada, where most joined Sitting Bull.

FIG. 52. Artillery near the Tongue River Cantonment. Artillery often
played a vital role in army operations against Indians. The gun
crews of a three-inch ordnance rifle and a twelve-pound Napoleon
gun pose with their weapons in the snow near the Tongue River
cantonment. LIBRARY OF CONGRESS, USZ62-46514.

The Great Sioux War was over. Across the plains, war, rather than peace,
had marked the final days of the Grant administration. To the south, the
Kiowas and Comanches had nearly been annihilated; to the north, the
Lakota-Cheyenne coalition had splintered. Crazy Horse would be bayo-
neted at the Red Cloud Agency guardhouse within the year. It had been
a bloody time: between early 1874 and May 1877, the army had engaged
in 144 combat actions against Indians, suffering nearly five hundred
casualties. Ironically, with the passage of the Custer crisis, the army
now faced its own harsh new political reality. In an era of limited federal
spending, frontier security no longer seemed such a high priority, and
the territorial delegates who tended to benefit most from the military had
no voting rights in the House. Furious with the deployment of federal
troops in recent contested elections in South Carolina and Louisiana,
the House Democratic leadership would brook no compromise in its
determination to emasculate what Tennessee's J. D. C. Atkins dubbed
"a political engine." The regulars, they insisted, must be reduced from

twenty-seven thousand to seventeen thousand, and language forbidding the use of soldiers to support any state government was included in that year's army appropriation bill. The Republican-controlled Senate refused to go along, so the 44th Congress adjourned on March 3, 1877, without having funded the army. Effective June 30—the close of the fiscal year—the regulars would go without pay.[34]

TWELVE

Conquest of a Continent

With Congress out of session and the army without its appropria-tions, hopes for a permanent borderlands peace were shattered in mid-June 1877, when young men among the Nez Perces (who called themselves the Nee-Me-Poo, or the real people), launched a series of attacks against white intruders in the Salmon River region of central Idaho. Although the assaults had been uncoordinated, they reflected the pent-up frustration with the incessant challenges to their lifestyle. The Nez Perces then routed a mixed command of regular cavalry, volunteers, and allied Indian scouts under Captain David L. Perry at White Bird Creek, killing thirty-three and wounding four others. "If there was any plan of attack," muttered one disgusted sergeant, "I never heard of it."[1]

War had come. Commanding the Department of the Columbia, Brigadier General Oliver O. Howard began organizing the chase. The collected followers of Looking Glass, Joseph, Ollokut, White Bird, and Toohoolhoolzote, numbering over seven hundred men, women, and children, fought Howard's main column on July 11–12 at the Clearwater, an engagement notable for the Nee-Me-Poos' inability to agree on tactics and Howard's unwillingness to aggressively pursue his defeated enemy. The Nez Perces then opted to make a break for the buffalo plains to the east, where they hoped to join their old friends, the Crows. Their slow pace enabled Colonel John Gibbon, leading two hundred men from the

District of Western Montana, to attack them on August 9–10 at the Big Hole. In a clash that Phil Sheridan described as being "one of the most desperate engagements on record," twenty-nine soldiers and volunteers were killed and another forty wounded. Nez Perce dead numbered twice that many.[2]

The trek nonetheless continued. Having trailed the nontreaty Nez Perces for over five hundred miles into Montana, on September 12 a dispirited Howard called for assistance from Miles, who had briefly served under his command on the eastern front during the Civil War. Vain, talented, and needing no further encouragement, Miles marched northwest from the Tongue River Cantonment with ten companies of mounted troops, two artillery pieces, and a squad of Cheyenne scouts. The Nez Perce cause was further hurt by a sharp engagement on the thirteenth at Canyon Creek with a Seventh Cavalry battalion and Crow scouts. Though the Nez Perces acknowledged only one man killed, they were nevertheless dispirited, as they realized that the Crows would offer no assistance. "My heart was just like fire," recalled one warrior. Canada now seemed the only alternative.[3]

Ridden by internal dissent and worn out from their three-month ordeal, the Nez Perces made their way north, their pace easing as they distanced themselves from Howard and Colonel Sturgis. Miles, having gone unnoticed by the Nez Perces until it was too late, attacked on the afternoon of September 30 in the Bear's Paw Mountains. The Nez Perces threw back the assault and began fortifying their position. Amid the snow and sleet, the army's cannon lobbed occasional shells into the enemy camp (though terrifying, the weapon's usefulness was limited because they had brought only twenty-four shells). Perhaps 170 Nez Perces managed to elude the army cordon and make their way to Canada, but the remainder were hemmed in. Howard, bringing with him influential Nez Perce leaders Captain John and Old George, arrived on the fourth. Negotiations intensified, and through these emissaries Joseph relayed what has come to be known as his surrender speech:

> I am tired of fighting. Our chiefs are killed. . . . It is cold and we have no blankets. The little children are freezing to death. My people, some of them, have run away to the hills, and have no blankets, no food; no one knows where they are—perhaps

freezing to death. . . . Hear me, my chiefs. I am tired; my heart
is sick and sad. From where the sun now stands I will fight no
more forever.[4]

Not all the Nez Perces followed Joseph's lead, as White Bird and
perhaps fifty others slipped through the soldier lines to Canada. In the
years to come, Joseph's unfulfilled desire to go with his people from
their exile in the Indian Territory back to their homelands came to symbolize the tragedy of the nation's Indian policy. Nor did the army receive
much credit for its operations against the Nez Perces. "It is impossible
to meet public expectation in Indian campaigns," Sheridan had once
complained to Sherman. "The Indians will not stand to receive such a
blow as would satisfy the public and end the campaign; therefore it has
to peter out, as the saying is."[5]

Military affairs along the Texas-Mexican border were to the army of
much more immediate political value. On June 1, 1877, Secretary of War
George W. McCrary authorized General Ord to "use his own discretion"
in pursuing fleeing raiders into Mexico. In late September, Lieutenant
Colonel William Shafter and four hundred men splashed across the Rio
Grande and burned a Lipan and Mescalero camp near Saragosa. Captain
Samuel Young and Lieutenant John L. Bullis led smaller forays that fall.
Mexico denounced the new policy, but Ord's aggressiveness earned him
the enduring gratitude of Texas Democrats. The general, Representative
Gustave Schleicher assured Sherman, was among "the most popular
and requested men in Texas."[6]

The Texas delegation was pivotal as the 45th Congress assembled in
late November. As a price for agreeing to the much-delayed army appropriations, House Democrats, who still held their majority, demanded
that the army reduce its enlisted men from twenty-five thousand to
twenty thousand. Washington's deployment of regulars to help end that
summer's railroad strikes gave critics further ammunition. Missouri's
Thomas T. Crittenden denounced its use "against the laboring men
of this country." James H. Blount, a former Confederate officer from
Georgia, complained that regulars "always regard the country as in a
state of war." But Texas representatives David B. Culberson, DeWitt C.
Giddings, Roger Q. Mills, and James W. Throckmorton joined Schleicher
in breaking party ranks to back a Senate amendment blocking the new

cuts. On November 17, the House accepted the Senate version by a narrow 134–129 count; eight Democrats (including the afore-mentioned Texans) had joined all 126 Republicans to form a slim proarmy majority. Three and a half months late, contractors would receive the money owed them by the government and soldiers their back pay. For the next two decades, War Department spending leveled off at between 12–17 percent of the total federal budget—a rate roughly equal to that of George Washington's first administration.[7]

Ord sought to capitalize on the alliance. "If the Texas delegation, will in a body call on the President to let Texas have that part of the Army, 5,000 men, for her protection, *which that delegation secured to it by their votes*," he advised Schleicher, "they can I am sure get it." Although Sherman had concluded "that a cooler & less spasmodic man" would be more suitable to command the Rio Grande Valley, he admitted that the regulars must "quiet the clamors of the Texas people, and of the Texas Representatives, who have us at their mercy." Without their support, he predicted that his army would be "slaughtered" in the next session.[8]

The Texans had demanded a price for blocking the army reduction: the return of Ranald Mackenzie to their state. The army complied, and in June 1878 Mackenzie stormed across the border into Mexico, bringing along three batteries of artillery for good measure. The Yankees encountered more Mexican soldiers than Indians, and on two occasions the rivals nearly came to blows. Fortunately, cooler heads prevailed, and that fall five thousand Mexican troops under General Jeronimo Trevino undertook a vigorous campaign against Lipans, Mescaleros, and Kickapoos. The marriage of Ord's daughter to Trevino seemed to symbolize the growing rapprochement along the Rio Grande.[9]

In addition to chasing Indians, the army brought national authority to Texas's southern borderlands. Valley civilians seemed less concerned, for example, that the garrison at Ringgold Barracks was comprised of black enlisted personnel than they were that the troopers represented an outside force intent on usurping local autonomy. As did other westerners, Anglos, Mexicans, and Tejanos frequently turned to the courts in their effort to limit the army's reach. But the army gradually asserted its control, as well as its legitimacy. That it had achieved legitimacy seemed especially clear in El Paso's 1877 "Salt War," when the arrival of nine companies of the Ninth Cavalry quelled a bloody local feud that

FIG. 53. "Hostile—but Accommodating." Through much of the war against the Nez Perce, the army went without pay. This cartoon poking fun at the 1877 reduction of the army bill was published on September 1, 1877, in *Frank Leslie's Illustrated Newspaper*.
LIBRARY OF CONGRESS, USZC2-770.

had left at least eleven persons dead. "For God sake, and the sake of humanity . . . do not allow the troops be removed from this county," wrote one resident.[10]

In Oregon, Bannock and Paiute grievances against the United States were as lengthy as those of their former neighbors, the Nez Perces. Tensions finally blew open in May and June of 1878, when seven hundred Bannocks and Paiutes bolted from the Fort Hall and Malheur agencies into southeastern Oregon. Peace emissaries having failed, on June 23 Captain Reuben F. Bernard and three companies of the First Cavalry hit the Indian camp. A former enlisted man, the remarkable Bernard would participate in over one hundred combat engagements during his forty-one years of military service. In their quintessential dawn attack, his troopers scattered the inhabitants and destroyed their property. On July 9, Bernard, now leading seven companies of horse soldiers through the rugged John Day River country, attacked the Indians' rocky defenses atop Birch Creek. Although, according to Howard, "the different sides of the hill were steeper than Missionary Ridge," Bernard's troopers managed to dislodge the defenders and captured over two hundred horses. The coalition soon scattered into small parties, with the last engagement coming on September 12. "I have never known officers and soldiers to encounter and overcome greater obstacles," asserted Howard.[11]

The most recent conflicts against the Indians had hardly ended as the second session of the 45th Congress opened. House Democrats— save the Texas delegation—resumed their attempts to reduce the army. "During the last ten years not one-half of our Army has been used for legitimate purposes," exclaimed Ohio's Milton L. Southard. "Its use has consisted mainly of running elections and keeping the dominant party in power." Illinois' William A. J. Sparks attributed the increasingly evident army-borderlands political alliance to greed. "Everybody knows," he insisted, "that when you have an Army in a thinly populated Territory the people of that Territory get high prices for their production." To attract support for that year's appropriations bill, Democrats linked army cutbacks to a popular *posse comitatus* measure that would have required congressional approval for using the regulars to quell internal disorder. They also promised to return the Office of Indian Affairs to the War Department, a move long advocated by army brass.[12]

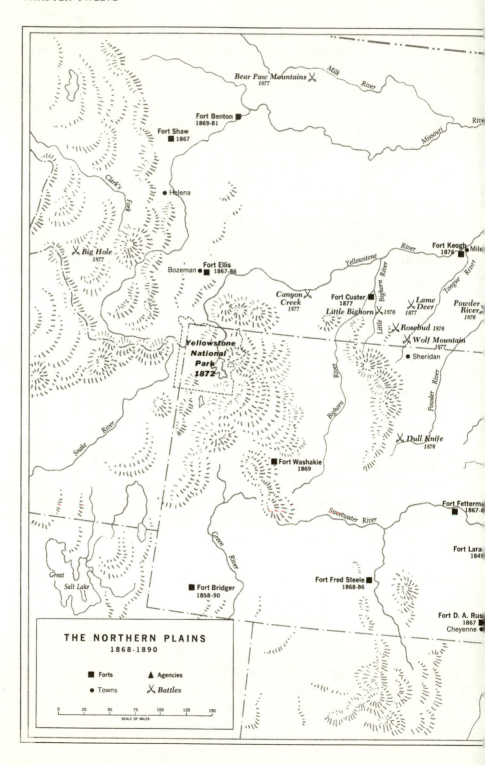

THE NORTHERN PLAINS
1868-1890

■ Forts   ▲ Agencies
● Towns   ✗ Battles

0   25   50   75   100   125   150
SCALE OF MILES

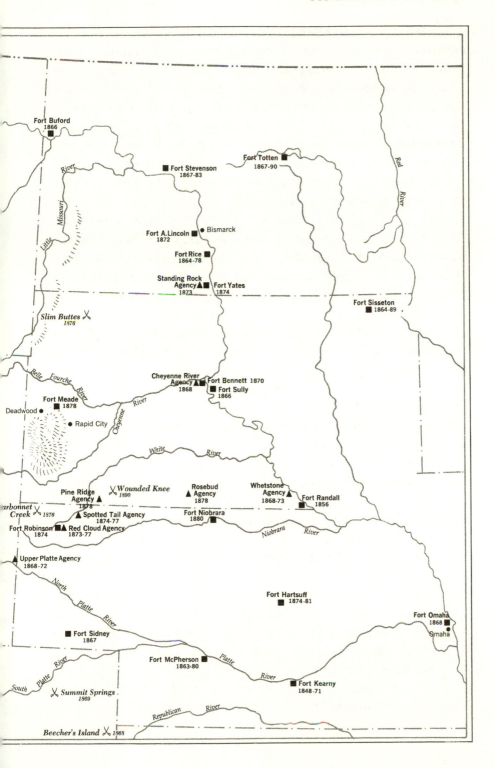

Fort Buford
1866

Fort Stevenson
1867-83

Fort Totten
1867-90

Missouri River

Little Missouri River

Red River

Fort A. Lincoln
1872

Bismarck

Fort Rice
1864-78

Standing Rock
Agency
1873

Fort Yates
1874

Fort Sisseton
1864-89

Slim Buttes
1876

Belle Fourche River

Cheyenne River
Agency
1868

Fort Bennett 1870

Fort Sully
1866

Fort Meade
1878

Deadwood

Rapid City

Cheyenne River

White River

Wounded Knee
1890

Rosebud
Agency
1878

Whetstone
Agency
1868-73

Fort Randall
1856

Pine Ridge
Agency
1878

Spotted Tail Agency
1874-77

Fort Niobrara
1880

Carbonnet
Creek 1876

Fort Robinson
1874

Red Cloud Agency
1873-77

Niobrara River

Upper Platte Agency
1868-72

North Platte River

Fort Hartsuff
1874-81

Fort Omaha
1868

Omaha

Fort Sidney
1867

Fort McPherson
1863-80

Platte River

Fort Kearny
1848-71

South Platte River

Summit Springs
1869

Republican River

Beecher's Island 1868

In May 1878, the increasingly exasperated Texan, Gustave Schleicher noted that "no one doubts that if they had the votes[,] the votes of Dakota and Montana and Idaho and every other Territory with an Indian frontier would be given against any reduction of the Army which protects them." Despite western protests, by a slim 120–116 majority the House cut the army to twenty thousand. All told, borderlands legislators voted against the final bill by a twenty-four-to-one count, with five of the six members of the Texas delegation crossing party lines to oppose the measure. The Senate refused to go along with either the transfer of the Indian Office or the army reductions. "It is entirely a question of the safety of the frontiers now," explained Aaron A. Sargent, a California Republican. Ten Senate Democrats, including Texans Richard Coke and Samuel Bell Maxey and Oregon's LaFayette Grover, joined Republicans to block the House package. A conference committee compromise accepted the *posse comitatus* restrictions and left the army intact but rejected the Indian bureau transfer.[13]

Despite hopes that the Indian wars had ended, violence still plagued the borderlands. In 1879, regulars spent three months chasing several dozen Sheepeaters (Mountain Shoshones), numbering about two dozen fighting men, through Idaho's tangled Salmon River country. "Should they discover us before we do them," complained Bernard, once more in the thick of the action, "they can hide in the timbered rocky mountains for a long time and go from point to point much faster than we can, even if we knew where to go." In late July at Vinegar Hill, the Sheepeaters ambushed and nearly burned alive Lieutenant Henry Catley and fifty troopers. As was so often the case, only Indian scouts hired by the government—in this instance twenty Umatillas led by Lieutenant Edward S. Farrow and Lieutenant William C. Brown—managed to find the enemy. On October 1 and 2, fifty-one exhausted men, women, and children surrendered to Farrow.[14]

Meanwhile, the aftereffects of the recent wars against the Lakotas and Northern Cheyennes were still being felt. In summer 1877, about a thousand Cheyennes were forced to relocate from the Red Cloud Agency to Indian Territory. Plagued by disease, irregular government annuities, and the destruction of the southern buffalo herds, in September 1878 some 360 homesick men, women, and children following Little Wolf, Wild Hog, and Dull Knife began a desperate trek back north. Well

FIG. 54. Officers and their families, at Fort Davis. Officers and their families pose above officers' row at Fort Davis, Texas. Enlisted barracks would be across the parade ground to the left. FORT DAVIS NATIONAL HISTORIC SITE.

armed and battle hardened, they routed two troops of the Fourth Cavalry at Turkey Springs, ambushed another pursuit column at Punished Woman's Fork, and killed thirty-two civilians unfortunate enough to be in their path until being overwhelmed by superior numbers. Dull Knife surrendered at Camp Robinson on October 23; the following January, at least twenty Cheyennes were cut down as they attempted yet another escape. Those with Little Wolf made it to Montana, where they finally gave themselves up in March. Once again, the army had hardly distinguished itself; as the *Omaha Bee* put it, "our military forces are covered with anything but glory."[15]

Conditions among the Utes in Colorado, which had secured its statehood in 1876, were no better. Well meaning but wholly impractical efforts by their agent, Nathan C. Meeker, to transform these horse people into sedentary farmers brooked trouble. Fearful for his life, in

1879 Meeker called in Major Thomas T. ("Tip") Thornburgh and the cavalry. On September 29 the two sides engaged in a bloody encounter at Milk Creek. The Utes admitted losing nearly two dozen of the 100 or so fighters engaged; of the 120 soldiers present, 11 were killed (including Thornburgh) and 23 were wounded, and three-quarters of their horses and mules were either killed or wounded. As the fighting progressed, Utes murdered Meeker and nine employees at the White River Agency, taking five women and children captive.

News of the affair electrified the country. Union Pacific Railroad officials "turned over their track" to nearly three thousand reinforcements. Secretary of the Interior Carl Schurz, however, convinced Sherman to delay the army's offensives in favor of renewed negotiations. Trying desperately to supply his men through the isolated White River Agency, Sheridan summed up the army's frustrations: "We went to the agency at the solicitation of the Indian Bureau, whose agent was murdered and our men killed and wounded, and now we are left in the heart of the mountains with our hands tied and the danger of being snowed in staring us in the face. I am not easily discouraged, but it looks as though we had been pretty badly sold out in this business." Much to Sheridan's surprise, the diplomatic offensive worked, and the Utes accepted reservations in Utah and southwestern Colorado.[16]

The presence of Sitting Bull and four thousand refugees over the Canadian border, where they endangered the ever-diminishing buffalo herds on which resident groups also depended, posed a considerably more serious military threat. Soldiers erected Fort Custer fifteen miles north of the battlefield at the Little Bighorn; five other forts—Assiniboine, McKinney, Meade, Maginnis, and Niobrara—completed the defenses. Major J. M. Walsh and a small detachment of the North-West Mounted Police could not force the newcomers out, and all feared that the situation would become intolerable. Operating from Fort Peck, in July 1879 Miles engaged in a running fight with Sitting Bull near the Canadian border. But Sherman had no intention of letting his ambitious nephew-in-law provoke an international incident. Bewildered by the flood of new immigrants into the Dakotas—a boom fueled by the presence of the soldiers, cheap land, unusually wet weather, and the railroads—most of Sitting Bull's followers drifted away. In July 1881, he and 187 others turned themselves in at Fort Buford.[17]

To the southwest, the Office of Indian Affairs' attempt to concentrate Apaches at desolate San Carlos spawned yet another disaster. "There was nothing but cactus, rattlesnakes, heat, rocks, and insects," recalled one resident bitterly. Colonel Benjamin Grierson, a former music teacher turned cavalryman, characterized it as "the most unsuitable place that could possibly have been selected." Resolved to accept no more false promises, in late summer 1879, Victorio, war leader of the Chihenne (Warm Springs) Apaches, broke with the government and launched a series of lightning strikes against herdsmen and travelers throughout southern New Mexico, far west Texas, and northern Chihuahua. Brilliantly employing traditional Apache tactics that relied on evasion, decoys, and ambushes, Victorio and his followers eluded their pursuers from a weakened Ninth Cavalry, their campaigns having effectively dismounted over half the regiment. Efforts by the regulars seeming to be futile, the New Mexico legislature appropriated $100,000 for local committees of public safety, and a squad of Texas Rangers hurried to El Paso.[18]

Adopting an unusually innovative approach the following year, Grierson, as commander of the District of the Pecos, won something of a strategic victory by garrisoning his Tenth Cavalry at the isolated waterholes of the Trans-Pecos. Twisting away from the spiderweb of Grierson's detachments, Victorio fell back into Mexico. Bluecoats who crossed the border in pursuit turned back when met by Colonel Joaquin Terrazas and about a thousand Mexican regulars, volunteers, and allied scouts. Terrazas meant business; tracking the Apaches to the Tres Castillos Mountains, on October 15 his troops attacked, killing Victorio, some sixty fighters, and eighteen women and children. The "Victorio Wars" were ended, courtesy of the Republic of Mexico.[19]

That same year, the *Army and Navy Journal* reminded readers of the importance of the army's "collateral" duties throughout the borderlands. Despite Congress's recent attempt, via *posse comitatus*, to limit such a use of the army, the army continued to engage in law enforcement activities. As Sherman explained it, "When there are no courts or civil authorities to hold and punish such malefactors, we must of necessity use the musket pretty freely." Officers tended to side with forces of order. Thus soldiers were deployed in New Mexico's Lincoln County War in 1878–79, and in the following decade they occupied Omaha, Seattle, and Rock Springs, Wyoming, in response to riots against immigrant Chinese workers. In 1892, elements of the Sixth Cavalry were called into Johnson County to rescue some hired bullies sponsored by the Wyoming Stock Growers' Association from the vengeance of the region's citizens. And under the guise of protecting the federal mails, fully two-thirds of the army was deployed, often in the West, to restore order during the widespread labor strikes of 1894.[20]

Checking illegal trespass onto lands reserved to Indians became especially complicated in the 1880s, when cattlemen began leasing large chunks of Cheyenne and Arapaho properties, and boomers like David L. Payne, a hard-drinking dreamer and populist, set their eyes on Indian Territory. Regulars hated the thankless job, made all the more difficult because they needed Interior Department authorization to enter the reservations. A full-scale crisis erupted in 1885, when key Cheyenne leaders refused to continue the leasing program. Sheridan, named the commanding general following Sherman's retirement two years earlier, ejected the cattlemen. But such measures were temporary, and two regiments of cavalrymen tried in vain to police squatters ("sooners") and control the pandemonium unleashed by the 1889 Oklahoma land rush.[21]

Given the emphasis on scientific observation at West Point and their own experiences in walking, riding, hunting, fishing, camping, exploring, and patrolling the American West, many officers readily embraced federal endeavors to preserve wilderness areas. In an age of limited federal government, only the army had the manpower—and the inclination—to do the job. The army, largely through the efforts of officers like Captain William Ludlow and General Sheridan, had protected Yellowstone National Park against the ravages of unpoliced tourists, hunters, loggers, and miners since its founding in 1872. Yosemite and Sequoia (along with nearby General Grant) were returned to federal control eighteen years later. Until the creation of the National Park Service in 1916, regulars, continuing the century-old practice whereby the army handled federal resource management tasks, safeguarded the areas. "Blessings on Uncle Sam's soldiers," gushed naturalist John Muir, "they have done the job well, and every pine tree is waving its arms for joy."[22]

The frontier army had also continued its borderlands explorations. Military posts supported—and often provided escorts for—surveys, such as those of Ferdinand V. Hayden and John Wesley Powell of the

FIG. 55. Meeting at Rock Springs with Chinese consuls. The army played a
major law enforcement role in the borderlands and in 1885 intervened
at Rock Springs, Wyoming, to prevent additional violence against
Chinese workers. Left to right: Colonel Alexander D. McCook;
Huang Sih Chuen, Chinese consul from New York; Frederick A.
Bee, Chinese consul from San Francisco; Tsang Hoy, interpreter;
Lieutenant S. W. Groesbeck. NATIONAL ARCHIVES, 111-SC-103556.

Rocky Mountains and the Colorado River country. Soldiers took a more
direct role in Lieutenant George Wheeler's "U.S. Geographical Surveys
West of the One Hundredth Meridian" (1869, 1871, 1872–79). Surveying
hundreds of thousands of square miles, Wheeler's military engineers
and civilian scientists identified 105 new species of animal and insect
life and brought back 61,659 specimens to the Smithsonian Institution.
Doctor Elliott Coues established an international reputation in orni-
thology, and officers Washington Matthews, William Philo Clarke,
William H. Corbusier, and John Gregory Bourke compiled pioneering
studies of Indian languages and life. Since 1814, surgeons had kept regular weather reports, and in 1870 Colonel Albert J. Myer used the Army

Signal Corps as an umbrella organization for what ultimately became the National Weather Service.[23]

The activities of the two hundred or so army surgeons also high-lighted the military's multiple roles in western life. Future surgeon general George M. Sternberg, perhaps the first American bacteriologist, as well as an inveterate fossil collector, participated in campaigns against the Cheyennes and the Nez Perces. Dissatisfied with the monotony of garrison duty, Dr. Leonard Wood volunteered for field service against Geronimo and would later be awarded a Medal of Honor. Others less adventurous than Wood expanded their clienteles beyond the confines of military reservations, combining their desire to generate a little extra income with sincere humanitarianism among populations with little access to professional care. Still others, like Corbusier, serviced nearby Indian reservations. During the 1870s, surgeons at Fort Riley initiated a systematic rural health program. The army sometimes even extended its supplies of preventive medicines to the public, as it did in the Department of Texas in 1873.[24]

The thirty post chaplains and four regimental chaplains (one for each of the African American regiments) who gained regular army status in 1867 also handled a multiplicity of western tasks. Chaplains supervised post gardens and bakeries, acted as librarians, oversaw treasuries, and served on councils. As high rates of illiteracy posed a major obstacle to military efficiency, their chief collateral responsibility included the education of children and enlisted men. Among the most capable was the dynamic George M. Mullins, whose efforts at Fort Davis led the post commander to characterize "the marked improvement" of his men as being "highly commendable."[25]

As it had since the nation's inception, the federal government—and more particularly the army—served as a cornerstone of many frontier economies. "Government contracts in those times were the greatest business plums, and often two or three firms would join forces in securing one of them," recalled Governor Miguel A. Otero of New Mexico. Benefiting from $46 million in army payments between 1869 and 1889, Texans took particular advantage of the system. "The whole state of Texas counts on expenditure of money for army supplies, and when a Congressman tackles the appropriation bill he joins issue with the whole state from Dan to Beersheba," fumed Samuel Smith,

FIG. 56. A presidential tour of yellowstone. Tours throughout the borderlands, featuring prominent guests, were a staple of army efforts to promote its image following the Civil War. This photo was taken during President Chester A. Arthur's 1883 expedition through Yellowstone National Park. The three seated men in the center are, from left to right, General Sheridan, President Arthur, and Secretary of War Robert Todd Lincoln. LIBRARY OF CONGRESS, USZ62-137259.

an acting assistant surgeon. "It seems to be bred in the bone to bleed 'Uncle Sam,' and the citizens of this state are fully aware of how the operation is performed."[26]

Members of the military community continued to find Indian policy frustrating and blamed Interior Department incompetence and the exaggerations of frontier residents eager to profit from their presence for the problems with it. "If the Army had more authority Indian wars would be shorter and less frequent," asserted John M. Schofield. There was "too much money in this Indian business," declared George Crook. "So many of these reports of Indian depredations are entirely without foundation, often times gotten up by someone who has corn to sell, and a company of cavalry coming into the neighborhood is a good thing for them," complained Caroline Winne, wife of a surgeon. "These frontier people are wholly unscrupulous," added another officer. "It is an outrage that we of the Army who have all the hardships to encounter should be made such catspaws of, mere tools of ambitious men who care only for their own interests."[27]

Most soldiers, on the other hand, saw nothing unethical in their own attempts to profit from the borderlands and regularly intermingled carrying out their official duty with engaging in regional development and personal advancement. Illustrative were the activities of General John M. Schofield, who in 1869 dispatched his brother, Major George Schofield, on an inspection tour into Colorado. As he surveyed the region between Fort Lyon and Fort Reynolds, George mixed official business with family interests and (ultimately) private land purchases, proclaiming the trip to have been "of service to both of us and to the Govt." Fort Davis, Texas, seemed to have been an epicenter for Gilded Age investors in blue. Colonel Benjamin Grierson gobbled up forty-five thousand acres of land and backed an unsuccessful effort to build a narrow gauge railroad that have would linked Fort Davis and the Southern Pacific. At least seven other officers followed their commander's lead in purchasing land, Lieutenant John R. Bullis claiming fifty-three thousand acres in Pecos County alone. Concurrently, Grierson and his comrades worked to keep property values high by insuring that the army kept a big base at Fort Davis, overseeing construction of new officers' quarters, barracks, commissary and quartermaster storehouses, and a water pipeline.[28]

Taking a slightly different tack in Montana, Colonel Miles attempted to link his personal ambitions with regional development. Establishing a separate military department under his command would, he explained to Delegate Martin Maginnis and Governor Benjamin F. Potts in 1878, bring lucrative federal investments. Eager to feast at the federal trough, one Helena businessman surmised that a new military post "would *really double* the value of our property." In return, territorial politicians lobbied for Miles's promotion to brigadier general. The fact that Montana did not get its separate military department, and that Miles did not immediately receive his promotion, should not blind us to the close ties that existed between the army and western political leaders.[29]

Even as borderlands populations increased, federal troops remained a major source of regional development. With the help of a special $100,000 appropriation, soldiers completed 1,218 miles of telegraph in Texas. Although officially a military system, civilians frequently used the services of these and other army-operated telegraphs. Similarly, Major Charles W. Howell's comprehensive report on the Missouri River between Omaha and Sioux City spurred considerable improvements by the Corps of Engineers. Commanding the Department of the Columbia from 1881–86, Miles, having finally won his brigadier's star, put the fifteen hundred soldiers under his command to work building military roads and telegraphs and conducting a variety of surveys and reconnaissances. Deeming the exploration of Alaska "beyond the reach of private enterprise," Miles dispatched several of his personal aides—Lieutenants Frederick Schwatka, Willis E. Everette, William R. Abercrombie, and Henry Allen—to explore the most northern reaches of his command.[30]

The arrival of railroads often had a negative effect on local borderlands economies, as cheaper transportation now connected garrisons with national markets. Subsistence, forage, and equipment could now be brought in at prices well below those once charged by small businessmen. Fort Riley, Kansas, offers a prime example. At the time that the Kansas Pacific Railroad reached the post in 1866, seven contractors were supplying corn to the base at ninety-one cents per bushel. By 1890, the price had fallen to thirty cents, and it took only one contractor to fill the order. New railroad connections also hurt the overland hauling industry, which had once been a major pillar of frontier economies. On the other hand, railroads encouraged ever-increasing numbers of non-Indians to move west: the population of borderlands states and territories grew by 488 percent between 1870 and 1900. The larger number of residents, of course, offered greater opportunities for private enterprise.[31]

No one grasped the connection between the army, railroads, and non-Indian western development better than William T. Sherman. "Prosperous farms and cattle ranches exist where ten years ago no man could venture," he wrote in 1880. "This is largely due to the soldier, but in equal, if not greater measure, to the adventurous pioneers themselves, and to that new and greatest of civilizers, the railroad." Following several grand tours of the West—during which he enjoyed the use of luxurious railroad cars, courtesy of his many friends in the industry—Sherman, now nearing retirement, recommended that the army abandon many posts inaccessible by rail. His successors, Phil Sheridan (1883–88), John M. Schofield (1888–95), and Nelson A. Miles (1895–1903), agreed. In 1880, the army had occupied 111 western posts; by 1897, that number had fallen to 47.[32]

As the nation changed, so did the frontier army, if with the same grudging caution of most large, inherently conservative institutions. By the late 1870s, with the size of the army now settled at about twenty-seven thousand officers and men, the officer corps had stabilized at just under twenty-two hundred. It was distinctly less southern than it had been before the Civil War: whereas 43.2 percent of officers had hailed from southern states in 1860, by 1877 only 17.2 percent had been born in the South. About half of all officers that year had gained their commissions during the Civil War or shortly thereafter; of these, just over half had originally come from the ranks. West Point's influence had declined accordingly. In 1860, 68 percent boasted military academy training, but by 1877, that percentage had been halved. Critics charged that the large number of rankers and volunteers had slowed the trend toward professionalization within the army, a movement counteracted—with varying degrees of success—by the efforts of leaders like Sherman, Sheridan, and Schofield to foster specialized training and reform.[33]

Regulars began to place greater emphasis on individual marksmanship, but the army resisted congressional efforts to ensure the commissioning of enlisted men. With annual desertion rates averaging about 15 percent, only in the late 1880s, when the reform-minded team of Secretary of War Redfield Proctor and commanding general Schofield took charge, did the army seriously address the problem. Better military codes of punishment and justice, closer scrutiny of recruits, a system of post canteens and athletics programs in place of the old sutlers, withholding more of the enlisted man's first year pay (with interest) until his discharge, a larger vegetable ration, more comfortable uniforms, authorization of civil officers to arrest deserters, and allowing disgruntled soldiers to purchase their discharge after a year of service helped to bring down annual desertion rates to less than 5 percent in the 1890s. Although desertion was still double that of the British Army, the Proctor-Schofield reforms had significantly improved conditions for American soldiers.[34]

Swarms of civilians followed the regulars to all but the most isolated

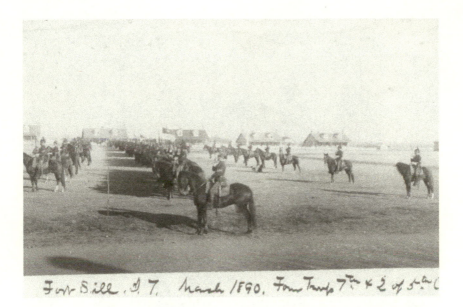

Fort Sill . I. T,   March 1890.   From Troops 7ᵗʰ & 2 of 5ᵗʰ (

FIG. 57. Cavalry maneuvers at Fort Sill, about 1890. Only the gradual concentration of troops made possible by railroads allowed the frontier army to conduct anything like large-scale military exercises. Here elements of the Fifth and Seventh Cavalry regiments are on maneuver at Fort Sill, Indian Territory. LIBRARY OF CONGRESS, USZ62-67502.

posts. In 1891, with the army officially numbering 24,234 officers and men, the surgeon general reported the presence of 14,450 civilians (2,831 adult males, 5,456 adult females, and 6,163 children) at military garrisons. Many had a direct association with the army as laundresses, servants, guides, civilian laborers, or family members. Seamstresses, merchants, farmers and ranchers, teamsters, station keepers, clerks, restaurant and barkeepers, cooks, tailors, mechanics, and laborers could be found in the larger communities.[35]

The boomtowns that sprang up near military posts sometimes become centers of vice, corruption, and immorality. Among the roughest was reputedly "the Flat," located next to Fort Griffin along the Clear Fork of the Brazos River. Frequented by soldiers, buffalo hunters, cowboys, and adventurers, the Flat's Griffin Avenue housed an exotic assortment

FIG. 58. Hispanic wood gatherers at Fort Davis. Civilians such as these constituted an integral part of almost every frontier military community. FORT DAVIS NATIONAL HISTORIC SITE.

of grog shops, gambling dens, dance halls, and two full blocks of broth-els. "Griffin," reported a Dallas newspaper, "which has long been the roost of a large quantity of 'soiled doves,' can now boast of a larger flock than any other town on the frontier." A local rancher described it as "a veritable robber's hole," where "they would throw a blanket over your head and take your money in a flash." But the boundaries of acceptable behavior, though wide, did have limits. Even during the Flat's spectac-ular heyday in the mid-1870s, local authorities usually tried to prose-cute cases of gratuitous violence, and the surrounding county housed hundreds of legitimate farmers, professionals, and skilled laborers. Moreover, the raucous times were relatively short; with the end of the buffalo trade, the close of the open range, the deactivation of the military post, and the arrival of the Texas Central Railroad to nearby Albany (the latter both occurring in 1881), the Flat withered away.[36]

As might be expected, the number of officers and wives living together in the borderlands seems to have increased as an area became more populated—in 1870, 40 percent of officers lived in households with their wives in Dakota and Wyoming; in 1870 the number had climbed to 56 percent. Children lived in roughly two-thirds of the married households. Though rarely challenging Victorian-era restrictions on their public roles, many wives saw promotion for their spouses as a means of elevating their own status. Thus Mary Sherman Miles, wife of the ambitious colonel, assiduously lobbied her uncle, William T. Sherman, on her husband's behalf. "You may be assured that I personally am well informed of his [Miles's] special merits," sighed the general. Alice Baldwin, whose husband, Frank, would win two Medals of Honor (the first for his actions during the Civil War at Peach Tree Creek, Georgia, and the second for his deeds against the Cheyennes at McClellan's Creek in 1874), angrily denounced the army's failure to grant him promotion. "If Indian warfare was only regarded as legitimate warfare," she observed astutely, "there would be encouragement for hard work & successful campaigning such as you have done." Most famously, Elizabeth Custer devoted much of her adult life to her husband, initially in furthering his military career and after his death in defending and embellishing his reputation. As Libbie's biographer, Shirley Leckie, puts it, "George Armstrong Custer's career was based on the efforts of two people."37

These women generally reflected the ethnic, racial, and class prejudices of the broader public in their views of the peoples of the frontier. They joined their husbands, for example, in routinely flouting post–Civil War legislation that officially forbade them from using enlisted men as their personal servants ("strikers"), assuming that it simply befit their status as gentlemen and ladies to use these soldiers for their daily household chores. Though generally sympathetic to Hispanic citizens of the Rio Grande Valley, Helen Chapman, wife of an army quartermaster, admitted that "it is impossible to live among a people so morally, physically and intellectually degraded without feeling assured that a more powerful race must before long subdue them." Mrs. Frances Roe complained that most Indians she encountered "were simply, and only, painted, dirty and nauseous smelling savages!" Anecdotal evidence suggests that greater personal familiarity with the tribes led many wives to soften, but not entirely forget, their preconceived biases. Almost

FIG. 59. Canteen at Fort Keogh. Among the reforms introduced in the late 1880s was the post canteen, intended to provide a more wholesome atmosphere for frontier soldiers than the old sutler's store or nearby grogshops. NATIONAL ARCHIVES, 111-SC-97981.

without exception, the lordly officers' wives chafed at their lack of official status in army regulations. Frances Anne Boyd, wife of Captain Orsemus Bronson Boyd, recalled that "many indignant meetings were held at which we discussed the matter, and rebelled at being considered camp followers." They perhaps gained a measure of selfish satisfaction in 1878, then, when the army forbade the designation of any new laundresses.[38]

In the public sphere, officers and their wives attempted to evoke class unity and a sense of refined gentility. Both their quarters (physically separate from those of others in the garrisons) and their pay ($1,400 per year for the lowest paid second lieutenant, plus bonuses for longevity, which meant about $30,000 in 2006 terms) distinguished them from others in the military communities. In his published reminiscences, Miles thus portrayed his fellow officers as being "as a rule, educated and intelligent gentlemen, while their wives and daughters were cultured and gentle." In reality, however, intense internal rivalries divided these military elites. "The idea of the army being 'one happy family' was a considerable exaggeration," remembered one officer's wife. Almost every Civil War veteran had seen his wartime rank diminished, and one army study indicated that it would take twenty-four to twenty-six years for a second lieutenant to reach the rank of major. West Pointers believed themselves superior to those without such formal training, and Civil War veterans found it difficult to accept those who had not participated in the terrible conflict as their equals. Wives often affected a similar clannishness, and the process of "ranking out," whereby a newly arriving officer could eject a subordinate (and his family) from choice quarters, was sure to stir resentment.[39]

By the 1880s, the expansion of railroads and reduction in the number of garrisons enabled the War Department to afford more attention to the "civilizing" nature of post architecture. The army had always seen itself as an agent of civilization, so most in the military community welcomed the trend. The old posts, largely products of improvisation, had endured a seemingly never-ending cycle of being built, repaired, rebuilt, and abandoned; now, however, they could import more comfortable cultural traditions from the East to posts designated as permanent. Thus parade grounds became village greens; trees were planted, lawns watered, and picket fences erected, especially along officers' row. Clapboard walls and bay windows now graced newer buildings, and bandstands showcased regimental musicians. Model plans for officers' quarters, barracks, hospitals, and assorted support buildings afforded a degree of standardization. By no means were the changes simply cosmetic: running water, ice machines, oil lamps, and bathrooms improved health and living conditions for everyone.[40]

To complete the military conquest of the Southwest, the army still needed to overcome Apache resistance. In August 1881, Colonel Eugene A. Carr set out from Fort Apache with two troops of cavalry and twenty-five Apache scouts to arrest a Cibecue medicine man, Nock-ay-det-klinne, believed to be whipping up opposition to white expansion. On their return, the scouts—about half of whom were Cibecues—joined Nock-ay-det-klinne's followers in attacking Carr's camp, killing five soldiers and wounding four others (two mortally). The army poured in

FIG. 60. Enlisted men's barracks at Fort Clark, 1880s. Bunks and lockers are ready for inspection at Fort Clark during the 1880s. LIBRARY OF CONGRESS, USZ6-1125.

reinforcements from California, Nevada, Colorado, New Mexico, and Texas. "I want this annual Apache stampede to end right now, and to effect that result will send every available man in the whole Army if necessary," vowed Sherman.[41]

The show of force overawed the Apaches of the White Mountain region, and Captain Adna R. Chaffee's victory in the Battle of Big Dry Wash took the steam out of another revolt. Three of the guilty scouts were hung. But the flood of bluecoats onto the reservations seems to have spooked the Chiricahuas, many of whom followed Juh, Nachez, and Geronimo to join Victorio's old supporters in Mexico. In April 1882 they thundered back into Arizona, killing dozens of people throughout the Gila River Valley, and the following spring Chato and two dozen warriors slipped into southeastern Arizona and southwestern New Mexico, killing at least eleven people before vanishing.[42]

No. 2—Apache Scouts, at Apache Lake, Sierra Blanca Range.

FIG. 61. Apache scouts. Despite the 1881 revolt against Carr, Indian auxiliaries, such as these Apaches, were indispensable to the army throughout the borderlands. LIBRARY OF CONGRESS, DIG-STEREO-1S00281.

Transferred back to Arizona and benefiting from a reciprocal cross-ing agreement made with the Díaz administration, on May 1, 1883, George Crook led 45 cavalrymen, 193 Apache scouts, and 350 mules car-rying sixty days' worth of supplies into Mexico. Moving into the Sierra Madres, they stormed the very heart of the Apache stronghold fifteen days later. Disheartened by internal divisions, ammunition shortages, and the presence of so many of their own people alongside the bluecoats, the key leaders agreed to return to the United States.[43]

But life under the army's watch at San Carlos was hardly conducive to traditional Chiricahua culture. In May 1885, Geronimo, forty-two warriors, and about one hundred women and children broke away, launching three weeks of raids in Arizona and New Mexico before reentering Mexico. Even the three thousand cavalrymen Crook had mobilized could not prevent the occasional incursions that followed. "I go to bed tonight," wrote President Grover Cleveland on December 22, "very much dejected and wondering if something cannot be done to better protect our citizens on the frontier and put a stop to these dreadful murders." Chasing the Apaches deep into Mexico, on January 11, 1886, Captain Emmet Crawford was killed during a skirmish with Mexican militia, and subsequent negotiations between Crook and Chiricahua leaders fell apart. Long skeptical of Crook's dependence on Apache scouts, in early April Sheridan happily accepted his request for a transfer.[44]

Crook's replacement, Miles, was urged to accept "the necessity of making active and prominent use of the Regular troops of your command." Possessing enormous advantages in manpower, supplies, and equipment, Miles carved southern New Mexico and Arizona into districts of observations, set up twenty-seven heliograph stations, and stationed infantry at key mountain passes and water holes. Mounted units were to exert "the most vigorous and persistent efforts" in following every trail. Yuma scouts replaced most of Crook's Apaches. Another Chiricahua raid that April prompted organization of a strike force of thirty-five cavalrymen, twenty infantry, thirty packers, twenty Indian scouts, and one hundred mules, commanded by Captain Henry Lawton. But after three months of exhausting marches in Sonora, Lawton's command returned empty handed. One rancher judged the officers as "either grossly inefficient . . . or damnably culpable."[45]

Meanwhile, Miles pursued other options. Friends and families of the raiders had remained on the reservations; removing them might induce Geronimo to turn himself in. Thus in late August, guards hustled 382 Indians onto railroad cars bound for Fort Marion, Florida. And although President Cleveland still insisted that "nothing . . . be done with Geronimo which will prevent our treating him as a prisoner of war, *if we cannot hang him, which I would much prefer,"* on September 3 Miles met with Geronimo at appropriately named Skeleton's Canyon. Explaining that they would rejoin their families in Florida and promising that "we shall not kill you but shall treat you justly," Miles won Geronimo's assent. Five days later, soldiers loaded the remaining Chiricahuas aboard waiting cars and packed them off to Florida. Amid bitter recriminations among Miles, the Cleveland administration, Crook, westerners, and Indian reform groups about the treatment accorded the Chiricahuas, the Geronimo wars were over.[46]

To the north, another major military campaign was still to come. The 1880s had been a miserable decade on the Standing Rock, Cheyenne River, Lower Brule, Pine Ridge, and Rosebud reservations. Hunting was poor, crop failures common, and government annuities unreliable. Many residents turned to spiritual means of better shaping their futures. In this case it was the Ghost Dance, popularized by a Northern Paiute religious figure named Wovoka. As understood by the Lakotas and Cheyennes, Wovoka's teachings promised the cataclysmic defeat of U.S. authority and their own spiritual rejuvenation. In fall 1890, the prospect of a messianic Indian awakening certainly terrified Daniel F. Royer, the new agent at Pine Ridge. A political hack called "Young-Man-Afraid-of-Indians" by his charges, on October 30 Royer concluded that "the only remedy for this matter is the use of the military." Two weeks later, bombarded by appeals from Royer and widespread speculation about a pending Indian outbreak, President Benjamin Harrison ordered in the army.[47]

Now bearing a second general's star and command of the Division of the Missouri, Miles again oversaw military operations. On November 20, Brigadier General John R. Brooke, commanding eight companies, a Hotchkiss cannon, and a Gatling gun rumbled onto Pine Ridge; that same day, Lieutenant Colonel A. T. Smith, leading five companies and a Hotchkiss gun, swept onto the Rosebud Reservation. Terrified Indians fled in droves, and the precipitous action unified the Ghost Dancers, who numbered about a third of the reservation peoples. On at least three occasions Miles warned Brooke not to allow his commands "to be mixed up with the Indians." He resisted immediate assaults, but a botched attempt to arrest Sitting Bull left the most famous Lakota, as well as seven of his supporters and six Indian policemen, dead.[48]

FIG. 62. Wounded Knee. Soldiers inspect the awful carnage and debris at Big Foot's camp. LIBRARY OF CONGRESS, USZ62-46006.

Among the most prominent of the remaining leaders was Big Foot, a respected Minneconjou traditionalist followed by as many as four hundred men, women, and children. On December 29 at Wounded Knee Creek, Colonel James W. Forsyth, commanding 438 men of the Seventh Cavalry, a platoon of Oglala scouts, and four Hotchkiss cannon, attempted to implement orders to disarm Big Foot's people. General instructions for the Indians to turn over their weapons producing only a few guns, Forsyth sent two officers and thirty men into the camp, a move that directly violated Miles's earlier warnings. Tensions mounted, with villagers resentful of yet another attempt to forcibly eradicate their culture. Hearing what they thought to be shots from the lodges, the soldiers surrounding the camp opened fire, their booming Hotchkiss shells ripping through the village and the snow-covered ravines as the Minneconjous tried to flee. A vicious mêlée ensued, with some soldiers trying to stop the carnage and others needlessly slaughtering noncombatants. In the end, three hundred Indians, mostly women and children, were killed or wounded. Twenty-five soldiers died, and thirty-nine had been wounded.[49]

As news of the disastrous bloodbath spread, the next day revenge-minded Lakotas nearly trapped Forsyth's command near the Drexel Mission, four miles from the Pine Ridge Agency. Only the arrival of a battalion of African American cavalrymen averted the possibility of a serious defeat. But the Lakotas faced overwhelming odds. Opposed by one-fifth of the entire U.S. Army, escape was impossible and open resistance futile. On January 21, 1891, the biggest military operation since the Civil War broke up after a final grand review.[50]

The Long Frontier

Eight months following the tragedy at Wounded Knee, Nelson A. Miles, who in 1895 would succeed John Schofield as commanding general, predicted that "the old theory that the destruction of a vast herd of buffalo had ended Indian wars, is not well-founded." Indeed, the notion that peace had come to the borderlands would have surprised most contemporary officers. In 1892, Brigadier General Alexander McD. McCook warned that "a conflict with the Navajoes, who are in great numbers and are well armed, would be a serious business." Only the arrival of regulars, reported Brigadier General John J. Coppinger three years later, had prevented conflict between whites and Bannock Indians near Jackson's Hole, Wyoming. One Navajo known as "the Kid," believed to be from the San Carlos Reservation, had bedeviled regulars stationed in the Southwest for years, and in 1896 U.S. soldiers pursued some Apaches 150 miles into Mexico, leading Brigadier General Frank Wheaton to call attention "to the extraordinary amount of field service and laborious scouting." And in a repeat of countless such efforts throughout the nineteenth century, several detachments of regulars were later dispatched to help moderate the chaos resulting from discoveries of gold in Alaska.[1]

Changes were nonetheless afoot. North and South Dakota, Montana, and Washington gained statehood in 1889, and Idaho and Wyoming followed the next year. Congress organized the Oklahoma Territory in 1890 and granted Utah its statehood six years later. Even more dramatic was the nation's expansion overseas. The government annexed Hawaii in 1898, and as a result of the war against Spain the United States acquired Guam, the Philippines, and Puerto Rico. Cuba's short-lived independence was quickly replaced by American hegemony, and in 1899 the United States acquired Wake Island and American Samoa.

On the surface, changes within the army seemed to mirror the transformation of the nation's borderlands. Beginning in 1890, the army attempted to institutionalize its long practice of hiring Native American scouts by setting aside one company per regiment for Indian enlisted men, who would serve five-year enlistments as regular soldiers. The War Department also made a concerted effort to reduce the flow of immigrants into military service. Seeking to pave the way for more reforms, in 1903 President Theodore Roosevelt and Secretary of War Elihu Root forced Miles, the aging frontier warrior, into retirement. Concurrently, the War Department abolished the office of commanding general in favor of a chief of staff, who would oversee a general staff. The rapid-fire creation of the Army War College (1901), introduction of smokeless, recoilless three-inch field guns (1902), and adaptation of new bolt-action Springfield rifles (1903) seemed further indications of a break from the past.[2]

But the army would be slow to complete its metamorphosis. Most officers were lukewarm about the effort to enlist Indians as regular soldiers, and the recruits had been mustered out by 1897. Miles proved not to be the obstacle; in the wake of his departure, army bureaucrats showed more interested in maintaining their bases of influence and power than in cultivating meaningful reform. Finally, the pacification of the Philippines bore an eerie resemblance to the army's long efforts to conquer the western borderlands. Diverse and fragmented enemies, physical discomfort, internal factionalism, ambivalence about native peoples, mixed messages from civilians about their mission, professionalism tinged with occasional misbehavior, lack of attention to counterinsurgency doctrine—such were the experiences of U.S. soldiers in the Philippines. "Young lieutenants soon discovered they must not only be warriors," explains historian Brian Linn, "but explorers, road builders, emissaries to tribal councils, provincial governors, customs officials, teachers, sanitation experts, and relief workers." The heritage of the frontier army was thus apparent in the soldiers who now occupied a new global empire.[3]

Historian Francis Paul Prucha has correctly described the regular army as being "a child of the frontier." Ironically, though created in direct response to frontier challenges, the army rarely structured itself in a manner consistent with borderlands realities. As Schofield reasoned in 1875, "There is no glory to be won in savage warfare." Save for Anthony Wayne's short-lived Legion of the United States—created in the wake of two humiliating defeats—the regulars never developed a coherent doctrine for fighting Indians, a foe most saw as being unworthy of systematic analysis or intellectual scrutiny. Their refusal to face the facts revealed a troubling institutional reluctance to grapple with the messy, unconventional disputes that so often characterized military affairs on the borderlands, a failure that would continue to plague the nation's armed forces for another century.[4]

The continual transfer of the regulars to newer frontiers had always produced some winners and some losers. "The Flat" at Fort Griffin died, as did Fort Stevenson, abandoned by the army in 1883 and now covered by the waters of Lake Sakakawea. Fort Churchill, erected in 1860 in the wake of the Pyramid Lake conflicts against the Paiutes and Bannocks, joined countless other former posts in eventually becoming a park. Other communities, by contrast, welcomed the army's departure. Fort Ellis had long been a staple to the economy of Bozeman, Montana, but by the mid-1880s local residents had come to see the thirty-two thousand-acre military reservation as an impediment to economic progress. Throwing open this land to private owners, explained one newspaper, would "contribute more to the development of the thrifty little city than its maintenance as a dilapidated two-company post."[5]

Elsewhere, military patronage remained a key segment of western economies. At Fort Riley, for example, voters in nearby communities approved a series of bond issues to make the post into the hub of a regional railroad network. The army turned the twenty-thousand-acre military reservation into an immense hay farm, from which it supplied garrisons far and wide well into the twentieth century. And in the late 1880s, the army's decision to establish its school for cavalry and light artillery brought over three quarters of a million dollars in renovations and expansion. "FORT RILEY BOOMS," gloated the editor of the *Junction*

FIG. 63. Nelson Miles and staff in Puerto Rico. The American frontiers
would expand overseas during the Spanish-American War.
Here Miles and his staff survey their campaign in Puerto
Rico, which the United States would acquire in the Treaty
of Paris (1898). LIBRARY OF CONGRESS, USZ62-117207.

City Union. The expansion of railroads allowed San Antonio, Texas, to
see even more direct benefits from the military's presence. Long headquarters for the Department of Texas, the city profited from the army's
decision to transfer additional troops and consolidate supply and quartermaster operations there. In 1891, editors of the *San Antonio Express*
giddily pronounced that "the presence of the troops in our market adds
over a million dollars annually."[6]

By design as well as by accident, peoples living in (or wanting to live in)
the North American borderlands often did things that antagonized their
rivals. The many cultures that contested the frontiers agreed on very little,
but almost everyone saw military conflict as a legitimate means of resolv-
ing disputes. Violence too often begat violence, and vengeance begat vengeance. Britain, Spain, Mexico, and the Confederacy lost their contests for
empire against the United States. For American Indians, the defeat was
particularly painful. The wars, the removals, and the horrors that too often

955. Group of Spaniards, Chinese, Filipinos and American Soldiers with Pet Goat.

FIG. 64. Soldiers and Filipino civilians. U.S. soldiers eventually came to understand that effective counterinsurgency efforts in the Philippines—the new frontier of the twentieth century—required close interaction with civilian communities. LIBRARY OF CONGRESS, USZ62-121603.

accompanied reservation life took an immense physical and emotional toll. By attempting to ally with Washington against their other enemies, some had delayed their removal or ameliorated their conditions, but even the Crows and the Pawnees had eventually been relocated. Yet the losses, while dispiriting, did not mean that they had been defeated as peoples, or had given up their efforts to improve themselves, or to maintain their own distinct identities. The conquest, to them, was by no means total.[7]

In the United States, regular soldiers were often ambivalent about these conflicts, but in the end they equated liberty and order with their American empire. "These territories are the safety valve of the Nation," insisted William Sherman, and "afford an outlet for the surplus population and add vastly to the wealth and property of all." The army could not remain neutral, whomever the designated enemy might be. Sherman's contemporary, Phil Sheridan, bluntly captured the army's perspective:

My duties are to protect these people [settlers]. I have nothing to do with Indians but in this connection. There is scarcely a day in which I do not receive the most heart rendering appeals to save settlers . . . and I am forced to the alternative of choosing whether I shall regard their appeals or allow them to be butchered in order to save myself from the hue and cry of the people who know not the Indians and whose families have not the fear, morning, noon, and night, of being ravished and scalped by them. The wife of the man at the center of wealth and civilization and refinement is not more dear to him than is the wife of the pioneer of the frontier. I have no hesitation in making my choice. I am going to stand by the people over whom I am placed and give them what protection I can.[8]

Between 1790 and 1900, regulars participated in over eleven hundred combat operations against Indians. The soldiers had left a mixed record of brilliant individual initiative, great courage in the face of skilled enemies and harsh conditions, unimaginative leadership dulled by the tedious monotony of garrison life, and shameful dereliction of duty. The individual fighting skills and small logistical demands of the Indians often rendered it extraordinarily difficult to bring them to battle, especially on the Great Plains and in the desert southwest. Most soldiers showed neither tactical nor strategic innovation. The vast majority of army patrols, reconnaissances, and expeditions never encountered any Indians, and the vast majority of the old army's regulars never fired a shot their way. Forcing the action often required taking great risks: operating against enemies attuned to the ways of hit-and-run warfare, the army suffered major defeats such as those of Harmar, St. Clair, and Custer.[9]

Only the toughest and most stubborn regulars had the fortitude to engage in the arduous pursuits necessary to bring their enemies to combat. In the end, officers like Wayne, Harrison, Crook, Miles, and Mackenzie learned to turn one of the Indians' greatest tactical strengths into a critical strategic weakness. Exploiting the cumbersome but seemingly inexhaustible logistical network that their nation-building efforts had done so much to create, soldiers relentlessly struck the homes and villages of those peoples whom their government deemed hostile. On the frontiers, distinctions between combatants and noncombatants had been blurred since the colonial era. Precariously balanced Indian economies fell into ruin; discouraged and distraught by their terrible physical and psychological losses, in the end even life on the reservation seemed a better option than continued military resistance. As historian Elliott West explains, "Cheyennes, Arapahoes, Lakotas, Comanches, and Kiowas were not muscled into reservations because soldiers defeated and sometimes butchered them. They ended up there because they lost command of the resources they needed to live as they wished."[10]

It is sometimes forgotten, however, that control of those resources had been wrested from the Indians as a result of things military. The United States won Florida and the Southwest by direct force of arms, and Texas's independence from Mexico had also been gained on the battle-field. Several Indian groups—most notably the Creeks and many peoples who had once occupied Washington state—had clearly been whipped. Others, such as many Apaches, Seminoles, Lakotas, and Cheyennes, rarely lost in pitched battle. But military affairs encompass more than combat. Simply put, soldiers built forts, which staked claim to sites that had once had been of real value to Indian opponents. Though immense, the borderlands' natural resources were not infinite. With many forts came a modicum of security and often the newcomers who wanted to take advantage of a developing market, the transportation networks that linked it to other places, and the assurance that a faraway government was, at least to a degree, interested.

Amid a heated appropriations debate in 1878, Representative Auburn L. Pridemore (D-Va.), a former Confederate officer turned lawyer and politician, sharply criticized Martin Maginnis, Montana's territorial delegate, for having stressed the army's importance in developing the American West. "I tell him that the history of this land will not bear him out in the assertation that the regular Army has cleared the forest and moved on to the West in that grand era of civilization which marks that country," argued Pridemore. "It has been the tiller of the soil who stood with loaded gun in his own field who has made his way through the savage land."[11]

Pridemore was correct in insisting that non-Indians would have continued to expand their borderlands without the army's presence, and no knowledgeable soldier would have claimed otherwise. Civilians would have flocked to the gold fields of California or to the promise of gold fields in the Black Hills had there been no regulars. They would have formed militias and volunteer organizations to protect themselves as they extended their own little empires in what they believed to be the name of liberty. But the congressman failed to recognize—or admit—that without the regular army, the loyalties of these people who staked out these claims might have been very different. Rather than Washington, they might have looked to Mexico City, or London, or to some independent regional power whose capital lay in the free state of Franklin, New Orleans, St. Louis, Salt Lake City, or San Francisco. And the Indians might have been able to continue to manipulate those varied loyalties to preserve their own interests and autonomy, as they had done so skillfully in the colonial era. But the army's presence showed that Washington cared, and in the end, it would be the Stars and Stripes that flew over the American frontiers.[12]

ABBREVIATIONS

ASPIA	*American State Papers: Indian Affairs*
ASPMA	*American State Papers: Military Affairs*
CL	Clements Library
HD	House Document
HED	House Executive Document
HR	House Report
LC	Library of Congress
LR/AGO	Letters Received, Adjutant General's Office
LR/OIA	Letters Received, Office of Indian Affairs
LR/SW	Letters Received, the Office of Secretary of War
LS	Letters Sent
LS/AGO	Letters Sent, Adjutant General's Office
LS/SW	Letters Sent by the Secretary of War Relating to Military Affairs
MPP	*Messages and Papers of the Presidents*
NARA	National Archives and Records Administration
OR	*Official Records of the Union and Confederate Armies*
PWD	Papers of the War Department
RG	Record Group
SBD	*Select British Documents*
SD	Senate Document

SED	Senate Executive Document
SR	Senate Report
Statutes	*Statutes at Large of the United States of America, 1789–1873*
TP	*Territorial Papers of the United States*
USAMHI	United States Army Military History Institute
WDAR	War Department, Annual Report
WGW	Writings of George Washington, Electronic Text Center

NOTES

PREFACE

1. WDAR, 1873, 40.
2. Tate, *Frontier Army in the Settlement of the West*, x.
3. *Letters of Delegates to Congress* 3:52–53.
4. Lee, "Early American Ways of War," and "Peace Chiefs and Blood Revenge," offers an excellent historiographical discussion of these issues.
5. Prucha, *Sword of the Republic*, 394 (first quotation); Prucha, *Broadax and Bayonet*; Howe, *What Hath God Wrought*, 5–6 (second quotation).
6. Grenier, *First Way of War*. For a different analysis of the period, which stresses the essential continuities of frontier conflict and the European reluctance to adopt frontier methods, see Starkey, *European and Native American Warfare*.
7. Linn, *Echo of Battle*; Wooster, *Military and U.S. Indian Policy*, 15; Cutrer, *Ben McCulloch*; Laver, *Citizens More Than Soldiers*.
8. McPherson, *For Cause and Comrades*; Wright and MacGregor, *Soldier-Statesmen*, 201–2 (quotation).
9. Maginnis to Lamont, Feb. 15, 1893, vol. 2, Lamont Papers (quotation).
10. Lamar and Thompson, eds., *The Frontier in History*; Dobak and Phillips, *Black Regulars*; Ostler, *Plains Sioux and U.S. Colonialism*, 22–23.

CHAPTER 1

1. Calloway, *American Revolution in Indian Country*, 273 (first quotation); Dowd, *Spirited Resistance*, 93 (second quotation).

2. Nobles, "Breaking into the Backcountry," 662 (first quotation); Grenier, *First Way of War*, 158–61; Washington to the Passamaquoddy chiefs, Dec. 24, 1776, vol. 6, WGW (second quotation).

3. Calloway, *American Revolution in Indian Country*, 278–79; Starkey, *European and Native American Warfare*, 131–32, 137–38, 167–69; Nobles, "Breaking into the Backcountry," 663–66; Slaughter, *Whiskey Rebellion*, 62; Aron, *How the West Was Lost*, 47–58.

4. Horsman, *Expansion and American Indian Policy*, 30 (quotation); O'Brien, "Conqueror Meets the Unconquered," 39–72.

5. Allen, *His Majesty's Indian Allies*, 56–57; Prucha, *Sword of the Republic*, 2–3; Hurt, *Indian Frontier*, 199; Dowd, *Spirited Resistance*, passim.

6. Washington to Steuben, Mar. 15, 1784, vol. 27, WGW (quotation); "Sentiments on a Peace Establishment," May 2, 1783, vol. 27, WGW.

7. Weigley, *History of the United States Army*, 77–78; Gallagher, "Reinterpreting the 'Very Trifling Mutiny.'"

8. Sword, *Washington's Indian War*, 89; Skelton, "Social Roots," and "Confederation's Regulars."

9. Prucha, *Sword of the Republic*, 7–9, 394; Calloway, *American Revolution in Indian Country*, 285; Hurt, *Indian Frontier*, 107; *Journals of the Continental Congress* 34:583 (quotation).

10. *ASPIA* 1:8–9 (quotation); Prucha, *Sword of the Republic*, 10–11, 44–45; Weigley, *History of the United States Army*, 83; Sword, *Washington's Indian War*, 37–41.

11. Hinderaker, *Elusive Empires*, 236; Wright and MacGregor, *Soldier-Statesmen*, 211 (quotations).

12. Weigley, *History of the United States Army*, 86–87; Stuart, *War and American Thought*, 65–66; *The Federalist, with Letters of "Brutus,"* 489–90, 493 (quotation).

13. *The Federalist, with Letters of "Brutus,"* 12, 110–19, 194–202.

14. Wright and MacGregor, *Soldier-Statesmen*, 241; Sword, *Washington's Indian War*, 82; Cayton, "'Separate Interests,'" 43, 47–49, 51–52; Hinderaker, *Elusive Empires*, 236–37, 269; Grenier, *First Way of War*, 191; *Papers of George Washington* 3:588 (first quotation); Bergmann, "Commerce and Arms," 16; *ASPIA* 1:5–14 (second quotation).

15. Allen, *His Majesty's Indian Allies*, 71; Starkey, *European and Native American Warfare*, 17–35; Hamtramck to Harmar, Apr. 11, 1789, vol. 10, Harmar Papers (first quotation); Frothingham to Harmar, Apr. 3, 1789, Harmar Papers; Heart to Harmar, Apr. 22, 1789, and May 10, 1789, Harmar Papers; *St. Clair Papers* 2:146–47 (second and third quotations); *ASPIA* 1:97–98 (fourth quotation).

16. Dowd, *Spirited Resistance*, 88–89, 99 (first quotation); *Outpost on the Wabash*, 236–37, 246, 255 (second, third, and fourth quotations); Sword, *Washington's Indian War*, 88, 91; Rowe, *Bulwark of the Republic*, 10; *St. Clair Papers* 2:161; *ASPMA* 1:23–24.

17. *St. Clair Papers* 2:186–87; Waghelstein, "U.S. Army's First War," 4–5; Knox to Harmar, Sept. 3, 1790, PWD (quotations); *Outpost on the Wabash*, 258–59.

18. Sword, *Washington's Indian War*, 96–99 (quotation), 108–20; Prucha, *Sword of the Republic*, 20–21; *ASPMA* 1:26–27.

19. Nelson, "General Charles Scott," 226–27 (first quotation); *ASPMA* 1:26, 30 (second quotation); Washington to Knox, Nov. 19, 1790, vol. 31, WGW (third and fourth quotations).

20. *ASPIA* 1:112–13, 171–73 (quotations); Prucha, *Sword of the Republic*, 22.

21. *ASPIA* 1:131–32, *St. Clair Papers*, 2:233–39 (quotation).

22. Sword, *Washington's Indian War*, 53, 146–50, 160–68; Starkey, *European and Native American Warfare*, 146; Nelson, "General Charles Scott," 219–20, 234 (first quotation); "Winthrop Sargent's Diary," 242 (second quotation), 244–50; *St. Clair Papers*, 2:241–46.

23. *St. Clair Papers*, 2:241–46.

24. "Winthrop Sargent's Diary," 244–50 (first quotation); *ASPIA* 1:136 (second quotation); Sword, *Washington's Indian War*, 168–70 (third and fourth quotations).

25. Allen, *His Majesty's Indian Allies*, 74–77 (first quotation); Sword, *Washington's Indian War*, 180–90 (second quotation); *ASPIA* 1:136–38 (third and fourth quotations).

26. Prucha, *Sword of the Republic*, 26 (quotation); Gaff, *Bayonets in the Wilderness*, 9–10; Sword, *Washington's Indian War*, 188–95; Eid, "American Indian Military Leadership," 71–88.

27. Nelson, "General Charles Scott," 234–35; *St. Clair Papers* 2:262–67, 276–77 (second and third quotations); *ASPMA* 1:36–39; *ASPIA* 1:197 (first quotation).

28. *ASPIA* 1:197–202 (quotations); Waghelstein, "U.S. Army's First War," passim.

29. *Annals*, 2nd Cong., 1st sess., col. 338–40; *Statutes* 1: 241–43; Sword, *Washington's Indian War*, 205–6; Gaff, *Bayonets in the Wilderness*, 28–32; "Opinion of the General Officers," [Mar. 9, 1792], vol. 31, WGW (quotations). In his notes of a meeting with the president, Knox, and Secretary of the Treasury Alexander Hamilton, Thomas Jefferson described Wayne as "brave and nothing else. Deserves credit for Stony Point but on another occasion run his head against a wall where success was both impossible and useless" (*Papers of Thomas Jefferson* 23:240–42).

30. Birtle, "Origins of the Legion," 1249–57; Starkey, *European and Native American Warfare*, 150; *ASPMA* 1:40–41. As early as 1789, Wayne had suggested that he be authorized to organize "a legionary Corps" along the Georgia frontiers.

31. *Campaign into the Wilderness* 1:15–16 (first quotation), 49, 58, 82, 90; Orders of the Legion, July 21, 1792, 4, Legion of the United States Papers; Wayne to Knox, Aug. 17, 1792, PWD (second quotation).

32. Wayne to Knox, July 24, 1792, Wayne Manuscripts; *Campaign into the Wilderness* 1:62–68 (quotation), 103–4, 109–10.

33. Wilkinson to Knox, Nov. 3, 1792, Wayne Manuscripts; Gaff, *Bayonets in the Wilderness*, 86; Sword, *Washington's Indian War*, 196–97, 217–22; Dowd, *Spirited Resistance*, 103–4.

34. Knox to Putnam, Aug. 7, 1792, Wayne Manuscripts; Wayne to Wilkinson, Jan. 5, 7, 1793, Wayne Manuscripts; Knox to Wayne, Jan. 12, 1793, Wayne Manuscripts; Wayne to Knox, Jan. 24, 1793, Wayne Manuscripts; Bergmann, "Commerce and Arms," 57–59; Gaff, *Bayonets in the Wilderness*, 144; Orders of the Legion, June 6, 1793, 59, and Sept. 5, 1793, 89, Legion of the United States Papers; *Campaign into the Wilderness* 2:127–28 (quotation).

35. *Campaign into the Wilderness* 2:129–39, 3:2–3; Gaff, *Bayonets in the Wilderness*, 170–86; Sword, *Washington's Indian War*, 249–52.

36. *Correspondence of Lieut. Governor John Graves Simcoe* 2:383; *Campaign into the Wilderness* 3:11–14, 36–42 (first quotation); Sword, *Washington's Indian War*, 257, 260–61; Wayne to Knox, Mar. 10, 1794, PWD (second quotation).

37. Gaff, *Bayonets in the Wilderness*, 234, 246–53; Sword, *Washington's Indian War*, 272–79; Starkey, *European and Native American Warfare*, 152–53; *Michigan Pioneer and Historical Collections* 20:364–65.

38. *Campaign into the Wilderness* 3:63–64 (first quotation); Gaff, *Bayonets in the Wilderness*, 256, 265–99; Sword, *Washington's Indian War*, 280–94; Starkey, *European and Native American Warfare*, 153; Orders of the Legion, July 25, 1794, 131, and Aug. 8, 1794, 135 (second quotation), Legion of the United States Papers. For criticism of Wayne's conduct, see *Greene Ville to Fallen Timbers*, 251–59.

39. Sword, *Washington's Indian War*, 295–98; Gaff, *Bayonets in the Wilderness*, 299; Dowd, *Spirited Resistance*, 113

40. Sword, *Washington's Indian War*, 299–307; Gaff, *Bayonets in the Wilderness*, 301–11; Howard, "Battle of Fallen Timbers," 46–47 (quotation); Starkey, *European and Native American Warfare*, 154–55; *Campaign into the Wilderness* 3:65–68. Lieutenant William Clark, serving with a rifle company in the Fourth Sub-Legion, argued that the American lines might have broken if the Indians "had kept themselves compact and advanced with judgment" (Jones, *William Clark*, 77–79).

41. *Campaign into the Wilderness* 3:65–68; Sword, *Washington's Indian War*, 306–11 (quotation); Gaff, *Bayonets in the Wilderness*, 326.

CHAPTER 2

1. Jones, *William Clark*, 79 (quotation); Gaff, *Bayonets in the Wilderness*, 334, 338–46.

2. *Campaign into the Wilderness* 3:70–73 (quotation); Rusche, "Treachery Within the United States Army," 478–91.

3. Brown to Hogdon, Sept. 28, 1796, plan for military encampment from Governor Sargent's papers (photocopy), Northwest Territory Collection; Starkey, *European and Native American Warfare*, 154–55; Bergmann, "Commerce and Arms," 96; Dowd, *Spirited Resistance*, 113–14.

4. Cayton, "'Separate Interests,'" 47; Hinderaker, *Elusive Empires*, 244–45, 252; Bergmann, "Commerce and Arms," 3, 14.

5. Hurt, *Indian Frontier*, 119–22; Prucha, *Sword of the Republic*, 54–56.

6. *Papers of James Madison* 12:220–21 (first and second quotations); Cayton, "'Separate Interests,'" 39–40, 54–55, 62, 66; *ASPMA* 1:67; Knox to Shelby, July 12, 1792, Wayne Manuscripts; Blount to Beard, May 31, 1793, War Department Collection of Post-Revolutionary War Manuscripts, roll 4, RG 94, NARA (third quotation); Grenier, *First Way of War*, 171–81; *Papers of Andrew Jackson* 1:49 (fourth quotation).

7. Kohn, *Eagle and Sword*, 301; Cress, *Citizens in Arms*, 132; *ASPMA* 1:112; *Statutes* 1:483–85; Prucha, *Great Father*, 31–37.

8. *ASPMA* 1:112, 267–68; Birtle, "Origins of the Legion," 1260–61 n. 19; Gaff, *Bayonets in the Wilderness*, xix; Waghelstein, "Preparing for the Wrong War," 18–25.

9. Prucha, *Sword of the Republic*, 57–58; Gough, "Officering the American Army, 1798," 460–71; *ASPMA* 1:124–27; Washington to Alexander Spotswood, Sept. 24, 1798, vol. 36, WGW (first quotation); McHenry to "Sir," [Apr. 10, 1799], McHenry Papers; Crackel, *Mr. Jefferson's Army*, 18–19 (second quotation); Kohn, *Eagle and Sword*, xii–xiii, 286; Murphy, "John Adams: The Politics of the Additional Army," 234–49; Ferling, *Adams*, 355–56, 372–73, 393–94.

10. *ASPIA* 1:543–44.

11. *ASPMA* 1:113; McHenry draft letter, Aug. 3, 1796, McHenry Papers; McHenry to "Sir," Feb. 25, 1797, McHenry Papers; McHenry draft, [Nov. 1798], McHenry Papers; *New ASPMA* 4:3–6 (quotation); Prucha, *Sword of the Republic*, 23, 54–56.

12. Prucha, *Sword of the Republic*, 58; *TP* 1:410–11; *Papers of Alexander Hamilton* 23:377–93 (first quotation), 402, 515; *ASPMA* 1:133–39, 142–44 (second and third quotations); McHenry to Otis, Feb. 11, 1800, McHenry Papers.

13. Jones, *William Clark*, 48 (quotation); Crackel, "Military Academy in the Context of Jeffersonian Reform," 99–117; Carp, "Problem of National Defense," 40–41.

14. Crackel, *Mr. Jefferson's Army*, 38–39, 45; Heitman, *Historical Register* 2:568–69; Coffman, *Old Army*, 8. The reduction in force fell more heavily on officers than enlisted men. Between December 1801 and June 1802, the number of enlisted men fell from 3,794 to 3,040, about 80 percent of the original force, whereas the number of officers declined from 248 to 172, just over 69 percent (Weigley, *History of the United States Army*, 109).

15. *ASPMA* 1:156; Dearborn to Wilkinson, Feb. 22, 1802, Letters Sent by the Secretary of War Relating to Indian Affairs, roll 1, RG 75, NARA; Crackel, *Mr. Jefferson's Army*, 100–101; Prucha, *Sword of the Republic*, 182–83; Nelson, "Military Roads for War and Peace," 3.

16. Charles Wilkins to McCormick, Feb. 25, 1802, Wilkins Papers (quotation); various articles of agreement, in Subsistence Contracts, 1803–12, RG 107, NARA, especially 41, 49, 69, 73, 85, 137, 145, 193, 197, 218, 251.

17. Jackson, "Jefferson, Meriwether Lewis," 91–93 (first four quotations); Coffman, *Old Army*, 8–10; Dearborn to Wilkinson, Feb. 22, 1802, Letters Sent by the Secretary of War Relating to Indian Affairs, roll 1, RG 75, NARA (fifth quotation); Crackel, *Mr. Jefferson's Army*, 50–51, 222 n. 52.

18. Morsman, "Securing America," 46 (quotation), 60–61; Prucha, *American Indian Policy in the Formative Years*; Dearborn to Claiborne, Harrison, and St. Clair, Feb. 23, 1802, Letters Sent by the Secretary of War Relating to Indian Affairs, roll 1, RG 75, NARA.

19. Prucha, *Sword of the Republic*, 84–85.

20. Prucha, *Sword of the Republic*, 87; *TP* 9:217 (quotation). Wilkinson had tipped off the Spanish to Freeman's presence. See *Jefferson and Southwestern Exploration*.

21. *TP* 13:5 (first quotation), 8; Crackel, *Mr. Jefferson's Army*, 102–4, 109–10; *TP* 9:71, 91–94, 96–98, 138–39 (second and third quotations). In 1811, about thirty regulars helped to put down "a formidable insurrection" of slaves upriver from Baton Rouge (Crackel, *Mr. Jefferson's Army*, 916–19).

22. *ASPMA* 1:176–77; *Campaign into the Wilderness* 4:8 (first quotation); Prucha, *Sword of the Republic*, 74; Crackel, *Mr. Jefferson's Army*, 111–14 (second quotation). The move was not without precedent, for Major General Arthur St. Clair had held a similar joint assignment as governor of the Northwest Territory.

23. Crackel, *Mr. Jefferson's Army*, 114–15.

24. *New ASPMA* 4:11–12; Crackel, *Mr. Jefferson's Army*, 126–31 (quotations).

25. *New ASPMA* 4:11, 14–16; *American State Papers: Miscellaneous Affairs* 1:574; Crackel, *Mr. Jefferson's Army*, 158–59. William B. Skelton concluded that "there can be little doubt that a significant minority of the officer corps participated to some degree" in the Burr conspiracy (*American Profession of Arms*, 80).

26. Crackel, *Mr. Jefferson's Army*, 152–54, 164–68; *Annals*, 6th Cong., 1st sess., 298; *Annals*, 10th Cong., 1st sess., 1395, 1932–34 (first quotation), 1939 (second quotation), 2061–62; Cress, "Reassessing American Military Requirements," 60–61; *ASPMA* 1:227–28; Hickey, "Federalist Defense Policy," 63–70.

27. Stagg, "Soldiers in Peace and War"; Stagg, "Enlisted Men in the United States Army"; Steinhauer, "'Sogers,'" 37; Coffman, *Old Army*, 146 (quotation).

28. Crackel, *Mr. Jefferson's Army*, 170–75; Dearborn to Eustis, May 2, 14, 1808, roll 1, Eustis Papers; Dearborn to Varnum, May 10 (quotation), June 12, 1808, Dearborn Miscellaneous Manuscripts Collection; *Boston Gazette*, July 14, 1808.

29. Coffman, *Old Army*, 12–14 (first and second quotations); Coles, "Peaceable Coercion to Balanced Forces," 79; Hamtramck to McHenry, Jan. 1798, McHenry Papers (third and fourth quotations); Stuart, *War and American Thought*, 68; Wagoner and McDonald, "Mr. Jefferson's Academy," 140 (fifth quotation); Crackel, *Mr. Jefferson's Army*, 116–20. For more positive interpretations of the officer corps, see Skelton, *American Profession of Arms*, 86, and Kohn, *Eagle and Sword*, 295.

30. Taylor to Jesup, June 18, 1821, box 17, Jesup Papers, LC (first quotation); Crackel, *Mr. Jefferson's Army*, 182; Kieffer, *Maligned General*, 4–5 (second and third quotations).

31. Allen, *His Majesty's Indian Allies*, 111–15 (first and second quotations); Dowd, *Spirited Resistance*, xiv, 129, 140, 145; *Messages and Letters of William Henry Harrison* 1:224 (third and fourth quotations); *New ASPMA* 8:99–134; Prucha, *Sword of the Republic*, 98–100.

32. Dowd, *Spirited Resistance*, 139; *Messages and Letters of William Henry Harrison* 1:402–5, 407–17, 429 (quotations).

33. *Messages and Letters of William Henry Harrison* 1:571–75, 604–5.

34. Harrison wrote two reports of the battle, dated November 8 and 18. The latter is considerably more detailed, and more optimistic (*Messages and Letters of William Henry Harrison*, 614–15, and *ASPMA* 1:776–79). See also Bergmann, "Commerce and Arms," 235.

35. *Annals*, 12th Cong., 1st sess., 731 (quotations); Prucha, *Sword of the Republic*.

CHAPTER 3

1. Hickey, *War of 1812*, 75; Prucha, *Sword of the Republic*, 106; *ASPMA* 1:313–17, 320; Weigley, *History of the United States Army*, 119; *Writings of Albert Gallatin*, 581–83 (quotations); Brown to Williams, Dec. 28, 1813, Brown Papers, CL.

2. *SBD* 1:272–77 (first, second, and third quotations), 432–34, 436–37 (fourth and fifth quotations); Antal, *A Wampum Denied*, 21.

3. Hickey, *War of 1812*, 81–85; Latimer, *1812*, 67; Hull to Eustis, Aug. 26, 1812, H-361, LR/SW, roll 45, RG 107, NARA; *SBD* 1:461 (second and third quotations); Cass to Eustis, Sept. 10, 1812, C-462, LR/SW, roll 43, RG 107, NARA (fourth quotation). Hull was court-martialed, convicted of cowardice and neglect of duty, and sentenced to death. President Madison accepted the court's recommendation of mercy on the grounds of Hull's Revolutionary War service. Hull spent the rest of his life in a futile attempt to regain his reputation.

4. *SBD* 1:498–99 (first quotation), 508 (second quotation), 358 (third quotation).

5. Hickey, *War of 1812*, 86–88; *New ASPMA* 5:111 (first quotation); *National Intelligencer*, Dec. 22, 1812 (second quotation).

6. Hickey, *War of 1812*, 85; Taylor to Harrison, Sept. 10, 1812, T-149, LR/SW, roll 44, RG 107, NARA; Grenier, *First Way of War*, 210–11; Cusick, *Other War of 1812*.

7. Hickey, *War of 1812*, 85–86; Skeen, *Citizen Soldiers*, 84–85; Stagg, *Mr. Madison's War*, 398–99; *New ASPMA*, 5:61–62.

8. Skeen, *John Armstrong*, 3–7, 124, 133–35, 139–41, 153; Gallatin to Madison, Mar. 5, 1813, Madison Papers, roll 5; *Official Letters . . . During the War with Great Britain*, 156 (first and second quotations); *SBD* 2:33–37, 44–46; *Centinel of Freedom*, May 18, 1813 (third quotation).

9. *SBD* 2:46, 323–27; Hickey, *War of 1812*, 136–37 (first quotation); Harrison to Armstrong, Oct. 9, 1813, H-1813, Letters Received by the Secretary of War, Unregistered Series, 1789–1861, roll 8, RG 107, NARA (second and third quotations); Grenier, *First Way of War*, 212–13; Starkey, *European and Native American Warfare*, 165; Dowd, *Spirited Resistance*, 184–85; Skeen, *Citizen Soldiers*, 93 (fourth quotation).

10. Hickey, *War of 1812*, 140–43; *ASPMA* 1:443–49, 487–88 (quotations).

11. Hickey, *War of 1812*, 128–83 (quotations); Weigley, *History of the United States Army*, 121; Scott to Irvine, May 27, 1814, Scott Papers; Stagg, *Mr. Madison's War*, 403–35.

12. Hickey, *War of 1812*, 185–89 (quotation); Brown to Armstrong, July 7, Aug. 7, 1814, Brown Papers, LC; Brown to Tompkins, Sept. 20, 1814, Brown Papers, LC; Skeen, *Citizen Soldiers*, 120–25.

13. Hurt, *Indian Frontier*, 123–25.

14. Grenier, *First Way of War*, 215–16; *Independent Chronicle*, Nov. 1, 1813 (first and second quotations); *Papers of Andrew Jackson* 2:428 (third quotation), 492–93 (fifth quotation); Starkey, *European and Native American Warfare*, 158–59; Remini, *Jackson and His Indian Wars*, 63–64 (fourth quotation); *Official Letters . . . During the War with Great Britain*, 255–56; Prucha, *Sword of the Republic*, 115.

15. Remini, *Jackson and His Indian Wars*, 73–76 (first quotation); Hurt, *Indian Frontier*, 127–29; *Papers of Andrew Jackson* 3:49, 52–55 (second quotation). Among the wounded was Lieutenant Sam Houston, who in subsequent years as president of the Republic of Texas and U.S. Senator would be an outspoken defender of Indian interests.

16. Remini, *Jackson and His Indian Wars*, 13–14, 57, 68–69, 88–90; Hurt, *Indian Frontier*, 130–33, 136; Prucha, *Sword of the Republic*, 117–18; Latimer, *1812*, 369–88 (quotation on 387).

17. Dowd, *Spirited Resistance*, 183, 190; Beers, *Western Military Frontier*, 37–38 (quotation); Stuart, *War and American Thought*, 150–51, 181.

18. Prucha, *Sword of the Republic*, 120–28; *TP* 10:535–37, 556–57, 573–75;

ASPIA 2:6 (quotation), 13–14; Dallas to Brown, May 17, 1815, Brown Papers, LC; Brown to Crawford, Nov. 30, 1815, Brown Papers, LC; Brown to Williams, Aug. 13, 1815, Brown Papers, CL.

19. Prucha, *Sword of the Republic*, 251–52; *TP* 15:55 (first quotation); *ASPMA* 1:696 (second and third quotations).

20. Rowe, *Bulwark of the Republic*, 53; Hickey, *War of 1812*, 139 (quotation); Stuart, *War and American Thought*, 174; Benn, *The Iroquois in the War of 1812*, 164, 172; Beltman, "Territorial Commands," 194–95; Skelton, "The Army in the Age of the Common Man," 94. Morris, *Sword of the Border*, argues that Brown enjoyed more influence.

21. Kretchik, "Peering Through the Mist," 60–67; Johnson, *Winfield Scott*, 67–68, 125; Starkey, *European and Native American Warfare*, 164; Waghelstein, "U.S. Army's First War," 16 (quotations).

22. *Albany Argus*, March 7, 1815; Fitzgerald, "'Nature Unsubdued,'" 14; *Annals*, 13th Cong., 3rd sess., col. 1215 (first quotation), 1225 (second quotation); Watts, *Republic Reborn*, 279–80. The House wanted a six-thousand-strong force, whereas the Senate had insisted on fifteen thousand (*Annals*, 13th Cong., 3rd sess., col. 1271–73; *Albany Argus*, March 7, 1815).

23. *MPP* 2:7–8 (first quotation); Randall to Cache, Nov. 22, 1817, Randall-Bache Collection (second and third quotations); Skelton, *American Profession of Arms*, 119–25; Wettemann, "'To the Public Prosperity,'" 48–51, 57–58; Calhoun to Brown, July 31, 1820, Confidential and Unofficial Letters Sent by the Secretary of War, roll 1, RG 107, NARA.

24. Larson, *Internal Improvement*, 59–63; *American State Papers: Miscellaneous* 1:724–921; *Papers of Andrew Jackson* 3:395–96; *ASPMA* 4:626–29; *TP* 10:785 (quotations).

25. Nelson, "Military Roads for War and Peace," 6–7; *Papers of John C. Calhoun* 2:229, 4:100 (third quotation), 4:342; *New ASPMA* 5:2–10 (first, second, and fourth quotations); Wettemann, "'To the Public Prosperity,'" 33–34, 57.

26. Taylor to Jesup, Sept. 18, 1820, box 17, Jesup Papers, LC (first and second quotations); Wool to Brown, June 18, 1820, Brown Papers, CL; Pegram to Anderson, Dec. 1, 1840, box 3, Anderson Papers (third quotation).

27. Coffman, *Old Army*, 154, 167 (first quotation); Nichols, "Soldiers as Farmers," 216–18; *Army Life*, 134, 138–40 (second and third quotations).

28. Lowe, *Five Years a Dragoon*, 21–23; Wooster, *Soldiers, Sutlers, and Settlers*, 168–72 (quotation).

29. Emerson, *Marksmanship*, 4–11; Archer to mother, Jan. 13, 1859, box 3, Archer Collection (first quotation); Mar. 28, 1852, Heintzelman Papers (second quotation); Coffman, *Old Army*, 156–57; Waghelstein, "Preparing for the Wrong War," 161–63.

30. Oliva, "Army and the Fur Trade," 21–26; *MPP* 2:16.

31. Watson, "National Territorial Expansion on the Western Frontier" (first and second quotations); Swagerty, "Leviathan of the North," 478–517;

Brown to Calhoun, Sept. 5, 1819, Brown Papers, LC; Calhoun to Brown, Mar. 6, 1819, Brown Papers, LC (third quotation); *ASPMA* 2:33 (fourth quotation).

32. *City of Washington Gazette,* Oct. 9, 1818, and *Niles' Register,* Oct. 17, 1818, both quoting the *St. Louis Enquirer* (first quotation); *ASPMA* 2:69 (second quotation).

33. Prucha, *Sword of the Republic,* 143–51; *Papers of John C. Calhoun* 3:639–40 (first quotation); Goetzmann, *Army Exploration,* 40–41; Calhoun to Brown, Mar. 6, 1819, Brown Papers, LC (second quotation).

34. *TP* 13:27 (first quotation); Prucha, *Sword of the Republic,* 171–78 (second and third quotations).

CHAPTER 4

1. Jesup to Monroe, Aug. 21, 1816 (first quotation), and Jesup to Monroe, Sept. 8, 1816 (second and third quotations), Jesup Papers, CL; Jesup to Jackson, Aug. 18, 21, 1816, box 2, Jesup Papers, LC; Jesup to Claiborne, Aug. 24, 1816, box 17, Jesup Papers, LC.

2. *ASPMA* 2:99–130; Heidler and Heidler, *Old Hickory's War,* x, 135, 169–70; Prucha, *Sword of the Republic,* 130–33; *Papers of Andrew Jackson* 4:213–15 (quotations).

3. *Diary of John Quincy Adams,* 198–200; *Annals,* 15th Cong., 2nd sess., 742, 1071–72; Scott to Brown, July 29, 1818, Brown Papers, CL (quotation); *ASPMA* 1:779–82; Calhoun to Brown, Aug. 15, 1819, Brown Papers, CL; Skeen, "Calhoun, Crawford, and the Politics of Retrenchment," 141–42; Fitzgerald, "Rejecting Calhoun's Expansible Army Plan," 160–85; Heidler and Heidler, *Old Hickory's War,* 229–30.

4. Goetzmann, *Army Exploration,* 43 (quotation); Morris, *Sword of the Border,* 220; Prucha, *Sword of the Republic,* 144–47; Watson, "National Territorial Expansion on the Western Frontier."

5. *Annals,* 16th Cong., 1st sess., 859, 1599–1602, 1611–15, 2232–34; Macomb to Calhoun, Nov. 9, 1819, M-121, LR/SW, roll 90, RG 107, NARA; Scott to Calhoun, Aug. 20, 1820, S-37, LR/SW, roll 91, RG 107, NARA (quotation); Jesup memorandum [March] 1820, Letters Sent by the Office of the Quartermaster General, Main Series, 1818–70, roll 1, RG 92, NARA; Atkinson to Calhoun, Oct. 18, 1820, A-29, LR/SW, roll 88, RG 107, NARA; *Papers of John C. Calhoun* 5:293–96, 317–19; Macomb to Calhoun, Sept. 30, 1820, M-122, LR/SW, roll 90, RG 107, NARA; *ASPMA* 2:188–91.

6. Heidler and Heidler, *Old Hickory's War,* 229–30; Fitzgerald, "Rejecting Calhoun's Expansible Army Plan," 160–85; *Annals,* 16th Cong., 2nd sess., 368 (first quotation); *Statutes* 3:615; Weigley, *History of the United States Army,* 142; Abert to Van Deventer, Jan. 25, 1821, box 4, Van Deventer Papers (second and third quotations).

7. *ASPMA* 2:188–91 (first and second quotations); *Papers of John C. Calhoun* 5:377–80 (third quotation); *Annals,* 16th Cong., 2nd sess., 374, 933.

"Borderlands" states in 1821 are defined as Alabama, Georgia, Illinois, Indiana, Kentucky, Louisiana, Mississippi, Ohio, and Tennessee.

8. Goetzmann, *Army Exploration*, 41–42 (quotation); *Statistical History*, 8, 1114–15.

9. Stanley Diary, Sept. 9, 1853, Center for American History (first quotation); Wall to Anderson, Aug. 19, 1836, box 2, Anderson Papers (second quotation); Skelton, *American Profession of Arms*, 310–11; Skelton, "Army in the Age of the Common Man," 103 (third quotation); Silver, "Edmund Pendleton Gaines and Frontier Problems," 333 (fourth and fifth quotations). See also *ASPIA* 2:161, and McLane to Mrs. McLane, Dec. 24, 1837, box 2, McLane Papers.

10. Hoffman, *Winter in the West* 2:86–87 (first quotation); Childs, "Recollections of Wisconsin," 180 (second and third quotations); *ASPMA* 5:506–10; Taylor to Jones, July 15, 1834, roll 1, Taylor Papers.

11. HD 219, 27th Cong., 3rd sess., serial 425, 20 (quotation); Prucha, *Great Father*, 58–67. See also *A Traveler in Indian Territory*.

12. Order of June 1, 1821, General Orders and Circulars of the War Department and Headquarters of the Army, roll 1, RG 94, NARA (quotation); *TP* 11:212, 243 (second quotation); Klyza, "The United States Army, Natural Resources, and Political Development," 5–7.

13. *TP* 21:710 (first and second quotations); *Making of a Soldier*, 42 (third and fourth quotations); Skelton, *American Profession of Arms*, 297–98 (fifth and sixth quotations).

14. Prucha, *Broadax and Bayonet*, 215–16 (first and second quotations); Thompson, *Civil War to the Bloody End*, 60–79; HD 144, 26th Cong., 1st sess., serial 365 (third and fourth quotations).

15. Hitchcock, *Fifty Years in Camp and Field*, 47 (first and second quotations); Coffman, *Old Army*, 66–70; Brown to Dallas, Nov. 20, 1815, Brown Papers, LC; Mitchell to Jesup, July 28, 1817, Jesup Papers, USAMHI; Gaines to Jesup, July 2, 1817, box 2, Jesup Papers, LC (fourth quotation); Randall to Bache, Mar. 4, 1818, Randall-Bache Collection; Calhoun to Scott, Mar. 5, 11, 1819, Confidential and Unofficial Letters Sent by the Secretary of War, roll 1, RG 107, NARA; Johnson, *Winfield Scott*, 97 (fifth and sixth quotations); Cunliffe, *Soldiers and Civilians*, 136.

16. Prucha, *Broadax and Bayonet*, 216–17 (first quotation); general orders, Nov. 10, 1798, General James Wilkinson's Order Book, roll 3, RG 94, NARA (second and third quotations); Coffman, *Old Army*, 99; Steinhauer, "'Sogers,'" 249–50; *ASPMA* 3:307–26 (fourth quotation); Order Book, 1834–35, Clinch Papers.

17. *Recollections of Western Texas*, 29 (first quotation); Stagg, "Soldiers in Peace and War"; McHenry to Wilkinson, Feb. 9, 1798, quoting the *Pittsburg Gazette* of Jan. 6, 1798, McHenry Papers (second and third quotations); Bandel, *Frontier Life*, 114 (fourth quotation); Vargas, "Progressive Agent of Mischief," 202 (fifth and sixth quotations); Coffman, *Old Army*, 137–41. Steinhauer, "'Sogers,'" 14, includes a list of "eminent enlisted

men" in the antebellum army, the most famous of whom was undoubtedly Edgar Allen Poe.

18. Skelton, "Army in the Age of the Common Man," 97; Skelton, "Social
Roots," 451–52; Skelton, "Confederation's Regulars," 783; Skelton,
American Profession of Arms, 146–49, 158, 261; Steinhauer, "'Sogers,'"
298, 300, 322–56. Correspondence regarding Hubbs is in Letters
Received by the Office of the Adjutant General, Main Series, 1822–60,
H-301 (1860), roll 642, RG 94, NARA; the quotation comes from a letter
to his father dated May 8, 1859. With the outbreak of the Civil War,
Hubbs got his wish, securing a lieutenancy in the Thirteenth Infantry
Regiment. Captured by the Confederates in 1864, he was dismissed from
the army in October 1865 (Heitman, *Historical Register* 1:551).

19. Vargas, "Progressive Agent of Mischief," 199–206 (first quotation);
Warfield Diary, July 17, 1830 (second quotation).

20. Coffman, *Old Army*, 193; *ASPMA* 3:228 (quotation), 274–77; Brown
to Calhoun, July 20, 1818, Brown Papers, LC; Steinhauer, "'Sogers,'"
288–90.

21. Ballentine, *Autobiography of an English Soldier*, 25–26; Coffman, *Old
Army*, 195–99; Vargas, "Military Justice System," 1–19.

22. *ASPMA* 4:287–91 (first quotation); Buchanan to Scott, Dec. 31, 1857, box
3, Buchanan Papers; Coffman, *Old Army*, 200; Warfield Diary, May 15, 16,
1831 (remaining quotations). Later, Warfield admitted that the "compromise" had been "a great faux pas" and provided a written description of
the affair to his superior officer.

23. Watson, "National Territorial Expansion on the Western Frontier"; Miller,
"U.S. Army Logistics Complex," passim (quotation on 70); Smith, "Army
Ordnance and the 'American System,'" 49–80.

24. Klyza, "United States Army, Natural Resources, and Political
Development," 3; *Statutes* 4: 22–23 (first quotation); Angevine, *The
Railroad and the State*, 18; Larson, *Internal Improvement*, table 2; Malone,
Opening the West, 31, 118–19; Wettemann, "'To the Public Prosperity,'"
2, 106; *ASPMA* 4:1–2 (second quotation); Jesup to Shriver, Jan. 17, 1824,
Letters Sent by the Office of the Quartermaster General, Main Series,
roll 3, RG 92, NARA; Prucha, *Sword of the Republic*, 188–89.

25. Prucha, *Broadax and Bayonet*, 34 (first quotation); *TP* 10:652 (second
quotation).

26. Atherton, "Western Foodstuffs," 167–68.

27. Tate, *Frontier Army in the Settlement of the West*, 123 (first two quotations);
HD 24, 27th Cong., 2nd sess., serial 402, 24; Holt, "Joined Forces";
Burrows, *Fifty Years in Iowa*, 43–48 (remaining quotations). For this and
subsequent approximations of relative dollar values, see Williamson, "Six
Ways to Compute the Relative Value of a U.S. Dollar Amount." I have
used the Consumer Price Index.

28. Prucha, *Sword of the Republic*, 251–53; *TP* 19:413, 462–63, 570–71, 602, 634, Morrison, "Fort Towson," 226 (quotation).

29. Prucha, *Sword of the Republic*, 155–57; Nester, *Arikara War*, 149–81; *ASPMA* 2:593–94 (quotation).

30. *New ASPMA* 8:321 (first, second, and third quotations); Jensen, "The Wright-Beauchampe Investigation," 134 (fourth quotation); Dougherty to Clark, Nov. 4, 1828, Letters Received by the Office of Indian Affairs, Upper Missouri Agency, roll 883, RG 75, NARA (fifth quotation); Fonterelle to Dougherty, Feb. 26, 1829, Letters Received by the Office of Indian Affairs, Upper Missouri Agency, roll 883, RG 75, NARA; Wright to Bliss, Apr. 11, 1829, Letters Received by the Office of Indian Affairs, Upper Missouri Agency, roll 883, RG 75, NARA; *St. Louis Enquirer*, Oct. 18, 1823 (sixth and seventh quotations). Cox, "A World Together, A World Apart," offers a sensible assessment of the effects of Leavenworth's expedition.

31. White, "Winning of the West."

32. *New ASPMA*, 15:61 (quotation); *ASPIA* 2:448–49, 595–609, 656; *ASPMA* 2:623–24; Prucha, *Sword of the Republic*, 158–63; *Papers of John C. Calhoun* 8:xxv; *Annals*, 18th Cong., 1st sess., 443–45, 449–61, 505–7, 752–53.

33. *ASPIA* 2:656 (quotation); Watson, "Subordination, Responsibility, and Discretion"; Wishart, *Fur Trade of the American West*, 53–65.

34. Brown to Calhoun, Mar. 21, 1823 (first and second quotations), and May 12, 1823 (third quotation), Brown Papers, LC; Brown to Barbour, Dec. 8, 1825, Brown Papers, LC; *ASPMA* 3:215–16, 330, 342.

35. Marston to Smith, March 30, 1820, Brown Papers, CL; *TP* 11:1093–95 (first quotation), 1102–3, 1109–10 (second quotation); "The Battle of Bad Axe," 119–35; Prucha, *Sword of the Republic*, 167; Barbour to Cass, Aug. 16, 1827, vol. 12; LS/SW, RG 107, NARA; HR 42, 19th Cong., 1st sess., serial 141, 6–18.

36. Barbour to Edwards, Sept. 10, 1827, vol. 12, LS/SW, RG 107, NARA (first quotation); *ASPMA* 3:618; HR 42, 19th Cong., 1st sess., serial 141, 13 (second quotation).

37. Lowery, *James Barbour*, 151–85; Skelton, "Commanding General and the Problem of Command," 117–22; *ASPMA* 4:1–2 (quotation); Hoxie, *Parading through History*, 63–67.

CHAPTER 5

1. *ASPMA* 4:154–55, 587; 5:26; [Cass], "Removal of the Indians," 77 (quotation). For conflicting interpretations of Andrew Jackson's views, see Remini, *Andrew Jackson and His Indian Wars*; Burstein, *Passions of Andrew Jackson*; Prucha, "Andrew Jackson's Indian Policy," and Case, "Abuse of Power."

2. *ASPMA* 4:588–89; 5:29–31; Cooke, *Scenes and Adventures in the Army*, 156–58 (quotation). Unless otherwise noted, discussion of the conflict is based on Jung, *Black Hawk War*.

3. *New ASPMA* 8:171–73 (quotation).

4. *New ASPMA* 8:179–85; *ASPMA* 5:29–31; "The Battle of Bad Axe," 57–58; Anderson to brother, Aug. 5, 1832, box 1, Anderson Papers (quotations).

5. Wright to Bliss, Apr. 11, 1829, W-39, LR/AGO, roll 48, RG 94, NARA; *ASPMA* 4:2, 5–6, 154, 277–80; Eaton to Miller, July 29, 1829, LS/SW, roll 12, RG 107, NARA (first quotation); Oliva, *Soldiers on the Santa Fe Trail*, 25–33; Cooke, *Scenes and Adventures*, 59 (second quotation).

6. *TP* 16:145–46; *ASPMA* 4:154, 219, 371, 585, 716; *Register of Debates*, 21st Cong., 1st sess., 272–73; *Register of Debates*, 22nd Cong., 1st sess., 3393 (first and second quotations), 1069 (third quotation); *Statutes* 4:533; Skelton, *American Profession of Arms*, 143. At least one officer complained bitterly about Jackson's appointments. "I have understood that the western members expect the appt. to that regt. of western people," ranted Ethan Allen Hitchcock. "This, to my mind, is a most preposterous presumption—altogether a new ridiculous species of local internal improvement. A Regt. of Dragoons is judged necessary for the defence of the western frontier. Who pays the troops? Not the western people. Who has the benefit of their services? The people, indeed, of the west, but what title does this give to them to enjoy a monopoly of the honors in the Regt.!" (Hitchcock to Garland, May 12, 1833, box 1, Hitchcock Papers).

7. Irving, *A Tour on the Prairies*, 59 (first quotation); *ASPMA* 5:19, 126; *Statutes* 4:652; Hildreth, *Dragoon Campaigns*, 14, 42–44 (second quotation); Hitchcock to brother, Mar. 31, 1834, box 1, Hitchcock Papers (third quotation).

8. Cass to McKean, Jan. 6, 1834, LS/SW, roll 15, RG 107, NARA (first and second quotations); *ASPMA* 5:170, 362, 627; 6:130–46; Catlin, *Letters and Notes*, 2:44, 84 (fourth quotation); Salter, ed., "Letters of Henry Dodge," 222 (third quotation); Prucha, *Sword of the Republic*, 357–58, 365–75; Hurt, *Indian Frontier*, 195–202; *TP* 12:991–92.

9. *ASPMA* 6:13–14 (second quotation), 150–53; *New ASPMA* 8:343–44 (first quotation). For the possible origins of the idea, see *ASPMA* 5:729–31 and 6:14–15.

10. Nelson, "Military Roads," 7–8; HR 42, 19th Cong., 1st sess., serial 141 (quotation); *ASPMA* 4:626–27, 815–16, 849–50; Prucha, *Sword of the Republic*, 191–92.

11. Coffman, *Old Army*, 152, 154, 193–94, 451 n. 125; Vargas, "Progressive Agent of Mischief"; *ASPMA* 4:708–9 (quotation); Prucha, *Sword of the Republic*, 325–26.

12. *ASPMA* 4:712 (first quotation); *ASPMA* 5:169, 630–31; *Register of Debates*, 24th Cong., 1st sess., 386–89, 1395–96; *ASPMA* 6:157–59 (second quotation); *Congressional Globe*, 24th Cong., 1st sess., appendix, 441 (third quotation). Cass later contradicted his conclusion that frontier security needs

held primacy. As part of an extensive report calling for millions of new dollars for coastal defenses that April, he insisted, "it is on our maritime frontier that we are most exposed" (*ASPMA* 6:366–68).

13. Laumer, *Dade's Last Command,* covers the episode in extraordinary detail; *ASPMA* 5:627; Clinch to Jones, Dec. 26, 1835, Clinch Papers.

14. Buchanan to Anderson, Jan. 13, 1836, box 1, Anderson Papers (first quotation); *ASPMA* 5:737; Remini, *Andrew Jackson and His Indian Wars,* 275 (second and third quotations); Jackson to Blair, Feb. 28, 1840, box 7, Jesup Papers, LC; Bemrose, *Reminiscences of the Second Seminole War,* 78; Prucha, *Sword of the Republic,* 278–81; Peskin, *Winfield Scott,* 92 (fourth and fifth quotations); *Papers of Andrew Jackson* 5:471.

15. *ASPMA* 6:417, 419–20; *TP* 21:1211, 1224–25; *New ASPMA* 8:348–49; Atkinson to Anderson, Mar. 28, 1836, box 2, Anderson Papers; Walraven and Walraven, "'Sabine Chute,'"; *Register of Debates,* 24th Cong., 1st sess., 3368 (quotation), 1387; Heitman, *Historical Register* 2:586–87.

16. Peskin, *Winfield Scott,* 95–96; Scott to Call, June 17, 1836, Scott Papers; Cass to Scott, June 24, 1836, box 6, Jesup Papers, LC; Cass to Jesup, July 11, 1836, Confidential and Unofficial Letters Sent by the Secretary of War, roll 2, RG 107, NARA; Prucha, *Sword of the Republic,* 282–85; Jesup to Butler, Jan. 21, 1837, LR/AGO, roll 166, RG 94, NARA; Jesup to Mills, Feb. 4, 1837, J-54, LR/AGO, roll 167, RG 94, NARA; Jesup to Jones, Feb. 7, 1837, J-19, LR/AGO, roll 166, RG 94, NARA; Grossman to Vinton, Feb. 23, 1837, Brown Papers, CL; *ASPMA* 7:864, 867–73 (quotations). For the terms of the capitulation, see HD 78, 25th Cong., 2nd sess., serial 323, 79–80.

17. Jesup to Jones, Feb. 7, 1837, J-19, LR/AGO, roll 166, RG 94, NARA; Poinsett to Jesup, July 25, 1837, LS/SW, roll 17, RG 107, NARA; Poinsett to Cummings, Armstrong, and Street, July 22, 1837, LS/SW, roll 17, RG 107, NARA; *ASPMA* 7:885–89; McLane to father, Jan. 6, 1837 (misdated; the year was 1838), box 2, McLane Papers (first quotation); Jesup to Taylor, Dec. 19, 1837, J-53, LR/AGO, roll 167, RG 94, NARA; Jesup to Whiting, Dec. 18, 1838, J-53, LR/AGO, roll 167, RG 94, NARA (second quotation); *ASPMA* 7:881–82; Prucha, *Sword of the Republic,* 286–93; Bauer, *Zachary Taylor,* 80–83; Finley to Chambers, Jan. 25, 1838, J-20, LR/AGO, roll 167, RG 94, NARA; Jesup to Jones, Jan. 26, 1838, LR/AGO, roll 167, RG 94, NARA; Jesup to Taylor, Feb. 8, 1838, J-54, LR/AGO, roll 167, RG 94, NARA (third quotation); Jesup to Call, Feb. 12, 1838, J-54, LR/AGO, roll 167, RG 94, NARA; Jesup to Wilkins, May 22, 1844, vol. 9, Jesup Papers, LC; "Concerns capture of Indian Chief Osceola" file, Jesup Papers, LC.

18. Jesup to Taylor, Feb. 2, 1838, J-56, LR/AGO, roll 167, RG 94, NARA; Jesup to Jones, Feb. 4, 1838, J-27, LR/AGO, roll 167, RG 94, NARA; Jesup to Jones, Feb. 9, 1838, J-30, LR/AGO, roll 167, RG 94, NARA; Jesup to Taylor, Feb. 14, 18 (first and second quotations), 1838, J-54, LR/AGO, roll 167, RG 94, NARA; Jesup to Taylor, Feb. 24, 1838, F-54, LR/AGO, roll 167, RG 94, NARA; Jesup to Poinsett, Feb. 24, 1838, J-44, LR/AGO, roll 167,

RG 94, NARA; Jesup to Jones, Feb. 28, 1838, J-42, LR/AGO, roll 167, RG 94, NARA; Poinsett to Jesup, Mar. 1, 1838, LS/SW, roll 18, RG 107, NARA; Jesup to Poinsett, Mar. 14, 1838, J-743, LR/AGO, roll 167, RG 94, NARA (third and fourth quotations); Jesup to Poinsett, Mar. 23, 1838, J-763, LR/ AGO, roll 167, RG 94, NARA.

19. Taylor to Jones, Mar. 10, 1838, J-49, LR/AGO, roll 167, RG 94, NARA; Taylor to Jesup, Mar. 20, 1838, J-67, LR/AGO, roll 167, RG 94, NARA; Taylor to Jesup, Mar. 30, 1838, J-76, LR/AGO, roll 167, RG 94, NARA; Taylor to Twiggs, Dec. 21, 1838, T-38, LR/AGO, roll 167, RG 94, NARA, roll 196; Bauer, *Zachary Taylor*, 86–90; Taylor to Jones, Jan. 5, 1839, T-13, LR/AGO, roll 196, RG 94, NARA (quotation). For more on the use of bloodhounds, see Campbell, "The Seminoles, the 'Bloodhound War' and Abolitionism."

20. Bauer, *Zachary Taylor*, 88–90; Taylor to Greene, Feb. 16, T-72, LR/AGO, roll 197, RG 94, NARA; Taylor to Twiggs, Feb. 16, 1838, T-72, LR/AGO, roll 197, RG 94, NARA; Taylor to Twiggs, Mar. 8, 1839, T-85, LR/AGO, roll 197, RG 94, NARA; Taylor to Jones, July 20, 1839, T-234, LR/AGO, roll 197, RG 94, NARA.

21. Bauer, *Zachary Taylor*, 91–95; Taylor to Poinsett, May 11, 1840, T-200, LR/ AGO, roll 218, RG 94, NARA; Gadsden to Poinsett, May 4, 1840, Poinsett Section, Gilpin Collection; Pegram to Anderson, Jan. 18, 1841, box 3, Anderson Papers (first and second quotations); Balch to president, May 4, 1840, box 3, Anderson Papers (third quotation).

22. Worth to Hitchcock, Mar. 10, 1841, box 1, Hitchcock Papers; Skelton, *American Profession of Arms*, 321; Waghelstein, "Preparing for the Wrong War," 159; Prucha, *Sword of the Republic*, 297–302; HD 262, 27th Cong., 2nd sess., serial 405, 11 (quotation).

23. Prucha, *Sword of the Republic*, 301; Waghelstein, "Preparing for the Wrong War," 161–62; Motte, *Journey into the Wilderness*, 199 (first quotation); Sherman, *Memoirs*, 25; McLane to father, Jan. 6, 1837 (misdated; the year was 1838), box 2, McLane Papers; Clark to King, May 18, 1841, King Papers; Birdsall to King, July 19, 1841, King Papers; Hitchcock to "Dear Sir" (marked, "not sent"), Dec. 5, 1840, box 1, Hitchcock Papers (second quotation); Hitchcock to Bell, Jan. 11, 1841, box 1, Hitchcock Papers (third quotation).

24. *ASPMA* 6:152–53 (first and second quotations), 7:779; Watson, "Professionalism, Social Attitudes, and Civil-Military Accountability," 1160 (third quotation).

25. *ASPMA* 7:575, 605, 777–85 (quotations), 905.

26. HD 311, 25th Cong., 2nd sess., serial 329; Silver, *Edmund Pendleton Gaines*, 253–54; Poinsett to Abert, Apr. 17, 1840, LS/SW, roll 22, RG 107, NARA; Gaines to Bell, July 7, 1841, vol. 129, LR/SW, RG 107, NARA. An early champion of the military use of railroads, Gaines in 1839 put forth an ambitious scheme for coastal defense, in which he envisioned a series of floating batteries, bristling with over a hundred cannon each. The job

could be done in six years and would cost about $66 million (HD 206, 26th Cong., 1st sess., serial 368).

27. *ASPMA* 7:578; Poinsett to Mason, July 15, 1837, LS/SW, roll 17, RG 107, NARA; Gaines to Bell, Apr. 21, 1841, LR/SW, vol. 127, RG 107, NARA; WDAR, 1838, 98–100; HED 278, 25th Cong., 2nd sess., serial 328; Cooper to Yell, Apr. 5, 1838, LS/SW, roll 19, RG 107, NARA; Poinsett to Linn, Jan. 11, 1839, LS/SW, roll 20, RG 107, NARA; SD 379, 26th Cong., 1st sess., serial 359; WDAR, 1839, 47, 114; WDAR, 1840, 19. See also "Map Illustrating the Plan of the Defences of the Western and Northwestern Frontier," map 75, Central Map Files, RG 75, NARA.

28. *ASPMA* 7:572–74 (first quotation), 589; Kemble to Poinsett, July 19, 1837, Poinsett Section, Gilpin Collection; Poinsett to [Kemble], July 31, 1837, Poinsett Section, Gilpin Collection; Routledge to Poinsett, Aug. 8, 1838, Poinsett Section, Gilpin Collection (second and third quotations); Skelton, *American Profession of Arms*, 133–34; *Congressional Globe*, 25th Cong., 2nd sess., 480–87; Wettemann, "'To the Public Prosperity,'" 7–8; *New ASPMA* 8:354; *Statutes* 5:256–60. Poinsett also tried, and failed, to reform the militia. See HD 2, 26th Cong., 1st sess., serial 363, 43–44; *Congressional Globe*, 26th Cong., 1st sess., 463, appendix, 577; HED 153, 26th Cong., 1st sess., serial 366; Brown to Poinsett, Sept. 23, 1840, Poinsett Section, Gilpin Collection; Wallace to Poinsett, June 13, 1840, Poinsett Section, Gilpin Collection; Kemble to Poinsett, Sept. 24, 1840, Poinsett Section, Gilpin Collection.

29. Wettemann, "'To the Public Prosperity,'" 6–9, 185–87, 235–92. Many of these former officers took leading roles in civilian management positions, especially railroads. Of the 1,058 graduates of West Point between 1802 and 1866, 35 became corporate presidents, 48 chief engineers, 41 superintendents or general managers, and 8 corporate treasurers (O'Connell, "Corps of Engineers and the Rise of Modern Management," 114–15).

30. *ASPMA* 7:878 (first and second quotations); Johnson, *Winfield Scott*, 120 (third quotation); Waghelstein, "Preparing for the Wrong War," 16, 160–61.

31. *Register of Debates*, 24th Cong., 1st sess., 3371 (first quotation); Smith, "West Point and the Indian Wars," 45–51 (second quotation); Atkinson to Anderson, May 1, 1839, box 2, Anderson Papers (third quotation).

32. Rowe, *Bulwark of the Republic* (first quotation); *ASPMA* 7:987–88 (remaining quotations); Taylor to Jesup, Nov. 26, Dec. 31, roll 1, Taylor Papers.

33. SD 356, 25th Cong., 2nd sess., serial 317 (first and second quotations); *Congressional Globe*, 25th Cong., 2nd sess., 182–83, 193 (third and fourth quotations); Taylor to Hitchcock, July 28, 1841, roll 1, Taylor Papers; Bauer, *Zachary Taylor*, 83; resolution, Missouri Senate and House, Feb. 13, 1839, B-69, LR/AGO, roll 202, RG 94, NARA (fifth quotation). For another defense of Taylor, see Henderson to King, Feb. 6, 13, 1838, King Papers.

CHAPTER 6

1. *Niles' National Register,* May 15, 1841, 164.

2. Bell to Gaines, May 22, 23:374, Aug. 25, 1841, 24:83–84, LS/SW, RG 107, NARA; WDAR, 1841, 61–62; *Congressional Globe,* 27th Cong., 2nd sess., 825, 838–39 (quotation), 844–45; *Statutes* 5:512. The House had originally voted to eliminate the Second Dragoons entirely. Borderlands representatives voting on the measure included thirteen Whigs and twelve Democrats. Congressional debates suggested that the Second Dragoons had been targeted because of the Democratic Party affiliations of its colonel, David Twiggs, and its lieutenant colonel, William S. Harney.

3. Cooke, *Scenes and Adventures,* 230 (quotation); *Statistical History,* 8, 1114–15.

4. Hildreth, *Dragoon Campaigns,* 85 (first quotation); *ASPMA* 1:781, 804 (second quotation); Coffman, *Old Army,* 150–51.

5. Wooster, *Soldiers, Sutlers, and Settlers,* 127 (first and second quotations); "Freeman's Report," 53:203; Parks, *General Edmund Kirby Smith,* 90–91 (third quotation).

6. Coffman, *Old Army,* 149–50; WDAR, 1857, HED 2, pt. 2, 35th Cong., 1st sess., serial 943, 49 (quotation); *Reminiscences of Zenas R. Bliss,* 18–19.

7. Coffman, *Old Army,* 154–55.

8. Coffman, *Old Army,* 24–26, 112–15, 138, 308; Talbot to mother, Dec. 21, 1848, Talbot Papers (first quotation); HR 354, 44th Cong., 1st sess., serial 1709, 46–47 (second quotation).

9. Holmes, "'And I Was Always with Him,'" 177–90; *Above a Common Soldier,* 33 (first, second, and third quotations); McConnell, *Five Years a Cavalryman,* 211 (fourth and fifth quotations). As a surgeon's mate put it in 1795, "where women are scarce, the men must not be dainty" ("Surgeon's Mate," 255).

10. Laurence, *Daughter of the Regiment,* 18 (quotation). For more general studies, see especially Stallard, *Glittering Misery,* and Nacy, *Members of the Regiment.*

11. Summerhayes, *Vanished Arizona,* 59 (first quotation); Vielé, *Following the Drum,* 131 (second quotation); Lane, *I Married a Soldier,* 22 (third quotation). Garrisons included the following forts: Gaines, later known as Fort Ripley (Mahkahta Co., Minn.), Snelling (Dakota Co., Minn.), Merrill (Nueces Co., Tex.), Duncan (Bexar Co., Tex.), Inge (Bexar Co., Tex.), Gates (Milan and Williamson Cos., Tex.), Martin Scott (Gillespie Co., Tex.), Lincoln (Medina Co., Tex.), Graham (Navarro Co., Tex.), and Worth (Tarrant Co., Tex.). These may be found in *Seventh Census of the United States,* 1850, manuscript census returns, 1850, rolls 367, 908, 910, 912, 913, RG 29, NARA.

    In 1870, Congress officially barred the use of soldiers as personal servants, but the law was commonly flouted (Coffman, *Old Army,* 306).

12. Coffman, *Old Army*, 306; Watson, "Flexible Gender Roles," 92, 104 n. 36; Skelton, *American Profession of Arms*, 208–9.

13. Abert to Van Deventer, box 3, Van Deventer Papers (first quotation); Skelton, *American Profession of Arms*, 192–99; Jesup to Croghan, Dec. 5, 1819, box 3, Jesup Papers, LC (second quotation).

14. Jesup to Croghan, Dec. 5, 1819, box 3, Jesup Papers, LC; Coffman, *Old Army*, 29–30, 49–50, 59, 63–64.

15. Steinhauer, "'Sogers,'" 338–39 (first and second quotations); Schofield, *Forty-six Years*, 18 (third quotation).

16. Steinhauer, "'Sogers,'" 332–37, 365.

17. Skelton, *American Profession of Arms*, 182, 285, 359.

18. Jesup to Heintzelman, Oct. 9, 1840, Poinsett Section, Gilpin Collection (quotations); Kaufman and Soares, "'Sagacious beyond Praise?'" 58, 81–82; Watson, "U.S. Army Officers Fight the 'Patriot War,'" 485–519. See also May, "Young American Males and Filibustering." Scott also enjoyed the use of "a small sum" of the $500,000 allotted for the defense of the northern boundary to use to develop confidential sources (Scott to Anderson, Apr. 15, 1839, box 2, Anderson Papers).

19. Utley, "The Frontier and the American Military Tradition," 9; Skelton, *American Profession of Arms*, 305; *New ASPMA* 12:287–91 (second and third quotations).

20. Brooks to unknown, Oct. 29, 1854, Brooks Papers (first and second quotations); Skelton, *American Profession of Arms*, 307–20 (third quotation).

21. Watson, "Militarily Effective but Politically Contingent," 5 (first quotation); Watson, "Subordination, Responsibility, and Discretion," 50–53; Skelton, *American Profession of Arms*, 134, 329; Oliva, *Soldiers on the Santa Fe Trail*, 42–49; Prucha, *Sword of the Republic*, 377–78 (second quotation).

22. *Traveler in Indian Territory*; West, *Contested Plains*; DeLay, "Wider World."

23. Hoxie, *Parading through History*, 60 (first quotation); SED 77, 40th Cong., 2nd sess., serial 1317, 51 (second quotation); Irving, *The Adventures of Captain Bonneville*, 166; van de Logt, "War Party in Blue," 2–4 (third and fourth quotations).

24. WDAR, 1842, 199–200; *Congressional Globe*, 28th Cong., 1st sess., 347, 415, 442 (quotations); WDAR, 1843, 52. The House voted ninety-four to fifty-six in favor of the measure, but no roll call vote was recorded. Democrats had regained a majority in the House, but debate regarding the bill evidenced no discernable party lines.

25. HD 2, 26th Cong., 1st sess., serial 363, 47 (quotation); Prucha, *Sword of the Republic*, 352–55, 363; Frazer, *Forts of the West*, passim.

26. Bearss and Gibson, *Fort Smith* (quotation p. 332); Jesup to Mackay, Mar. 23, 1844, box 9, Jesup Papers, LC; Jesup to unknown, Apr. 6, 1846, box 10, Jesup Papers, LC.

27. Thomas Cutrer, "Army of the Republic of Texas," *Handbook of Texas Online* (accessed May 4, 2008).

28. Craig H. Roell, "Linnville Raid of 1840," *Handbook of Texas Online* (accessed May 4, 2008); Anderson, *Conquest of Texas*, 153–94.

29. Nance, *Attack and Counterattack*; Haynes, *Soldiers of Misfortune*.

30. Spencer to Linn, Mar. 23, 1842, 24:349, LS/SW, RG 107, NARA; Ott, "'Ruining' the Rivers in the Snake Country" (quotation); WDAR, 1844, 126.

31. WDAR, 1845, 194–97, 208–13, 217–20.

32. Goetzmann, *Army Exploration*, 18, 21, 65–108.

33. Winders, *Mr. Polk's Army*, 9–11, 34 (first and second quotations), 37; *Statutes* 9:11, 13; *MPP* 4:413 (third and fourth quotations).

34. Weber, *Mexican Frontier*, 83–121, 276 (quotation p. 120); Blackhawk, *Violence over the Land*, 119–44; HED 60, 30th Cong., 1st sess., serial 520, 153, 168, 242; SED 7, 30th Cong., 1st sess., serial 505, 14; Oliva, *Soldiers on the Santa Fe Trail*, 63–76; Eisenhower, *So Far from God*, 205–9.

35. Eisenhower, *So Far from God*, 210–14.

36. Hagan, *This People's Navy*, 119–20, 131–32; Bauer, *Surfboats and Horse Marines*, 136–50; HED 60, 30th Cong., 1st sess., serial 520, 231 (quotations); Eisenhower, *So Far from God*, 214–16.

37. Eisenhower, *So Far from God*, 205, 215–32; WDAR, 1846, 513–17 (first quotation); SED 7, 30th Cong., 1st sess., serial 505, 109–13 (second quotation).

38. HED 60, 30th Cong., 1st sess., serial 520, 153 (quotation); Howarth, *To Shining Sea*, 162; Eisenhower, *So Far from God*, 205, 230–32, 397 n. 29.

39. Eisenhower, *So Far from God*, 231–43.

40. SED 1, 30th Cong., 1st sess., serial 503, 497–502 (quotations). Dawson, *Doniphan's Epic March*, provides an outstanding secondary account.

41. HED 60, 30th Cong., 1st sess., serial 520, 1128 (first and second quotations); *Democratic Telegraph and Texas Register*, May 28, 1847, quoting the *New Orleans Delta* (third quotation).

42. McNitt, "Navajo Campaigns," 179–91; SED 1, 30th Cong., 1st sess., serial 503, 69–70; Oliva, *Soldiers on the Santa Fe Trail*, 84–91; WDAR, 1848, 136–40.

43. *MPP* 4:631.

CHAPTER 7

1. Prucha, *Great Father*, 112; SR 156, 39th Cong., 2nd sess., serial 1279, 328.

2. Wooster, *Frontier Crossroads*, 39.

3. Smith, *The U.S. Army and the Texas Frontier Economy*, 11–13; Frazer, *Forts and Supplies*, 189; Conrad to Rusk, Jan. 24, 1852, LS/SW, roll 32, RG 107, NARA (quotations).

4. Talbot to sister, Oct. 24, Dec. 25, 1850, box 1, Talbot Papers.

5. Skelton, *American Profession of Arms*, 298 (first and quotations), 301–4; Ball, *Army Regulars*, 18 (third quotation), 154–55, 169.

6. Ball, *Army Regulars*, 19 (first and second quotations); Ord to James Ord, Nov. 8, 1854, Ord Family Papers; Brooks to unknown, May 28, 1854, Brooks Papers (third quotation).

7. General order 12, Aug. 9, 1855, in William W. Chapman Papers (first and second quotations); Wooster, "'The Whole Company Have Done It,'" 19–28 (third quotation); Jordan, Chapla, and Sutton, "'Notorious as the Noonday Sun,'" 456–508. The dragoon major implicated in the Taos riot was probably Philip R. Thompson, who was cashiered effective September 4, 1855. Reynolds later became a brigadier general in the Confederate army, and served for a time in the Egyptian army before returning to the United States, where he died, penniless, in 1876.

8. Etulain, *Beyond the Missouri*, 161–65; Mason to Jones, June 18, 1847, July 19, 1847, April 18, 1848, HED 17, 31st Cong., 1st sess., serial 573, 748–55; Sherman to Burton, Sept. 6, 1847, HED 17, 31st Cong., 1st sess., serial 573, 776–80; Sherman to Stevenson, May 8, 31, 1848, HED 17, 31st Cong., 1st sess., serial 573, 842–43; Ball, *Army Regulars*, 8–10.

9. WDAR, 1848, 61–62, 66; *Congressional Globe*, 31st Cong., 1st sess., appendix, 10; Riley to Jones, Apr. 16, 25, 1849, Records of the Tenth Military Department, roll 1, RG 393, NARA; Sherman, *Memoirs*, 82; *Statues* 9:505.

10. *MPP* 5:21; *Congressional Globe*, 31st Cong., 1st sess., 1047–61 (quotations), 1179–81, and appendix, 10–11; *Statutes* 9:438–39. Borderlands states included Wisconsin, Iowa, Missouri, Arkansas, Florida, and Texas.

11. *New ASPMA* 4:108–9; WDAR, 1850, 4–55 (first quotation); Conrad to Mallory, Aug. 2, 1852, vol. 33, LS/SW, RG 107, NARA; WDAR, 1852, 5 (second quotation); WDAR, 1851, 105, 113 (third quotation).

12. Utley, *Indian Frontier*, 59–60.

13. Crawford to Brooke, June 4, 1849, LS/SW, vol. 29, RG 107, NARA; Utley, *Frontiersmen in Blue*, 71–72; *Texas State Gazette*, Jan. 12, 1850 (quotation); WDAR, 1850, 35–36, 52; Conrad to Brooke, Mar. 8, 1851, LS/SW, vol. 31, RG 107, NARA.

14. Conrad to Smith, Apr. 30, 1851, LS/SW, vol. 31, RG 107, NARA (first quotation); Utley, *Frontiersmen in Blue*, 72–75; "Freeman's Report," 54:215; *Texas State Gazette*, May 17, 1851; Smith to Bell, Aug. 9, 1852, LR/SW, roll 163, RG 107, NARA; Conrad to Howard, Sept. 7, 1852, vol. 33, LS/SW, RG 107, NARA (second quotation); Conrad to Bell, Sept. 30, 1852, vol. 33, LS/SW, RG 107, NARA.

15. SED 7, 30th Cong., 1st sess., serial 505, 27–28 (first quotation); WDAR, 1851, 125–26 (second quotation).

16. Utley, *Frontiersmen in Blue*, 67, 87–90; WDAR, 1852, 23–25 (first quotation), 5–6 (second, third, and fourth quotations).

17. WDAR, 1850, 8; WDAR, 1851, 109–11, 161 (quotations), 164–65, 216–25; *Congressional Globe*, 31st Cong., 1st sess., 1967; Utley, *Frontiersmen in Blue*, 68.

18. WDAR, 1851, 142–43 (first quotation), 145 (second quotation); Utley, *Frontiersmen in Blue*, 65–66, 103–7; WDAR, 1852, 30.

19. Hitchcock, *Fifty Years in Camp and Field*, 390–91; WDAR, 1853, 41–42 (first quotation); Lyon to Canby, May 22, 1850, L-105, LR/AGO, roll 430, RG 94, NARA (second quotation).

20. SED 34, 34th Cong., 3rd sess., serial 880, 252, 254.

21. Ball, *Army Regulars*, 89–105; Davis to Wool, Jan. 12, 1854, LS/SW, vol. 35, RG 107, NARA; HED 88, 35th Cong., 1st sess., serial 956, 52.

22. Davis to Bell, Sept. 19, 1853, LS/SW, vol. 34, RG 107, NARA; *Laws of Texas* 4:258–59; WDAR, 1856, 4; Anderson, *Conquest of Texas*, 246–57, 267 (quotation). Anderson contends that Smith's double line of posts, which he dubs "brilliant," had created conditions that allowed the state to act.

23. WDAR, 1855, 12; WDAR, 1856, 17; Tate, *Frontier Army and the Settlement of the West*, 55–57; Goetzmann, *Army Exploration*, 262–304; Crawford to Abert, July 11, 1849, LS/SW, vol. 29, RG 107, NARA; WDAR, 1853, 16–23, 55–63; Davis to Sandridge, Jan. 29, 1856, LS/SW, vol. 37, RG 107, NARA; SED 29, 33rd Cong., 1st sess., serial 695.

24. WDAR, 1853, 24–25; Davis to Wayne, May 10, 1856, LS/SW, vol. 37, RG 107, NARA; WDAR, 1856, 5–6 (first quotation), 22–23; WDAR, 1857, 14; WDAR, 1860, 33–50; "Freeman's Report," 53:206 (second quotation); Paul, *Blue Water Creek*, 51–52; Utley, *Frontier Regulars*, 26–28, 57.

25. Morrison, *"The Best School in the World,"* 114–16; SED 1, 35th Cong., Senate Special Session, serial 916, 277 (quotations); Moten, *Delafield Commission*, 183–92.

26. Talbot to sister, Jan. 20, 1852, box 1, Talbot Papers (quotation); WDAR, 1853, 11–12; *MPP* 5:215, 287.

27. Paul, *Blue Water Creek*, 12–24, 29.

28. *Daily Missouri Republican*, Sept. 10, 1854 (first quotation); Scott to Hitchcock, Mar. 23, 1855, box 2, Hitchcock Papers; *New ASPMA* 8:443–53; Paul, *Blue Water Creek*, 29–47 (second quotation). See also Adams, *General William S. Harney*.

29. Paul, *Blue Water Creek*, 55, 60–64, 85–107; Bandel, *Frontier Life*, 84–88 (quotation); Todd to Sumner, Sept. 6, 1855, Sumner Family Papers; WDAR, 1855, 4, 49–51; "Harney Expedition," 110–14; Utley, *Frontiersmen in Blue*, 118–20.

30. Ostler, *Plains Sioux and U.S. Colonialism*, 40–43; *Explorer on the Northern Plains*, 52 (quotations).

31. *Congressional Globe*, 33rd Cong., 2nd sess., appendix, 334–41 (first and second quotations); *Congressional Globe*, 33rd Cong., 2nd sess., 461, 520 (third quotation). Roll call votes are in *Congressional Globe*, 33rd Cong., 2nd sess., 525, 1064. Borderlands states are defined as Wisconsin, Iowa, Missouri, Arkansas, Texas, Florida, and California.

32. Utley, *Frontiersmen in Blue*, 32 n. 60; Coffman, *Old Army*, 60; Skelton, *American Profession of Arms*, 146.

33. Missall and Missall, *The Seminole Wars*, 209–18.

34. Missall and Missall, *The Seminole Wars*, 218–22.

35. Davis to Lane, Nov. 27, 1854, vol. 36, LS/SW, RG 107, NARA; Davis to Curry, Jan. 2, 1855, vol. 36, LS/SW, RG 107, NARA; Utley, *Frontiersmen in Blue*, 175–82, 193 (first and second quotations); HED 93, 34th Cong., 1st sess., serial 858, 48 (third quotation); McConaghy, "The Old Navy in the Pacific West," 18–28.

36. Utley, *Frontiersmen in Blue*, 183–92 (first and second quotations); WDAR, 1856, 153–57, 194 (third quotation).

37. Utley, *Frontiersmen in Blue*, 194–98.

38. Utley, *Frontiersmen in Blue*, 142–48; Rodenbough, *From Everglade to Canyon*, 178–80; WDAR, 1855, 56–57, 62–69 (quotation).

39. WDAR, 1855, 56–61 (quotations); Utley, *Frontiersmen in Blue*, 148–52; Rodenbough, *From Everglade to Canyon*, 199–202; Davis to Bell, Sept. 19, 1853, vol. 34, LS/SW, RG 107, NARA; WDAR, 1853, 3; *Texas State Gazette*, Apr. 14, 1855.

40. WDAR, 1856, 2–8. For Davis's sympathies with France, see Vandervort, "France's Conquest of Algeria."

CHAPTER 8

1. For events in Kansas, I have depended unless otherwise noted on Mullis, *Peacekeeping on the Plains*, and Ball, *Army Regulars*. For congressional inquiries, see HED 50, 33rd Cong., 2nd sess., serial 783, SED 50, 33rd Cong., 2nd sess., serial 752, and SED 58, 33rd Cong., 2nd sess., serial 782.

2. SED 97, 34th Cong., 1st sess., serial 823, 3 (quotation); WDAR, 1856, 35–146.

3. *Congressional Globe*, 34th Cong., 1st sess., 1381–83, 1388–95, 1790–94, 2239–40; *Congressional Globe*, 34th Cong., 2nd sess., 5 (quotation), 83.

4. Skelton, *American Profession of Arms*, 216, 352; Lee to F. Lee, Nov. 1, 1856, 196, Adams, "An Annotated Edition of the Personal Letters of Robert E. Lee," 196 (first quotation); *General George Crook*, 10, 19; *Making of a Soldier*, 76 (second and third quotations); Coffman, *Old Army*, 59.

5. Scott to McDowell, Apr. 11, 1857, Scott Papers (quotation); Ball, *Army Regulars*, 180–88; Floyd to Walker, Aug. 1, 1857, LS/SW, vol. 39, RG 107, NARA; *New ASPMA* 10:316.

6. Ball, *Army Regulars*, 153–60; WDAR, 1855, 168; MacKinnon, "Gap in the Buchanan Revival," 43.

7. WDAR, 1857, 21–38; Metcalf, "Nauvoo Legion," 318–21; Ball, *Army Regulars*, 162–65 (first and second quotations); Moorman and Sessions, *Camp Floyd*, 45 (third quotation). MacKinnon, "Epilogue to the Utah War," 238–39, suggests that the economic windfall might have been less than earlier believed.

8. Moorman and Sessions, *Camp Floyd*, 127, 133–50; Floyd to Greenwood, Mar. 11, 1858, LS/SW, vol. 40, RG 107, NARA; MacKinnon, "Stranger in a Strange Land," 17; HD 605, 57th Cong., 1st sess., serial 4377, 1–17 (quotation); Bagley, *Blood of the Prophets*.

9. Ball, *Army Regulars*, 167–71; MacKinnon, "Stranger in a Strange Land," 22.

10. Ball, *Army Regulars*, 170 (quotation); Moorman and Sessions, *Camp Floyd*, 260–71.

11. Ball, *Army Regulars*, 139–49; HED 98, 36th Cong., 1st sess., serial 1057; HED 65, 36th Cong., 1st sess., serial 1059.

12. Ball, *Army Regulars*, 127–31; *Rip Ford's Texas*, 195–202; *Texas Indian Papers* 3:254–55 (quotation).

13. Knight, "Cart War," 319–36; WDAR, 1859, 359; HED 52, 36th Cong., 1st sess., serial 1050, 55, 86, 96–98; Thompson, *Civil War to the Bloody End*, 86–95; *Fifty Miles and a Fight*, 119–56 (quotation on 141); Utley, *Lone Star Justice*, 319 n. 6; Ball, *Army Regulars*, 131–35. For a superb biography of an often-misunderstood figure, see Thompson, *Cortina*.

14. Ball, *Army Regulars*, 136–37; HED 52, 36th Cong., 1st sess., serial 1050, 116 (first quotation), 133 (second quotation); HED 81, 36th Cong., 1st sess., serial 1056, 80–84 (third quotation).

15. Wood to Senate, November 30, 1849, "Wood to the Texas Senate," Texas State Library and Archives Commission, http://www.tsl.state.tx.us/governors/earlystate/wood-2-1.html (accessed Apr. 28, 2008) (first quotation); Olmsted, *Journey through Texas*, 182–83 (second quotation); *Congressional Globe*, 35th Cong., 1st sess., 493 (third quotation); WDAR, 1849, 143 (fourth and fifth quotations).

16. Utley, *Frontiersmen in Blue*, 120–23; WDAR, 1856, 106–11; Chalfant, *Cheyennes and Horse Soldiers*, 127–86; WDAR, 1857, 98–99; Lowe, *Five Years a Dragoon*, 197–203; *New ASPMA* 4:210–12; SED 11, pt. 1, 35th Cong., 1st sess., serial 919, 435.

17. Utley, *Frontiersmen in Blue*, 122–23 (first four quotations); WDAR, 1857, 98–99 (fifth quotation); Chalfant, *Cheyennes and Horse Soldiers*, 186–208.

18. SED 1, 35th Cong., 2nd sess., serial 974, 450 (quotations); West, *Contested Plains*, 199–202.

19. WDAR, 1858, 346–48 (quotation); Schlicke, *General George Wright*, 141–51.

20. WDAR, 1858, 348 (quotation), 364, 388; Utley, *Frontiersmen in Blue*, 207–10. The future generals included Wright (USA); Captain Erasmus D. Keyes (USA), Captain Edward O. C. Ord (USA), and Captain John H. Winder (CSA); and Lieutenant Henry B. Davidson (CSA), Lieutenant David M. Gregg (USA), Lieutenant William Dorsey Pender (CSA), and Lieutenant Robert O. Tyler (USA).

21. Of these, twelve became Confederate generals: Colonel Albert S. Johnston; Lieutenant Colonel Robert E. Lee; Major William J. Hardee; Captain Edmund K. Smith and Captain Earl Van Dorn; and Lieutenant George B. Cosby, Lieutenant Nathan G. Evans, Lieutenant Charles W. Field, Lieutenant John Bell Hood, Lieutenant Fitzhugh Lee, Lieutenant James P. Major, and Lieutenant Charles W. Phifer. Five, including Major George H. Thomas, Captain Innis W. Palmer and Captain George Stoneman, and Lieutenant Kenner Garrard and Lieutenant Richard W. Johnson, served as Union generals during the Civil War. Lieutenant Abraham K. Arnold became a brigadier general during the Spanish-American War, and bugler Edward M. Hayes was appointed a brigadier general in 1903, shortly before his retirement. See Arnold, *Jeff Davis's Own*, 330–40, and Heitman, *Historical Register*.

22. Anderson, *Conquest of Texas*, 286–310; WDAR, 1858, 253–54 (first and second quotations); *Texas State Gazette*, May 22, 29 (third quotation), 1858; *Rip Ford's Texas*, 229–36.

23. Anderson, *Conquest of Texas*, 307–12 (first quotation); Floyd to Runnels, Aug. 28, 1858, LS/SW, vol. 40, RG 107, NARA; WDAR, 1858, 258–74 (second and third quotations); Utley, *Frontiersmen in Blue*, 130–32.

24. Utley, *Frontiersmen in Blue*, 132–34; Twiggs to Thomas, Nov. 20, 1858, T-216, LR/AGO, roll 592, RG 94, NARA; WDAR, 1859, 358, 365–71 (quotation).

25. WDAR, 1859, 357, 371–72; Utley, *Frontiersmen in Blue*, 137–38.

26. Utley, *Frontiersmen in Blue*, 138–40; *New ASPMA* 8:539; WDAR, 1860, 5, 13–25, 56–61.

27. WDAR, 1857, 135–41 (quotation); Utley, *Frontiersmen in Blue*, 153–57.

28. Utley, *Frontiersmen in Blue*, 157–60; HED 69, 36th Cong., 1st sess., serial 1051, 34 (quotation).

29. WDAR, 1860, 74–75 (first quotation), 88–91 (second, third, and fourth quotations); Greer, *Colonel Jack Hays*, 312–22.

30. Brooks to Dave, June 29, 1856, Brooks Papers (first quotation); Utley, *Frontiersmen in Blue*, 81, 166–70; WDAR, 1859, 258–68, 323–54 (second quotation).

31. WDAR, 1860, 52–56 (quotations), 203–4.

32. WDAR, 1860, 60–68.

33. Archer to mother, Jan. 27, Apr. 14 (first quotation), May 1, 1861, Archer Collection; Peters to sister, Aug. 13, 1861, Peters Papers (second quotation); Talbot to sister, Oct. 22, 1860, box 2, Talbot Papers (third quotation); Lee to Custis Lee, Jan. 23, 1861, in Adams, "An Annotated Edition of the Personal Letters of Robert E. Lee," 721–22 (fourth and fifth quotations).

34. Skelton, *American Profession of Arms*, 352–58; Coffman, *Old Army*, 92–96, 205–7; Josephy, *The Civil War in the American West*, 35; Utley, *Frontiersmen in Blue*, 212; OR 53:492–93; WDAR, 1860, 218–21.

35. Wooster, *Texas and Texans*, 14–19. For the best primary account, see *Reminiscences of Major General Zenas R. Bliss.*

36. Josephy, *The Civil War in the American West*, 233–38; *OR* 50, pt. 1:463–64, 472; Sodergren, "Exercising Restraint." For a more critical assessment of the army's activities, see Chandler, "Fighting Words," 4–17.

37. Ball, *Army Regulars*, 70–71, 198–200.

38. *Chronological List of Actions*, 11–23; WDAR, 1860, 214–29.

CHAPTER 9

1. Weigley, *History of the United States Army*, 197–200; Utley, *Frontiersmen in Blue*, 212–16; *OR* 26, 1:720; *The Civil War Book of Lists*, 15–20, 187–88. The numbering system for mounted regiments was changed accordingly. The First and Second dragoons became the First and Second cavalries and the Mounted Riflemen became the Third Cavalry. The units previously designated as the First and Second cavalries became the Fourth and Fifth cavalries. A newly created regiment was named the Sixth Cavalry.

2. For Missouri's strategic value, see Belser, "Military Operations in Missouri and Arkansas."

3. Josephy, *The Civil War in the American West*, 319–35, 354–56; Utley, *Indian Frontier*, 73–75; Wooster, *Texas and Texans*, 34.

4. Josephy, *The Civil War in the American West*, 319–49; *Dakota Republican*, May 24, 1862 (quotations); *OR* 8:795–96.

5. *OR* 4:24–25 (quotation). In describing the Union-Confederate struggles in the Southwest in 1862, I have relied on Frazier, *Blood and Treasure*, unless otherwise noted. For the Union perspective, see Flint Whitlock, *Distant Bugles.*

6. Josephy, *The Civil War in the American West*, 38.

7. *OR* 50, 1:1013 (first quotation), 942 (second and third quotations).

8. SR 156, 39th Cong., 2nd sess., serial 1279, 124 (quotations). In describing the campaigns against Indians in Arizona and New Mexico during the Civil War, I have relied on Utley, *Frontiersmen in Blue*, unless otherwise noted.

9. *OR* 15:579–80 (quotations).

10. SR 156, 39th Cong., 2nd sess., serial 1279, 116, 160, 245–47; *OR* 26, 1:234–38, 250–57; *OR* 34, 1:71–75; *OR* 36, 1:71–77 (quotations).

11. *OR* 50, 2:256–57, 422; Josephy, *The Civil War in the American West*, 273–79.

12. Utley, *Frontiersmen in Blue*, 248, 254–56 (second quotation); Lamar, *The Far Southwest*, 432–34; SR 156, 39th Cong., 2nd sess., serial 1279, 140 (first quotation).

13. SR 156, 39th Cong., 2nd sess., serial 1279, 177–79 (first and third quotations); *OR* 34, 3:387 (second and fourth quotations).

14. *OR* 34, 1:917–20.

15. Josephy, *The Civil War in the American West*, 251–53; *OR* 50, 2:56, 119, 144 (quotations).

16. *OR* 50, 1:185–87 (first, second, and third quotations); Josephy, *The Civil War in the American West*, 257–59 (fourth quotation); Schindler, "Bear River Massacre," 307 (fifth quotation).

17. Utley, *Frontiersmen in Blue*, 224–25; *OR* 50, 1:199, 228–30; *OR* 50, 2:658–59, 903, 909–10 (second quotation), 1184–86; Josephy, *The Civil War in the American West*, 262–63.

18. Josephy, *The Civil War in the American West*, 264–65, 267; *OR* 50, 2:177–78, 830–31, 843, 881–82, 1075–76; Utley, *Frontiersmen in Blue*, 226–29; HED 1, pt. 2, 39th Cong., 1st sess., serial 1248, 651; *OR* 50, 1:168–69, 907 (quotation); San Francisco *Evening Bulletin*, June 18, 1862.

19. Josephy, *The Civil War in the American West*, 355–59; *OR* 13:484–85 (quotation), 841–44, 971–74.

20. Josephy, *The Civil War in the American West*, 361–71; Wooster, *Texas and Texans*, 80.

21. Castel, *Frontier State*, 139–45; *OR* 22, 2:470; *OR* 22, 1:576; Carney to Schofield, Aug. 25, 1863, box 3, Schofield Papers (quotation).

22. *OR* 22, 2:471–77 (first quotation), 482–88, 523; *OR* 22, 1:573–77, 585–87; Castel, *Frontier State*, 145–53; "Diary of Events in Dept. of Missouri 1863," box 1, 69–85, Schofield Papers; Carney to Schofield, containing undated clipping of the *Leavenworth Times*, Aug. 28, 1863, box 3, Schofield Papers (second quotation); Schofield to Ewing, Sept. 19, 1863, box 68, Ewing Family Papers; Josephy, *The Civil War in the American West*, 373, 380.

23. Josephy, *The Civil War in the American West*, 374–85.

24. Wooster, *Texas and Texans*, 32–33, 105–6, 133, 152–53, 170–71; Wooster, *Lone Star Regiments in Gray*, 218–20; *OR* 41, 1:885–87; *OR* 48, 1:27–28 (quotation).

25. *OR* 26:405 (quotation); Thompson and Jones, *Civil War and Revolution on the Rio Grande Frontier*; Dupree, *Planting the Union Flag in Texas*.

26. Dupree, *Planting the Union Flag in Texas*; *Rip Ford's Texas*, 383.

27. Anderson, *Kinsmen of Another Kind*.

28. *Through Dakota Eyes*, 32 (first quotation); Utley, *Indian Frontier*, 76–81; Josephy, *The Civil War in the American West*, 99–120 (second quotation).

29. *OR* 13:597 (first quotation), 613 (second quotation); *OR* 50:617–18; Cozzens, *General John Pope*, 200–201.

30. Josephy, *The Civil War in the American West*, 137–38. Another was granted last minute clemency.

31. *OR* 13:685–86 (quotation); *OR* 22, 1:555–68; Cozzens, *General John Pope*, 228–35; Josephy, *The Civil War in the American West*, 138–46; Utley, *Frontiersmen in Blue*, 271–74.

32. Cozzens, *General John Pope*, 235–42; *OR* 41, 2:228 (first quotation); *OR* 41, 1:141–45; Utley, *Frontiersmen in Blue*, 274–80; Josephy, *The Civil War in the American West*, 148–51.

33. Utley, *Frontiersmen in Blue*, 281–86; West, *Contested Plains*; *OR* 34, 4:402–4 (quotations).

34. Josephy, *The Civil War in the American West*, 296–305.

35. Lamar, *The Far Southwest*, 245–47; SR 156, 39th Cong., 2nd sess., serial 1279, 55 (first and second quotations); HED 1, pt. 5, 38th Cong., 2nd sess., serial 1220 (third quotation); Josephy, *The Civil War in the American West*, 305–8 (fourth quotation); *OR* 41, 3:462; *OR* 41 4:62, 433.

36. SED 26, 39th Cong., 2nd sess., serial 1277, 47 (quotations), 212; Josephy, *The Civil War in the American West*, 308–10.

37. Josephy, *The Civil War in the American West*, 308–10; Utley, *Frontiersmen in Blue*, 293–95; SR 156, pt. 3, 39th Cong., 2nd sess., serial 1279, 67 (first quotation), 74 (second and third quotations), 42.

38. Dunlay, *Kit Carson and the Indians*, 325–37; *OR* 41, 4:213–14 (first quotation); *OR* 41, 1:939–44 (second and third quotations).

39. Cozzens, *General John Pope*, 242–43; Utley, *Frontiersmen in Blue*, 300–303; *OR* 48, 1:41–43; 735–36, 793–94 (quotations).

40. Cozzens, *General John Pope*, 253–54; *OR* 48, 1:972–73, 1295–96 (quotation); Pope to Grant, June 19, 1865, series 5, roll 24, Grant Papers. In fall 1864, the Federals began to supplement their forces with six regiments of "Galvanized Yankees," Confederate prisoners who had agreed to join the war against the Indians.

41. Utley, *Frontiersmen in Blue*, 309–23, 333–36; *OR* 48, 2:412–13, 868–69; *OR* 48, 1:1172–74, 1181–82; Utley, *Lance and the Shield*, 66–68.

42. Utley, *Frontiersmen in Blue*, 323–30; *OR* 48, 1:366–83; *OR* 48, 2:1049 (quotation), 1129–30.

43. *New York Times*, July 23, 1865 (first quotation); Grant to Pope, June 19, 1865, ser. 5, roll 20, Grant Papers; Stanton to Grant, Aug. 12, 21, ser. 5, roll 24, Grant Papers; *OR* 48, 1:356–57 (second and third quotations).

CHAPTER 10

1. Sherman to Grant, Nov. 6, 1865, roll 10, Sherman Papers.

2. Utley, *Frontier Regulars*, 10–12; *Statutes* 14:332–38; Taylor to Hitchcock, May 19, 1841, roll 1, Taylor Papers (quotation).

3. Coffman, *Old Army*, 328–31 (quotation), 348–50; Adams, "'Common People With Whom I Shall Have No Relation,'" v; WDAR, 1875, 177.

4. Dobak and Phillips, *Black Regulars*, 92, 190, 280 (first, second, and third quotations); HR 384, 43rd Cong., 1st sess., serial 1624, 19 (fourth quotation).

5. HR 1061, 51st Cong., 1st sess., serial 2810, 4 (first quotation); *Ninth Census of the United States, 1870*, manuscript census returns, roll 528 (Maverick

County), RG 29, NARA; Knapp to Mead, Jan. 12, 1867, Knapp Papers (second quotation).

6. Kenner, *Black and White Together*, 27 (first quotation); Dobak and Phillips, *Black Regulars*, 238 (second and third quotations), 85–86; Wooster, *Frontier Crossroads*, 131.

7. Dobak and Phillips, *Black Regulars*, 237, 241.

8. Kinevan, *Frontier Cavalryman*, 232 (quotations); Robinson, "Don't Ruin a Good Story." For Flipper's account, see *Black Frontiersman: The Memoirs of Henry O. Flipper*. For Alexander, see Kenner, *Black and White Together*.

9. Thian, *Notes Illustrating the Military Geography of the United States*, 14–16.

10. Hutton, *Phil Sheridan and His Army*, 20–22 (first quotation); Schofield, *Forty-six Years*, 385 (second quotation). For the Schofield venture, see Wooster, "John M. Schofield and the 'Multipurpose' Army."

11. HED 70, 39th Cong., 1st sess., serial 1256, 308–13 (quotations).

12. WDAR, 1866, 48 (first quotation); Sheridan to Grant, Apr. 5, 1867, roll 24, Grant Papers (second quotation).

13. Utley, *Frontier Regulars*, 166–68; WDAR, 1869, 144–45; Anderson, *Conquest of Texas*, 346.

14. WDAR, 1867, 36; Sherman to Grant, May 27, 1867, roll 24, Grant Papers (quotation); Angevine, *The Railroad and the State*, 165–92.

15. Tate, *Frontier Army in the Settlement of the West*, 131–32.

16. Miller, *Soldiers and Settlers*, xiv (first quotation), 350; SED 74, 40th Cong., 2nd sess., serial 1317, 1–3; "The Statistics of the Wealth and Industry of the United States," 10, 82; Tate, *Frontier Army in the Settlement of the West*, 115 (second quotation). Assessed value of property in Arizona in 1870 was $1,410,295, but the Census Bureau set the "true" value at $3,440,791.

17. Hinckley, *Americanization of Alaska*, 67, 95–98; Tate, *Frontier Army in the Settlement of the West*, 92–93, 217–20.

18. Wooster, "John M. Schofield and the 'Multipurpose' Army" (quotation on 180).

19. Utley, *Frontier Regulars*, 93; Sherman to Grant, Aug. 29, 1866, roll 24, Grant Papers (first quotation); HED 23, 39th Cong., 2nd sess., serial 1288 (second, third, and fourth quotations); WDAR, 1866, 20–21.

20. Utley, *Frontier Regulars*, 100–106; Larson, *Red Cloud*, 93–101.

21. Larson, *Red Cloud*, 93–101; SED 15, 39th Cong., 2nd sess., serial 1277, 4 (quotation), 8, 14; Bray, *Crazy Horse*, 83–102.

22. Utley, *Indian Frontier*, 106–7; Utley, *Frontier Regulars*, 120–22; SED 156, 39th Cong., 2nd sess., serial 1279.

23. Sherman to Grant, Feb. 18, May 27, 1867, roll 24, Grant Papers; HED 240, 41st Cong., 2nd sess., serial 1425, 12–13, 82 (first quotation); WDAR, 1867, 67; Utley, *Cavalier in Buckskin*, 45–56; Statutes 15:589–97 (second quotation).

24. Larson, *Red Cloud*, 109–25; Bray, *Crazy Horse*, 108–15; Wooster, *The Military and United States Indian Policy*, 14; Grant to Sherman, March 2, 1868, roll 21, Grant Papers; *Statutes* 15:635–40 (quotation).

25. SED 13, 40th Cong., 3rd sess., serial 1360, 18–20 (first quotation); WDAR, 1868, 12 (second quotation). Unless otherwise noted, discussion of the conflicts on the southern plains in 1868–69 is based on Greene, *Washita*, and Utley, *Frontier Regulars*, 140–62.

26. WDAR, 1868, 12; Sheridan to Bradley, Sept. 28, 1868, Bradley Papers (quotations); Grant to Sherman, Sept. 25, 1868, roll 13, Sherman Papers.

27. SED 18, 40th Cong., 3rd sess., serial 1360, 4–5; WDAR, 1868, 21 (first quotation); WDAR, 1869 (second quotation).

28. WDAR, 1869, 44–45 (quotation). See Greene, *Washita*, for the best account of the battle.

29. Utley, *Frontier Regulars*, 155–64.

30. *General George Crook*, 143–59 (quotation); Utley, *Frontier Regulars*, 177–81.

31. Roberts, *Once They Moved Like the Wind*, 54–59; *Arizona Weekly Miner*, Apr. 22, 1871 (quotation); Utley, *Frontier Regulars*, 169–73; *Chronological List of Actions*, 26–27.

32. WDAR, 1866, 33; Ord to Logan, Dec. 29, 1869, Logan Papers (first quotation); WDAR, 1869, 124 (second and third quotations); Sherman to Belknap, Jan. 7, 1870, LS/AGO, roll 38, RG 94, NARA.

33. Grant to Sherman, Sept. 18, 1867, roll 12, Sherman Papers.

34. Sherman to president, Mar. 26, 1869, roll 45, Sherman Papers; Sherman to Schofield, Mar. 29, 1869, box 28, Barney Collection; Sherman to Sheridan, Apr. 10, 1869, roll 17, Sheridan Papers; Utley, *Indian Frontier*, 131; Sherman to Schofield, June 9, 1869, LS/AGO, roll 37, RG 94, NARA (quotations).

35. Schofield to Lowe, Feb. 11, 1869, box 49, Schofield Papers; *Congressional Globe*, 40th Cong., 3rd sess., 925–27 (first and second quotations), 950 (third and fourth quotations), 1384–85; *Statutes* 15:315–18.

36. Hutton, *Phil Sheridan*, 189–96; *Congressional Globe*, 41st Cong., 2nd sess., 1576–77 (quotation); Sheridan to Townsend, Oct. 21, 1869, box 91, Sheridan Papers; WDAR, 1870, 29–30.

37. Sheridan to Sherman, Jan. 29, 1870, box 53, Sheridan Papers; Sherman to Sheridan, Mar. 24, 1870, LS/AGO, roll 38, RG 94, NARA; Hutton, *Phil Sheridan*, 192–96 (first quotation); *New York Times*, Mar. 10, 1870 (second quotation); *Congressional Globe*, 41st Cong., 2nd sess., 1577 (fourth quotation), 1581 (third quotation).

38. *Congressional Globe*, 41st Cong., 2nd sess., appendix, 146–47 (quotations); *Congressional Globe*, 41st Cong., 2nd sess., 2275–77, 3316–27; *Statutes* 16:315–21. By a twenty-one-to-thirty-one vote, the Senate rejected a Stewart amendment that would have eliminated the reduction to thirty thousand. Six borderlands senators favored the larger

army, whereas nine voted to keep the limitation (*Congressional Globe*, 41st Cong., 2nd sess., 3388).

39. Schofield to Sherman, Sept. 16, 1872, box 49, Schofield Papers (quotation); Utley, *Frontier Regulars*, 192–93.

40. Utley, *Frontier Regulars*, 194–98 (first quotation); Crook to adjutant general, Sept. 4, 19, 1871, Crook Papers; Grant to Schofield, Mar. 6, 1872, box 4, Schofield Papers; WDAR, 1872, 78–79; *Chronological List of Actions*, 52–54; *Diaries of John Gregory Bourke* 1:51 (second quotation); Bourke, *On the Border with Crook*, 212–13 (third quotation).

41. Utley, *Indian Frontier*, 168–70; Canby to assistant adjutant general, Jan. 15, 1873, LS, Department of the Columbia, RG 393, NARA; Canby to Sherman, Jan. 30, 1873, LS, Department of the Columbia, RG 393, NARA; Kelton to Schofield, Feb. 5, 1873, box 41, Schofield Papers; Schofield to Gillem, Apr. 16, 22, 1873, box 49, Schofield Papers; Schofield to Sherman, Apr. 26, 1873, box 49, Schofield Papers; Schofield to Davis, Apr. 30, 1873, box 49, Schofield Papers (quotations).

42. Utley, *Indian Frontier*, 169–71; Utley, *Frontier Regulars*, 205–7; Schofield to Sherman, June 4, 1873, box 49, Schofield Papers; Schofield to Davis, June 5, 6, 7, 9, 1873, box 49, Schofield Papers; Schofield to Whipple, July 2, 1873, box 49, Schofield Papers; Wheaton to Schofield, May 10, 1873, box 9, Schofield Papers; Van Vliet to Sherman, May 4, roll 19, Sherman Papers (quotation).

43. Clarke to secretary of war, received Jan. 17, 1870, Indian Affairs, Department of the Missouri file, box 78, Schofield Papers (first quotation); Utley, *Indian Frontier*, 141–43; Marszalek, *Sherman*, 394–95; HED 1, pt. 1, 42nd Cong., 3rd sess., serial 1560, 612 (second quotation).

44. Robinson, *Bad Hand*, 126–44 (second and third quotations); Wooster, "The Army and the Politics of Expansion," 154–55; Grant, *Memoirs and Selected Letters*, 772 (first quotation); Carter, *On the Border with Mackenzie*, 419–69.

45. Mackenzie to Augur, June 28, 1873, Mackenzie Papers (quotation); Carter, *On the Border with Mackenzie*, 457–59; Crook to adjutant general, July 7, 1873, Crook Papers; HED 1, 43rd Cong., 2nd sess., serial 1634, 768–69.

46. *Chronological List of Actions*, 23–56. I have only included those actions involving army personnel. Heitman, *Historical Register* 2:426–39, counts 594 engagements involving regulars.

CHAPTER 11

1. Lubetkin, *Jay Cooke's Gamble*, 282 (first quotation); *New York Times*, Sept. 19, 1873 (second quotation).

2. *Congressional Record*, 43rd Cong., 1st sess., 986 (first and second quotations); HR 384, 43rd Cong., 1st sess., serial 1624, iii–xi, 5 (third quotation).

3. *Congressional Record*, 43rd Cong., 1st sess., 1017–20, 1170.

4. *Congressional Record*, 43rd Cong., 1st sess., 1237 (first quotation), 2308–12; Schofield to assistant adjutant general, Oct. 30, 1874, box 49, Schofield Papers (second and third quotations). For spending levels, see *Statistical History of the United States*, 8, 1114–15.

5. *Statistical History of the United States*, 8, 1114–15; Sherman to Stanton, Aug. 18, 1865, Belknap Papers; WDAR, 1873, 26; Marszalek, *Sherman*, 385–88, 566 n. 23; Sheridan to Sherman, May 26, 1874, box 11, Sheridan Papers.

6. Van Vliet to Sherman, May 4, 1873, roll 19, Sherman Papers (first and second quotations); Belknap to Delano, July 16, 20, 1874, LS/SW, roll 68, RG 107, NARA; Pope to Sheridan, July 16, 1874, LS, Department of the Missouri, RG 393, NARA; Sheridan to Pope, July 18, 1874, box 56, Sheridan Papers; Sheridan to Pope, July 22, box 11, Sheridan Papers (third and fourth quotations).

7. Pope to Price, Aug. 12, 1874, LS, Department of the Missouri, RG 393, NARA (first quotation); Pope to Miles, July 29, 1874, LS, Department of the Missouri, RG 393, NARA (second quotation); Augur to Mackenzie, July 23, 1874, LS, Department of Texas, RG 393, NARA; *Mackenzie's Official Correspondence*, 80–82; Augur to Mackenzie, Aug. 28, 1874, LS, Department of Texas, RG 393, NARA.

8. Hunt to Miles, Dec. 12, 1878, Miles Collection, USAMHI (first quotation); Marshall, *Miles Expedition*, 20, 24 (second quotation).Unless otherwise noted, details on the Red River War and its aftermath are from Utley, *Frontier Regulars*, 220–32.

9. *Indian Campaign on the Staked Plains*, 28–31; WDAR, 1874, 86; Marshall, *Miles Expedition*, 20, 24 (quotation).

10. Baldwin diary, Nov. 4–9, Baird Papers; *Indian Campaign on the Staked Plains*, 109.

11. *Indian Campaigns on the Staked Plains*, 91, 102, 96, 179, 183–84; WDAR, 1875, 88–94.

12. Wooster, "The Army and the Politics of Expansion," 155–57.

13. "Fort Laramie Treaty, 1868," (accessed November 1, 2007) (first quotation); Utley, *Lance and the Shield*, 91–93; Utley, *Indian Frontier*, 175 (second quotation); Lubetkin, *Jay Cooke's Gamble*, 93–113.

14. Lubetkin, *Jay Cooke's Gamble*, 114–61.

15. Lubetkin, *Jay Cooke's Gamble*, 241–90; *New York Times*, September 11, 1873; Bray, *Crazy Horse*, 165–69.

16. Bray, *Crazy Horse*, 179–81; Hoxie, *Parading through History*, 89, 107. For the debate on the army's role in the slaughter of buffalo, see Smits, "The Frontier Army and the Destruction of the Buffalo"; Dobak, "The Army and the Buffalo: A Demur"; Smits, "More on the Army and the Buffalo," and Isenberg, *Destruction of the Bison*.

17. Utley, *Cavalier in Buckskin*, 132–41 (first quotation); Jackson, *Custer's Gold*, 88–91 (second and third quotations), 108–13; *Chicago Inter-Ocean*,

Aug. 27, 1874 (fourth quotation); Bailey, *Pacifying the Plains*, 107–9; Terry to assistant adjutant general, Mar. 9, 1875, LS, Department of Dakota, RG 393, NARA (fifth quotation).

18. Hedren, *Fort Laramie and the Great Sioux War*, 13–15; SED 51, 44th Cong., 1st sess., serial 1664, 56 (first and second quotations); *Inter-Ocean*, May 30, 1875 (third quotation).

19. Utley, *Cavalier in Buckskin*, 145–47; Sheridan to Terry, Nov. 9, 1875, box 13, Sheridan Papers; Watkins to Smith, Nov. 9, 1875, box 91, Sheridan Papers (quotation).

20. Chandler to Secretary of War, Dec. 3, 1875, box 91, Sheridan Papers; Crook to assistant adjutant general, Dec. 22, 1875, LS, Department of the Platte; Terry to assistant adjutant general, Dec. 28, 1875, box 91, Sheridan Papers; Sheridan to Sherman, Jan. 3, 1876, box 14, Sheridan Papers; Sheridan to Terry, Feb. 9, 1876, box 58, Sheridan Papers (quotations).

21. Sheridan, endorsement of May 17, 1876, box 15, Sheridan Papers (first quotation); Bray, *Crazy Horse*, 193–99; Reynolds to Sherman, Apr. 11, 1876, roll 22, Sherman Papers (second and third quotations).

22. Utley, *Frontier Regulars*, 252–53; Sherman to Sheridan, Apr. 1, 1876, roll 22, Sherman Papers; Sheridan to Sherman, Apr. 3, 1876, Sherman Papers; Sheridan to Terry, May 16, 1876, box 58, Sheridan Papers (quotation). For other examples reflecting Sheridan's assertion that the enemy could not long stay together, see Sheridan to Sherman, Mar. 3, 1874, box 10, ibid.; and May 29, 1876, box 15, Sheridan Papers.

23. Utley, *Lance and the Shield*, 133–42; Marquis, *A Warrior Who Fought Custer*, 178–79 (quotation), 198–203.

24. Bray, *Crazy Horse*, 203–12; Crook to Sheridan, July 23, 1876, Crook Papers (quotation).

25. Utley, *Cavalier in Buckskin*, 158–64; *New York Times*, Mar. 25, 30, May 28, 1876; Dobak and Phillips, *Black Regulars*, 70–72; *Congressional Record*, 44th Cong., 1st sess., 3355–58, 3457–62, 3467–69.

26. *Congressional Record*, 44th Cong., 1st sess., 4144, 4155. Republicans from border states voting for the measure included Allison (Iowa), Hamilton (Texas), Harvey (Kansas), Hitchcock (Nebraska), Ingalls (Kansas), Jones (Nevada), and Paddock (Nevada). Twelve Senate Democrats, none of whom represented borderlands states, voted against it.

27. Utley, *Cavalier in Buckskin*, 175–77, 195 (second and third quotations); *The Little Big Horn, 1876*, 22–23 (first quotation). Unless otherwise noted, this account of the Little Bighorn campaign is based upon Utley, *Cavalier in Buckskin*; Utley, *Lance and the Shield*; Bray, *Crazy Horse*; Sklenar, *To Hell with Honor*; and Robinson, *Good Year to Die*. Samuel D. Sturgis, who had been the Seventh's colonel since 1869, was on detached duty.

28. Utley, *Cavalier in Buckskin*, 194.

29. Sheridan to Sherman, Feb. 10, 1877, roll 23, Sherman Papers (quotations); Utley, *Frontier Regulars*, 271.

30. *Duluth Weekly Tribune*, July 7, 1876 (first and second quotations); *New York Times*, July 8 (third quotation), 20, August 4, 13, 1876; Cameron to chairman, Senate Committee on Appropriations, July 13, 1876, LS/SW, roll 72, RG 107, NARA; *Statutes* 19:95, 97–101, 204; *Congressional Record* 44th Cong., 1st sess., 5674–75, 5694–96.

31. Utley, *Lance and the Shield*, 167–73; Wooster, *Nelson A. Miles*, 82–85 (quotation).

32. Smith, *Sagebrush Soldier*, 72–87 (first quotation); *Diaries of John Gregory Bourke* 2:181–94 (second quotation); Powell, *Sweet Medicine* 1:167.

33. Wooster, *Nelson A. Miles*; Greene, *Yellowstone Command*; Bray, *Crazy Horse*.

34. *Cong. Record*, 44th Cong., 2nd sess., 2111–18 (quotations), 2241. Combat engagements and casualties are from *Chronological List of Actions*, 56–64.

CHAPTER 12

1. This account of the Nez Perce conflict follows Greene's exhaustive *Nez Perce Summer* (quote on 43).

2. Greene, *Nez Perce Summer*, 139.

3. Greene, *Nez Perce Summer*, 232.

4. Greene, *Nez Perce Summer*, 309.

5. Sheridan to Sherman, Feb. 10, 1877, roll 21, Sheridan Papers.

6. McCrary to Sherman, June 1, 1877, LS/SW, roll 82, RG 107, NARA (first quotation); Schleicher to Sherman, Apr. 2, 1877, roll 24, Sherman Papers (second quotation).

7. *Congressional Records*, 45th Cong., 1st sess., 287–301, 513–14. For spending, see *Statistical History of the United States*, 8, 114–15.

8. Ord to Schleicher, Nov. 24, 1877, Ord Papers (first quotation); Sherman to Sheridan, Nov. 29, 1877, roll 24, Sherman Papers (second, third, and fourth quotations).

9. Sherman to Sheridan, Mar. 9, 1879, roll 17, Sheridan Papers; Robinson, *Bad Hand*, 239; Wooster, "The Army and the Politics of Expansion," 160–62.

10. Leiker, *Racial Borders*, 43–68 (quotation on 67).

11. Utley, *Frontier Regulars*, 322–43; WDAR, 1878, 170 (first quotation), 235 (second quotation). For Bernard, see Russell, *One Hundred and Three Fights and Scrimmages*.

12. *Congressional Record*, 45th Cong., 2nd sess., 3677, 3574, 3724, 3669.

13. *Congressional Record*, 45th Cong., 2nd sess., 3537, 3853, 4648, 4685–86. John Reagan, the lone Texan to support the cutbacks, represented an eastern district of the state.

14. WDAR, 1879, 157–59 (quotations); Utley, *Frontier Regulars*, 329–32.

15. Hoig, *Perilous Pursuit*, 194 (quotation).

16. Utley, *Frontier Regulars*, 332–42; *Diaries of John Gregory Bourke* 3:302; Bourke, *On the Border with Crook*, 426 (first quotation); SED 30, 46th Cong., 2nd sess., serial 1882, 90 (second quotation).

17. Sherman to Miles, Feb. 9, 1878, roll 45, Sherman Papers; Sherman to Miles, Mar. 30, Apr. 23, July 30, 1878, box 4, Miles Papers; Sherman to Sheridan, July 25, 1878, roll 17, Sheridan Papers; Utley, *Lance and the Shield*, 199–235.

18. Utley, *Indian Frontier*, 187 (first quotation); WDAR, 1880, 155–57 (second quotation); Chamberlain, *Victorio*, 178–79. Watt, "Ízisgo At'éé: Victorio's Military and Political Leadership of the Warm Springs Apaches," offers the best treatment of Victorio's military leadership.

19. Vandervort, *Indian Wars*, 204–5; Chamberlain, *Victorio*, 191–207.

20. *Army and Navy Journal*, July 17, 1880 (first quotation); Tate, *Frontier Army in the Settlement of the West*, 93–110 (second quotation), 338–39 n. 73–77; Kenner, "Guardians in Blue"; Laurie, "Filling the Breech."

21. Lincoln to Attorney General, May 26, 1882, LS/SW, roll 85, RG 107, NARA; Wickett, *Contested Territory*, 47–52; Hutton, *Phil Sheridan and His Army*, 360–63.

22. Meyerson, *Nature's Army*, viii (quotations).

23. Bartlett, *Great Surveys of the American West*; Tate, *Frontier Army in the Settlement of the West*, 12–14, 168–71, 183–91; Gillett, *Army Medical Department, 1865–1917*, 63–95; Coffman, *Old Army*, 382–83.

24. Coffman, *Old Army*, 382–83; Craig, "Medicine for the Military."

25. Budd, *Serving Two Masters*, 64–91; Wooster, *Frontier Crossroads*, 82 (quotations); HR 354, 44th Cong., 1st sess., serial 1709, 20, 45, 188. Until 1896, another chaplain served the U.S. Military Academy.

26. Miller, *Soldiers and Settlers*, 354 (first quotation); Smith, *The U.S. Army and the Texas Frontier Economy*, 11; Neilson, ed., "'I Long to Return to Fort Concho,'" 164–65 (second and third quotations).

27. Schofield to Townsend, May 22, 1873, box 49, Schofield Papers (first quotation); Crook to Hayes, Nov. 28, 1871, Crook Papers (second quotation); "Letters of Caroline Frey Winne," 6 (third quotation); Major Hough's March," 109 n. 16 (fourth and fifth quotations).

28. Tate, *Frontier Army in the Settlement of the West*, 286–92; G. W. Schofield to Schofield, June 12, 1869, box 8, Schofield Papers (quotation); Schofield, *Forty-six Years*, 425–26; Wooster, *Frontier Crossroads*, 110–14. For Schofield's land investments, see his papers, especially boxes 4, 5, 8, 9, 10, 12, 37, 49, 50, and 60. Subsequent Schofield ventures included land in Kansas, a silver mine in California (in partnership with his former aide, Captain William Wherry), a cattle ranch in Arizona (co-owned with Colonels Eugene A. Carr and Luther P. Bradley), and numerous railroad bonds.

29. Hauser to Maginnis, Dec. 11, 1877, box 2, Maginnis Papers (quotation); Miles to Maginnis, Nov. 8, 1878, Maginnis Papers; Potts to Maginnis, Feb. 5, 1879, Maginnis Papers; Potts to Miles, Aug. 27, Oct. 7, 1878, box 3, Miles Papers. Grateful for his efforts in driving away Indians, civilians near the military post at Fort Keogh named their community Miles City.

30. Belknap to House Appropriations Committee, Apr. 14, 1874, LS/SW, roll 68, RG 107, NARA; Tate, *Frontier Army in the Settlement of the West*, 69–75; Miles, *Personal Recollections*, 397–403, 416–31; Miles to AAG, Nov. 2, 1881, 6247 AGO 1881, LR/AGO, roll 58, RG 94, NARA (quotation); Miles to Allen, Oct. 24, 1885, box 5, Allen Papers.

31. Miller, *Soldiers and Settlers*, 287–355; Dobak, *Fort Riley and Its Neighbors*, 79–88. Borderlands states and territories are defined as Arizona, Colorado, Idaho, Kansas, Montana, Nebraska, Nevada, New Mexico, North Dakota, South Dakota, Texas, Utah, and Wyoming.

32. WDAR, 1880, 4 (quotations); Utley, *Frontier Regulars*, 47; WDAR, 1897, 102–8.

33. Grandstaff, "Preserving the 'Habits and Usages of War.'"

34. Coffman, *Old Army*, 225, 278–80, 371–75; WDAR, 1889, 8.

35. WDAR, 1891, 605; WDAR, 1888, 737.

36. Cashion, *A Texas Frontier*, 194 (first quotation), 202 (second and third quotations).

37. Sherman to Howard, Mar. 29, 1877, Howard Papers (first quotation); Alice to Baldwin, Mar. 31, 1877, box 9, Baldwin Papers (second and third quotations); Leckie, *Elizabeth Bacon Custer*, xx (fourth quotation). Calculations are based on *Ninth Census of the United States, 1870*, manuscript census returns, rolls 118 (Dakota, 1870) and 1748 (Wyoming, 1870) T 9, rolls 111–15 (Dakota, 1880), and roll 1454 (Wyoming, 1880), RG 29, NARA. Twenty-five of the eighty-five officer/wife households in Dakota had children born in that territory.

38. Smith, *View from Officers' Row*; *News from Brownsville*, 109 (first quotation); Roe, *Army Letters*, 10 (second quotation); McInnis, "Expanding Horizons," 108; Boyd, *Cavalry Life in Tent and Field*, 142 (third quotation); Coffman, *Old Army*, 308.

39. *Statutes* 16:320; Miles, *Personal Recollections*, 62 (first quotation); Paulding Memoirs, 10; Utley, *Frontier Regulars*, 19–20; Coffman, *Old Army*, 288–97.

40. Hoagland, *Army Architecture in the West*, offers a brilliant examination of these changes.

41. Collins, *Apache Nightmare*; WDAR, 1881, 144 (quotation). Unless otherwise noted, I have depended on Utley, *Frontier Regulars*, 370–93, for analysis of these campaigns against the Apaches.

42. Privately, Sherman hinted that Carr's heavy use of alcohol had dulled his abilities. Sherman to Willcox, Dec. 29, 1881, roll 47, Sherman Papers.

43. Roberts, *Once They Moved Like the Wind*, 226–38; WDAR, 1883, 173–78; Bourke, *On the Border with Crook*, 452–53.

44. Cleveland to Endicott, Dec. 22, 1885, series 2, roll 26, Cleveland Papers (quotations).

45. WDAR, 1886, 72–73 (first quotation), 166–67 (second quotation), 170–81; Wood, diary, May–June, 1886, box 1, Wood Papers; Henley to Miles, May 29, 1886, box 5, Gatewood Collection (third quotation); Gatewood to wife, June 25, 1886, box 7, Gatewood Collection.

46. Drum to Miles, Aug. 25, 1886, LS/SW roll 98, RG 107, NARA (first quotation); WDAR, 1886, 12–13; Miles, *Personal Recollections*, 520–21 (second quotation); SED 117, 49th Cong., 2nd sess., se. 2449, 144–62.

47. Royer to Belt, Oct. 30, 1890, Reports and Correspondence Relating to the Army Investigations of the Battle of Wounded Knee and to the Sioux Campaign of 1890–1891, roll 1, RG 94, NARA (quotation); Chandler to president, Nov. 13, 1890, Reports and Correspondence, roll 1, RG 94, NARA; Harrison to Secretary of War, Nov. 15, 1890, Reports and Correspondence, roll 1, RG 94, NARA.

    Two interpretations divide scholarly thought on Wounded Knee. The traditional view, stated in its most complete and forceful form in Utley, *Last Days*, portrays the disaster as "a regrettable, tragic accident of war that neither side intended" (230). Ostler, *Plains Sioux and U.S. Colonialism*, characterizes the Ghost Dance as an "anticolonial movement" (262), which the army, and particularly Miles, intentionally magnified in order "to open the door to a massive military operation, designed in part to demonstrate the continued relevance of the western army" (9).

    The present work seeks to blend Ostler's nuanced interpretation of Lakota culture with Utley's mastery of the army and military affairs. Although Miles certainly was not above such a gambit, Ostler understates the military capabilities of the Indians and presupposes that Miles, and the army, somehow knew that the wars against the Indians were over. They didn't. For a sharp rebuke of Ostler, see Lookingbill, "Killing Fields of Wounded Knee," 379–86.

48. Wooster, *Nelson A. Miles*, 180–84; Utley, *Last Days*, 112. For the orders, see Williams to Brooke, Nov. 18 and 23, 1890, Reports and Correspondence Relating to the Army Investigations of the Battle of Wounded Knee and to the Sioux Campaign of 1890–1891, roll 1, RG 94, NARA; Miles to Brooke, Dec. 7, 1890, Reports and Correspondence Relating to the Army Investigations of the Battle of Wounded Knee and to the Sioux Campaign of 1890–1891, roll 1, RG 94, NARA. Forsyth later asserted that Brooke had not forwarded these instructions to his subordinate officers, as they had been marked confidential. Wooster, *Nelson A. Miles*, 190.

49. Utley, *Last Days*, 200–228; Ostler, *Plains Sioux and U.S. Colonialism*, 328–53.

50. Utley, *Last Days*, 231–70.

EPILOGUE

1. WDAR, 1891, 144 (first quotation); WDAR, 1892, 131 (second quotation); WDAR, 1895, 4, 137, 163; WDAR, 1896, 4, 142–48; WDAR, 1898, 180–81.

2. Schofield, *Forty-six Years*, 488–89; Dunlay, *Wolves for the Blue Soldiers*, 195–97; Coffman, *Old Army*, 330–31.

3. Linn, "Long Twilight of the Frontier Army," 166 (quotation). Ironically, as Durwood Ball has suggested, only after it had taken up these overseas missions would the regular army be "incorporated into national mythology." And perhaps the supreme irony is that "stories inspired by the frontier experience"—many of them mythologized and stereotyped—would do much to engender this newer, more comfortable relationship between the nation and its professional soldiers (*Army Regulars*, 208).

4. Prucha, *Sword of the Republic*, 394 (first quotation); WDAR, 1875, 122 (second quotation); Utley, "The Frontier and the American Military Tradition," 9. See also Birtle, *U.S. Army Counterinsurgency and Contingency Operations Doctrine*.

5. Rust, "Settlers, Soldiers, and Scoundrels," 138.

6. Dobak, *Fort Riley and Its Neighbors*, 5 (first quotation); *Chicago Inter-Ocean*, Aug. 3, 1887; Tate, *Frontier Army in the Settlement of the West*, 135 (second quotation).

7. See for example Hoxie, *Parading through History*, and Ostler, *Plains Sioux and U.S. Colonialism*.

8. Sherman to Burnside, July 15, 1878, roll 45, Sherman Papers (first quotation); Hutton, *Phil Sheridan and His Army*, 185–86 (second quotation).

9. Heitman, *Historical Register* 2:390–449; *Chronological List of Actions*.

10. West, *Contested Plains*, 280–81. For a brief but enlightening assessment of logistical issues, see Vandervort, *Indian Wars*, 49.

11. *Congressional Record*, 45th Cong., 2nd sess., 3724.

12. For the conceptual links between empire and liberty, see especially Anderson and Cayton, *Dominion of War*.

BIBLIOGRAPHY

PRIMARY SOURCES

Manuscript Collections

Allen, Henry T. Papers. Library of Congress. Washington, D.C.

Anderson, Robert. Papers. Library of Congress. Washington, D.C.

Archer, James Jay. Collection. Maryland State Historical Society. Baltimore.

Baird, George F. Papers. Kansas State Historical Society, Center for Historical Research. Topeka.

Baldwin, Frank D. Papers. Huntington Library. San Marino, Calif.

Barney, Hiram. Collection. Huntington Library. San Marino, Calif.

Belknap, William W. Papers. Library of Congress. Washington, D.C.

Bradley, Luther. Papers. U.S. Army Military History Institute. Carlisle, Pa.

Brooks, William T. H. Papers. U.S. Army Military History Institute. Carlisle, Pa.

Brown, Jacob. Papers. Clements Library. University of Michigan, Ann Arbor.

Brown, Jacob. Papers. Library of Congress. Washington, D.C.

Buchanan, Robert C. Papers. Maryland State Historical Society. Baltimore.

Chapman, William W. Papers. Center for American History. University of Texas, Austin.

Cleveland, Grover. Papers. Library of Congress. Washington, D.C.

Clinch, Duncan. Papers. Library of Congress. Washington, D.C.

Crook, George. Papers. Hayes Library. Fremont, Ohio.

Dearborn, Henry. Miscellaneous Manuscripts Collection. Library of Congress. Washington, D.C.

Dunn Family Papers. Center for American History. University of Texas, Austin.

Eustis, William. Papers. Library of Congress. Washington, D.C.

Ewing, Thomas. Family Papers. Library of Congress. Washington, D.C.

Fynn, John. Papers. U.S. Army Military History Institute. Carlisle, Pa.

Gatewood, Charles B. Collection. Arizona Historical Society, Tucson.

Grant, Ulysses S. Papers. Library of Congress. Washington, D.C.

Greene, Francis V. Papers. New York Public Library. New York, N.Y.

Harmar, Josiah. Papers. Clements Library. University of Michigan, Ann Arbor.

Heintzelman, Samuel Peter. Papers. Library of Congress. Washington, D.C.

Hitchcock, Ethan Allen. Papers. Library of Congress. Washington, D.C.

Howard, Oliver O. Papers. Bowdoin College. Brunswick, Me.

Jesup, Thomas. Papers. Clements Library. University of Michigan, Ann Arbor.

Jesup, Thomas. Papers. Library of Congress. Washington, D.C.

Jesup, Thomas. Papers. U.S. Army Military History Institute. Carlisle, Pa.

King, Benjamin. Papers. Library of Congress. Washington, D.C.

Knapp, Obadiah H. Papers. Center for American History. University of Texas, Austin.

Lamont, Daniel. Papers. Library of Congress. Washington, D.C.

Legion of the United States Papers. U.S. Army Military History Institute. Carlisle, Pa.

Logan, John. Papers. Library of Congress. Washington, D.C.

Mackenzie, Ranald. Papers. U.S. Army Military History Institute. Carlisle, Pa.

Madison, James. Papers. Library of Congress. Washington, D.C.

Maginnis, Martin. Papers. Montana Historical Society. Helena.

McHenry, James. Papers. Clements Library. University of Michigan, Ann Arbor.

McLane, Louis. Papers. Library of Congress. Washington, D.C.

Miles, Nelson A. Collection. U.S. Army Military History Institute. Carlisle, Pa.

Miles, Nelson A. Papers. Library of Congress. Washington, D.C.

Northwest Territory Collection. Clements Library. University of Michigan, Ann Arbor.

Nourse, Charles J. Photocopies. U.S. Army Military History Institute. Carlisle, Pa.

Ord, E. O. C. Papers. Bancroft Library. University of California, Berkeley.

Ord Family Papers. Georgetown University Library. Special Collections. Washington, D.C.

Paulding, Grace and William. Memoirs. U.S. Army Military History Institute. Carlisle, Pa.

Peters, DeWitt C. Papers. Bancroft Library. University of California, Berkeley.

Poinsett Section. Henry D. Gilpin Collection. Historical Society of Pennsylvania. Philadelphia.

Randall-Bache Collection. U.S. Army Military History Institute. Carlisle, Pa.

Schofield, John. Papers. Library of Congress. Washington, D.C.

Scott, Winfield. Papers. Clements Library. University of Michigan, Ann Arbor.

Sheridan, Philip. Papers. Library of Congress. Washington, D.C.

Sherman, William. Papers. Library of Congress. Washington, D.C.

Stanley, David. Diary. Center for American History. University of Texas, Austin.

Sumner Family Papers. Library of Congress. Washington, D.C.

Talbot, Theodore. Papers. Library of Congress. Washington, D.C.

Taylor, Zachary. Papers. Library of Congress. Washington, D.C.

Van Deventer, Christopher. Papers. Clements Library. University of Michigan, Ann Arbor.

Warfield, William H. Diary. Maryland State Historical Society. Baltimore.

Wayne, Anthony. Manuscripts. Historical Society of Pennsylvania. Philadelphia.

Wilkins, James C. Papers. Center for American History. University of Texas, Austin.

Wood, Leonard. Papers. Library of Congress. Washington, D.C.

National Archives and Records Administration. Washington, D.C.
RECORD GROUP 29, RECORDS OF THE BUREAU OF THE CENSUS
Seventh Census of the United States, 1850. M 432.
Eighth Census of the United States, 1860. M 653.
Ninth Census of the United States, 1870. M 593.
Tenth Census of the United States, 1880. T 9.

RECORD GROUP 75, RECORDS OF THE BUREAU OF INDIAN AFFAIRS
Central Map Files.
Letters Received by the Office of Indian Affairs, 1824–80, Upper Missouri Agency. M 234.
Letters Sent by the Secretary of War Relating to Indian Affairs, 1800–24. M 15.

RECORD GROUP 77, RECORDS OF THE OFFICE OF THE CHIEF OF ENGINEERS
Civil Works Map File.
Published Maps Series.
War Department Map Collection.

RECORD GROUP 92, RECORDS OF THE OFFICE OF THE QUARTERMASTER GENERAL
Letters Sent by the Office of the Quartermaster General, Main Series,
1818–70. M 745.

RECORD GROUP 94, RECORDS OF THE ADJUTANT GENERAL'S OFFICE, 1780s–1917
General James Wilkinson's Order Book. M 654.
General Orders and Circulars of the War Department and Headquarters
of the Army, 1809–60. M 1094.
Letters Received by the Office of the Adjutant General, Main Series,
1822–60. M 567.
Letters Received by the Office of the Adjutant General, Main Series,
1881–89. M 689.
Letters Sent by the Office of the Adjutant General, Main Series, 1800–90.
M 565.
Reports and Correspondence Relating to the Army Investigations of the
Battle of Wounded Knee and to the Sioux Campaign of 1890–91. M 983.
War Department Collection of Post-Revolutionary War Manuscripts. M 904.

RECORD GROUP 107, RECORDS OF THE OFFICE OF THE SECRETARY OF WAR
Confidential and Unofficial Letters Sent by the Secretary of War. M 7.
Contracts, 1799–1810. Entry 44.
Letters Received by the Secretary of War, Main Series, 1801–70. M 221.
Letters Received by the Secretary of War, Unregistered Series, 1789–1861.
M 222.
Letters Sent by the Secretary of War Relating to Military Affairs, 1800–89.
M 6.
Miscellaneous Letters Sent by the Secretary of War, 1800–1809. M 370.
Subsistence Contracts, 1803–12. Entry 45.

RECORD GROUP 393, RECORDS OF THE U.S. ARMY CONTINENTAL COMMANDS
Letters Sent, Department of the Columbia.
Letters Sent, Department of Dakota.
Letters Sent, Department of the Missouri.
Letters Sent, Department of the Platte.
Letters Sent, Department of Texas.
Records of the Tenth Military Department, 1846–51. M 210.

Federal Government Documents

American State Papers: Indian Affairs. 2 vols. Washington, D.C.: Gales and Seaton, 1832–34.

American State Papers: Military Affairs. 7 vols. Washington, D.C.: Gales and Seaton, 1832–61.

American State Papers: Miscellaneous. 2 vols. Washington, D.C.: Gales and Seaton, 1834.

Annals of the Congress of the United States, 1789–1824. 42 vols. Washington, D.C.: Gales and Seaton, 1834–56.

Congressional Globe. 46 vols. Washington, 1834–73.

Congressional Record. 154 vols. to date. Washington, 1874– .

Journals of the Continental Congress, 1774–1789. 34 vols. Ed. Worthington C. Ford et al. Washington, D.C.: Government Printing Office, 1904–37.

Letters of Delegates to Congress, 1774–1789. 26 vols. Ed. Paul H. Smith. Washington, D.C.: Government Printing Office, 1976–2000.

New American State Papers: Indian Affairs. 13 vols. Ed. Thomas C. Cochran. Wilmington, Del.: Scholarly Publications, 1972.

New American State Papers: Military Affairs. Ed. Benjamin Franklin Cooling. 19 vols. Wilmington, Del.: Scholarly Publications, 1979.

Register of Debates in Congress. 14 vols. Washington, D.C.: Gales and Seaton, 1825–37.

"The Statistics of the Wealth and Industry of the United States . . . Compiled from the Original Returns of the Ninth Census." Washington, D.C.: Government Printing Office, 1872.

Statutes at Large of the United States of America, 1789–1873. 17 vols. Boston: Little, Brown, 1850–73.

The Territorial Papers of the United States. 26 vols. Ed. Clarence Carter. Washington, D.C.: Government Printing Office, 1934– .

U.S. War Department. *The War of the Rebellion: A Compilation of the Official Records of the Union and Confederate Armies.* 128 vols. Washington, D.C.: Government Printing Office, 1880–1901.

U.S. Congressional Serial Set

House Report 42, 19th Cong., 1st sess., serial 141. *Military Road in Michigan.*

Senate Doc. 356, 25th Cong., 2nd sess., serial 317. *Statement of the Officers of the Missouri Volunteers.*

House Doc. 78, 25th Cong., 2nd sess., serial 323. *Court of Inquiry— Operations in Florida.*

House Doc. 278, 25th Cong., 2nd sess., serial 328. *Military road, Western Frontier, etc.*

House Doc. 311, 25th Cong., 2nd sess., serial 329. *Defence of the Western Frontier . . . Furnished by Major General Gaines.*

Senate Doc. 379, 26th Cong., 1st sess., serial 359. *Defense of the Western Frontier.*

House Doc. 144, 26th Cong., 1st sess., serial 365. *Reservation at Fort Snelling.*

House Doc. 206, 26th Cong., 1st sess., serial 368. *National Defence and National Foundries.*

House Doc. 262, 27th Cong., 2nd sess., serial 405. *Correspondence— Secretary of War and Commanding Officer in Florida.*

House Doc. 219, 27th Cong., 3rd sess., serial 425. *Report of Lieutenant Colonel Hitchcock, Respecting the Affairs of the Cherokee Indians, etc.*

Senate Ex. Doc. 7, 30th Cong., 1st sess., serial 505. *Notes of a Military Reconnaissance, from Fort Leavenworth, in Missouri, to San Diego, in California, including parts of the Arkansas, Del Norte, and Gila Rivers.*

House Ex. Doc. 60, 30th Cong., 1st sess., serial 520. *Mexican War.*

House Ex. Doc. 17, 31st Cong., 1st sess., serial 573. *California and New Mexico.*

Senate Ex. Doc. 29, 33rd Cong., 1st sess., serial 695. *Reports of Explorations and Surveys to Ascertain the Most Practicable and Economical Route for a Railroad from the Mississippi River to the Pacific Ocean.*

Senate Ex. Doc. 50, 33rd Cong., 2nd sess., serial 752. *Fort Leavenworth.*

Senate Ex. Doc. 58, 33rd Cong., 2nd sess., serial 782. *Fort Leavenworth.*

House Ex. Doc. 50, 33rd Cong., 2nd sess., serial 783. *Delaware Indians.*

Senate Ex. Doc. 97, 34th Cong., 1st sess., serial 823. *Instructions Sent to Military Officers in Kansas.*

House Ex. Doc. 93, 34th Cong., 1st sess., serial 858. *Indian Hostilities in Oregon and Washington.*

Senate Ex. Doc. 34, 34th Cong., 3rd sess., serial 880. *Pay and Emoluments of Lieutenant General Scott.*

Senate Ex. Doc. 1, 35th Cong., Special Senate Session 1, serial 916. *Report of Captain George B. McClellan, One of the Officers Sent to the Seat of War in Europe, 1855 and 1856.*

Senate Ex. Doc. 11, pt. 1, 35th Cong., 1st sess., serial 919. *Commissioner of Indian Affairs, Annual Report.*

House Ex. Doc. 88, 35th Cong., 1st sess., serial 956. *Correspondence between the Late Secretary of War and General Wool.*

House Ex. Doc. 52, 36th Cong., 1st sess., serial 1050. *Difficulties on Southwestern Frontier.*

House Ex. Doc. 69, 36th Cong., 1st sess., serial 1051. *Indian Hostilities in New Mexico.*

House Ex. Doc. 81, 36th Cong., 1st sess., serial 1056. *Troubles on Texas Frontier.*

House Ex. Doc. 98, 36th Cong., 1st sess., serial 1057. *Correspondence with General Harney.*

House Ex. Doc. 65, 36th Cong., 1st sess., serial 1059. *Affairs in Oregon.*

House Ex. Doc. 70, 39th Cong., 1st sess., serial 1256. *Wagon Road from Niobrara to Virginia City.*

Senate Ex. Doc. 26, 39th Cong., 2nd sess., serial 1277. *Sand Creek Massacre.*

Senate Report 156, 39th Cong., 2nd sess., serial 1279. *Condition of the Indian Tribes.*

House Ex. Doc. 23, 39th Cong., 2nd sess., serial 1288. *Protection across the Continent.*

Senate Ex. Doc. 74, 40th Cong., 2nd sess., serial 1317. *Expense of Maintaining the Military Establishment in the Territories of New Mexico and Arizona.*

Senate Ex. Doc. 77, 40th Cong., 2nd sess., serial 1317. *Report of Brevet Brig. Gen. W. F. Raynolds on the Exploration of the Yellowstone.*

Senate Ex. Doc. 13, 40th Cong., 3rd sess., serial 1360. *Battle of the Washita River.*

House Ex. Doc. 240, 41st Cong., 2nd sess., serial 1425. *Difficulties with Indian Tribes.*

House Ex. Doc. 1, pt. 1, 42nd Cong., 3rd sess., serial 1560. *Commissioner of Indian Affairs, Annual Report.*

House Report 1061, 51st Cong., 1st sess., serial 2810. *Desertions from the Army.*

House Doc. 605, 57th Cong., 1st sess., serial 4377. *Mountain Meadows Massacre.*

War Department, Annual Reports

1828 Senate Doc. 1, 20th Cong., 2nd sess., serial 181.

1838 Senate Doc. 1, 25th Cong., 3rd sess., serial 338.

1839 House Doc. 2, 26th Cong., 1st sess., serial 363.

1840 Senate Doc. 1, 26th Cong., 2nd sess., serial 373.

1841 Senate Doc. 1, 27th Cong., 1st sess., serial 395.

1842 Senate Doc. 1, 27th Cong., 2nd sess., serial 413.

1843 Senate Doc. 1, 28th Cong., 1st sess., serial 431.

1847 Senate Doc. 1, 30th Cong., 1st sess., serial 503.

1848 House Doc. 1, 30th Cong., 2nd sess., serial 537.

1849 House Ex. Doc. 5, 31st Cong., 1st sess., serial 569.

1850 Senate Ex. Doc. 1, pt. 2, 31st Cong., 2nd sess., serial 587.

1851 Senate Ex. Doc. 1, 32nd Cong., 1st sess., serial 611.

1852 Senate Ex. Doc. 1, 32nd Cong., 2nd sess., serial 659.

1853 Senate Ex. Doc. 1, 33rd Cong., 1st sess., serial 691.

1854 Senate Ex. Doc. 1, 33rd Cong., 2nd sess., serial 747.

1855 Senate Ex. Doc. 1, 34th Cong., 1st sess., serial 811.

1856 Senate Ex. Doc. 5, 34th Cong., 3rd sess., serial 876.

1857 Senate Ex. Doc. 11, 35th Cong., 1st sess., serial 920.

1858 Senate Ex. Doc. 1, pt. 2, 35th Cong., 2nd sess., serial 975.

1859 Senate Ex. Doc. 2, 36th Cong., 1st sess., serial 1024.

1860 Senate Ex. Doc. 1, 36th Cong., 2nd sess., serial 1079.

1866 House Ex. Doc. 1, 39th Cong., 2nd sess., serial 1285.

1867 House Ex. Doc. 1, 40th Cong., 2nd sess., serial 1324.

1868 House Ex. Doc. 1, 40th Cong., 3rd sess., serial 1367.

1869 House Ex. Doc. 1, pt. 2, 41st Cong., 2nd sess., serial 1413.

1870 House Ex. Doc. 1, pt. 2, 41st Cong., 3rd sess., serial 1446.

1871 House Ex. Doc. 1, pt. 2, 42nd Cong., 2nd sess., serial 1503.

1872 House Ex. Doc. 1, pt. 2, 42nd Cong., 3rd sess., serial 1558.

1873 House Ex. Doc. 1, pt. 2, 43rd Cong., 1st sess., serial 1597.

1874 House Ex. Doc. 1, pt. 2, 43rd Cong., 2nd sess., serial 1635.

1875 House Ex. Doc. 1, pt. 2, 44th Cong., 1st sess., serial 1674.

1876 House Ex. Doc. 1, pt. 2, 44th Cong., 2nd sess., serial 1742.

1877 House Ex. Doc. 1, pt. 2, 45th Cong., 2nd sess., serial 1794.

1878 House Ex. Doc. 1, pt. 2, 45th Cong., 3rd sess., serial 1843.

1879 House Ex. Doc. 1, pt. 2, 46th Cong., 2nd sess., serial 1903.

1880 House Ex. Doc. 1, pt. 2, 46th Cong., 3rd sess., serial 1952.

1881 House Ex. Doc. 1, pt. 2, 47th Cong., 1st sess., serial 2010.

1882 House Ex. Doc. 1, pt. 2, 47th Cong., 2nd sess., serial 2091.

1883 House Ex. Doc. 1, pt. 2, 48th Cong., 1st sess., serial 2182.

1884 House Ex. Doc. 1, pt. 2, 48th Cong., 2nd sess., serial 2277.

1885 House Ex. Doc. 1, pt. 2, 49th Cong., 1st sess., serial 2369.

1886 House Ex. Doc 1, pt. 2, 49th Cong., 2nd sess., serial 2461.

1887 House Ex. Doc. 1, pt. 2, 50th Cong., 1st sess., serial 2533.

1888 House Ex. Doc. 1, pt. 2, 50th Cong., 2nd sess., serial 2628.

1889 House Ex. Doc. 1, pt. 2, 51st Cong., 1st sess., serial 2715.

1890 House Ex. Doc. 1, pt. 2, 51st Cong., 2nd sess., serial 2831.

1891 House Ex. Doc. 1, pt. 2, 52nd Cong., 1st sess., serial 2921.

1892 House Ex. Doc. 1, pt. 2, 52nd Cong., 2nd sess., serial 3077.

1893 House Ex. Doc. 1, pt. 2, 53rd Cong., 2nd sess., serial 3198.

1894 House Ex. Doc. 1, pt. 2, 53rd Cong., 3rd sess., serial 3295.

1895 House Doc. 2, 54th Cong., 1st sess., serial 3370.

1896 House Doc. 2, 54th Cong., 1st sess., serial 3478.

1897 House Doc. 2, 55th Cong., 2nd sess., serial 3630.

1898 House Doc. 2, 55th Cong., 3rd sess., serials 3744, 3745.

1899 House Doc. 2, 56th Cong., 1st sess., serials 3899, 3901, 3902, 3903.

1900 House Doc. 2, 56th Cong., 2nd sess., serials 4070, 4072, 4073, 4074, 4076.

1901 House Doc. 2, 57th Cong., 1st sess., serials 4269, 4271, 4273.

1902 House Doc. 2, 57th Cong., 2nd sess., serials 4443, 4451.

1903 House Doc. 2, 58th Cong., 2nd sess., serials 4628, 4630, 4631.

Newspapers

Albany Argus

Arizona Weekly Miner (Prescott)

Army and Navy Journal

Boston Gazette

Centinel of Freedom (Newark)

City of Washington Gazette

Chicago Inter-Ocean

Daily Missouri Republican (St. Louis)

Daily State Register (Des Moines)

Dakota Republican (Vermillion)

Duluth Weekly Tribune

Evening Bulletin (San Francisco)

Freedom's Champion (Atchison City, Kansas)

Independent Chronicle (Boston)

National Intelligencer (Washington)

New York Times

New York Tribune

Niles' Register (Baltimore, Washington, Philadelphia)

St. Louis Enquirer

Telegraph and Texas Register (Houston)

Texas State Gazette (Austin)

Internet Resources

"Fort Laramie Treaty, 1868." http://www.yale.edu/lawweb/avalon/ntreaty/ntoo1.htm.

"Papers of the War Department, 1784 to 1800." Center for History and New Media. George Mason University. http://wardepartmentpapers.org.

Wood to the Texas Senate. Texas State Library and Archives Commission. http://www.tsl.state.tx.us/governors/earlystate/wood-2-1.html.

Writings of George Washington. Electronic Text Center. University of Virginia Library. http://etext.virginia.edu/washington.

Books

Above a Common Soldier: Frank and Mary Clarke in the American West and Civil War. Rev. ed. Ed. Darlis Miller. Albuquerque: University of New Mexico Press, 1997.

Adjutant General's Office. *Chronological List of Actions, etc., with Indians, from January 15, 1837 to January, 1891.* 1891; rpt., Old Army Press, 1979.

Anthony Wayne, a Name in Arms: Soldier, Diplomat, Defender of Expansion Westward of a Nation; the Wayne-Knox-Pickering-McHenry Correspondence. Ed. Richard C. Knopf. Pittsburgh: University of Pittsburgh Press, 1960.

Army Life on the Western Frontier: Selections from the Official Reports Made between 1826 and 1845. Ed. Francis Paul Prucha. Norman: University of Oklahoma Press, 1958.

Ballentine, George. *Autobiography of an English Soldier in the United States Army.* 2 vols. London: Hurst and Blackett, 1853.

Bandel, Eugene. *Frontier Life in the Army, 1854–1861.* Ed. Ralph P. Bieber. Glendale: Arthur H. Clarke, 1932.

Bemrose, John. *Reminiscences of the Second Seminole War.* Ed. John K. Mahon. Gainesville: University of Florida Press, 1966.

Black Frontiersman: The Memoirs of Henry O. Flipper. Ed. Theodore D. Harris. Fort Worth: Texas Christian University Press, 1997.

Bourke, John G. *On the Border with Crook.* 1891; rpt., Lincoln: University of Nebraska Press, 1971.

Boyd, Mrs. Orsemus Bronson. *Cavalry Life in Tent and Field.* 1894; rpt., Lincoln: University of Nebraska Press, 1982.

Burrows, J. M. D. *Fifty Years in Iowa.* Davenport, Iowa: Glass and Co., 1888.

Michigan Pioneer and Historical Collections. 2nd ed. 40 vols. Ed. Clarence M. Burton. Lansing, Mich., 1877–1929.

Campaign into the Wilderness: The Wayne-Knox-Pickering-McHenry Correspondence. 5 vols. Ed. Richard C. Knox. Columbus: Anthony Wayne Parkway Board, Ohio State Museum, 1955.

Carter, Robert G. *On the Border with Mackenzie.* 1935; rpt., Austin: Texas State Historical Association, 2007.

Catlin, George. *Letters and Notes on the Manners, Customs, and Conditions of the North American Indians.* 2 vols. 1844; rpt., New York: Dover, 1973.

A Compilation of the Messages and Papers of the Presidents, 1789–1908. 10 vols. Ed. James D. Richardson. [New York]: Bureau of National Literature and Arts, 1908.

Cooke, Philip St. George. *Scenes and Adventures in the Army; or, Romance of Military Life.* 1857; rpt., New York: Arno Press, 1973.

"Correspondence of John C. Calhoun." Ed. J. Franklin Jameson. American Historical Association, *Annual Report, 1899.* Washington, D.C.: Government Printing Office, 1900.

The Correspondence of Lieut. Governor John Graves Simcoe. 5 vols. Ed. Ernest A. Cruikshank. Toronto: Ontario Historical Society, 1923–26.

Crane, Charles J. *Experiences of a Colonel of Infantry.* New York: Knickerbocker Press, 1923.

The Diaries of John Gregory Bourke. 3 vols. to date. Ed. Charles M. Robinson III. Denton: University of North Texas Press, 2003– .

The Diary of John Quincy Adams, 1794–1845: American Political, Social, and Intellectual Life from Washington to Polk. Ed. Allen Nevins. New York: Ungar, 1951.

Explorer on the Northern Plains: Lieutenant Gouverneur K. Warren's Preliminary Report of Explorations in Nebraska and Dakota, in the Years 1855–'56–'57. Washington, D.C.: Government Printing Office, 1982.

The Federalist, with Letters of "Brutus." Ed. Terence Ball. Cambridge: Cambridge University Press, 2003.

Fifty Miles and a Fight: Major Samuel Peter Heintzelman's Journal of Texas and the Cortina War. Ed. Jerry Thompson. Austin: Texas State Historical Association, 1998.

From Greene Ville to Fallen Timbers: A Journal of the Wayne Campaign, July 28–September 14, 1794. Ed. Dwight L. Smith. Indiana Historical Society Publications 16, no. 3. Indianapolis: Indiana Historical Society, 1952.

General George Crook: His Autobiography. Ed. Martin F. Schmitt. 1946; rev. ed., Norman: University of Oklahoma Press, 1986.

Gibbon, John. *Adventures on the Western Frontier.* Ed. Alan and Maureen Gaff. Bloomington: Indiana University Press, 2002.

Governors Messages and Letters: Messages and Letters of William Henry Harrison. 2 vols. Ed. Logan Esarey. Indianapolis: Indiana Historical Commission, 1922.

Grant, Ulysses S. *Memoirs and Selected Letters.* New York: Library of America, 1990.

Hildreth, James. *Dragoon Campaigns to the Rocky Mountains by a Dragoon.* 1836; rpt., New York: Arno Press, 1973.

Hitchcock, Ethan Allen. *Fifty Years in Camp and Field.* Ed. W. A. Croffut. New York: G. P. Putnam's Sons, 1909.

Hoffman, Charles F. *A Winter in the West.* 1835; rpt., Ann Arbor, Mich.: University Microfilms, 1966.

The Indian Campaign on the Staked Plains, 1874–1875: Military Correspondence from War Department, Adjutant General's Office, File 2815–1874. Ed. Joe F. Taylor. Canyon, Tex.: Panhandle-Plains Historical Society, 1962.

Irving, Washington. *The Adventures of Captain Bonneville, U. S. A., in the Rocky Mountains and the Far West.* Ed. Edgeley W. Todd. Norman: University of Oklahoma Press, 1961.

————. *A Tour on the Prairies*. Ed. John Francis McDermott. Norman: University of Oklahoma Press, 1956.

Jefferson and Southwestern Exploration: The Freeman and Custis Accounts of the Red River Expedition of 1806. Ed. Dan L. Flores. Norman: University of Oklahoma Press, 1984.

Kip, Lawrence. *Indian War in the Pacific Northwest: The Journal of Lieutenant Lawrence Kip*. Lincoln: University of Nebraska Press, 1999.

Lane, Lydia. *I Married a Soldier; or, Old Days in the Old Army*. 1893; rpt., Albuquerque, N.Mex.: Horn and Wallace, 1964.

Latrobe, Charles J. *The Rambler in North America*. 2 vols. 2nd ed. London: R. B. Seeley and W. Burnside, 1836.

Laurance, Mary Leefe. *Daughter of the Regiment: Memoirs of a Childhood in the Frontier Army, 1878–98*. Ed. Thomas T. Smith. Lincoln: University of Nebraska Press, 1999.

The Laws of Texas 1822–1897. Comp. H. P. N. Gammel. Austin, Tex.: Gammel Book Co., 1898.

The Little Big Horn 1876: The Official Communications, Documents and Reports, with Rosters of the Officers and Troops of the Campaign. Comp. Lord J. Overfield II. 1967; rpt., Lincoln: University of Nebraska Press, 1990.

Lowe, Percival Greene. *Five Years a Dragoon ('49 to '54) and other Adventures on the Great Plains*. Norman: University of Oklahoma Press, 1965.

The Making of a Soldier: Letters of General R. S. Ewell. Ed. Percy Gatling Hamlin. Richmond, Va.: Whitter and Shepperson, 1935.

Marshall, J. T. *The Miles Expedition of 1874–1875: An Eyewitness Account of the Red River War*. Ed. Lonnie J. White. Austin, Tex.: Encino Press, 1971.

McConnell, H. H. *Five Years a Cavalryman; or, Sketches of Regular Army Life on the Texas Frontier, 1866–1871*. 1889; rpt., Norman: University of Oklahoma Press, 1996.

Miles, Nelson A. *Personal Recollections and Observations of General Nelson A. Miles*. 1896; rpt., Lincoln: University of Nebraska Press, 1996.

Motte, Jacob R. *Journey into the Wilderness: An Army Surgeon's Account of Life in Camp and Field during the Creek and Seminole Wars, 1836–1838*. Ed. James F. Sunderman. Gainesville: University of Florida Press, 1953.

The News from Brownsville: Helen Chapman's Letters from the Texas Military Frontier, 1848–1852. Ed. Caleb Coker. Austin Texas State Historical Association, 1992.

Official Letters of the Military and Naval Officers of the United States during the War with Great Britain in the Years 1812, 13, 14, and 15, with Some Additional Letters and Documents Elucidating the History of That Period. Ed. John Brannan. Washington, D.C.: Way and Gideon, 1823.

Olmstead, Frederick Law. *A Journey through Texas; or, A Saddle-trip on the Southwestern Frontier*. Lincoln: University of Nebraska Press, 2004.

Outpost on the Wabash, 1787–1791: Letters of Brigadier General Joseph Harmar and Major John Francis Hamtramck and Other Letters and Documents from the Harmar Papers in the William L. Clements Library. Ed. Gayle Thornbrough. Indiana Historical Society Publications 19. Indianapolis: Indiana Historical Society, 1957.

The Papers of Alexander Hamilton. Vol. 22. Ed. Harold C. Syrett. New York: Columbia University Press, 1975.

The Papers of Andrew Jackson. 7 vols. to date. Ed. Sam B. Smith and Harriet Chappell Owsley. Knoxville: University of Tennessee Press, 1980– .

The Papers of George Washington. Vol. 3. Ed. Dorothy Twohig. Charlottesville: University of Virginia Press, 1989.

The Papers of James Madison. Vol. 12. Ed. Charles F. Hobson and Robert A. Rutland. Charlottesville: University Press of Virginia, 1979.

The Papers of John C. Calhoun. Vols. 1–10. Ed. Clyde N. Wilson and W. Edwin Hemphill. Columbia: University of South Carolina Press, 1959–77.

The Papers of Thomas Jefferson. Vol. 7. Ed. Julian P. Boyd. Princeton, N.J.: Princeton University Press, 1953.

The Papers of Thomas Jefferson. Vol. 23. Ed. Charles T. Cullen. Princeton, N.J.: Princeton University Press, 1990.

The Papers of Thomas Jefferson. Vol. 30. Ed. Barbara B. Oberg. Princeton, N.J.: Princeton University Press, 2003.

Ranald S. Mackenzie's Official Correspondence Relating to Texas, 1871–1873. Ed. Ernest Wallace. Lubbock: West Texas Museum Association, 1967.

Recollections of Western Texas, Descriptive and Narrative, including an Indian Campaign, 1852–55, Interspersed with Illustrative Anecdotes by Two of the U.S. Mounted Rifles. Ed. Robert Wooster. Lubbock: Texas Tech University Press, 2001.

The Reminiscences of Major General Zenas R. Bliss, 1854–1876: From the Texas Frontier to the Civil War and Back Again. Ed. Thomas T. Smith et al. Austin: Texas State Historical Association, 2007.

Rip Ford's Texas. Ed. Stephen Oates. Austin: University of Texas Press, 1963.

Rodenbough, Theo F. *From Everglade to Canyon with the Second United States Cavalry.* 1875; rpt., Norman: University of Oklahoma Press, 2000.

Roe, Frances M. A. *Army Letters from an Officer's Wife, 1871–1888.* New York: Appleton, 1909.

Schofield, John M. *Forty-six Years in the Army.* 1897; rpt., Norman: University of Oklahoma Press, 1998.

Select British Documents of the Canadian War of 1812. 3 vols. Ed. William C. Wood. 1920–28; rpt., New York: Greenwood Press, 1968.

Sherman, William Tecumseh. *Memoirs.* New York: Library of America, 1990.

The St. Clair Papers: The Life and Public Service of Arthur St. Clair. 2 vols. Ed. William Henry Smith. Cincinnati: Robert Clarke, 1882.

Summerhayes, Martha. *Vanished Arizona: Recollections of the Army Life of a New England Woman.* 1911; rpt., Lincoln: University of Nebraska Press, 1979.

Texas Indian Papers. 4 vols. Ed. Dorman Winfrey and James M. Day. Austin: Texas State Library, 1959–61.

Through Dakota Eyes: Narrative Accounts of the Minnesota Indian War of 1862. Ed. Gary Anderson and Alan R. Woolworth. St. Paul: Minnesota Historical Society Press, 1988.

A Traveler in Indian Territory: The Journal of Ethan Allen Hitchcock, Late Major-General in the United States Army. Ed. Grant Foreman. 1930; rpt., Norman: University of Oklahoma Press, 1996.

Vielé, Theresa Griffin. *Following the Drum: A Glimpse of Frontier Life.* 1858; rpt., Lincoln: University of Nebraska Press, 1984.

The Writings of Albert Gallatin. 3 vols. Ed. Henry Adams. Philadelphia: J. B. Lippincott, 1879.

The Works of Thomas Jefferson. Vol. 12. Ed. Paul L. Ford. New York: G. P. Putnam's Sons, 1905.

Articles

"The Battle of Bad Axe: General Atkinson's Report." Ed. Roger L. Nichols. *Wisconsin Magazine of History* 50 (Autumn 1966): 54–58.

[Cass, Lewis]. "Removal of the Indians." *North American Review* (Jan. 1830): 62–121.

Childs, Ebenezer. "Recollections of Wisconsin Since 1820." *Report and Collections of the State Historical Society of Wisconsin* 4 (1859): 153–95.

"The Civil War of Private Morton." Ed. James T. King. *North Dakota History* 35 (Winter 1968): 8–19.

Denny, Ebenezer. "A Military Journal, Kept by Major E. Denny, 1781–1795." *Memoirs of the Historical Society of Pennsylvania* 7 (1860): 237–412.

Dick, Helen D. "A Newly Discovered Diary of Colonel Josiah Snelling." *Minnesota History* 18 (Dec. 1937): 399–406.

Dresden W. H. Howard, "The Battle of Fallen Timbers as told by Chief Kin-Jo-I-No." *Northwest Ohio Quarterly* 20 (Jan. 1948): 37–49.

"Freeman's Report on the Eighth Military Department." Ed. Martin L. Crimmins. *Southwestern Historical Quarterly* 51 (July 1947): 54–58; 51 (Oct. 1947): 167–74; 51 (Jan. 1948): 252–58; 51 (Apr. 1948): 350–57; 52 (July 1948): 100–108; 52 (Oct. 1948): 227–33; 52 (Jan. 1949): 349–53; 52 (Apr. 1949): 444–47; 53 (July 1949): 71–77; 53 (Oct. 1949): 202–8; 53 (Jan. 1950): 308–19; 53 (Apr. 1950): 443–73; 54 (Oct. 1950): 204–18.

"The Harney Expedition Against the Sioux: The Journal of Capt. John B. S. Todd." Ed. Ray H. Mattison. *Nebraska History* 43 (June 1962): 92–130.

"'I Long to Return to Fort Concho': Acting Assistant Surgeon Samuel Smith's Letters from the Texas Military Frontier, 1878–1879." Ed. John Neilson. *Military History of the West* 24 (Fall 1994): 123–86.

"Letters of Caroline Frey Winne from Sidney Barracks and Fort McPherson, Nebraska, 1874–1878." Ed. Thomas R. Buecker. *Nebraska History* 62 (Spring 1981): 1–46.

"Letters of Henry Dodge to General George W. Jones." Ed. William Salter. *Annals of Iowa*, 3rd series, 3 (Oct. 1897): 220–23.

"Lt. Sylvester Mowry's Report on His March in 1855 from Salt Lake City to Fort Tejon." Ed. Lynn R. Bailey. *Arizona and the West* 7 (Winter 1965): 329–46.

"*Major Hough's* March into Southern Ute Country." Ed. Robert G. Athearn. *Colorado Magazine* 25 (May 1948): 97–109.

Schindler, Harold. "The Bear River Massacre: New Historical Evidence." *Utah Historical Quarterly* 67 (Fall 1999): 300–308.

"A Surgeon's Mate at Fort Defiance: The Journal of Joseph Gardner Andrews for the year 1795." Ed. Richard C. Knopf. *Ohio Historical Quarterly* 66 (Jan., Apr., July 1957): 57–86, 159–86, 238–68.

"Winthrop Sargent's Diary While with General Arthur St. Clair's Expedition against the Indians." *Ohio Archaeological and Historical Society Publications* 33 (1924): 237–73.

SECONDARY SOURCES
Books

Adams, George Rollie. *General William S. Harney: Prince of Dragoons.* Lincoln: University of Nebraska Press, 2001.

Allen, Robert S. *His Majesty's Indian Allies: British Indian Policy in the Defence of Canada, 1774–1815.* Toronto: Dundurn Press, 1992.

Anderson, Fred, and Andrew Cayton. *The Dominion of War: Empire and Liberty in North America, 1500–2000.* New York: Viking Penguin, 2005.

Anderson, Gary Clayton. *The Conquest of Texas: Ethnic Cleansing in the Promised Land, 1820–1875.* Norman: University of Oklahoma Press, 2005.

———. *Kinsmen of Another Kind: Dakota-White Relations in the Upper Mississippi Valley, 1650–1862.* St. Paul: Minnesota Historical Society Press, 1984.

Angevine, Robert G. *The Railroad and the State: War, Politics, and Technology in Nineteenth-Century America.* Stanford, Calif.: Stanford University Press, 2004.

Antal, Sandy. *A Wampum Denied: Procter's War of 1812.* Ottawa: Carleton University Press, 1997.

Arnold, James R. *Jeff Davis's Own: Cavalry, Comanches, and the Battle for the Texas Frontier*. New York: John Wiley, 2000.

Aron, Stephen. *How the West was Lost: The Transformation of Kentucky from Daniel Boone to Henry Clay*. Baltimore, Md.: Johns Hopkins University Press, 1996.

Athearn, Robert G. *Forts of the Upper Missouri*. Lincoln: University of Nebraska Press, 1967.

Bagley, Will. *Blood of the Prophets: Brigham Young and the Massacre at Mountain Meadows*. Norman: University of Oklahoma Press, 2002.

Bailey, John W. *Pacifying the Plains: General Alfred Terry and the Decline of the Sioux, 1866–1890*. Westport, Conn.: Greenwood Press, 1979.

Ball, Durwood. *Army Regulars on the Western Frontier, 1848–1861*. Norman: University of Oklahoma Press, 2001.

Bartlett, Richard A. *Great Surveys of the American West*. Norman: University of Oklahoma Press, 1962.

Bauer, K. Jack. *Surfboats and Horse Marines: U.S. Naval Operations in the Mexican War, 1846–48*. Annapolis, Md.: U.S. Naval Institute, 1969.

———. *Zachary Taylor: Soldier, Planter, Statesman of the Old Southwest*. Baton Rouge: Louisiana State University Press, 1985.

Bearss, Ed, and Arrell M. Gibson. *Fort Smith: Little Gibraltar on the Arkansas*. Norman: University of Oklahoma Press, 1969.

Beers, Henry Putney. *The Western Military Frontier, 1815–1846*. 1935; rpt., Philadelphia: Porcupine Press, 1975.

Benn, Carl. *The Iroquois in the War of 1812*. Toronto: University of Toronto Press, 1998.

Birtle, Andrew J. *U.S. Army Counterinsurgency and Contingency Operations Doctrine, 1860–1941*. Washington, D.C.: Center of Military History, 2001.

Blackhawk, Ned. *Violence over the Land: Indians and Empires in the Early American West*. Cambridge, Mass.: Harvard University Press, 2006.

Bray, Kingsley M. *Crazy Horse: A Lakota Life*. Norman: University of Oklahoma Press, 2006.

Budd, Richard M. *Serving Two Masters: The Development of American Military Chaplaincy*. Lincoln: University of Nebraska Press, 2002.

Burstein, Andrew. *The Passions of Andrew Jackson*. New York: Knopf, 2003.

Byler, Charles A. *Civil-Military Relations on the Frontier and Beyond, 1865–1917*. Westport, Conn.: Praeger Security International, 2006.

Calloway, Colin G. *The American Revolution in the Indian Country: Crisis and Diversity in Native American Communities*. Cambridge: Cambridge University Press, 1995.

———. *The Scratch of a Pen: 1763 and the Transformation of North America*. New York: Oxford University Press, 2006.

Carter, Harvey Lewis. *The Life and Times of Little Turtle: First Sagamore of the Wabash.* Urbana: University of Illinois Press, 1987.

Cashion, Ty. *A Texas Frontier: The Clear Fork Country and Fort Griffin, 1849–1887.* Norman: University of Oklahoma Press, 1996.

Castel, Albert. *Frontier State at War.* Ithaca, N.Y.: Cornell University Press, 1958.

Cayton, Andrew. *The Frontier Republic: Ideology and Politics in the Ohio Country, 1780–1825.* Kent, Ohio: Kent State University Press, 1986.

Chalfant, William Y. *Cheyennes and Horse Soldiers: The 1857 Expedition and the Battle of Solomon's Fork.* Norman: University of Oklahoma Press, 1989.

Chamberlain, Kathleen P. *Victorio: Apache Warrior and Chief.* Norman: University of Oklahoma Press, 2007.

The Civil War Book of Lists: Over 300 Lists, from the Sublime . . . to the Ridiculous. Conshohocken, Pa.: Combined Books, 1993.

Clodfelter, Mark. *The Dakota War: The United States Army Versus the Sioux, 1862–1865.* Jefferson, N.C.: McFarland, 1998.

Coakley, Robert W. *The Role of Military Forces in Domestic Disorders, 1789–1878.* Washington, D.C.: Center of Military History, 1988.

Coffman, Edward M. *The Old Army: A Portrait of the American Army in Peacetime, 1784–1898.* New York: Oxford University Press, 1986.

Collins, Charles. *Apache Nightmare: The Battle at Cibecue Creek.* Norman: University of Oklahoma Press, 1999.

Cozzens, Peter. *General John Pope: A Life for the Nation.* Urbana: University of Illinois Press, 2000.

Crackel, Theodore J. *Mr. Jefferson's Army: Political and Social Reform of the Military Establishment, 1801–1809.* New York: New York University Press, 1987.

Cress, Lawrence. *Citizens in Arms: The Army and the Militia in American Society to the War of 1812.* Chapel Hill: University of North Carolina Press, 1982.

Cunliffe, Marcus. *Soldiers and Civilians: The Martial Spirit in America, 1775–1865.* Boston: Little, Brown, 1968.

Cusick, James G. *The Other War of 1812: The Patriot War and the American Invasion of Spanish East Florida.* University Press of Florida, 2003.

Cutrer, Thomas W. *Ben McCulloch and the Frontier Military Tradition.* Chapel Hill: University of North Carolina Press, 1993.

Dawson, Joseph G., III. *Doniphan's Epic March: The First Missouri Volunteers in the Mexican War.* Lawrence: University Press of Kansas, 1999.

Dobak, William A. *Fort Riley and Its Neighbors: Military Money and Economic Growth, 1853–1895.* Norman: University of Oklahoma Press, 1998.

Dobak, William A., and Thomas D. Phillips. *The Black Regulars, 1866–1898.* Norman: University of Oklahoma Press, 2001.

Doubler, Michael D. *Civilian in Peace, Soldier in War: The Army National Guard, 1636–2000.* Lawrence: University Press of Kansas, 2003.

Dowd, Gregory Evans. *A Spirited Resistance: The North American Indian Struggle for Unity, 1745–1816.* Baltimore, Md.: Johns Hopkins University Press, 1992.

Dunlay, Tom. *Kit Carson and the Indians.* Lincoln: University of Nebraska Press, 2000.

———. *Wolves for the Blue Soldiers: Indian Scouts and Auxiliaries with the United States Army, 1860–90.* Lincoln: University of Nebraska Press, 1982.

Dupree, Stephen A. *Planting the Union Flag in Texas: The Campaigns of Major General Nathaniel P. Banks in the West.* College Station: Texas A&M University Press, 2008.

Eisenhower, John S. D. *So Far from God: The U.S. War with Mexico, 1846–1848.* 1989; rpt., Norman: University of Oklahoma Press, 2000.

Emerson, William K. *Marksmanship in the U.S. Army: A History of Medals, Shooting Programs, and Training.* Norman: University of Oklahoma Press, 2004.

Etulain, Richard. *Beyond the Missouri: The Story of the American West.* Albuquerque: University of New Mexico Press, 2006.

Ferling, John. *John Adams: A Life.* Knoxville: University of Tennessee Press, 1992.

Frazer, Robert W. *Forts and Supplies: The Role of the Army in the Economy of the Southwest, 1846–1861.* Albuquerque: University of New Mexico Press, 1983.

———. *Forts of the West: Military Forts and Presidios, and Posts Commonly Called Forts, West of the Mississippi River to 1898.* Norman: University of Oklahoma Press, 1965.

Frazier, Donald S. *Blood and Treasure: Confederate Empire in the Southwest.* College Station: Texas A&M University Press, 1995.

Gaff, Alan D. *Bayonets in the Wilderness: Anthony Wayne's Legion in the Old Northwest.* Norman: University of Oklahoma Press, 2004.

Gillett, Mary C. *The Army Medical Department, 1818–1865.* Washington, D.C.: Center of Military History, 1987.

———. *The Army Medical Department, 1865–1917.* Washington, D.C.: Center of Military History, 1995.

Goetzmann, William H. *Army Exploration in the American West 1803–1863.* New Haven, Conn.: Yale University Press, 1959.

Greene, Jerome A. *Fort Randall on the Missouri, 1856–1892.* Pierre: South Dakota State Historical Society, 2005.

———. *Morning Star Dawn: The Powder River Expedition and the Northern Cheyennes, 1876.* Norman: University of Oklahoma Press, 2003.

———. *Nez Perce Summer, 1877: The U.S. Army and the Nee-Mee-Poo Crisis.* Helena: Montana Historical Society Press, 2000.

———. *Washita: The U.S. Army and the Southern Cheyennes, 1867–1869.* Norman: University of Oklahoma Press, 2004.

———. *Yellowstone Command: Colonel Nelson A. Miles and the Great Sioux War, 1876–1877.* Lincoln: University of Nebraska Press, 1991.

Greer, James K. *Colonel Jack Hays: Texas Frontier Leader and California Builder.* Rev. ed. College Station: Texas A&M University Press, 1987.

Grenier, John. *The First Way of War: American War Making on the Frontier, 1607–1814.* Cambridge: Cambridge University Press, 2005.

Gump, James O. *The Dust Rose Like Smoke: The Subjugation of the Zulu and the Sioux.* Lincoln: University of Nebraska Press, 1994.

Hagan, Kenneth J. *This People's Navy: The Making of American Seapower.* New York: Free Press, 1991.

Haynes, Sam W. *Soldiers of Misfortune: The Somervell and Mier Expeditions.* Austin: University of Texas Press, 1990.

Hedren, Paul. L. *Fort Laramie and the Great Sioux War.* 1988; rpt., Norman: University of Oklahoma Press, 1998.

Heidler, David S., and Jeanne T. Heidler. *Old Hickory's War: Andrew Jackson and the Quest for Empire.* Baton Rouge: Louisiana State University Press, 2003.

Heitman, Francis B. *Historical Register and Dictionary of the United States Army, from its Organization, September 29, 1789, to March 2, 1903.* 2 vols. 1903; rpt., Urbana: University of Illinois Press, 1965.

Hickey, Donald R. *The War of 1812: A Forgotten Conflict.* Urbana: University of Illinois Press, 1989.

Hinckley, Ted C. *The Americanization of Alaska, 1867–1897.* Palo Alto, Calif.: Pacific Books Publishers, 1972.

Hinderaker, Eric. *Elusive Empires: Constructing Colonialism in the Ohio Valley, 1673–1800.* Cambridge: Cambridge University Press, 1997.

Hoagland, Alison K. *Army Architecture in the West: Forts Laramie, Bridger, and D. A. Russell, 1849–1912.* Norman: University of Oklahoma Press, 2004.

Hoig, Stan. *Perilous Pursuit: The U.S. Cavalry and the Northern Cheyennes.* Boulder: University Press of Colorado, 2002.

Horsman, Reginald. *Expansion and American Indian Policy, 1783–1812.* East Lansing: Michigan State University Press, 1967.

Howarth, Stephen. *To Shining Sea: A History of the United States Navy, 1775–1991.* New York: Random House, 1991.

Howe, Daniel Walker. *What Hath God Wrought: The Transformation of America, 1815–1848.* New York: Oxford University Press, 2007.

Hoxie, Frederick E. *Parading through History: The Making of the Crow Nation in America, 1805–1935.* Cambridge: Cambridge University Press, 1995.

Hurt, R. Douglas. *The Indian Frontier, 1763–1846.* Albuquerque: University of New Mexico Press, 2002.

Hutton, Paul A. *Phil Sheridan and His Army.* Lincoln: University of Nebraska Press, 1985.

Isenberg, Andrew C. *The Destruction of the Bison, 1750–1920.* Cambridge: Cambridge University Press, 2000.

Jackson, Donald. *Custer's Gold: The United States Cavalry Expedition of 1874.* 1966; rpt., Lincoln: University of Nebraska Press, 1972.

Johnson, Timothy D. *Winfield Scott: The Quest for Military Glory.* Lawrence: University Press of Kansas, 1998.

Jones, Landon Y. *William Clark and the Shaping of the West.* New York: Hill and Wang, 2004.

Josephy, Alvin M., Jr. *The Civil War in the American West.* New York: Knopf, 1991.

Jung, Patrick J. *The Black Hawk War of 1832.* Norman: University of Oklahoma Press, 2007.

Kenner, Charles L. *Black and White Together: Buffalo Soldiers and Officers of the Ninth Cavalry, 1867–1898.* Norman: University of Oklahoma Press, 1999.

Kerstetter, Todd M. *God's Country, Uncle Sam's Land: Faith and Conflict in the American West.* Urbana: University of Illinois Press, 2006.

Kieffer, Chester. *Maligned General: The Biography of Thomas Sidney Jesup.* San Rafael, Calif.: Presidio Press, 1979.

Kime, Wayne R. *Colonel Richard Irving Dodge: The Life and Times of a Career Army Officer.* Norman: University of Oklahoma Press, 2006.

Kinevan, Marcos. *Frontier Cavalryman: Lieutenant John Bigelow with the Buffalo Soldiers in Texas.* El Paso: Texas Western Press, 1998.

Klunder, Willard Carl. *Lewis Cass and the Politics of Moderation.* Kent, Ohio: Kent State University Press, 1996.

Kohn, Richard H. *Eagle and Sword: The Federalists and the Creation of the Military Establishment in America, 1782–1802.* New York: Free Press, 1975.

Koistinen, Paul A. C. *Beating Plowshares into Swords: The Political Economy of American Warfare, 1865–1919.* Lawrence: University Press of Kansas, 1997.

Lamar, Howard. *The Far Southwest, 1846–1912: A Territorial History.* New Haven, Conn.: Yale University Press, 1966.

Lamar, Howard, and Leonard Thompson, eds. *The Frontier in History: North American and Southern Africa Compared.* New Haven, Conn.: Yale University Press, 1981.

Larson, John Lauritz. *Internal Improvement: National Public Works and the Promise of Popular Government in the Early United States.* Chapel Hill: University of North Carolina Press, 2001.

Larson, Robert W. *Red Cloud: Warrior-Statesman of the Lakota Sioux.* Norman: University of Oklahoma Press, 1997.

Latimer, Jon. *1812: War with America.* Cambridge, Mass.: Harvard University Press, 2007.

Laumer, Frank. *Dade's Last Command.* Gainesville: University Press of Florida, 1993.

Laurie, Clayton, and Ronald H. Cole. *The Role of Federal Military Forces in Domestic Disorders, 1877–1900.* Washington, D.C.: Center of Military History, 1997.

Laver, Harry S. *Citizens More Than Soldiers: The Kentucky Militia and Society in the Early Republic.* Lincoln: University of Nebraska Press, 2007.

Leckie, Shirley A. *Elizabeth Bacon Custer and the Making of a Myth.* Norman: University of Oklahoma Press, 1993.

Leiker, James N. *Racial Borders: Black Soldiers along the Rio Grande.* College Station: Texas A&M University Press, 2002.

Linn, Brian McAllister. *The Echo of Battle: The Army's Way of War.* Cambridge, Mass.: Harvard University Press, 2007.

Lowery, Charles D. *James Barbour, a Jeffersonian Republican.* University: University of Alabama Press, 1984.

Lubetkin, M. John. *Jay Cooke's Gamble: The Northern Pacific Railroad, the Sioux, and the Panic of 1873.* Norman: University of Oklahoma Press, 2006.

Mahon, John K. *History of the Militia and the National Guard.* New York: Macmillan, 1983.

Malone, Laurence J. *Opening the West: Federal Internal Improvements Before 1860.* Westport, Conn.: Greenwood Press, 1998.

Marquis, Thomas B. *A Warrior Who Fought Custer.* Minneapolis: Midwest Co., 1931.

Marszalek, John F. *Sherman: A Soldier's Passion for Order.* New York: Free Press, 1993.

McConnell, Michael. *Army and Empire: British Soldiers on the American Frontier.* Lincoln: University of Nebraska Press, 2004.

McPherson, James M. *For Cause and Comrades: Why Men Fought in the Civil War.* New York: Oxford University Press, 1997.

Meyerson, Harvey. *Nature's Army: When Soldiers Fought for Yosemite.* Lawrence: University Press of Kansas, 2001.

Miller, Darlis A. *Soldiers and Settlers: Military Supply in the Southwest, 1861–1885.* Albuquerque: University of New Mexico Press, 1989.

Missall, John, and Mary Lou Missall. *The Seminole Wars: America's Longest Indian Conflict.* Gainesville: University Press of Florida, 2004.

Moneyhon, Carl. *Texas after the Civil War: The Struggle of Reconstruction.* College Station: Texas A&M University Press, 2004.

Monnett, John H. *Tell Them We Are Going Home: The Odyssey of the Northern Cheyennes.* Norman: University of Oklahoma Press, 2001.

Moorman, Donald R., and Gene A. Sessions. *Camp Floyd and the Mormons: The Utah War.* Salt Lake City: University of Utah Press, 1992.

Morris, John D. *Sword of the Border: Major General Jacob Jennings Brown, 1775–1828.* Kent, Ohio: Kent State University Press, 2000.

Morrison, James L. *"The Best School in the World": West Point, the Pre–Civil War Years, 1833–1866.* Kent, Ohio: Kent State University Press, 1986.

Moten, Matthew. *The Delafield Commission and the American Military Profession.* College Station: Texas A&M University Press, 2000.

Mullis, Tony R. *Peacekeeping on the Plains: Army Operations in Bleeding Kansas.* Columbia: University of Missouri Press, 2004.

Nacy, Michele J. *Members of the Regiment: Army Officers' Wives on the Western Frontier, 1865–1890.* Westport, Conn.: Greenwood Press, 2000.

Nance, Joseph Milton. *Attack and Counterattack: The Texas-Mexican Frontier, 1842.* Austin: University of Texas Press, 1964.

Nester, William R. *The Arikara War: The First Plains Indian War, 1823.* Missoula, Mont.: Mountain Press Publishing, 2001.

Nichols, Roger L. *General Henry Atkinson: A Western Military Career.* Norman: University of Oklahoma Press, 1965.

O'Brien, Sean Michael. *In Bitterness and in Tears: Andrew Jackson's Destruction of the Creeks and Seminoles.* Westport, Conn.: Praeger, 2003.

Oliva, Leo E. *Soldiers on the Santa Fe Trail.* Norman: University of Oklahoma Press, 1967.

Ostler, Jeffrey. *The Plains Sioux and U.S. Colonialism from Lewis and Clark to Wounded Knee.* Cambridge: Cambridge University Press, 2004.

Parks, Joseph Howard. *General Edmund Kirby Smith, C. S. A.* Baton Rouge: Louisiana State University Press, 1954.

Paul, R. Eli. *Blue Water Creek and the First Sioux War, 1854–1856.* Norman: University of Oklahoma Press, 2004.

Peskin, Allan. *Winfield Scott and the Profession of Arms.* Kent, Ohio: Kent State University Press, 2004.

Pinheiro, John C. *Manifest Ambition: James K. Polk and Civil-Military Relations during the Mexican War.* Westport, Conn.: Praeger Security International, 2007.

Powell, Peter J. *Sweet Medicine: The Continuing Role of the Sacred Arrows, the Sun Dance, and the Sacred Buffalo Hat in Northern Cheyenne History.* 2 vols. Norman: University of Oklahoma Press, 1998.

Prucha, Francis Paul. *American Indian Policy in the Formative Years: The Indian Trade and Intercourse Acts, 1790–1834.* 1962; rpt., Lincoln: University of Nebraska Press, 1970.

———. *Broadax and Bayonet: The Role of the United States Army in the Development of the Northwest, 1815–1860.* 1953; rpt., Lincoln: University of Nebraska Press, 1967.

———. *The Great Father: The United States Government and the American Indians.* Abridg. ed. Lincoln: University of Nebraska Press, 1986.

———. *The Sword of the Republic: The United States Army on the Frontier, 1783–1846.* 1969; rpt., Bloomington: University of Indiana Press, 1977.

Remini, Robert V. *Andrew Jackson and His Indian Wars.* New York: Viking Penguin, 2001.

Richter, William L. *The Army in Texas During Reconstruction, 1865–1870.* College Station: Texas A&M University Press, 1987.

Roberts, David. *Once They Moved Like the Wind: Cochise, Geronimo, and the Apache Wars.* New York: Simon and Schuster, 1993.

Robinson, Charles M., III. *Bad Hand: A Biography of General Ranald S. Mackenzie.* Austin, Tex.: State House Press, 1993.

———. *A Good Year to Die: The Story of the Great Sioux War.* Norman: University of Oklahoma Press, 1995.

Rowe, Mary Ellen. *Bulwark of the Republic: The American Militia in the Antebellum West.* Westport, Conn.: Praeger, 2003.

Russell, Don. *One Hundred and Three Fights and Scrimmages: The Story of General Reuben F. Bernard.* Mechanicsburg, Pa.: Stackpole Books, 2003.

Schlicke, Carl P. *General George Wright: Guardian of the Pacific Coast.* Norman: University of Oklahoma Press, 1988.

Secoy, Raymond. *Changing Military Patterns on the Great Plains (17th Century through Early 19th Century).* Locust Valley, N.Y.: J. J. Augustin, 1953.

Silver, James W. *Edmund Pendleton Gaines: Frontier General.* Baton Rouge: Louisiana State University Press, 1949.

Skeen, C. Edward. *Citizen Soldiers in the War of 1812.* Lexington: University Press of Kentucky, 1999.

———. *John Armstrong, Jr., 1758–1843: A Biography.* Syracuse, N.Y.: Syracuse University Press, 1981.

Skelton, William B. *An American Profession of Arms: The Army Officer Corps, 1784–1861.* Lawrence: University Press of Kansas, 1992.

Sklenar, Larry. *To Hell with Honor: Custer and the Little Bighorn.* Norman: University of Oklahoma Press, 2000.

Skowronek, Stephen. *Building a New American State: The Expansion of National Administrative Capacities, 1877–1920.* Cambridge: Cambridge University Press, 1982.

Slaughter, Thomas P. *The Whiskey Rebellion: Frontier Epilogue to the American Revolution*. New York: Oxford University Press, 1986.

Smith, Sherry L. *Sagebrush Soldier: Private William Earl Smith's View of the Sioux War of 1876*. Norman: University of Oklahoma Press, 1989.

———. *The View from Officers' Row: Army Perceptions of Western Indians*. Tucson: University of Arizona Press, 1990.

Smith, Thomas T. *The U.S. Army and the Texas Frontier Economy, 1845–1900*. College Station: Texas A&M University Press, 1999.

Stagg, J. C. A. *Mr. Madison's War: Politics, Diplomacy, and Warfare in the Early American Republic, 1783–1830*. Princeton, N.J.: Princeton University Press, 1983.

Stallard, Patricia Y. *Glittering Misery: Dependents of the Indian Fighting Army*. San Rafael, Calif.: Presidio Press, 1978.

Starkey, Armstrong. *European and Native American Warfare, 1675–1815*. Norman: University of Oklahoma Press, 1998.

The Statistical History of the United States: From Colonial Times to the Present. New York: Basic Books, 1976.

Stuart, Reginald C. *War and American Thought: From the Revolution to the Monroe Doctrine*. Kent, Ohio: Kent State University Press, 1982.

Sword, Wiley. *President Washington's Indian War: The Struggle for the Old Northwest, 1790–1795*. Norman: University of Oklahoma Press, 1985.

Tate, Michael L. *The Frontier Army in the Settlement of the West*. Norman: University of Oklahoma Press, 1999.

Thian, Raphael P. *Notes Illustrating the Military Geography of the United States, 1813–1880*. Ed. John M. Carroll. Austin: University of Texas Press, 1979.

Thompson, Jerry. *Civil War to the Bloody End: The Life and Times of Major General Samuel P. Heintzelman*. College Station: Texas A&M University Press, 2006.

———. *Cortina: Defending the Mexican Name in Texas*. College Station: Texas A&M University Press, 2007.

Thompson, Jerry, and Lawrence T. Jones. *Civil War and Revolution on the Rio Grande Frontier: A Narrative and Photographic History*. Austin: Texas State Historical Association, 2004.

Utley, Robert M. *Cavalier in Buckskin: George Armstrong Custer and the Western Military Frontier*. Norman: University of Oklahoma Press, 1988.

———. *Frontier Regulars: The United States Army and the Indian, 1866–1891*. 1973; rpt., Lincoln: University of Nebraska Press, 1984.

———. *Frontiersmen in Blue: The United States Army and the Indian, 1848–1861*. 1967; rpt., Lincoln: University of Nebraska Press, 1981.

———. *Indian Frontier, 1846–1890*. Rev. ed. Albuquerque: University of New Mexico Press, 2003.

———. *The Lance and the Shield: The Life and Times of Sitting Bull*. New York: Henry Holt, 1993.

———. *The Last Days of the Sioux Nation*. New Haven, Conn.: Yale University Press, 1963.

———. *Lone Star Justice: The First Century of the Texas Rangers*. New York: Oxford University Press, 2002.

Vandervort, Bruce. *Indian Wars of Mexico, Canada, and the United States*. New York: Routledge, 2006.

Warren, Stephen. *The Shawnees and Their Neighbors, 1795–1870*. Urbana: University of Illinois Press, 2005.

Watts, Steven. *The Republic Reborn: War and the Making of Liberal America, 1790–1820*. Baltimore, Md.: Johns Hopkins University Press, 1987.

Weber, David. *The Mexican Frontier, 1821–1846: The American Southwest under Mexico*. Albuquerque: New Mexico University Press, 1982.

Weigley, Russell F. *The American Way of War: A History of United States Military Strategy and Policy*. New York: Macmillan Press, 1973.

———. *History of the United States Army*. Enlrg. ed.; Bloomington: Indiana University Press, 1984.

West, Elliott. *The Contested Plains: Indians, Goldseekers, and the Rush to Colorado*. Lawrence: University Press of Kansas, 1998.

Whitlock, Flint. *Distant Bugles, Distant Drums: The Union Response to the Confederate Invasion of New Mexico*. Boulder: University Press of Colorado, 2006.

Wickett, Murray R. *Contested Territory: Whites, Native Americans, and African Americans in Oklahoma, 1865–1907*. Baton Rouge: Louisiana State University Press, 2000.

Winders, Richard Bruce. *Mr. Polk's Army: The American Military Experience in the Mexican War*. College Station: Texas A&M University Press, 1997.

Wishart, David J. *The Fur Trade of the American West, 1807–1840: A Geographical Synthesis*. Lincoln: University of Nebraska Press, 1979.

Woodman, Lyman L. *Duty Station Northwest: The U.S. Army in Alaska and Western Canada, 1867–1987*. 3 vols. Anchorage: Alaska Historical Society, 1996–99.

Wooster, Ralph A. *Lone Star Regiments in Gray*. Austin, Tex.: Eakin Press, 2002.

———. *Texas and Texans in the Civil War*. Austin, Tex.: Eakin Press, 1995.

Wooster, Robert. *Frontier Crossroads: Fort Davis and the West*. College Station: Texas A&M University Press, 2006.

———. *The Military and United States Indian Policy, 1865–1903*. New Haven, Conn.: Yale University Press, 1988.

———. *Nelson A. Miles and the Twilight of the Frontier Army*. Lincoln: University of Nebraska Press, 1993.

————. *Soldiers, Sutlers, and Settlers: Garrison Life on the Texas Frontier.* College Station: Texas A&M University Press, 1987.

Wright, Robert K., and Morris J. MacGregor, Jr. *Soldier-Statesmen of the Constitution.* Washington, D.C.: Center of Military History, 1987.

Internet Resources

The Handbook of Texas Online. Texas State Historical Association. http://www.tshaonline.org/handbook/online.

Williamson, Samuel. "Six Ways to Compute the Relative Value of a U.S. Dollar Amount, 1774 to Present." http://www.measuringworth.com/uscompare.

Articles and Essays

Atherton, Lewis. "Western Foodstuffs in the Army Provisions Trade." *Agricultural History* 14 (Oct. 1940): 161–69.

Beltman, Brian W. "Territorial Commands of the Army: The System Refined but Not Perfected, 1815–1821." *Journal of the Early Republic* 11 (Summer 1991): 185–218.

Birtle, Andrew J. "The Origins of the Legion of the United States." *Journal of Military History* 67 (Oct. 2003): 1249–62.

Caldwell, Norman W. "The Frontier Army Officer, 1794–1814." *Mid-America: An Historical Review* 37 (Apr. 1955): 101–28.

Campbell, John. "The Seminoles, the 'Bloodhound War' and Abolitionism, 1796–1865." *Journal of Southern History* 72 (May 2006): 259–302.

Carp, E. Wayne. "The Problem of National Defense in the Early American Republic." In *The American Revolution: Its Character and Limits*, ed. Jack P. Greene, 14–50. New York: New York University Press, 1987.

Case, Alfred A. "Abuse of Power: Andrew Jackson and the Indian Removal Act of 1830." *The Historian* 65 (Winter 2003): 1330–53.

Cayton, Andrew "'Separate Interests' and the Nation-State: The Washington Administration and the Origins of Regionalism in the Trans-Appalachian West." *Journal of American History* 79 (June 1992): 39–67.

Chandler, Robert J. "Fighting Words: Censoring Civil War Journalism in California." *California Territorial Quarterly* 51 (Fall 2002): 4–17.

Coles, Harry L. "From Peaceable Coercion to Balanced Forces, 1807–1815." In *Against All Enemies: Interpretations of American Military History from Colonial Times to the Present*, ed. Kenneth J. Hagan and William R. Roberts, 71–89. Westport, Conn.: Greenwood Press, 1986.

Crackel, Theodore J. "The Military Academy in the Context of Jeffersonian Reform." In *Thomas Jefferson's Military Academy: Founding West Point*, ed. Robert M. S. McDonald, 99–117. Charlottesville: University of Virginia Press, 2004.

Craig, Stephen C. "Medicine for the Military: George M. Sternberg on the Kansas Plains, 1866–1870." *Kansas History* 21 (Autumn 1998): 188–206.

Cress, Lawrence Delbert. "Reassessing American Military Requirements, 1783–1807." In *Against All Enemies: Interpretations of American Military History from Colonial Times to the Present*, ed. Kenneth J. Hagan and William R. Roberts, 49–69. Westport, Conn.: Greenwood Press, 1986.

DeLay, Brian. "The Wider World of the Handsome Man: Southern Plains Indians Invade Mexico, 1830–1848." *Journal of the Early Republic* 27 (Spring 2007): 83–113.

Dobak, William A. "The Army and the Buffalo: A Demur." *Western Historical Quarterly* 26 (Summer 1995): 197–202.

Eid, Leroy V. "American Indian Military Leadership: St. Clair's Defeat." *Journal of Military History* 57 (Jan. 1993): 71–88.

———. "'A Kind of Running Fight': Indian Battlefield Tactics in the Late Eighteenth Century." *Western Pennsylvania Historical Magazine* 71 (1988): 147–71.

Fitzgerald, Michael S. "'Nature Unsubdued': Diplomacy, Expansion and the American Military Buildup of 1815–1816." *Mid-America* 77 (Winter 1995): 5–32.

———. "Rejecting Calhoun's Expansible Army Plan: The Army Reduction Act of 1821." *War in History* 3 (Apr. 1996): 161–85.

Flores, Dan. "Bison Ecology and Bison Diplomacy: The Southern Plains from 1800 to 1850." *Journal of American History* 78 (Sept. 1991): 465–85.

Herrera, Ricardo A. "Self-Governance and the American Citizen as Soldier, 1775–1861." *Journal of Military History* 65 (Jan. 2001): 21–52.

Hickey, Donald R. "Federalist Defense Policy in the Age of Jefferson, 1801–1812." *Military Affairs* 45 (Apr. 1981): 63–70.

Holmes, Alice D. "'And I Was Always with Him': The Life of Jane Thorpy, Army Laundress." *Journal of Arizona History* 38 (Summer 1997): 177–90.

Holt, Marilyn Irvin. "Joined Forces: Robert Campbell and John Dougherty as Military Entrepreneurs." *Western Historical Quarterly* 30 (Summer 1999): 183–202.

Gallagher, Mary A. Y. "Reinterpreting the 'Very Trifling Mutiny' at Philadelphia in June 1783." *Pennsylvania Magazine of History and Biography* 119 (July 1995): 3–35.

Gough, Robert. "Officering the American Army, 1798." *William and Mary Quarterly*, 3rd series, 43 (July 1986): 460–71.

Grandstaff, Mark R. "Preserving the 'Habits and Usages of War': William Tecumseh Sherman, Professional Reform, and the U.S. Army Officer Corps, 1865–1881, Revisited." *Journal of Military History* 62 (July 1998): 521–45.

Jackson, Donald. "Jefferson, Meriwether Lewis, and the Reduction of the United States Army." *Proceedings of the American Philosophical Society* 124 (Apr. 1980): 91–96.

Jensen, Richard E. "The Wright-Beauchampe Investigation and the Pawnee Threat of 1829." *Nebraska History* 79 (Fall 1998): 133–43.

Jordan, Weymouth T., Jr., John D. Chapala, and Shan C. Sutton. "'Notorious as the Noonday Sun': Capt. Alexander Welch Reynolds and the New Mexico Territory, 1849–1859." *New Mexico Historical Review* 75 (Oct. 2000): 456–508.

Kanon, Thomas. "'A Slow, Laborious Slaughter': The Battle of Horseshoe Bend." *Tennessee Historical Quarterly* 58 (Spring 1999): 2–15.

Karsten, Peter. "The 'New' American Military History: A Map of the Territory, Explored and Unexplored." *American Quarterly* 36 (Summer 1984): 389–418.

Kaufman, Scott, and John A. Soares. "'Sagacious beyond Praise?' Winfield Scott and Anglo-American–Canadian Border Diplomacy, 1837–1860." *Diplomatic History* 30 (Jan. 2006): 57–82.

Kenner, Charles. "Guardians in Blue: The United States Cavalry and the Growth of the Texas Range Cattle Industry." *Journal of the West* 34 (Jan. 1995): 46–54.

Klyza, Christopher McGrory. "The United States Army, Natural Resources, and Political Development in the Nineteenth Century." *Polity* 35 (Fall 2002): 1–28.

Knight, Larry. "The Cart War: Defining American in San Antonio in the 1850s." *Southwestern Historical Quarterly* 109 (Jan. 2006): 319–35.

Larson, John Lauritz. "'Bind the Republic Together': The National Union and the Struggle for a System of Internal Improvements." *Journal of American History* 74 (Sept. 1987): 363–87.

Laurie, Clayton D. "Filling the Breech: Military Aid to Civil Power in the Trans–Mississippi West." *Western Historical Quarterly* 25 (Summer 1994): 149–62.

Lee, Wayne E. "Early American Ways of War: A New Reconnaissance, 1600–1815." *The Historical Journal* 44 (Mar. 2001): 269–89.

———. "Fortify, Fight, or Flee: Tuscarora and Cherokee Defensive Warfare and Military Culture Adaptation." *Journal of Military History* 68 (July 2004): 713–70.

———. "Peace Chiefs and Blood Revenge: Patterns of Restraint in Native American Warfare, 1500–1800." *Journal of Military History* 71 (July 2007): 701–41.

Linn, Brian M. "*The American Way of War* Revisited." *Journal of Military History* 66 (Apr. 2002): 501–30.

———. "The Long Twilight of the Frontier Army." *Western Historical Quarterly* 27 (Summer 1996): 141–67.

Lookingbill, Brad. "The Killing Fields of Wounded Knee." *Reviews in American History* 33 (Sept. 2005): 379–86.

MacKinnon, William P. "And the War Came: James Buchanan, the Utah Expedition, and the Decision to Intervene." *Utah Historical Quarterly* 76 (Winter 2008): 22–37.

———. "The Buchanan Spoils System and the Utah Expedition: Careers of W. M. F. Magraw and John M. Hockaday." *Utah Historical Quarterly* 31 (Spring 1963): 127–50.

———. "Epilogue to the Utah War: Impact and Legacy." *Journal of Mormon History* 29 (Fall 2003): 186–248.

———. "The Gap in the Buchanan Revival: The Utah Expedition of 1857–58." *Utah Historical Quarterly* 45 (Winter 1977): 36–46.

———. "Stranger in a Strange Land: My Forty-five Years with the Utah War and What I Have Learned." *Yale University Library Gazette* (Oct. 2005): 17–22.

Mahon, John K. "Anglo-American Methods of Warfare, 1676–1794." *Mississippi Valley Historical Review* 45 (Sept. 1958): 254–78.

May, Robert E. "Young American Males and Filibustering in the Age of Manifest Destiny: The United States Army as a Cultural Mirror." *Journal of American History* 78 (Dec. 1991): 857–86.

McConaghy, Lorraine. "The Old Navy in the Pacific West: Naval Discipline in Seattle, 1855–1856." *Pacific Northwest Quarterly* 98 (Winter 2006–7): 18–28.

McKenna, Marian C. "Above the Blue Line: Policing the Frontier in the Canadian and American West, 1870–1900." In *The Borderlands of the American and Canadian Wests: Essays on Regional History of the Forty-ninth Parallel,* ed. Sterling Evans, 81–106. Lincoln: University of Nebraska Press, 2006.

McNitt, Frank. "Navajo Campaigns and the Occupation of New Mexico, 1847–1848." *New Mexico Historical Review* 43 (July 1968): 173–94.

Metcalf, Brandon J. "The Nauvoo Legion and the Prevention of the Utah War." *Utah Historical Quarterly* 72 (Fall 2004): 300–321.

Morrison, James L., Jr. "Military Education and Strategic Thought, 1846–1861." In *Against All Enemies: Interpretations of American Military History from Colonial Times to the Present,* ed. Kenneth J. Hagan and William R. Roberts, 113–31. Westport, Conn.: Greenwood Press, 1986.

Morrison, W. B. "Fort Towson." *Chronicles of Oklahoma* 8 (June 1930): 226–32.

Morsman, Jenry. "Securing America: Jefferson's Fluid Plans for the Western Perimeter." In *Across the Continent: Jefferson, Lewis and Clark, and the Making of America,* ed. Douglas Seefeldt, Jeffrey L. Hantman, and Peter S. Onuf, 46–61. Charlottesville: University of Virginia Press, 2005.

Murphy, William J., Jr. "John Adams: The Politics of the Additional Army, 1798–1800." *New England Quarterly* 52 (June 1979): 234–49.

Nelson, Harold B. "Military Roads for War and Peace, 1791–1836." *Military Affairs* 19 (Spring 1955): 1–14.

Nelson, Paul D. "General Charles Scott, the Kentucky Mounted Volunteers, and the Northwest Indian Wars, 1784–1794." *Journal of the Early Republic* 6 (Autumn 1986): 219–51.

Nichols, Roger L. "Soldiers as Farmers: Army Agriculture in the Missouri Valley, 1818–1827." *Agricultural History* 44 (Apr. 1970): 213–22.

Nobles, Gregory H. "Breaking into the Backcountry: New Approaches to the Early American Frontier, 1750–1800." *William and Mary Quarterly*, 3rd ser., 46 (Oct. 1989): 641–70.

O'Brien, Greg. "The Conqueror Meets the Unconquered: Negotiating Cultural Boundaries on the Post–Revolutionary Southern Frontier." *Journal of Southern History* 67 (Feb. 2001): 39–72.

O'Connell, Charles F., Jr. "The Corps of Engineers and the Rise of Modern Management, 1827–1856." In *Military Enterprise and Technological Change: Perspectives on the American Experience*, ed. Merritt Roe Smith, 87–116. Cambridge, Mass.: MIT Press, 1985.

Oliva, Leo. "The Army and the Fur Trade." *Journal of the West* 26 (Fall 1987): 21–26.

Ott, Jennifer. "'Ruining' the Rivers in the Snake Country: The Hudson's Bay Company Fur Desert Policy." *Oregon Historical Quarterly* 104 (Summer 2004): 166–95.

Posey, John Thornton. "Rascality Revisited: In Defense of General James Wilkinson." *Filson Club History Quarterly* 74 (Fall 2000): 309–52.

Prucha, Francis Paul. "Andrew Jackson's Indian Policy: A Reassessment." *Journal of American History* 56 (Dec. 1969): 527–39.

Robinson, Charles M., III. "Don't Ruin a Good Story with the Facts: An Analysis of Henry Flipper's Account of His Court-Martial in *Black Frontiersman*." *Southwestern Historical Quarterly* 111 (July 2007): 51–71.

Rusche, Timothy M. "Treachery Within the United States Army." *Pennsylvania History* 65 (Autumn 1998): 478–91.

Russell, Peter. "Redcoats in the Wilderness: British Officers and Irregular Warfare in Europe and America, 1740 to 1760." *William and Mary Quarterly*, 3rd series, 35 (Oct. 1978): 629–50.

Rust, Thomas C. "Settlers, Soldiers, and Scoundrels: Economic Tension in a Frontier Military Town." *Military History of the West* 31 (Fall 2001): 117–38.

Silver, James W. "Edmund Pendleton Gaines and Frontier Problems, 1801–1849." *Journal of Southern History* 1 (Aug. 1935): 320–44.

Skeen, C. Edward. "Calhoun, Crawford, and the Politics of Retrenchment." *South Carolina Historical Magazine* 73 (July 1972): 141–55.

Skelton, William B. "The Army in the Age of the Common Man, 1815–1845." In *Against All Enemies: Interpretations of American Military History from Colonial Times to the Present*, ed. Kenneth J. Hagan and William R. Roberts, 91–112. Westport, Conn.: Greenwood Press, 1986.

——. "The Commanding General and the Problem of Command in the United States Army, 1821–1841." *Military Affairs* 34 (Dec. 1970): 117–22.

——. "The Confederation's Regulars: A Social Profile of Enlisted Service in America's First Standing Army." *William and Mary Quarterly*, 3rd series, 46 (Oct. 1989): 770–85.

——. "Social Roots of the American Military Profession: The Officer Corps of America's First Peacetime Army, 1784–1789." *Journal of Military History* 54 (Oct. 1990): 435–52.

Smith, Carlton. "Congressional Attitudes towards Military Preparedness during the Monroe Administration." *Military Affairs* 40 (Feb. 1976): 22–25.

Smith, Merritt Roe. "Army Ordnance and the 'American System' of Manufacturing, 1815–1861." In *Military Enterprise and Technological Change: Perspectives on the American Experience*, ed. Merritt Roe Smith, 39–86. Cambridge, Mass.: MIT Press, 1985.

——. Introduction. In *Military Enterprise and Technological Change: Perspectives on the American Experience*, ed. Merritt Roe Smith, 1–37. Cambridge, Mass.: MIT Press, 1985.

Smith, Sherry L. "Lost Soldiers: Re-searching the Army in the American West." *Western Historical Quarterly* 29 (Summer 1998): 149–64.

Smith, Thomas T. "West Point and the Indian Wars, 1802–1891." *Military History of the West* 24 (Spring 1994): 24–56.

Smits, David D. "'Fighting Fire with Fire': The Frontier Army's Use of Indian Scouts and Allies in the Trans-Mississippi Campaigns, 1860–1890." *American Indian Culture and Research Journal* 22 (Spring 1998): 73–116.

——. "The Frontier Army and the Destruction of the Buffalo, 1865–1883." *Western Historical Quarterly* 25 (Autumn 1995): 312–38.

——. "More on the Army and the Buffalo." *Western Historical Quarterly* 26 (Summer 1995): 203–8.

Sodergren, Steven E. "Exercising Restraint: Military Responses to Southern Sentiment in California during the Civil War." *Military History of the West* 37 (2007): 1–27.

Spiller, Roger J. "Calhoun's Expansible Army: The History of a Military Idea." *South Atlantic Quarterly* 79 (Spring 1980): 189–203.

Stagg, J. C. A. "Enlisted Men in the United States Army, 1812–1815: A Preliminary Survey." *William and Mary Quarterly*, 3rd series, 43 (Oct. 1986): 615–45.

———. "Soldiers in Peace and War: Comparative Perspectives on the Recruitment of the United States Army, 1802–1815." *William and Mary Quarterly*, 3rd series, 57 (Jan. 2000): 79–120.

Swagerty, William R. "'The Leviathan of the North': American Perceptions of the Hudson's Bay Company, 1816–1846." *Oregon Historical Quarterly* 104 (Winter 2003): 478–517.

Utley, Robert M. "The Frontier and the American Military Tradition." In *The American Military on the Frontier: Proceedings of the 7th Military History Symposium*. Ed. James P. Tate. Washington, D.C.: Office of Air Force History, 1978.

Vargas, Mark A. "The Military Justice System and the Use of Illegal Punishments as Causes of Desertion in the U.S. Army, 1821–1835." *Journal of Military History* 55 (Jan. 1991): 1–19.

———. "The Progressive Agent of Mischief: The Whiskey Ration and Temperance in the United States Army." *The Historian* 67 (Summer 2005): 199–216.

Wade, Arthur P. "The Military Command Structure: The Great Plains, 1853–1891." *Journal of the West* 15 (July 1976): 5–22.

Waghelstein, John D. "Preparing the U.S. Army for the Wrong War, Educational and Doctrinal Failure, 1865–91." *Small Wars and Insurgencies* 10 (Spring 1999): 1–33.

———. "The United States Army's First War: War in the Northwest Territory, 1790–1795." *Small Wars and Insurgencies* 12 (Summer 2001): 1–18.

Wagoner, Jennings L., Jr., and Christine Coalwell McDonald. "Mr. Jefferson's Academy." In *Thomas Jefferson's Military Academy: Founding West Point*, ed. Robert M. S. McDonald, 118–53. Charlottesville: University of Virginia Press, 2004.

Walraven, Bill, and Margorie K. Walraven. "The 'Sabine Chute': The U.S. Army and the Texas Revolution." *Southwestern Historical Quarterly* 107 (Apr. 2004): 573–601.

Watson, Samuel J. "Flexible Gender Roles During the Market Revolution: Family, Friendship, Marriage, and Masculinity among U.S. Army Officers, 1815–1846." *Journal of Social History* 29 (Fall 1995): 81–106.

———. "How the Army Became Accepted: West Point Socialization, Military Accountability, and the Nation-State During the Jacksonian Era." *American Nineteenth Century History* 7 (June 2006): 219–51.

———. "United States Army Officers Fight the 'Patriot War': Responses to Filibustering on the Canadian Border, 1837–1839." *Journal of the Early Republic* 18 (Autumn 1998): 485–519.

Wettemann, Robert P., Jr. "A Part or Apart: The Alleged Isolation of Antebellum U.S. Army Officers." *American Nineteenth Century History* 7 (June 2006): 193–217.

White, Richard. "The Winning of the West: The Expansion of the Western Sioux in the Eighteenth and Nineteenth Centuries." *Journal of American History* 65 (Sept. 1978): 319–43.

Wood, Cynthia A. "The Lieutenants and the Lady: The Trials of Elizabeth Easton Morton." *Journal of Arizona History* 40 (Summer 1990): 157–80.

Wooster, Robert. "The Army and the Politics of Expansion: Texas and the Southwestern Borderlands, 1870–1886." *Southwestern Historical Quarterly* 93 (Oct. 1989): 151–68.

———. "'A Difficult and Forlorn Country': The Military Looks at the Southwest, 1850–1881." *Arizona and the West* 28 (Winter 1986): 339–56.

———. "Fort Davis and the Close of a Military Frontier." *Southwestern Historical Quarterly* 105 (Oct. 2006): 173–92.

———. "John M. Schofield and the 'Multipurpose' Army." *American Nineteenth Century History* 7 (June 2006): 173–91.

———. "'The Whole Company Have Done It': The U.S. Army and the Fort Davis Murder of 1860." *Journal of the West* 32 (Apr. 1993): 19–28.

Dissertations and Unpublished Materials

Adams, Francis R. "An Annotated Edition of the Personal Letters of Robert E. Lee, April 1855–April 1861." Ph.D. diss., University of Maryland, 1955.

Adams, Kevin John. "'Common People with Whom I Shall Have No Relation': Class, Race, and Ethnicity in the Post–Civil War Frontier Army." Ph.D. diss., University of California, Berkeley, 2004.

Belser, Thomas A. "Military Operations in Missouri and Arkansas, 1861–1865." Ph.D. diss., Vanderbilt University, 1958.

Bergmann, William H. "Commerce and Arms: The Federal Government, Native Americans, and the Economy of the Old Northwest, 1783–1807." Ph.D. diss., University of Cincinnati, 2005.

Cox, J. Wendel. "A World Together, a World Apart: The United States and the Arikaras, 1803–1851." Ph.D. diss., University of Minnesota, 1998.

Kretchik, Walter Edward. "Peering Through the Mist: Doctrine as a Guide for U.S. Army Operations, 1775–2000." Ph.D. diss., University of Kansas, 2001.

McInnis, Verity. "Expanding Horizons: Officers' Wives on the Military Frontiers, 1846–1903." M.A. thesis, Texas A&M University-Corpus Christi, 2006.

Miller, Cynthia Allen. "The U.S. Army Logistics Complex: A Case Study of the Northern Frontier." Ph.D. diss., Syracuse University, 1991.

Steinhauer, Dale Richard. "'Sogers': Enlisted Men in the U.S. Army, 1815–1860." Ph.D. diss., University of North Carolina, 1992.

van de Logt, Martinus Johannes Maria. "War Party in Blue: Pawnee Indian Scouts in the United States Army, 1864–1877." Ph.D. diss., Oklahoma State University, 2002.

Vandervort, Bruce C. "France's Conquest of Algeria: Template for the Winning of the American West?" Paper presented at the annual meeting of the Western History Association, Oklahoma City, 2007.

Waghelstein, John David. "Preparing for the Wrong War: The United States Army and Low Intensity Conflict, 1755–1890." Ph.D. diss., Temple University, 1990.

Watson, Samuel J. "Militarily Effective but Politically Contingent: Evaluating U.S. Army Pacification Efforts on the Northwestern Trans-Mississippi Frontier, 1820–1846." Paper presented at the annual meeting of the Society for Military History, Ogden, Utah, Apr. 2008.

———. "National Territorial Expansion on the Military Frontiers: Military Strategy, Operations, and Implications." Unpublished manuscript in author's possession.

———. "Professionalism, Social Attitudes, and Civil-Military Accountability in the United States Officer Corps, 1815–1844." Ph.D. diss., Rice University, 1996.

———. "Subordination, Responsibility, and Discretion." Unpublished manuscript in author's possession.

Watt, Robert N. "Ízisgo At'éé: Victorio's Military and Political Leadership of the Warm Springs Apaches." Unpublished manuscript in author's possession.

Wettemann, Robert Paul, Jr. "'To the Public Prosperity': The United States Army and the Market Revolution, 1815–1844." Ph.D. diss., Texas A&M University, 2001.

borderland policemen, 64; brought national authority to Texas's southern borderland, 241; casualties increase, 161; chaplains in, 252; combat with Indians increases in 1850s, 119; Congress increases cavalry regiments, 188; cornerstone of frontier economies, 252; destroyed homes and villages, 273; importance to regional development, 33; individuals purchase land on frontier, 254; and infrastructure work, 27; and internal improvements, 70, 134; in Kansas, 143–44; largest civilian employer in New Mexico, 121; and law enforcement activities, 249; main mission tied to borderlands, 70; meeting with Union Pacific at Ft. Sanders, 198; national military policy in the West, xv; nation growing faster than, 135; one quarter of commissioned personnel left and entered Confederate service, 160; other uses of, 249–50; pay declines for enlisted personnel, 189; place in society of, 7; protects Chinese workers, **251**; racial composition, 189; rates of officer resignation, 145; reducing lawlessness in Texas, 194; and regional prosperity, 71; role in expansion of nation, xii; role in marketing borderlands, 7; role in nation building, 143; single largest purchasing and employment agency, **197**; small size preferred, xiv, 96; as source of nation building, 26; surgeons in, 252; and territorial expansion, 20; ties with western political leaders, 254; troops as source of regional development, 255; in Utah, 143, 145. *See also* officers

U.S. Civil War, xiv, 134; frontier life changes during, 163; majority of soldiers were volunteers during, 164

U.S. Congress: adjourns without having funded Army, 237; cuts spending on Army, 216, 217

U.S. Navy, 112

Van Buren, Martin, 93
Van Dorn, Earl, 156, 157, 165
Vásquez, Rafael, 109
Victorio, 249, 262
Vielé, Egbert L., 101
Vielé, Teresa, 101
violence: civilians blamed for, 122
Voorhees, Daniel, 210

Wade, Benjamin, 186
Waite, Stand, 164, 176
Wall, William, 63
Walsh, J. M., 248
war: level of destruction, 1
War Department: spending at, 241
Warfield, William H., 68, 69
Warner, William H., 123
War of 1812, 39, 51, 60, 80; and balance of power with Indians, 48; disputes stemming from, 66
Washington, George, 7, 8, 14, 24, 26, 30, 32, 241; and need for professional army, 4
Wayne, Anthony, 16, 17, 20, 23, 27, 37, 88, 124, 270, 273; emphasis on marksmanship and use of war gaming, 15; enforced iron discipline, 14; in painting, **17**; and stable economic infrastructure, 21; and whiskey ration, 18
weaponry: improvements in, 134
Weer, William, 175
Weir, Thomas B., 228
West, Joseph R., 168
West Point, N.Y., 49, 50, 68, 69, 90, 94, 103, 111, 117, 128, 140, 174, 206, 250, 256, 261; establishment of military academy at, 26
Wheaton, Frank, 268
Wheeler, George, 251
Wheeler, William A., 216, 217
whiskey ration: abolishment of, 83
Whitman, Marcus, 128
Wilkinson, James, 17, 21, 22, 25, 26, 30, 31, **32**, 32, 33
Williams, Thomas, 104
Winchester, James, 42
Woll, Adrián, 109

CPSIA information can be obtained
at www.ICGtesting.com
Printed in the USA
LVHW11202522072O
661296LV00002B/140